The Effective, Efficient Professor

Related Titles of Interest

Successful College Teaching: Problem-Solving
Strategies of Distinguished Professors
Sharon A. Baiocco and Jamie N. DeWaters
ISBN: 0-205-26654-1

Colleges and Universities as Citizens
Robert G. Bringle, Richard Games, and
Reverend Edward A. Malloy, CSC
ISBN: 0-205-28696-8

Faculty Work and Public Trust: Restoring
the Value of Teaching and Public Service in
American Academic Life
James S. Fairweather
ISBN: 0-205-17948-7

Emblems of Quality in Higher
Education: Developing and Sustaining
High-Quality Programs
Jennifer Grant Haworth and Clifton F. Conrad
ISBN: 0-205-19546-6

Writing for Professional Publication: Keys to
Academic and Business Success
Kenneth T. Henson
ISBN: 0-205-28313-6

Learner-Centered Assessment on
College Campuses: Shifting the Focus
from Teaching to Learning
Mary E. Huba and Jann E. Freed
ISBN: 0-205-28738-7

Revitalizing General Education in a Time
of Scarcity: A Navigational Chart for
Administrators and Faculty
Sandra L. Kanter, Zelda F. Gamson, and
Howard B. London
ISBN: 0-205-26257-0

The Adjunct Professor's Guide to Success:
Surviving and Thriving in the College Classroom
Richard E. Lyons, Marcella L. Kysilka, and
George E. Pawlas
ISBN: 0-205-28774-3

Multicultural Course Transformation in
Higher Education: A Broader Truth
Ann Intili Morey and Margie K. Kitano
(Editors)
ISBN: 0-205-16068-9

Teaching Tips for College and University
Instructors: A Practical Guide
David Royse
ISBN: 0-205-29839-7

Creating Learning-Centered Courses
for the World Wide Web
William B. Sanders
ISBN: 0-205-31513-5

Designing and Teaching an On-Line Course:
Spinning Your Web Classroom
Heidi Schweizer
ISBN: 0-205-30321-8

Leadership in Continuing and Distance
Education in Higher Education
Cynthia C. Jones Shoemaker
ISBN: 0-205-26823-4

Shaping the College Curriculum:
Academic Plans in Action
Joan S. Stark and Lisa R. Lattuca
ISBN: 0-205-16706-3

For further information on these and other related titles, contact:
College Division
Allyn and Bacon
75 Arlington Street
Boston, MA 02116
www.ablongman.com

The Effective, Efficient Professor

Teaching, Scholarship and Service

Phillip C. Wankat

Clifton L. Lovell Distinguished Professor and
Head of Division of Interdisciplinary Engineering Studies

Purdue University

Allyn and Bacon

Boston ▪ London ▪ Toronto ▪ Sydney ▪ Tokyo ▪ Singapore

Executive editor and publisher: *Stephen D. Dragin*
Series editorial assistant: *Barbara Strickland*
Manufacturing buyer: *Chris Marson*
Marketing manager: *Stephen Smith*
Cover designer: *Suzanne Harbison*
Editorial-production service: *Stratford Publishing Services, Inc.*
Electronic composition: *Stratford Publishing Services, Inc.*

Copyright © 2002 by Allyn & Bacon
A Pearson Education Company
75 Arlington Street
Boston, MA 02116

Internet: www.ablongman.com

Library of Congress Cataloging-in-Publication Data

Wankat, Phillip C.
     The effective, efficient professor : teaching, scholarship and service / Phillip C. Wankat.
          p.   cm.
     Includes bibliographical references (p.   ) and index
     ISBN 0-205-33711-2
       1. College teaching.   2. teacher effectiveness.   3. Effective teaching.   I. Title

     LB2331 .W317 2002
     378.1'25—dc21   2001022873

Printed in the United States of America

10   9   8   7   6   5   4   3   2   1   05   04   03   02   01

To Dot, Charles, and Jennifer,
who give meaning to my life.

CONTENTS

LIST OF FIGURES AND TABLES

Figures

Tables

PREFACE

Professors need to be both effective and efficient. Effectiveness is doing the right thing in a way that works. For example, the students of effective teachers learn. Efficiency is doing something in a fashion that minimizes time or maximizes the amount of work accomplished. The efficient person gets work done in a timely fashion. A common myth is that effectiveness and efficiency are incompatible. Although there are situations where this is true (e.g., in advising students), most of the time efficiency complements effectiveness.

This book is built on several assumptions. First, I believe that to a large extent people control their own feelings and their own destinies. Effective people accept personal responsibility and learn to control their interpretations of events (Burns, 1989; Csikszentmihalyi, 1990). Second, I believe that teaching, scholarship, and service are all important and that the relative importance of each depends on context. Third, I believe that people can change and grow. Although habits are often difficult to change, people *can* change them. Fourth, I believe that the tacit knowledge necessary to function effectively as a professor can be taught and can be learned. Professors can learn to improve their teaching, scholarship, writing, time management, committee service, and so forth. Also, it is better to decide voluntarily to change than to have your institution try to force you to change. Finally, changes by individual professors are necessary but may not be sufficient to change colleges and universities.

Unfortunately, the only function for which most professors have been trained is disciplinary scholarship. Although the lack of education and training in teaching is most obvious (and is being addressed at some institutions), new professors also often lack time management, writing, interpersonal relations, teamwork, and administrative skills. Though useful, on-the-job training is often not sufficient. Understanding also requires a knowledge based on research. Ideally, future professors would learn in graduate school about other types of scholarship, pedagogy, time management, use of technology, and certain aspects of service (e.g., how to run effective committee meetings). Those who missed this experience, which includes almost the entire professoriate, must learn these aspects after graduation if they are to come close to their potentials as professors. Given that the tasks of a full professor are not that different from those of an assistant professor, these skills will be useful throughout much of one's career. This is true until one becomes, as many professors do, a department chair. Then a whole new catalog of attitudes and skills is needed. Although graduate schools could certainly prepare students better, development is needed throughout one's career. The ideas in this book are easy to understand and can facilitate such development throughout professors' careers. The hard part is translating our theoretical understanding into action. Translating ideas into action is interwoven throughout this book in the form of hypothetical, occasionally autobiographical, examples and as tips.

Academic positions at all institutions have several characteristics in common. First, professors teach and want their students to learn. Second, professors are expected to be scholarly and, at many institutions, to write scholarly works. Third, professors are expected to be involved in the service, administrative, and leadership functions of their institutions. Finally, professors need to have a life outside of academe. Balancing these competing needs is difficult. Research universities expect more emphasis on scholarship and publication, liberal arts colleges expect more emphasis on teaching, and community colleges often expect a dual emphasis on teaching and service. The appropriate balance can differ significantly, but the functions that professors perform are similar regardless of their environment. This similarity makes it possible to write a book that will be useful to professors and future professors at all types of institutions.

Because my experiences as a student and as a professor are mainly at research universities, I have relied on extensive reading of the literature to broaden my knowledge base. I have extensively supported my statements so that few suggestions are based solely on my opinion. Many of the suggestions are supported by extensive research based on teaching and scholarship; others are based on informed opinion or common sense. When there are conflicts in the literature, I have cited the conflicting sources so that readers can decide what will work for them. Since I tend to read and cite the literature obsessively, some readers will feel that certain statements are obvious and do not need a reference. Others, however, will argue about the validity of these same statements. Because of the breadth of topics covered, I have relied to a large extent on secondary resources instead of the primary research literature.

Part I applies classical time management techniques to academic positions. Sections 2.1 to 2.3, particularly section 2.1 on personal missions, are important bases for the remainder of the book. Since teaching is the activity professors spend the most time on, over half the book focuses on teaching and students (Parts II and III, respectively). Part IV focuses on scholarship, writing, service, and administration. This book was purposely designed so that it need not be read in a linear fashion. After reading sections 2.1 to 2.3, feel free to skip around. For example, if teaching a lecture class is most important to you now, read Chapters 4 and 5. You may later want to read parts of Chapters 7 and 8 to improve your understanding of and rapport with students. And still later, when you want to consider other teaching methods, read Chapter 6. If writing or the lack of writing time is your most important concern, read sections 10.4 and 10.5. If you are having difficulty mentoring graduate students, read sections 9.1, 9.2, and 9.5. And so forth.

I have been aided by many people in my quest to become a professor, starting with my parents, Grace Pryor Wankat and Charles Wankat. Two high school teachers that stand out are Dr. Norman Ladd, who taught me calculus, and Dr. Kirkpatrick, who taught chemistry. As an undergraduate at Purdue University, I encountered many excellent teachers, including Professors Robert Benkesser, Roger Eckert, Alden Emery, Robert Greenkorn, David Kessler, Lowell Koppel, Lester Lahti, and Jack Myers. My research advisor at Princeton University, Professor Bill Schowalter, was my model for the ideal adviser discussed in Chapter 9. I was also influenced by other inspiring teachers and researchers, including Professors Ron Andres, Leon Lapidus, Dudley Saville, and Richard Wilhelm, and by the other graduate students in my class.

Although I served as a teaching assistant twice, I had no formal training in how to teach. Fortunately, assistant professors at Purdue first taught recitation sections for a lecture course taught by an experienced professor—in my case Professor Bob Greenkorn. Frequent luncheon discussions on teaching and dealing with problem students with Professors Ron Barile and Neal Houze were also helpful. The first course I taught on my own was a semidisaster that encouraged me to take Professor John Feldhusen's course "Educational Psychology for College Teachers." This course was the catalyst that started me in the scholarship of teaching and served as the model for my own course on college teaching.

I was later able to convince Professor Harold ("Dick") Hackney to admit me into his course "Counseling Theories and Techniques" despite my lack of background. This eventually led to my obtaining a master's degree in education. I had the pleasure of taking many good courses from teachers in the Education Department, including Professors Janine Bernard, Kent Davis, John Feldhusen, Dick Hackney, Lee Isaacson, and Alan Segrist.

After completing the master's degree in education, I convinced the Chemical Engineering graduate committee to allow me to teach an experimental course titled "Educational Methods in Engineering." The department head, Professor Ron Andres, suggested that I collaborate with the newly hired communications specialist, Dr. Frank Oreovicz. The trial course was successful, and over the years we expanded the course and eventually used a National Science Foundation grant to write a textbook, *Teaching Engineering,* that is now available free at http//:unitflops.ecn.purdue.edu/ChE/News/ Book. Over the years I have also presented teaching workshops that have allowed me to collaborate with some of the best known teachers in engineering, including Professors Richard Felder, Stewart Slater, Karl Smith, Jim Stice, and Don Woods.

While learning to teach, I was also developing a research program. Over the years the direction of my research and my research methods were greatly affected by Professors Norman Sweed, Robert Greenkorn, and C. Judson King. I worked with a number of excellent graduate students and collaborated on research with Professors Alden Emery, Fritz Friedlander, Georges Grevillot, David Kessler, Michael Ladisch, Narsi Narsimhan, Richard Noble, Martin Okos, Daniel Tondeur, and Linda Wang.

Until I was promoted to full professor, I did only modest amounts of service and administration. After I became head of Freshman Engineering, I received invaluable assistance from my two associate heads, Professors Dick McDowell and John Gaunt; from my administrative assistant, Ms Judy Anderson; and from the associate dean, John McLaughlin. Professor Phil Swain, Mrs. Shelley Applegate, Mrs. Mary Bonhomme, and Mrs. Julayne Moser guided me through the difficulties of being interim director of Continuing Engineering Education. I have just returned to the administrative front as head of the Department of Interdisciplinary Engineering Studies. If I am willing to listen, people will be willing to help me learn this job also. These years as an administrator have convinced me that administrators need to keep active in teaching and research.

I wrote the first draft of this book over two summers and a one-semester sabbatical. I appreciate the sabbatical from Purdue University, the editing done by Dr. Frank Oreovicz, the continued interest and encouragement of Professor Jim Caruthers, and the understanding and forbearance of my wife, Dot, as she endured two summers without pay. My children, Charles and Jennifer, proved very understanding that their father needed to work even when he was home. To improve the book, I have gratefully incorporated into the final manuscript the efforts of my editor, Steve Dragin, at Allyn and Bacon and of the reviewers, Robert G. Bringle of Indiana University—Purdue University Indianapolis, Helena Waddy of the State University of New York at Geneseo, and Harold Hackney of Fairfield University.

Phillip C. Wankat
West Lafayette, Indiana

The Effective, Efficient Professor

1 Introduction: Effectiveness and Efficiency in Academe

Professor Albert Forrest nibbled on his sandwich while he finished writing tomorrow's test. Al usually enjoyed teaching and received good teaching ratings. He liked to talk with the students, but they interrupted his other work. He wished he could give his students the individual attention they deserved and still have time for his other work. The only way he seemed to get anything done now was to come in to work on weekends, when all the students were gone. He seemed to work all the time.

Work was also less fun than it used to be. Al always seemed to have something new to do, but never enough time to be sure it was done correctly. Right now the new president was pushing professors to develop Internet home pages for their courses, but Al had never found time to learn how to use his computer for more than word processing and e-mail. And he wasn't convinced that a home page would improve his teaching. His dean wanted professors to write more proposals and bring in money. Al was trying to develop a proposal with two colleagues, but it was not moving very quickly. He had been working on a textbook for five years, but at the rate it was going it would take another five years. Al had expected the paper he published last year to stir up some interest, but only his friends and former students seemed to have read it. After congratulating him, his department chair had immediately pushed for more "output." And today he had a committee meeting between class and the university senate meeting. As he cleaned the crumbs off his desk, Al wondered where all his time went.

There are professors who are embarrassingly productive (e.g., Schneider, 1998a). Even Huber (1992, 142), who is otherwise scathing in his attacks on professors, admits, "Some scholars are so productive they must be on steroids." But most professors are not superstars (Felder, 1994a), and it is rare to be highly productive in both teaching and service (Fairweather, 1999). An appropriate question is, how can the average professor be more productive and effective at teaching, scholarship, and service without sacrificing his or her personal life?

Professors work long hours. Bowen and Schuster (1986, 72) and Fairweather (1996, 25) report that many studies found that professors work 55 to 62 hours per week during the academic year and only somewhat less during vacation periods. Despite these long hours, we are attacked for a variety of sins, including laziness, excessive self-interest, and a lack of productivity (e.g., Huber, 1992; P. Smith, 1990; C. J. Sykes, 1988). Unfortunately, many of the critics are in positions of power, such as members of boards of trustees, state and federal legislators, governors, members of the U.S. Congress, and college and university administrators (Meyer, 1998, 29–38). These influential people, along with the majority of students and their parents, expect and demand change.

Improving productivity does *not* require more hours per week than most professors already invest. But "time management," "effectiveness," and "efficiency" tend to be pejorative terms to many professors, who equate a drive for more productivity with the university administration and the state legislature (collectively a.k.a. the enemy). Increasing productivity involves changing habits—always difficult, even when the reasons and principles are clear. Some professors worry that students will be short-changed. However, effective teaching is often efficient teaching, and efficiency can create more time to interact with students.

Many "unfair" institutional-based situations can overwhelm professors' best efforts. Professors who are hired to do one job (e.g., teach) can be stuck in a bad situation if their institution changes and they are asked to do another job (e.g., research). It is quite possible for administrators to demand "productivity" from professors without providing the necessary resources. That this is an administrative failure does not reduce the impact on the professors. An unfair, untrustworthy, unstable, ineffective, tyrannical, or just plain mean dean or department chair will make a professor's life difficult (Getman, 1992, 97–100). Unfair behaviors by administrators and governing boards are certainly not new (C. J. Lucas, 1994, 197–200). Excesses led to the establishment of the American Association of University Professors in 1915 and to more recent unionization drives (Getman, 1992, 73–90, 101–109; C. J. Lucas, 1994, 197–200; Nelson, 1997). Fortunately, college presidents and governing boards have less arbitrary power today than they had in the old days, when firing without cause was common.

Tenured professors can often insulate themselves from institutional politics and wait until there is a change of administrators. Untenured and part-time faculty are much more at the mercy of the boss. Solutions to these institution-based problems often require structural changes at the university and educational-system levels (Mac-Taggart and associates, 1996) that are beyond the scope of this book. Individual faculty may have the choice of changing jobs. Effective, efficient professors are more likely to have other opportunities and thus the chance to control their destinies.

Time management and efficiency methods are tools that help professors control the conflict between their traditional autonomy and the demands for accountability now being placed on them. The results of controlling our time and becoming more effective and efficient are more freedom and more productivity.

1.1. What Is the Problem?

Professor Forrest is not alone. Many professors feel that they do not have enough time. In a survey of professors by the Carnegie Foundation for the Advancement of Teaching (Boyer, 1990), 44 percent of respondents strongly agreed or agreed with reservations to the statements "I hardly ever get time to give a piece of work the attention it deserves" and "My job is a source of considerable personal strain."

Why do so many professors feel they do not have enough time and are always straining to finish tasks? First, there are too many tasks competing for their time. The mission statements of most higher education institutions are broad. Menges (1999a) found that new faculty at community colleges were the least stressed and explained this by noting that expectations of faculty at community colleges are clearer than those of faculty at other institutions. The fewer tasks people have to do, the easier it is to focus on them.

Students and their parents want professors to teach and be accessible. Administrators want them to do research that will enhance the institution's reputation and bring in money. State governors and legislators want faculty to teach, but they also want them to do research that will drive the economy or help solve pressing social problems. Representatives from companies, news organizations, and various levels of government want professors to apply their expertise to understand and solve problems. Graduate students want to consult with faculty on research. Other professors want time for committees and sometimes just to socialize. Related to these demands are the large number of interruptions. Students come to the door with questions, the phone rings, e-mail never stops, and the daily mail and e-mail can bring hours of work.

Surveys illustrate the variety of faculty duties. Faculty spend about 60 percent of their time teaching (Menges, 1999a). New faculty reported spending two-thirds of their time on teaching activities, except at research universities, where half their time was spent teaching and half on research (Menges, 1999a). Most felt that their schools expected them to devote more time to research and less to teaching. More than 99 percent of the respondents to a 1995–96 faculty survey by the Higher Education Research Institute at the University of California, Los Angeles (UCLA; Almanac, 1998, 32), thought that being a good teacher was essential or very important. Almost 87 percent thought that being a good colleague was essential or very important, and 55 percent thought that engaging in research was essential or very important.

The demands on college professors' time are not going to decrease (Tierney, 1999, xi–xviii). Altbach (1995, 31) notes that periods of limited resources for higher education are actually the norm. The new calls for accountability and productivity will not go away (Layzell, 1999; Meyer, 1998).

A second problem is that overcommitment is easy but reducing the load is difficult (Getman, 1992). Professors have considerable autonomy and can choose what to work on, but many tasks, such as writing a book, serving as department chair or as officer in a professional society, and developing a major research group, can swallow available time for years. The result can be overcommitment and a life of little but work. Forty-one percent of the respondents to the Carnegie faculty survey either strongly agreed or agreed with reservations to the statement "I tend to subordinate all aspects of my life to my work" (Boyer, 1990, Table A-34).

A third problem is that professors are not trained for many aspects of their jobs. Often, graduate students learn how to do the scholarship of discovery (disciplinary research), but not how to do broader forms of scholarship, including the scholarships of integration, application, and teaching (Boyer, 1990). And what they do learn about research they learn in an environment very different from that of professors, who must juggle myriad duties. Although they have one experience—good, bad, or indifferent—at being mentored, they do not study mentoring. Unfortunately, most never formally study teaching. They learn teaching by watching their own professors and getting on-the-job practice. Most do not learn the pedagogical tools to conceptualize what they know about teaching and share it with their colleagues.

What it boils down to is that most professors have never studied and some have never learned either the extrinsic or the intrinsic tasks necessary to function as a professor. These tasks involve effectively and efficiently teaching, doing scholarship, working with others, mentoring, and providing service within the university. It is also important that time be found to have some unscheduled time and a satisfying personal life.

Fortunately, solutions to the second and third problems are under professors' control. We can learn how to prevent or cope with overcommitment and perform our myriad duties. Dealing with these two problems will help us cope with the first problem. The purpose of this book is to help professors gain mastery over these problems. By learning to become more effective and efficient, professors can relieve some of the pressure on their time.

1.2. Why Effectiveness and Efficiency?

Effectiveness means doing the right thing. Consider your values when developing goals and setting priorities. Ask, "What is the right thing to do?" Effectiveness also involves doing something so that it achieves the right goals. Effective teaching is, above all, teaching that fosters student learning. Most professors believe effective teaching is one of the right things to do. Efficiency is doing something well without wasting steps. Efficiency without effectiveness—such as efficiently teaching a class in which students do not learn—is hollow. Effectiveness without efficiency means the professor and often the students waste time. Both are needed (Covey, 1989).

As another example, consider writing a paper. Effectiveness is writing a paper that is correct and adds positively to the literature. It should be published and have impact within the discipline. Without effectiveness, why bother writing? Efficiency means that the paper is written in a reasonable length of time. Without efficiency, effectiveness can be lost—the paper may never be finished or, if finished, may no longer be timely.

Some professors think a focus on productivity is detrimental to the spirit of the university (Wilshire, 1990, 31–32). Students deserve and need personal attention, and giving it to them is not always "productive" for professors. Although efficiency does not solve all problems, inefficiency is not the answer, either. A balance is needed between efficiency that does not impair academic functioning and allowing time for seemingly inefficient activities. Efficiency, where it is possible, provides time for critically important activities that cannot be done efficiently.

Methods to improve effectiveness and efficiency will not always work (McGee-Cooper, 1994, 11–21; Wankat & Oreovicz, 1993, 26–27). Professors need to help students learn and need to keep learning themselves. There are effective strategies to help one learn, and relatively efficient ways to use them, but in the short term, the process of learning often seems neither effective nor efficient. We need to have faith that with diligent effort learning will occur, and this faith needs to be shared with our students. In teaching there are times when planning is helpful and times when the effective teacher must seize the unexpected teachable moment.

Doing creative work does not appear to be either efficient or effective, yet, once a good idea is created and developed, the whole process can become both (see section 10.4). Time spent on creative tasks often flows and does not fit the limits imposed by rigid schedules. Efforts to be creative can enhance teaching, scholarship, and even service.

Many teaching and advising activities require personal contact (see Chapter 7 and section 9.5). Most students need some personal attention to thrive—but not too much. Providing personal attention is time consuming and doesn't appear efficient, but without it effectiveness is lost. Excellent teaching requires rapport with students, which is hard to develop without giving them some personal attention. Good academic advising, which requires highly focused attention, is often taken for granted, while bad advising is often obvious. A key reason for being efficient in other tasks is to have time to spend with your students.

1.3. The Potential Satisfactions of Faculty Life

If you ask Al Forrest if he is satisfied with his job, he will first give you a catalog of woes and then say he can't think of anything else he would rather do. Most faculty are satisfied with their jobs. The UCLA Higher Education Research Institute faculty survey (Almanac, 1998, 32) found that "overall job satisfaction" was noted as very satisfactory or satisfactory by 76 percent of the respondents. The job aspect with the highest rating was "autonomy and independence," which was marked as very satisfactory or satisfactory by 86 percent of the respondents.

People choose to become professors for a variety of reasons:

- They love their discipline.
- They are interested in teaching.
- They want to work with students.
- They want to have an impact on students' lives.
- They want the freedom, autonomy, and flexibility to pursue their intellectual interests.
- They enjoy doing research.
- They are attracted by the chance to learn continuously.
- They hope for supportive and stimulating colleagues.
- They are attracted by the financial rewards and job security (Austin & Rice, 1998, 737–738; Layzell, 1999; Reis, 1997, 99).

Full-time, tenure-track faculty positions are often very satisfying, since they can usually be structured to maximize the opportunities for *flow*. For example, on rare occasions in Professor Forrest's lectures everything seems to work: the examples click, the jokes *are* funny, the timing is exquisite, and the students pay rapt attention. During these lectures Al feels he has the students in the palm of his hand. When these wonderful lectures are over, the class spontaneously claps. During the flow experience Al feels very much alive, and when he reflects on the experience he is happy. After these lectures, he feels that being a professor is the greatest job in the world.

Flow, or optimal experiences, can occur in "situations in which attention can be freely invested to achieve a person's goals" (Csikszentmihalyi, 1990, 40). The conditions for flow are:

1. A sense of control
2. The ability to set realistic, feasible goals and subgoals
3. Meaningful rules, such as in sports and games
4. Feedback on progress toward achieving goals and subgoals
5. Focused attention
6. A balance between challenge and skills
7. Increased challenge and skill to prevent boredom (Csikszentmihalyi, 1990, 74, 97, 180–184; 1997, 29–33)

Flow can occur in a variety of situations, such as interactions with people, mental activities, and physical performances, including both work and leisure. Sports and hobbies are particularly likely to result in flow, because they often include interactions with people and either physical or mental activity (Csikszentmihalyi, 1997, 67–68). Faculty work such as teaching and research often combines interactions with people with mental activity (and sometimes physical activity) and includes a number of possibilities to experience flow. According to Csikszentmihalyi (1990, 118), the conditions for enjoying a mental activity are:

1. Skill in a symbolic domain
2. Clear rules
3. A goal
4. Feedback
5. Concentration and interaction at one's skill level

Both research and teaching can produce flow and enjoyment (Duffy & Jones, 1995, 28–29).

Although most faculty positions allow one to experience flow, if we asked four professors in identical positions, we would find that three are essentially satisfied and one is unsatisfied. Satisfaction at work depends on the person (Csikszentmihalyi, 1990, 154). People can refuse to remain unhappy (Henderson, 2000). Professors are responsible for making the most of their opportunities.

Early in their careers, faculty often find the challenges of academia too great for their skill levels. This can be particularly true in areas that professors are not trained for, such as teaching and advising. Later, the job can become boring, since it feels like everything has been done before. Boredom because of lack of variety and challenge is the number one problem for all jobs (Csikszentmihalyi, 1990, 161). One of the unfortunate characteristics of faculty positions is that little changes after each promotion. To stay motivated throughout a career, faculty "need to be competent, pursue worthwhile goals, feel autonomous, have social support, and receive affirming feedback" (Walker & Hale, 1999). When boredom occurs, professors need to either change their goals (e.g., change the focus to administration for a period) or ratchet up the challenge level (e.g., learn and use new teaching or research skills). Professors usually have enough control that they can keep their jobs interesting.

1.4. Using This Book

There's no one-size-fits-all method for improving effectiveness and efficiency. You have to adapt teaching, scholarship, and service methods to fit yourself.

Jung (1971) observed that people could be classified according to three continua. In the *extravert–introvert continuum* extraverts are energized by interacting with people whereas introverts are energized by working alone. This continuum does not say anything about the relative effectiveness of extraverts versus introverts. An extravert may be wonderful at working with people or may simply be a bore. An introvert may be shy or may have a gift for drawing others out. Extraverts are less likely to want to do projects that must be done alone, but they may be good at these tasks nevertheless.

The extreme ends of the *perception continuum* are *sensing* and *intuition*. People who prefer sensing would rather perceive the world with their senses; those who prefer intuition want to use their thought processes. We all have both abilities, but tend to use our preferred style. Sensing students like to learn in a step-by-step fashion and appreciate examples. Intuitive students appear to be much quicker, but often are not as accurate. Intuitive students clearly have an advantage on timed multiple-choice tests, but this advantage does not extend to most jobs.

The methods people use to make decisions vary along the *thinking and feeling continuum*. People who prefer thinking processes to make decisions want to use rational, logical processes. People who prefer to use feeling processes naturally include subjective, personal values in the decision process. Again, we have both abilities, but tend to use our preferred style. Differences in making judgments can cause disagreements and hard feelings. People who prefer a feeling process often see those who don't as cold, while they are perceived as being overly emotional. People who use the thinking process tend to be more efficient, but not necessarily more effective, at making decisions. People using the feeling process can adapt the structured rating methods used by people who use the thinking process by including subjective factors in the rating scheme.

Myers and Briggs (see Carskadon, 1994; Fairhurst & Fairhurst, 1995; McCaulley, 1987; Myers, 1991; Myers & McCaulley, 1985; Myers & Myers, 1980) developed metrics for Jung's three continua and added a fourth continuum that identifies how individuals choose to live in the world. This fourth continuum stretches from highly *judging* to highly *perceptive* individuals. People who prefer the judging mode want to control life and avoid surprises. They are often superb planners, but may not adapt well when things do not work out as planned. People who prefer the perceiving mode are happier to go with the flow and adapt to whatever happens. They tend to be better at activities such as advising or interactive teaching, which require one to adapt, but are criticized for not planning enough. There is some overlap between the perceiving style and right brain preferences (Herrmann, 1990; Lumsdaine & Lumsdaine, 1993).

Assistant professors are often pushed so hard to accomplish and build their resumes that they may be forced into a judging mode of life, even if it is not natural.

After five or six years, this behavior can become habitual. This is unfortunate, since the judging mode is not necessarily better than the perceptive mode. They can relearn how to enjoy life more from their more laid-back colleagues. We all need to continually work at balancing our lives.

Changing any habit is difficult. For the purposes of changing work habits, the judging versus perceptive continuum is most important. Books on efficiency and time management are usually written by people who prefer judging, since we are usually more interested in goals and scheduling. Although I have attempted to include ideas for everyone, this book is naturally permeated by my judging preference. Thus, people who prefer judging will probably find the book fits their style well. However, professors who prefer a perceptive style are likely to benefit more from this book than those who prefer planning, since the latter are probably already using many of these techniques.

Value judgments are required to prioritize both institutional and individual goals. Since these goals affect everything professors and institutions do, please read section 2.1 on personal missions. Most of the ideas in this book contain a nugget of truth that can be adapted to fit your circumstances. Of course, most professors are not at research universities and some parts will not apply. For example, faculty at colleges without graduate programs may choose to skip Chapter 9. Pick and choose what is applicable to you, but be willing to try something new. And remember that the appropriate action, particularly with respect to people, always depends on context. For example, I discuss two very different teaching styles (Chapters 5 and 6) without making a value judgment about which is better. The appropriate style depends on the context. If any of my suggestions do not fit the context of your job, disregard or adapt them.

People can be resistant to change. Although many of the ideas in this book are easy to understand, they are difficult to put into action. The most important advice is *start now.* Don't wait. Pick a few items that will make an impact and start using them. Most efforts to change habits fail because the effort is structured in such a way that failure is almost inevitable. Don't expect to be perfect. Treat any lapse as a learning experience, not a failure, and persist. Chapter 12 presents more formal methods for changing habits.

CHAPTER

2 Missions, Goals, and Activities

"Goals! Don't preach to me about goals and being efficient," exclaimed Professor Susan Smith. "I know all about goals. I set goals before every semester. But then I get dumped into a class I've never taught before with 72 students. And I still have my other classes, committees, and research to do. Plus I have a family. I can't be efficient when I'm struggling to survive." Chapters 2 and 3 are about goals and efficiency, explaining how you can go beyond just surviving to achieve your most important goals. The first part of this chapter discusses how you can determine your own mission, goals, and activities, and the second presents tactics to accomplish them.

This book is based on the premise that people are personally responsible for their lives. It is your life, and you are responsible for how you live it. To develop a degree of control in an uncertain world, it helps to see unfortunate situations not as disasters but as challenges or problems to be solved. Expect difficulties. Taking the attitude "If there's a problem here, I caused it" (Lair, 1972) is often the first step to resolution of problems between people. Effective, efficient people accept personal responsibility and learn to control their interpretations of events (Burns, 1989; Csikszentmihalyi, 1990, 1997).

Picture yourself in an airplane going to your discipline's annual conference. For the two-hour flight you brought three hours of work. But the plane took off an hour late, and it has been circling for over an hour, waiting to land, so you've finished the work and have nothing to do. You pick up the airline magazine. It is likely to contain an article about time management, organization, or setting goals, and you are likely to read it. Many professors have read one of the bestsellers on these topics. Thus, many readers of this book will be familiar with goals and priorities, to-do lists, calendars, efficient handling of mail, efficient travel, and other classic topics in the time management literature. Other readers will be unfamiliar with these topics. We have all faced similar situations in class. A diversity of backgrounds is a challenge for the teacher, and in this case for the author.

As a teacher, I am interested in individualizing this chapter and the entire book. If everything is new to you, read the entire chapter. Then go back and reread some of the parts that appear to be important for you. If most of the topics are familiar, skim the chapter and slow down to a reading pace when you come to something new. Take the same approach when reading other chapters.

2.1. Personal Missions

Although it is not essential to have a personal mission or calling in life, having one can provide almost limitless energy. It makes life more holistic, makes one more authentic, so that "the walk fits the talk," and reduces self-doubts. People with a mission in life find it easier to determine which goals they want to accomplish. They are also more likely to find happiness while focusing on their mission (Csikszentmihalyi, 1990, chapter 1; Henderson, 2000).

Bolles (1981), Covey (1989), Csikszentmihalyi (1990), McWilliams (1991), Palmer (1998, 25–33), and Zelinski (1997) all discuss personal missions (though they may call them other things). Everyone has the right to detect and live his or her personal mission as long as others' rights are not destroyed. A personal mission does not have to be grandiose, such as conquering cancer, developing a unified field theory, improving teaching in all universities, or eliminating poverty—although these would be fine missions. A personal mission can be much more localized and down to earth. It can be raising one's children to become responsible adults, continually working to develop one's marriage, striving to improve one's teaching and students' learning, maintaining a positive attitude, and acting in a collegial fashion. Note that the verbs used are action verbs, indicating a continuing process. A mission is a process, not a result.

Ultimately, people must detect and follow their personal mission to live a satisfying, fulfilling life. "A musician must make music, an artist must paint, a poet must write, if he is to be ultimately at peace with himself" (Abraham Maslow, quoted by Zelinski, 1997, 61). I would add that the teacher must teach and the researcher must search after truth.

People *detect,* not *invent,* their missions in life (Covey, 1989, 128). The personal mission is an integration of who we are and what we value and what gives us energy at our deepest levels. Covey's examples show that the personal mission statement is often complex, since it covers many areas of life.

Mature individuals' personal mission statements will be congruent with the center of their interests if they have sorted through conflicting messages and detected their true personal missions (Schumacher, 1973, 95). Part of the difficulty is that we hear so many messages about what we *should* be that we have difficulty separating what we *are* from the noise. Uncovering one's personal mission can be time-consuming but rewarding. Zelinski (1997, 62–63) suggests the following four questions:

1. "What are all your passions?"
2. "What are your strengths?"
3. "Who are your heroes?"
4. "What do you want to discover or learn?"

It is important to be honest about what interests and excites you. "Personal missions" that are really the wishes of others, such as our parents or spouse, are not really personal missions and cannot be as fulfilling as our inherent, real personal missions.

Growth and change occur throughout life, and both the center of one's interest and one's personal mission can change as a result of either slow maturing or a traumatic event such as the death of a parent. Children start out as self-centered. As they grow, they go through phases with different centers. Many college students appear to be friend centered (Covey, 1989, 115). As people mature, a stronger, longer lasting center of interest usually develops. This center describes to a large extent their character. Professors are often knowledge centered, student centered, or fame centered. Because of changes, people must work to redetect their personal missions periodically. As people age it becomes easier for them to discover their own mission.

> EXERCISE: Take the time to determine your personal mission statement. If you have never done this before, plan on revisiting your analysis periodically until your ideas have coalesced into a statement that feels right. If you have already determined your personal mission statement, review and renew it.

Fit between Institutional and Personal Missions

Professors choose to work at institutions for a variety of reasons. New Ph.D.s are not necessarily the most introspective and self-insightful people in the world. They often do not know their personal mission and misunderstand the institution's mission.

I once heard a radio interview with the U.S. national champion in horseshoes. Mastering the game of horseshoes was his passion, and being the best at horseshoes was his mission in life. This mission gave him the will and energy to excel. However, he deeply lamented that it brought him no recognition and monetary rewards. Although people have the right and the obligation to discover their own personal missions, there are absolutely no guarantees that they will receive external rewards for accomplishing them. Any professor whose personal interests and mission are not aligned with the mission and reward system of his or her institution can tell you this.

"All institutions of higher education have, or should have, one thing in common: the primary mission of educating students," states Kennedy (1997, 24). But institutional missions are more complicated than this. Flagship state universities are under pressure from their state legislators to improve undergraduate teaching *and* use research to drive technological development in the state (Clark, 1995, 132). Community colleges are pressured to improve their students' success in transferring to four-year institutions *and* improve job training (C. J. Lucas, 1996, 43–49). Comprehensive universities are asked to do everything. Such mixed messages invariably result in muddled mission statements. Institutions need to have clear mission statements and goals, but many do not follow them (Gardiner, 1994, 107–109). Detecting an institution's true mission priorities requires looking past the boilerplate at how the institution allocates its resources and rewards professors.

Since prestige in the U.S. university system lies with research and graduate education, universities with limited resources—all but a handful of private universities— are pulled toward favoring the graduate program and research over undergraduates, regardless of their official mission statement (Clark, 1995, 130). Fairweather (1994, 1996) found that faculty pay correlates strongly with number of publications. One of the major problems in higher education is that many institutions claim that one value—teaching undergraduates—is their highest priority, but tending to other goals prevents them from attending closely to this central goal (Fairweather, 1996; Gardiner, 1994, 131).

Even if the match between the personal mission and the institutional mission is initially close, either one or both may change over time. The match may become a mismatch. What can professors do if their personal mission does not coincide with their institution's mission?

The answer depends on the degree of mismatch. If the mismatch is slight, we can adjust and both missions can be fulfilled. After all, being a professor is a job and there are parts of jobs that we do not particularly want to do, but as professionals we do them at least as well as necessary. Ideally, we do them efficiently so we can move on to the parts more important to us.

If the most important parts of the two missions match, there are usually few problems. But the match may be between the professor's primary mission and a secondary part of the institution's mission. For example, a professor's primary mission may be teaching and fostering growth in students, but this is really a secondary part of the institution's mission. Some professors find it suffocating to work in such a situation and feel they must change positions to survive. Palmer (1998, 13–16) discusses the need for people to work in a nurturing or "life-giving" environment and implies that modern universities are not life-giving for many professors. Other professors are able to adapt to these contradictions.

Unfortunately, we can't change our personal mission statement at will. For example, we can't make research our personal mission just because that is what the university rewards. However, a variety of accommodations are possible. Missions are often broader than they appear at first. Some institutions have been willing to broaden the definition of research to include a variety of types of scholarship (see section 10.2). As other ways to add to the institution's prestige become acceptable (e.g., other types of scholarship, government consulting, teaching on television, writing textbooks, and developing multimedia presentations), professors' personal missions may become better aligned with their institution's. In other words, *become famous and local recognition and rewards usually follow*. Another possibility is that teaching, although still secondary, is important enough to the institution that professors whose personal missions are in teaching can receive adequate resources and rewards (Schulz, 1998).

Sometimes there is no congruence between the professor's personal mission in life and the institution's mission. Professors may choose to move to an institution that is a closer match. Writers and artists often decide to do these pursuits full-time. Professors who have become interested in business often consider starting a second career. If travel and time with family have become all important, perhaps it is time to retire.

In some cases, none of these solutions is possible. Many professors, particularly older ones, feel trapped because their personal mission is no longer aligned with their institution's, yet they are unwilling to quit or retire. It is vitally important to seek a personal accommodation with the institution and avoid bitterness. Tenured professors interested in students can decide to do what they want and seek their rewards (nonmonetary) from the students. If the situation at work is tolerable, the tenured professor may be able to treat the position as a forty-hour-per-week job and search for primary satisfactions outside of work. Although it's certainly not ideal, I have seen this accommodation work reasonably well when the professor was willing to fill roles (e.g., lab coordinator or schedule deputy) that no one else wanted to fill.

Finally, if you hate your job, Zelinski (1997, 57–58) has advice for you: Quit! "It is not impossible to leave a job, just difficult. Don't fool yourself by thinking something is impossible when it is only hard. If you want to do something, and are committed to doing it, you can do it. There is a price to pay, but it will be worth it in the long run."

2.2. Goals and Priorities

The purpose of saving time is to have more time to pursue our goals. At least some of our goals should be related to our life mission. Goals are needed in all areas of life, not only work. The most useful parts of this section and the next are the work *you* do to develop your own lists of goals, priorities, and activities.

Developing Goals

We all want to accomplish both the things we have to do (being a professor *is* a job) and the things we want to do (our work goals), and still have time for a personal life. If we work too much, we tend to lose the motivation to be efficient. The brain seems to ask itself, "Be efficient for what? So I can do more work?" Thus, we need goals outside of work, and these personal goals must go beyond relaxing from work, since that really is a work-related goal. Find at least one leisure activity that you enjoy, will be continually challenging, and can lead to growth. Such an activity can result in *flow* (see section 1.3). Examples that work for different people are exercises such as jogging, swimming, walking, and weight lifting; sports such as fishing, golf, sailing, and tennis; hobbies such as gourmet cooking, model building, and woodworking; and reading.

It is useful to develop goals for various time frames (Lakein, 1973). For professors, the term (quarter or semester) and summer are natural time frames. It is also useful to list goals for longer periods of time, such as three or five years, in addition to lifetime goals. For assistant professors, the time until promotion documents need to be prepared is a natural period. Associate professors can choose the number of years until it is reasonable to be considered for promotion to full professor.

GOAL DEVELOPMENT EXERCISE **1.** Pick a natural time frame from one to four years. On a sheet of paper list your goals for this period. Be sure to list both personal and work goals. When you feel you have exhausted your ideas, leave the list alone. While you are doing other tasks, there is a good chance your subconscious will develop additional goals. After a day or so, come back to the list and add more goals. Keep doing this until the well dries up.

GOAL DEVELOPMENT EXERCISE **2.** On a separate sheet of paper, list your personal and work-related lifetime goals. Follow the same procedure as in Exercise 1. Compare your two lists. Are a reasonable number of lifetime goals included in the first list? Feel free to change your goal lists at any time.

One goal that most people have but may forget to put on their lists is maintaining or obtaining good health—an enabling goal that makes it easier to reach other goals. If this goal was inadvertently missed, add it to your lists. In many cases, improving one's health is a reasonable goal. However, an incurable illness or a chronic health condition is not an excuse to give up.

Major goals should be broken down into subgoals so a sense of accomplishment is felt more frequently. For example, writing a book can be broken down into these subgoals: outline the book, outline each chapter, write each chapter, and rewrite each chapter. Accomplishment of the subgoals is obviously easier and provides positive feedback as one moves toward the major goal. The same procedure can be used in teaching. If your goal is to do an outstanding job teaching, your immediate subgoal is to do an excellent job *today*. Feedback from the students will tell if you accomplished that goal or at least came close today. A series of successful days will lead to accomplishing the major goal.

Classification of Goals

Goals That You Alone Decide You Have Achieved versus Goals That Others Decide You Have Achieved.   Goals can be classified in a variety of ways. The most important distinction is whether you alone decide that you have achieved the goal or this is a joint decision with others. When others must agree that you have achieved a goal, the criteria that they will use should have a major impact on your subgoals. For example, one critically important goal for most new professors is getting tenure. In 1992 about 73 percent of candidates were awarded tenure (D. W. Leslie, 1998, 669). Although institutions and departments have different standards, on average tenure became more difficult to attain in the last three decades of the twentieth century. Research publication requirements, in particular, increased (D. W. Leslie, 1998, 666, 670). Denial of tenure usually occurs because a professor does not meet the institution's criteria. Professors who teach well *and* meet the research criteria are usually promoted. Tenure is thoroughly explored in Firkin's (1996) and Tierney's (1998) collections of papers and from a different viewpoint by Silber (1989, 139–159). Van Alstyne (1971) and Firkin (1996, 92–97) discuss the legal meaning of tenure.

Professor John Johnson has decided to work hard to present a good case for his promotion/tenure, but the final decision is made by his institution. Development of a good case requires that John understand the institutional criteria. Since there are both written and unwritten requirements, he reads the documentation and talks to people. Although the criteria are purposely vague, subjective, and subject to change, John's diligent efforts to understand them result in an accurate enough fix.

John may not agree with some of the promotion criteria. He has the right to argue against the criteria, since they are based on value judgments. (Personally, I feel that a narrow focus on research is not in the best interest of colleges and universities.) However, *he does not have the right to win*. Since the institution ultimately decides, professors who argue about the appropriate criteria by doing different subgoals often are not promoted. Often the decision to deny promotion is a joint decision, even if the professor's part is not acknowledged. However, professors who take the risk of doing something different but do it very well may be promoted.

If Professor Johnson fails to realize that he has chosen to argue against his institution's criteria, he may be setting himself up for a disaster. He needs to accept what *is* (Krishnamurthi, 1954). Then he can take charge of his life and make a conscious decision whether to play by the institution's rules (setting and achieving subgoals that meet the institution's criteria). If personal values prevent John from doing this, at least he will know what risks he is taking. Unfortunately, *fear* may prevent him from accepting what *is* (Krishnamurthi, 1954; Palmer, 1998, 35–60).

Promotion or any other reward decisions can be unfair, impossible, and perhaps unethical. John's institution may hide the actual criteria it will use. The criteria can be set at one level initially and then new requirements can be added. John may be denied tenure regardless of merit, because the institution decided it cannot afford or does not want more tenured professors in his department. (In rare situations this decision may be necessary.) There is also evidence that women are often treated differently than men, sometimes given a higher workload, which can result in fewer publications (Creamer, 1998).

Who determines whether goals have been achieved affects many areas of life, although often less dramatically than in the tenure decision. Tenured professors can choose to ignore projects that meet their institution's expectations and work on other projects. The ability to pick and choose what to work on within broad limits is one of the privileges and joys of being tenured. However, this privilege does *not* require the institution to reward professors who don't meet expectations. Professors have the right to argue about the criteria, but not the right to win. Taking responsibility for their actions requires that professors who ignore their institution's expectations realize that the institution's rewards may be withheld from them. The paradox is that professors who follow their personal missions and do what they feel is right often do it so well that they are ultimately rewarded for their efforts. Tenure provides the time to wait for these rewards.

Routine versus Nonroutine Goals.   A second distinction is between routine or automatic goals and nonroutine goals. For example, graduating from college becomes automatic for seniors. They have to continue to go to class and study at least a bit, but they know how to do that. For many first-year students, graduating from college is a scary, nonroutine goal. Automatic goals are much easier to accomplish than nonroutine goals. One of the purposes of education is to make many scary, nonroutine goals automatic or close to automatic.

Work versus Personal Goals.   The third distinction, between work and personal goals, may be fuzzy. If John decides to improve his health, that is a personal goal, but it will probably also make him more effective and efficient at work. Intellectual activities can also affect both work and personal life. For example, for this book I wanted to learn about the concept of flow. Unexpectedly, this concept also affected my leisure activities and my family life.

Idealistic versus Realistic Goals.   It is useful to have both idealistic and realistic goals. An example of an idealistic goal is to write a textbook that will change the way a subject is taught and learned, while a more realistic goal is to write a book that will be adopted. I aim for the former but accept the latter.

Growth Goals.   Finally, it is useful to have at least one growth goal (Covey, 1989, 287–307; McCay, 1995, 155–156). Examples of growth goals are earning a master's degree in another discipline, learning a new language, developing a new computer skill, reading a challenging but rewarding book, improving skill in a sport, and learning more about oneself. Professors who develop a second area of expertise in addition to their discipline often have an advantage, since they stand out. For example, professors who develop expertise in pedagogy in addition to their disciplinary skills stand out from other professors who are also good teachers. Earning a master's degree in your second area of expertise is one way to certify your interest and competence.

> GOAL DEVELOPMENT EXERCISE 3. Return to your goal lists and add any goals that were missed.

Priorities

Most professors find they have too many goals. There is no way to accomplish all of them. We need *priorities.* Ask yourself, Which goals are most important now? Often, the most important goals are clear. List them first in your priorities. If you leave all your goals on the list as high priority, you are not prioritizing. Successful professors set only a few high-priority goals (Walker & Hale, 1999). Some goals may be important to you but will interfere with achieving other goals. Conflicting demands are "an essential fact of academic existence" (Eble, 1988, 222). One way to accomodate goals that are not work related, such as sailing alone across the Atlantic Ocean, is to use them as rewards when the higher priority work goals are met. Your department and institution may not understand, but they will tolerate the behavior, since their criteria were met first.

   If your priorities are not clear to you, they can usually be made clear by comparing each goal with each other goal (Mayer, 1990, 55–56). If we compare goal A separately to goals B, C, D, and so on and each time find that goal A is more important, then goal A has the highest priority. Goal B can next be compared separately to each of the remaining goals. It often helps to sleep on the priority decision.

> PRIORITY EXERCISE. Prioritize the goals on each of your lists. Sleep on this decision and then revisit your priorities.

   Both goals and priorities change with time (Lakein, 1973). A presentation that will be delivered on November 15th may be a low priority in August, a moderate priority in October, and a very high priority the second week in November. Dramatic events such as getting a new job, being promoted, getting married, having a child, or the death of a parent may cause a rethinking of our goals and priorities. Occasionally, there is an epiphanic moment. One such moment came to me when I was interviewing for positions while finishing my Ph.D. In the middle of a presentation to a company, I thought, "What am I doing here? I really want to teach." The goals and priorities belong to you. Change them whenever you want.

2.3. Activities

Activities are what we *do* to achieve our goals (Lakein, 1973). For example, Professor Susan Smith has set a goal of being promoted to full professor, and, toward this end, her mentor has identified two subgoals for her: improving her teaching and her publication record. She looks at these subgoals and decides that improving her teaching is the most important work goal this semester. With a little bit of help, she develops the following list of activities to improve her teaching:

- Attend a teaching workshop.
- Analyze last year's student evaluations to see if there are things that are irritating the students.
- Take photographs of the students and learn their names.
- Develop objectives for the course and share them with the students.
- Set office hours that are convenient for the students.
- Ask a master teacher to visit her class and provide feedback.
- Smile more.
- Pass out incomplete lecture notes to the students.
- Have at least one small-group activity each class period.

Obviously, Susan can generate more ideas for activities than she can do. She needs to prioritize them. She starts by noting that some activities need to be done only once, while others will have to be done most class periods. Since it is easier to find the time and energy to do the one-shot activities, she chooses two of them and one ongoing activity to work on. To change her work habits, Susan needs to stay with these tasks for at least one month, preferably the whole term.

Family and personal life are important. A balance between work and love is needed, although juggling between family and professional responsibilities is difficult. Maybe it is time to drop scheduled activities, simplify, and have some free time instead (e.g., the children and the parents may all be tired of the annual Christmas show). Turning off the television may also free up a significant amount of time (Csikszentmihalyi, 1990, 83, 119–120, 168–171; Zelinski, 1997, 127–128).

It is efficient to find one activity that will help you achieve two or more goals (McGee-Cooper, 1994, 179–185). For example, Susan decides that maintaining her good health and spending more fun time with her children are both important goals. One activity that she lists to maintain her health is to exercise more. Her son enjoys bike riding, and her daughter wants to be a basketball star. She decides to ride regularly with her son and play basketball with her daughter. Susan is *not* trying to do two things at once. When she rides her bike with her son or plays basketball with her daughter, she is doing a single activity and enjoys doing it. These activities are efficient because they help her meet two important goals simultaneously.

ACTIVITY DEVELOPMENT EXERCISE. Develop a list of activities that will help you accomplish one of your high-priority goals. Be creative. Force yourself to add items that are not readily obvious. Once you've come up with a long list, let it sit overnight and then go back and prioritize the activities. Commit yourself to doing one or two of these activities.

Deciding to do everything is *not* prioritizing. Some possibilities must be left out. One of the reasons for developing a long list is to force you to choose. Reflection will often show that things are on the list because they have always been there, not because they are effective.

Some activities may not be feasible. For example, some professors are able to run one or two marathons a year. Setting a goal of running a marathon is reasonable if you are in good health and fairly good shape and you check with your physician. A training schedule (the activities) can be developed to achieve this goal. Expecting to run a marathon every month is infeasible. The time and energy commitments are too great.

2.4. Workloads and Time Logs

How many hours should you work each day and each week? In the course of history there have been "no strict formulas" (Csikszentmihalyi, 1990, 143). Currently, in the United States the forty-hour workweek is an approximate standard, although professionals tend to work more. Most professors clearly work more. But forty hours a week is probably the minimum a full-time professor can work without incurring the wrath of department chairs, deans, trustees, and state legislatures.

If you are trying to get promoted, become famous, or compete with other professors, a forty-hour workweek is clearly not enough, but working more hours per week is productive only up to a point. During World War II, a study in England found that factory workers produced more when they increased their workweek from five to six days. Since this initial experiment was a success, the workweek was increased further to seven days. The total output, not just output per day, decreased. When the workweek was returned to six days, total output went back up. People need a day off every week.

For most people, around 55 hours of work per week will get the most work done (Harrisberger, 1994, 167, 240). Regularly working more hours often leads to burnout and stagnation. Since professors have considerable discretion on how they use their time, perhaps half of the 55 hours per week could be spent on work for the institution and the other half on projects of their own choosing. Of course, working fewer hours per week is an option, particularly for professors who are past the promotion/tenure grind or are not in a tenure-track position.

Professors who are trying to earn promotion and tenure may feel that the tenure probation period is similar to wartime, since almost total dedication is required. But they will accomplish more over the five- to six-year probationary period if they take off one day a week and *reduce* their average workweek to approach 55 hours. Occasional bursts of more work are not detrimental if they are rewarded by relaxation. Professors will also probably benefit from a yearly vacation and mini-vacations, such as spending an extra day as a tourist at conventions. Vacations and other outings "help to clear the mind, to change perspectives, to look at one's situation with a fresh eye" (Csikszentmihalyi, 1997, 45).

Workaholics

Unfortunately, most companies and universities want workaholics (Zelinski, 1997, 42, 50). Workaholics think of work constantly (Freudenberger, 1980; McGee-Cooper, 1994, 203–207). They give up all other goals and can experience flow only at work (Csikszentmihalyi, 1997, 63). They never take a day off to enjoy leisure activities. If they take a day off, it is to rest so that they will be better prepared for work. They take vacations either for work purposes or because they are nagged to do so by their spouses. And when they return from vacation, they can't wait to get back to work.

For most people this is a recipe for burnout. The exceptions who thrive on continual work find that their mission in life, job, and avocation are all the same. Unfortunately, many assistant professors adopt the workaholic pattern, believing it is the only path to tenure. They, and other faculty, may work frequently at home, and the job can consume all their time (Tack & Patitu, 1992, 42–44). However, in addition to being more productive, people who take time off are usually more creative and make fewer mistakes at work (Zelinski, 1997).

The solution to avoid workaholism is to find at least one other interest in life. Activities such as sports, games, or hobbies that allow one to set goals, focus entirely, and experience flow are particularly good. They distance one from work and help prevent staleness.

Having It All

Another problematic syndrome is believing one can have it all: a full load at the university, including awards in both teaching and research; a busy travel schedule; a happy family life with home-cooked meals; well-adjusted children who receive lots of focused attention; a well-kept house and yard; a busy social life, including many cultural events; and so forth. More women than men think this way, because women face more family pressures (Tack & Patitu, 1992, 45–50). The impossibility of having it all is discussed by Peters and Austin (1985, 496). Although being superorganized helps, trying to have it all is a recipe for stress and burnout.

This syndrome occurs because professors refuse to prioritize and institutions are not attuned to the complex family pressures experienced by women professors (Tack & Patitu, 1992). To prioritize, realize that some things are not necessary. Skip a meeting occasionally. A simpler home life will be easier to manage. Substitute money for time. For example, gourmet food or at least very good food can be purchased for carry-out. When you are promoted into a position with power, remember to work for institutional change to provide more flexibility for working parents.

Time Logs

How many hours are you really working per week? Many professors overestimate their actual work hours until they keep track. To determine your work practices, keep a time log or diary (Boice, 1992, 135; Csikszentmihalyi, 1997, 40–41; Di Yanni, 1997, chapter 2; Marvin, 1974; Walesh, 1995, 42). One way to do this is create a log in which you record everything you do during one day, at fifteen-minute intervals. Include everything—the work you do on your highest priority task, other work, phone calls, rest and daydreaming breaks, coffee breaks, visitors and other interruptions, visits to the rest room, checking your e-mail, and time spent recording the log. The log needs to be kept up-to-the-minute throughout the day. If you wait until the end of the day, you will miss many small interruptions that can add up to a significant portion of your time. Fortunately, time logs need to be done infrequently.

Be sure you keep the time log on a fairly typical day. If you want to check your work habits during the academic year, keep the log during a typical academic week—not the first week of the term or the day before a major vacation. Check on your summer work habits with a log during summer break.

Look for patterns in your log. What fraction of your time is spent on task? My time logs show that I am lucky to spend 60 percent of my time on task. Interruptions are my major problem. What are your most productive times for getting "alone" work done? My time logs consistently show that I get the most done from 7:30 or 8:00 to about 9:30 in the morning. If I don't have a lunch meeting, there is often a second productive period around lunch time. A third productive period often occurs from around 4:00 P.M. until I go home for the evening; this period is invariably productive on Friday afternoons. These periods are productive because there are fewer interruptions at these times.

What are your time wasters? Interruptions, mail, and e-mail can consume a significant amount of time. Do you or interrupters manage your time? Do you work on the high-priority items, or do you let yourself become sidetracked to less important but more urgent or more fun tasks? Procrastinating by working on fun or urgent tasks is common. Do you work alone at your most effective times? Many people do not know what their most effective times are (Csikszentmihalyi, 1997, 40). If you work at home, do you stay on task or let distractions pull you away? Home has an entirely different set of distractions than work.

TIME LOG EXERCISE: Keep a time log for one or two days.

After you have kept a time log and analyzed it, think about ways to improve. Results, not hours of work, are what count (Moran, 1993). Don't keep busy just to look busy. Look at your goals and work on the important items. The difference between busy and happy versus overworked and frazzled is probably only a 5 to 10 percent increase in workload.

There are lots of methods you can use to control your time better and ensure that you spend more of it on high-priority tasks.

2.5. To-Do Lists, Calendars, and Schedules

Some people cringe when they hear the words "to-do list" and "schedule," thinking they smack of overregimentation. However, the variety of calendars, schedules, and electronic devices available (Covey, 1989, 146–182; Lakein, 1973; Mackenzie, 1972, chapters 3 and 4; Mayer, 1990, section 18; McGee-Cooper, 1994, part 2; Di Yanni, 1997, chapter 2) is large enough that everyone can find a system that works. Despite claims to the contrary, no one system is best for everyone. Professors who strongly prefer perceptive (or right brain) behavior may find that the suggestions in McGee-Cooper (1994) are the most in tune with their preferred styles. Lakein (1973, 14–17) warns to watch out for the overorganizer. Try different procedures until you find a method that works. Find the appropriate balance between organization and moderate chaos. If nothing seems to work, be creative and develop your own scheme. Borrow a little from the different experts and add your own touches. What is needed is a balance between being scheduled and being flexible. Continual balancing is difficult, but appears to be part of the life of a professor.

To-Do Lists

The to-do list includes the things that need to be done and important goals (Lakein, 1973; Mackenzie, 1972; McGee-Cooper, 1994; Van Blerkom, 1995, 39). Including goals focuses our attention and reduces distractions (Csikszentmihalyi, 1997, 137), making it more likely we will get things done. You can see your to-do list as a flexible tool to help you accomplish what you want to, or as a sword hanging over your head, ready to drop if you ever falter.

As an example of customization, consider the technique that Susan found works for her. Her semester to-do list of major projects and unusual tasks (those that do not occur every week) is a useful guide for preparing weekly and daily lists. If the project or task has a deadline, Susan lists the deadline on the semester list. Of course, she usually puts more items on the semester list than she can accomplish. She thinks of the list as part deadline items and part wish list. She prioritizes the long-term goals, but includes currently low-priority goals as a reminder of what she would like to do in the future.

Susan's weekly list includes items from the semester list plus routine items, such as preparing lectures, that need to be done every week. She makes sure that at least one high-priority, long-term goal is on her weekly list and schedules at least one time period, preferably more, to work on this goal during the week. She also lists important personal activities. The busier she is, the more she feels a need to organize.

Calendars

Susan writes her daily list on her desk calendar, on the blank side of the page. This list includes must-do items, such as preparing a lecture or writing a test. Listing an item, such as writing a test, several days early is helpful. If something does not get worked on, she transfers it to the next day. Sometimes this transferring can go on for two weeks if there is no deadline. On the side of the calendar with half-hour time blocks she lists appointments (both work and personal) and classes. She also schedules one morning a week to work at home. She tries hard to protect this time block, since it allows her to move forward on a long-term project every week.

Professors are often asked if they are available for committee meetings or oral examinations, but the person asking is unable to make a firm commitment until he or she has asked everybody involved. Susan tells the person what times are open on her calendar, but always adds that this can change. She will not commit to be available until she is given a firm date and time. She does tentatively schedule meetings in her calendar in pencil but prefers not to because canceled appointments may not be removed from the calendar.

Schedules

Lakein (1973, 48–50) notes that people have *internal prime time*s, when they work best alone, and *external prime time*s, when they work best with others. An important scheduling goal is to have alone time during internal prime times and interaction during external prime times (Lakein, 1973; Mayer, 1990, chapters 5 and 25; McGee-Cooper, 1994, 121–123; Walesh, 1995, 36). It is important to have some alone time every day. The more introverted you are, the more you will value this alone time. Some professors find they automatically have alone time and see no need to schedule it. Others know that if it is not scheduled, this time will evaporate. Professors also need to be sure there is enough external prime time.

Susan's internal prime time is in the early morning. Although she does not enjoy getting up early, mornings are very productive if she gets up around 6:30, eats a light breakfast, helps get her children ready for school, and starts work promptly. After lunch, she has trouble focusing on creative tasks such as writing. She reserves this external prime time for meetings, office hours, answering mail and e-mail, teaching class, and other interaction activities. This schedule provides sufficient time at work so that she is available to people who need to interact with her, and it provides time at home to write.

Susan often works half a day on Saturdays. She uses this time either to get caught up on work tasks that slipped by during the week or to work on long-term goals. She also rests and does things with her family on Saturday. (Moran [1993] advises not working on weekends.) Except for rare emergencies, she does not work on Sundays.

This is Susan's personal schedule. Following this schedule requires self-discipline. She must set the alarm clock and get up in the morning. She also has to force herself to work when she is at home, despite distractions. When her children were little, working at home was not effective. When circumstances changed, she adjusted her schedule. The only magical thing about this schedule is it works for Susan. Determine a personal schedule that works for you.

Schedule growth or professional development time every week (Marvin, 1974; McCay, 1995). This is a time for learning new skills, such as new research methods in your discipline, new computer hardware, or new software. Pick skills that you find inherently interesting, that you can use, or that will prevent stagnation. Self-directed growth time is often sufficient to keep up with evolutionary changes in your field. Truly revolutionary changes may require taking a short course or workshop.

> SCHEDULING EXERCISE. Determine what daily schedule works for you. Remember that professors need interaction time and alone time. Arrange your daily calendar to follow this schedule as much as possible. If you really do not know what schedule will be effective, experiment. Try different schedules for a week and record daily what you did and how effective you were. After several weeks, look for patterns of what works and what does not. For example, you may find that mornings are effective if you get to bed early but are totally ineffective when you get to bed late. Or perhaps you are never effective in the morning. Some of the important patterns can be subtle. You may find that one cup of coffee and a bowl of cereal are sufficient for a good morning of work, but skipping breakfast or eating too large a breakfast doesn't work.

Procrastination

For many people procrastination is the number one devil that prevents them from meeting their goals. Unfortunately, the more important the task, the easier it is to procrastinate. One major reason is *fear* (Lakein, 1973, 128–133). Because we are afraid (often subconsciously) of not accomplishing the goals, we never start. This is particularly true of writing tasks (see sections 10.4 and 10.5). Large projects often seem to be overwhelming because they cannot be finished with a single burst of energy.

It is usually easier to control behavior than fear. Once you start working on a project, the fears usually recede. Mayer (1990, 73–80) suggests some ways to stop procrastinating:

- Don't allow yourself to do trivia instead.
- Reward yourself for getting started.
- If a reward for starting doesn't spur you, think of a punishment for not starting.
- Nibble at big projects to get started.
- Break the big project into parts and develop subgoals (see section 10.3). When you do one small part, reward yourself for accomplishing a subgoal.
- Schedule the times and places to work on the project. Several small time blocks are likely to be more effective than one large block.
- Discuss your fears with someone you trust or write them in a private diary. Consider rational arguments to counteract these fears.
- Force yourself to do the task.
- Bore yourself to death. Do absolutely nothing.

People often procrastinate doing something because they do not really want to do it. Do a goal check. Will this task, as distasteful as it is, help you accomplish a high-priority goal? Reminding yourself of the goal can get you started. I find this technique to be helpful in writing research proposals. I dislike asking for money, but doing research is a high-priority goal. So, somewhat grudgingly, I write proposals. If the goal check shows that the task is not a means toward high-priority goal, maybe you should not do it.

Another trick is to use procrastination creatively to get things done. Put a task that someone else wants you to do high on your to-do list. Then "procrastinate" on this task by working on other projects that are interesting and important to you.

2.6. Summary

If you want to change, *start now*. Don't wait for that magical moment when you have gotten yourself organized and caught up. You may wait a long time.

Start by working to detect your personal mission. It has to feel right to you and not be what others tell you to do. If your mission does not align with your institution's, look for accommodations that will close the gap. Develop goals in a number of areas, including work, leisure, and growth. Pick one or two goals and brainstorm activities that will help you meet them. Prioritize the activities and pick one or, at most, two to focus on for each goal. Develop a method to remember the goals daily.

If you get less done than you think you should, keep a time log for a few days. The results may show where improvements can be made. Try using to-do lists and some form of calendar. Although they are not magic bullets, many people find that one of these methods helps to organize their days, makes the days less hectic and ensures that the important tasks get done. Experiment to find a variation that works for you.

Trying to become a totally new person overnight invariably leads to failure. You have to find changes that work, but that takes at least a month. Be patient. And be gentle on yourself. When you backslide into your old habits, chuckle at your weakness and then return to the new behavior pattern. When you are successful, congratulate and reward yourself. Positive change requires, first, belief that you are responsible for yourself and, second, self-discipline (Covey, 1991, 49–51; Csikszentmihalyi, 1990, 1997; Glasser, 1984, chapters 5 and 6; S. Johnson & Johnson, 1986). No one is going to do it for you.

3 Applying Time Management Methods

In Chapter 2, Professor Susan Smith decided to organize her life. She detected her mission and goals. She developed to-do lists and a schedule that worked for her. But this is not sufficient. She has to actually *do* things to meet her goals. The literature on time management covers a large number of techniques to help people accomplish tasks. In this chapter, I discuss how academics can use these to improve their effectiveness and efficiency.

3.1. Increasing Attention and Energy

Attention

One of the secrets to success is to simply pay attention (Zelinski, 1997, 16). Learning to pay attention is a major part of many spiritual teachings (Easwaran, 1991). Unfortunately, paying attention and focusing are sometimes difficult. Professors are preoccupied by other things, see what they expect to see, and do things out of habit. Our time becomes contaminated when we are supposedly doing one thing, such as working on a paper, but are really focusing on another, perhaps a fight with the department chair. This is an unproductive worry, since we are not doing anything to resolve the problem and it is interfering with other work (McGee-Cooper, 1994, 164–167).

Although we normally don't work at it, alertness can be cultivated. McCay (1995, 42–45) suggests three alertness exercises:

1. Occasionally change your routines. Do things differently.

Susan tried taking notes at departmental seminars and found that this helped her pay attention and she no longer fell asleep.

2. Every day, practice an activity that you enjoy and requires all your attention.

Susan returned to playing her flute and found she felt much more mellow afterwards. Meditation is another possibility (Easwaran, 1991).

3. Cultivate at least one interest based on observation.

Susan's husband enjoys bird-watching.

Then use these skills. Pay attention to what happens at work. Observe students and other faculty. Pay attention while doing research.

Energy

Paying attention requires energy, and if attention needs to be shifted from one thing to another, even more energy is demanded. Being a professor is a high-energy occupation. Where does this energy come from? Do things that you enjoy and are passionate about. Determine what activities help you regain your energy and engage in some of them every day. Introverts are energized by working alone, whereas extraverts are energized by interacting with people. Arrange your daily schedule to give yourself periods to recover after activities that drain your energy.

Increase your available energy by focusing less on negative activities, because they are tremendous energy sinks. Conserve energy by avoiding interactions that involve criticism and the resulting defensiveness. To stay energetic and alert and gain productive time, McCay (1995, 47–70) recommends that we frequently check seven areas and control our response if something negative has occurred.

1. *Thinking*. Since the symbols and words we use affect all other factors, thinking is the most important area. Watch for the use of absolutes such as "must," "mustn't," "should," and "shouldn't" and words that imply failure such as "can't," "try," and "but." Professors often do this to themselves and to their students; for example, compare the different connotations of "You shouldn't sleep in class" and "You would do better in class if you stayed awake." When you catch yourself thinking in negative patterns, stop! Use words such as "it would be better" instead of "should" or "must."

2. *Feelings*. The immediate, short-lived feeling you have in response to an event (e.g., a flash of anger when another car bumps into yours) appears to be a hardwired response that is not under conscious control. However, longer term reactions (e.g., continued anger about a minor car accident) are under conscious control (Borysenko, 1987; Easwaran, 1991; Ellis, 1973; Ellis & Harper, 1997). When you become aware of these negative feelings, explore the thoughts behind them.

3. *Movement*. Gritting your teeth, crossing your arms, stomach pains, talking fast or incessantly, laughing nervously, and other body and muscular patterns are often early warnings that something negative is occurring. Analyze the thinking behind the physical problem and move. Stand up, go for a walk, relax your jaw, do a deep breathing exercise, or go to the rest room. Regular, daily exercise helps people stay healthy and have more energy (Rowe & Kahn, 1998, 97–111).

4. *Food and Beverages*. Watch what you eat and drink. To determine patterns, log your eating and drinking habits every 10 or 15 minutes for several days. Determine if there are patterns that distress your system and stay away from them.

5. *Environment*. The environment is everything around us, including lighting, decorations, air quality, and the people we interact with. Negative factors in the environment may include bare or ugly walls, smokers, and excessive noise. A short-term solution is to try a temporary change. If the hallways are being painted and your office smells, go to the library or borrow another office. If your office is ugly, take charge and beautify it. Note that some people are much more sensitive to the environment than others.

6. *Past Experiences*. People make their own memories and have significant control on how much past experiences affect their lives. The brain will bring up old, often unpleasant memories, when it is not kept occupied (Csikszentmihalyi, 1990, 119, 128). Professor Smith found that she spent quite a bit of time stewing over old injustices. She decided to allow herself the luxury of doing this for two minutes and then she would move on with her life.

7. *Expectations*. Unrealistic expectations can sour an otherwise enjoyable experience. For example, many assistant professors expect that promotion will make their world a brighter place. And it is—momentarily. Then the new associate professors find that little has actually changed. This can lead to disappointment, blaming the institution, and a search for greener pastures.

Take charge of your life and use your energy on what interests you.

3.2. Computer Technology

Computers will continue to affect how professors do their jobs, but exactly how much is debatable. Both the pro-technology side (e.g., Borchardt, 1996; Finlayson, 1996) and the skeptics (e.g., Attewell, 1996; Mayer, 1990, 146–149) make valid points. Taking a middle course between obsessing over the new technology and shunning it altogether appears to work for most professors. As far as computer use in teaching is concerned, I believe that (1) computers have clear-cut advantages for some, but not all, forms of teaching (see section 4.5), and (2) the best teaching will always involve personal contact with the instructor.

Advantages and Disadvantages of Computers

Computers have brought many advantages. Students are more willing to rewrite when they use computers, since word processing programs make writing a rough draft and rewriting much easier. Producing a clean copy with a variety of type styles is simpler. With spreadsheets and graphing programs, graphs can be drawn more quickly and neatly than they can be drawn by hand. Word processing and presentation software such as PowerPoint produces neat, readable transparencies. E-mail and the Worldwide Web have revolutionized the way we communicate and obtain information. Approximately 85 percent of Internet use is estimated to be e-mail (Harper, 1999). Simulation programs provide enormous power and can present realistic scenarios. Many new research areas would not be possible without the power and storage capacity of modern computers. The best educational software has shown increased student time on task and corresponding increases in learning.

Yet every one of these advances has a dark side. The disadvantages due to technological limitations will eventually be fixed; however, most of the disadvantages are caused by operator error. Computers often magnify human faults. Although word processors are in many ways wonderful, they seem to encourage excessive rewriting and in most cases have *not* changed productivity (Attewell, 1996).

Students will readily produce fancy graphs, but they often understand less. Since producing graphs by hand is laborious, in the past most students made them only when it was absolutely necessary. Production of excellent transparencies is indeed easier, but many people keep "improving" transparencies past the point where communication is improved. Also, producing graphs on the computer often hinders interpretation by separating the student from the data.

There is too much e-mail. And it is too easy to send messages that are not ready to be sent or should never be sent. The web is a highly seductive medium that can suck people into hunting for information for hours. Since it is easy for individuals to post whatever they want, the web is much less reliable than books. Web pages that have inoperative links or Java bugs can cause computers to crash. The web has proven to be a poor substitute for actual contact with people and evidence is mounting that web addiction is real (Fearing, 1996; Kinch, 1996; Young, 1998).

As for simulations, they are certainly powerful, but virtual reality is not a substitute for reality. Although the power of computers and calculators is incredible, people who were trained with slide rules had a much better feel for the correctness of their answers. With a slide rule, the user had to determine where the decimal point was. A flaw in slide rule technology forced the operator to make order-of-magnitude estimates. Computers can store huge amounts of information, but retrieving it can be difficult. Well-designed educational software is indeed effective, but poorly designed software is not. Using computers and other modern technology can also increase stress (Baldwin, 1989).

Finally, people have a tendency to let the computer "think" for them. They become less flexible in seeking alternative solutions and paralyzed when the computer is not working. For example, if computer registration is done in a particular way, they assume things cannot be done any other way. This, of course, ignores that a person programmed the computer to operate in this way and could have programmed it to operate in another way. Or if the network is down they assume they cannot communicate with another person forgetting that they can make a disk and walk to the other person's office ("the sneaker net"). Students seem to be particularly susceptible to these problems and often assume that even ridiculous answers must be correct if they are from the computer.

Institutions have found it difficult to measure the return on their computing investments. The use of computers has resulted in a "productivity paradox." People believe that using computers should increase productivity, but most studies have been unable to point to measurable increases in productivity (DeLoughry, 1994; J. Leslie, 1998). Productivity paradoxes have occurred in the past when a new technology was introduced. It took approximately fifty years for productivity increases to become obvious after the introduction of electric motors, which was also an extremely versatile technology with thousands of applications (J. Leslie, 1998).

Effective, Efficient Use of Computers

What can professors do to avoid being snared by the seductions and pitfalls of computer technology yet not be branded a Luddite?

- Balance doing things by hand with doing things on the computer. For example, if you can't determine how to put a figure where you want it in a file on the computer, revert to cut and paste on the hard copy.
- Ask for help. Often the best help is from people who know how to use the software or the machine but are not experts. The experts tend to clog their explanations with too many options. Secretaries are usually good sources of information on office software.
- Stay one step behind technology and software. The first version of any major innovation invariably has bugs.
- Don't get too far behind technology, though, or you will have trouble functioning. For example, many professional societies now conduct a substantial portion of their business via e-mail and the web.
- Avoid perfectionism. To a certain extent, perfectionism is in the eye of the reader. Stop revising after a reasonable number of revisions.
- Save everything and back up frequently. One chapter of this book was lost when my computer "lost" the file. Fortunately, I had saved an earlier version on a floppy disk.
- Avoid excessive and frequent customization, such as fancy wallpaper, desktops, and fonts. The line between computer work and play often becomes blurred.
- Read at least the first section of the manual.
- Document all web sources. Make bookmarks or write down your sources.
- Retrieve changed or eliminated web sites through the Alexa search engine <http://www.alexa.com> (Selingo, 1998).
- A good place to learn better web search techniques is the "Bare Bones 101" tutorial at <http://www.sc.edu/beaufort/library/bones.html>. Lesson 5 of this tutorial and the site <http://lib.nmsu.edu/instruction/eval.html> are good sources on evaluating web sites.
- Since it is no longer possible to be caught up on your reading, limit your web time.
- Have a reason to save files. Don't automatically save everything.

Certain devices and—even more important—attitudes can help you use the computer more effectively and efficiently:

- Buy a monitor with a large screen.
- Get more memory.

- Buy a high-speed modem, such as digital subscriber line (DSL) or cable.
- Consider a Zip drive for backing up files.
- If you don't mind carrying an expensive piece of machinery that is a favorite target of thieves, and you can afford it, invest in a laptop. Talk to ordinary users about what they like and don't like about them. Go light, since the "necessary" add-ons increase the weight.
- Don't use pirated software, and don't look the other way if your students do.
- Get tips from others about what hardware and software work.
- Organize your hard disk with either long lists of folders or layers of embedded folders, but not both (Borchardt, 1996). Or purchase software that allows other styles. Use the Find command. Use logical file names.
- Periodically clean out your files. Use a pre-trash file for a second chance after something is thrown away.
- Use e-mail efficiently (see Table 3.3).

3.3. Conventions and Networking

Conventions help academics catch up on the latest research, network and socialize with other professors, find jobs and collaborators, and attend committee meetings to get the business of the professional society done. They can provide new ideas and regenerate professors. The downside is that "almost everyone . . . is on the make" professionally (Getman, 1992, 231).

Traveling to conventions can be a major time commitment and expense. Too much travel can reduce your ability to get things done, and your long-term goals can suffer. Gain control through these three steps:

1. Decide if you really want or need to go. If there is no goal for the trip, don't go.
2. Look at the big picture before deciding. List all the travel you are aware of for three months before and three months after the meeting to see if you will have enough time and energy to go.
3. Say no if there are good reasons for staying home.

Tips for efficient travel are listed in Table 3.1. The principles of *Zen driving* are given in Table 3.2. Zen driving is both easy and very difficult to maintain. It is certainly the safest way to drive in any large city. Focusing on the task of driving instead of doing other things, such as using a car phone, will reduce accidents.

Plan ahead for conventions and meetings (Panitz, 1996). Decide ahead of time which programs you want to attend, but be sure to schedule some free time for networking, fun, and relaxation. An afternoon off to work in the hotel room or visit a local museum alone can do wonders for the energy level of introverts. However, the more involved you are in the convention, the more you will gain from it. If you want to spend some time catching up with an old friend, make arrangements ahead of time. Since

TABLE 3.1.   Commonsense Tips for Efficient Travel

General:

- *Call home every night.*
- Ask local people for directions and suggestions.

Airplane Travel:

- Find a good travel agent or become familiar with making arrangements through the web. There are huge differences in the convenience of airline flights and their cost. Nonstop flights are preferable.
- Give yourself plenty of time to get to the airport. The number one priority is the trip, not doing 15 more minutes of work.
- Develop a standard checklist for packing. If you pack light and carry on everything, you save time and don't have to worry about lost luggage. Packing light also makes it easier to use local public transportation at your destination.
- Pack snacks in your carry-on bag.
- Pack enough work in your carry-on for at least two hours longer than your flight is *supposed* to last (Mackenzie, 1972, 73; McGee-Cooper, 1994, 124; Walesh, 1995, 41). Bring along some variety, such as reading and writing, and bring items such as magazines that can be thrown away after they are read to make room for items you pick up on the trip.
- McGee-Cooper (1994, 124) strongly suggests using laptop computers.
- Carry on *critical* items such as medicine and the slides or transparencies for your talk. *Always* carry your tickets and (if needed) passport with you.
- If there is a problem such as a mix-up in seat assignments, politely ask the flight attendant for help.
- Part of the hassle of travel is caused by the unpleasant environment of airplanes, which can be noisy, crowded, too dry, and too hot or too cold, and by jet lag. Dress comfortably and bring a sweater or light jacket. Stretch in your seat and get up out of it every hour or two. Walk during layovers. Drink noncaffeinated, nonalcoholic drinks. Use a decongestant if you have a stuffy nose. Eat lightly throughout the trip, and if you don't like standard airline food (if it is served), ask for a special diet plate.
- Bring any device, such as an inflatable pillow, eye shades, or earplugs, that will help you relax on the plane.
- Before you arrive, switch your watch to local time. There will be fewer misunderstandings and chances for error.

Automobile Travel:

- Study the map and write down instructions for the highways you plan to take before you leave. Have the instructions and map handy during the trip.
- Either switch drivers or give the driver a break every two hours. Snacks and beverages will help keep the driver fresh.
- If you have work to do or are tired, get someone else to drive.
- Listening to music or a sporting event will make the trip seem to go faster.
- If you rent a car, obtain directions from the agent. Familiarize yourself with the car in the lighted parking lot before driving off.
- Use the principles of Zen driving listed in Table 3.2.

TABLE 3.2.   The Principles of Zen Driving

1. Accept that you already know how to drive in a relaxed but attentive manner.
2. Sit in the driver's seat, strap on the seatbelt, and let the ever present inner chatter pass on by. Focus on being in the car.
3. Decide the route to where you are going, put the car in gear, and drive without consciously paying attention to the mechanical aspects of driving, since you already know them.
4. Practice "moving meditation." Sit erect and attentive in your moving car and be aware of everything around you. If thoughts of work, family, or other drivers intrude, acknowledge them and return to awareness of everything happening.
5. Maintain your attention of everything happening within a 360-degree radius. Move your head, look at the mirrors, be aware of your speed, hear the sound of your tires, smell the air, and feel the entire experience. Let your mind comment on everything happening and then let it slide past. Acknowledge the distractions of your judgments of other drivers and of yourself and let them pass. First tolerate and then let pass your feelings of fear or anger.
6. As in any meditation, you must refocus when the brain's inner chatter reoccurs.
7. Assert yourself effortlessly, without thinking, to respond to whatever happens. For example, if a driver swerves into your lane, swerve assertively and automatically into the free space you are aware of.
8. Return to awareness whenever you are distracted.
9. Practice regularly to keep your skill level high.

Source: Adapted from K.T. Berger, *Zen Driving* (New York: Ballantine Books, 1988), pp. 15, 32–33, 35–43, 46–55, 65–70.

convenient hotels can fill up rapidly, make reservations as soon as you know which days you will attend. I prefer staying at hotels that are close to the convention but are not formal convention hotels. These hotels are usually less expensive, and the atmosphere tends to be saner. (Panitz [1996] recommends staying at the convention hotel.) Restaurants away from the convention hotels also tend to be less crowded and less expensive. If the waiters and waitresses call customers by name, you have found a place where locals eat.

If you will make a presentation at the meeting, practice ahead of time. Never check your computer disk, slides, or transparencies with your luggage. If you plan to give a computer presentation, always have a backup plan, such as transparencies, in case the technology doesn't work. Arrive at the meeting room early to become comfortable with the room and any equipment you will use. The early arrival of speakers also helps the session chair relax. After the presentation, debrief yourself. What worked, and what could be improved? Record the questions you were asked.

It is impossible to pay attention for three or four straight hours of presentations. Don't try. Take a break when there is a talk that is not of interest to you. Go out into the hall, get a drink of water, talk to people, or sit in a quiet corner and generate new ideas, meditate, or read. I find that taking notes on both the content and the style of the presentation helps me concentrate. You can also use this time as a "student" to reflect on presenters' actions and learn what's effective and not effective.

Immediately after a session is a good time to mingle and meet people (a.k.a. networking). Stick around after the morning session and become part of a lunch group. If you hear any important tidbits during these informal discussions, record them as soon as you have a chance. Hand out your business card and collect others' cards freely. When you collect a card, write the date and location plus a short note about the person's interests on the back. This information can come in handy years later. For example, if you want to invite someone to present a seminar at your school, it is nice to be able to remind the person that you met in Paris in June 2001.

Since face-to-face interactions have not been replaced by virtual ones (Agre, 1994), conventions are a prime place to network effectively. Be willing to talk respectfully with everyone, not just the stars in your discipline. Senior faculty, who can be very helpful to junior faculty and graduate students, may be surprised at the useful information and support they receive back. Junior faculty and graduate students are usually the ones who know the research details. Senior faculty can help junior faculty and graduate students network by introducing them to people and including them in informal groups. Junior faculty and graduate students can prepare for these discussions by studying the research articles of professors they want to meet (Agre, 1994).

Good networking is a two-way exchange of ideas, information, and resources that is beneficial to both parties (Agre, 1994; Bloom et al., 1998, 83–89; Woods & Ormerod, 1993). You must share some of your knowledge and resources, even if it often seems that you give more than you receive. In the long run, the givers are appreciated and rewarded, often in unexpected ways (Nowak & Sigmund, 2000). Professors who know many people and give of themselves are often elected to more professional offices and receive more awards than can be accounted for by a dispassionate analysis of their accomplishments. Networking is enhanced by truly caring for people. People respond to warmth, enthusiasm, and trust. Be genuinely happy to see people, and let this show. The hardest part of networking for introverts is showing their caring. Arrange to spend time with people and learn quality things about them. These attitudes also work in teaching.

Susan found it difficult to mingle and talk to people at meetings. She improved when she realized that many people draw a distinction between casual, breezy conversations and in-depth conversations. Casual conversation is superficially hearty and formulaic (Csikszentmihalyi, 1997, 114). With a little practice, Susan mastered this form. Deep conversations involve an interest in at least one of the other person's goals, and then a mutual follow-up on this interest (Csikszentmihalyi, 1997, 114–115). Deep conversations are difficult to fake.

On the trip home, collect your notes and thoughts and create a to-do list of things you promised. You may have promised reprints to several people, the address of a colleague to a friend, and the outline of a proposed session to the program chair of the next meeting. Delivering what you promise is necessary to maintaining a network. Don't promise things that you cannot or are unwilling to deliver. It is better to say no or not volunteer.

Some effort to maintain contact via telephone, e-mail, or letter in addition to occasional contacts at meetings is also necessary to maintain a network. Don't wait until you need a favor. For example, a short note of congratulations when someone wins an award or is promoted is always appreciated. Or consult with colleagues for advice before organizing a seminar or meeting (Agre, 1994).

When you give a seminar at another university, take the same approach as just described for conferences. Prepare the talk ahead of time and plan ahead. Study the school's brochure to connect names with research. Notice who went to the same graduate or undergraduate school you did, since it gives you a connection to talk about. If your school is interested in recruiting graduate students, arrange to meet with undergraduate students to talk about the opportunities of graduate school. Most schools are happy to arrange these meetings. On the trip home, debrief yourself. And when you get home, deliver what you promised.

3.4. Coping with Stress

For all the talk about ivory towers, academic life is often stressful (Boyer, 1990, tables A-30 and A-31; Gmelch, 1993; Menges, 1999a; Seldin, 1987; Sorcinelli, 1994c). Although a certain amount of stress actually improves performance (Csikszentmihalyi, 1997, 157; Gmelch, 1993, 12), many faculty, particularly new faculty, are *too* stressed (Gmelch, 1993, 24–25). A 1998–99 University of California, Los Angeles (UCLA), survey of faculty (Magner, 1999b) found that the worst stressors for faculty are:

1. Lack of reward and recognition.
2. Time constraints. This number one source of stress in the UCLA survey was cited by 85.6 percent of respondents. Related to time pressures were "lack of personal time," cited by 79.7 percent, and "managing household responsibilities," cited by 71.2 percent.
3. Influences within the department, mainly interactions with the chair. "Institutional procedures and red tape" was cited as a source of stress by 69.4 percent of respondents in the UCLA survey.
4. Professional identity. Trying to maintain a professional identity (e.g., as a sociologist) while working as a professor.
5. Student interactions.
6. "Keeping up with information technology" was cited by 67.2 percent of respondents.

Female faculty are less satisfied with their positions and feel more job-related stress than do male faculty. Female faculty's dissatisfaction is greatest in male-oriented departments (Tack & Patitu, 1992, 36–42). Married women experience more stress from time constraints and professional identity than do other faculty (Gmelch, 1993, 25; Tack & Patitu, 1992, iv–v, 43–50). New faculty are particularly stressed by tenure anxiety and concerns for the future (Trautvetter, 1999, 85). The clearer the mission and goals of the institution, the less stress faculty feel (Menges, 1999a).

Handling Stress

Resilient people use a variety of coping strategies (Whitman et al., 1986). Professors can make sure they get enough sleep, eat properly, and exercise (Rowe & Kahn, 1998).

They can also try *changing the environment* (Wankat, 1993a). Uncomfortable office furniture can cause physical distress. Noisy environments can cause stress and reduce productivity. Although *changing the academic environment is appealing, it usually is not possible, and other coping strategies need to be explored.*

A second strategy is to change our perception of the stress. *Stress is caused by our interpretations of stimuli* (Borysenko, 1987; Ellis, 1973; Ellis & Harper, 1997; Seligman, 1990). Changing the interpretation can markedly decrease the stress. One way to do this is to list all the tasks we need to do and then prioritize them (Csikszent-mihalyi, 1997, 106–107). Many of the tasks may be unimportant or may take only five minutes to complete. What appears to be a hopelessly busy schedule may look much more manageable after it is analyzed. And doing something about at least some of our goals tends to make us feel better (Csikszentmihalyi, 1997, 137).

Talking to someone will also help you sort out and defuse issues. It's a good idea to check your self-talk, too. For example, suppose that an article Susan submitted to a journal receives a bad review and the editor questions the suitability of the paper for publication. Susan can interpret this several different ways. A mature way to deal with the disappointment is first to feel sadness and irritation that the work was not appreciated and additional work is now needed. After the luxury of a few minutes or hours of feeling sorry for ourselves, we can start improving the manuscript. But many professors react irrationally. One response, which is usually irrational, is to blame the entire problem on the reviewers and the editor, insist that the original manuscript was perfect, and refuse to change anything. Unless you are famous, this is a recipe for frustration. Another irrational response is to take the rejection personally and believe that it means you are a bad person. This is caused by an irrational belief system. Change your belief system to a more accepting one, and you will reduce your stress (Borysenko, 1987; Ellis, 1973; Ellis & Harper, 1997; Seligman, 1990).

A third way to cope with stress is to use *recreation and relaxation*. Playing basketball, golf, or tennis, doing some other sport, or just walking is an effective way to cope with moderate stress, and the exercise is good for your health (Gmelch, 1993, 29; Rowe & Kahn, 1998, 97–111). Effective relaxation methods include breathing exercises (Borysenko, 1987; Humphrey, 1988; Whitman et al., 1986), progressive relaxation (Humphrey, 1988; Jacobson, 1962), muscle exercises (Borysenko, 1987), meditation (Benson, 1975; Easwaran, 1991; Humphrey, 1988), and repetition of a mantra (Easwaran, 1991). When I was a graduate student, I became very stressed and anxious while preparing for the departmental general examination. Daily practice of progressive relaxation based on Jacobson's (1962) book brought the problem under control. Daily use of any of these proven methods would probably have worked.

Saying No

People have trouble saying no (Ellis & Harper, 1997; Lakein, 1973, 84–88; Mackenzie, 1972, 54–56; Mayer, 1990, 84–89; McGee-Cooper, 1994, 193–198; McWilliams, 1991, 166, 410). It may be comforting to have the reputation of being the person everyone can count on—"Good old Susan. You can always count on her"—but the effort to keep that reputation may burn you out. Saying no may give you the time to do what you really want to do. An attitude change and perhaps assertiveness training (Alberti & Emmons, 1974) may be necessary to learn to say no. Think of all the important things you could do if you said no more often!

You do not have to give a reason when you say no. Reasons invite argument, and a determined individual can find ways around every excuse you come up with. Either just say "No" or say, "Let me think about it." This is a reasonable request, and it gives you the initiative. Who knows, you may change your mind. And if you really are not sure, "let me think about it" *is* an appropriate response. After a while, you can send a note or e-mail stating that after due deliberation you have decided to decline. Don't call, since you may have to defend your decision.

If you are not sure about doing something, try mapping out the commitment on the calendar to see how long it will take (McGee-Cooper, 1994). Since professors routinely underestimate how long something will take, if it appears to be too heavy a commitment, it probably is. If there is time available but you still are not sure, try listing the alternative uses for this time. If one of the alternatives is much more appealing, schedule that instead.

Of course, there may be good reasons to say yes. I routinely serve on the advisory committees for other professors' graduate students, and they do the same for me. I say yes to these requests because there is a *quid pro quo* that helps me achieve the important goal of helping my own students graduate.

3.5. Efficiency Tips

Communications can be a time sink for most professors, who may spend hours reading and responding to mail, e-mail, and memos and answering and returning telephone calls. As shown in Table 3.3, there are a variety of methods for efficiently dealing with communications, which may be categorized as valid, semivalid, or invalid. Valid mail (or e-mail or telephone calls), which comprises 80 percent of the communication useful to you, consists of necessary mail, including bills, checks, personal letters, responses to your inquiries, journals you subscribe to, catalogs you requested, and so forth. Fortunately, valid mail is usually easy to spot, since it is addressed to you, has a recognizable return address, and is more or less expected. Express mail or packages from air express companies are usually valid. Unfortunately, even valid mail such as bills often contains invalid portions, such as offers for merchandise.

Invalid communications include unwanted advertising and various "deals." Slogans such as "You may have already won," "Dated offer!" "3.9% APR," and "The favor of a reply is requested" and items addressed to "Occupant" are normally invalid mail. There is no law saying that invalid mail or e-mail must be opened. Since many professional societies have started fund-raising through offering credit cards, invalid mail may well come from valid return addresses. This mail may need to be opened, but a quick perusal will show it is invalid.

Semivalid mail is the mail that cannot be classified quickly. It needs to be opened and scanned so that it can be reclassified as valid or invalid. Many university memos

TABLE 3.3.   Ways to Make Your Communication More Efficient

Mail:

- The goal is to handle each item only once.
- Do not handle mail (or e-mail) during your prime work-alone times (Lakein, 1973, 80).
- Sort the mail into valid, invalid, and semivalid. Discard invalid mail or save it for a very low energy period (Delaney, 1981).
- Open the semivalid mail, scan it, and reclassify it.
- Open the valid mail, and as much as possible complete whatever you have to do—respond, file it, talk to someone about it, or discard it—at one sitting.
- Do *something* to move mail forward every time you pick it up (Mackenzie, 1972, 71–73).
- Write directly on the letter to respond to the sender or to make notes for yourself.
- Respond immediately to the rare truly urgent item by fax, e-mail, or telephone.
- When you send mail, include your e-mail address, telephone, and fax numbers, and perhaps the URL to your homepage on the letterhead.
- Envelopes should have return addresses.
- Letters should be polite, short, and to the point.
- If you are really angry about something, write a letter to calm down, but do *not* send it. After you have calmed down, put this "hot" letter in the trash.

E-mail:

- Assume that your e-mail messages are *not* private.
- *Never* write a "hot" e-mail message. It is too easy for it to be sent by accident. Don't ever send messages when you are angry.
- Make e-mail brief, and proofread it before you hit send.
- Don't read other people's e-mail.
- Respond to e-mail in batches.
- If you will be away from your e-mail, have the e-mail automatically respond that you will respond when you return.
- Aliases are convenient for sending e-mail to a number of people, but the message loses its personal touch.
- Requests for people to do work are much more effective if they are addressed to only one person instead of to a group.

Telephone:

- If the telephone rings at a truly bad time, such as the moment you're leaving for class, do not answer it.
- If a call is going to take more time than you have available, it is polite to ask if you can call back.
- With salespeople you do not want to talk to, be polite but firm—"I'm really not interested." If the caller is rude and ignores this, repeat the statement and hang up.
- If you leave an important message on an answering machine, make sure you provide a way (e-mail or a return call) for the recipient to let you know the message was received and understood.

are in this category. Most do not contain useful information, but enough of them do that you shouldn't toss any campus memo without skimming it first.

Tips that professors may find useful from a number of time management and efficiency books are listed in Table 3.4 (e.g., Lakein, 1973; MacKenzie, 1972; Mayer, 1990; McCay, 1959; McGee-Cooper, 1994; McWilliams, 1991).

TABLE 3.4.   A Grab Bag of Efficiency Tips

"The single most important time saving technique to learn is to *write it down*" (Mayer, 1990, 117). This is a little too strong, but it remains excellent advice. Carry a sheet of paper and a pen with you, and date everything.

The 80:20, or Pareto, principle states that 80 percent of the value of comments, ideas, or tasks comes from 20 percent of the items (Lakein, 1973, 70–73; Mackenzie, 1972, 51–53; McGee-Cooper, 1994, 221–223; Walesh, 1995, 37–38, 201–203). Spend prime time on the important 20 percent of tasks and either don't do or develop efficient routines for handling the remaining 80 percent.

Use odd moments of down time throughout the day productively (Lakein, 1973, 58–59). For example, bring along work such as a book or article to read while you wait at the doctor's office.

Label as "urgent" tasks listed on your calendar that will help you meet your high-priority goals. This makes it much more likely they will be done than the common "back-burner" approach.

To control interruptions, try closing your door while retaining open access (Walesh, 1995, 40). Working at home is often a solution to interruptions but has its own pitfalls. There are different interruptions at home, and work life can consume home life. If you work at home, follow a schedule similar to your work schedule.

If at all possible, arrange your office into a private work area and a meeting area that is visitor friendly.

The efficiency of clean desks is vastly overrated (McGee-Cooper, 1994, 67–79). If you like a clean desk, by all means keep a clean desk. However, having a modest number of piles around makes an office look worked in, and if you can work this way, don't feel you have to make your office cleaner.

Arrange your office to have the items you use often physically close to you and those you seldom use at a distance (Borchardt, 1996). Put the books and journals you use frequently within reach. Store the files that you routinely use in the most convenient file cabinets.

Every employee should have an ergonomic office chair. A properly fitted chair is the first line of defense against back pain and carpal tunnel syndrome (Sauter et al., 1985).

Appropriately delegating work will help professors reduce workloads. Effective delegation requires that the task be clear and the person doing it be allowed some control over exactly how and when to accomplish the task.

Perhaps the way to save the most time and reduce your workload in teaching is to *delegate work to students*. Teaching methods to do this are explored in Chapter 6.

When it comes to interacting with people, "attention is all there is" (Bob Waterman, quoted by Peters & Austin, 1985, 312).

3.6. Summary

Efficient work habits require both an overall strategy (e.g., goals, priorities, and to-do lists), as discussed in Chapter 2, and tactics for doing things on a daily basis, as discussed in this chapter.

People can improve their attention and energy levels. This isn't really difficult, but it does require getting out of our comfortable ruts. We need to be sure that we are not wasting energy. I know professors who waste huge amounts of time complaining, but don't realize that they are their own worst enemies.

Computers have allowed people to accomplish much more, but they have also helped people waste time. Treat the computer as another tool—use it when it is useful to you and use something else when it isn't.

Many professors spend a fair amount of their time traveling. This time can be relatively productive or unproductive. Professors who never travel will benefit from adding a trip a year, whereas those who travel too much need to learn to say no. One of the main benefits of attending conventions is networking, which is often more edifying than attending sessions. We often learn more while networking because we are being active learners.

Stress is part of academic life. Most professors can learn to cope with it by developing a variety of strategies, including changing the environment, changing their interpretation of events, participating in recreation, and practicing relaxation techniques. During particularly stressful periods be sure you use your coping mechanisms.

Several actions help us to accomplish tasks daily. For example, learn to say no. Keep mail, e-mail, and telephone calls from becoming time sinks by categorizing them as important and less important.

To make progress, start with an inventory of how you work. Adapt suggestions from time management books such as this one to the context of your life and work. Ignore suggestions that do not fit. When you recognize yourself wasting time or procrastinating, work to change your habits. The more aware you are of your habits, the easier it will be to effect improvements. But do not berate yourself for past or current failures. Try something new and reward yourself when it works.

4 Teaching and Learning

"By a crude mathematical formula, it can be suggested that what students teach students should be one-third of an undergraduate education, what professors teach students should be another third, and what each student does alone in the library, the laboratory, and the study should be the remaining third" notes Pelikan (1992, 61). Kuh et al. (1991, 8) report that 70 percent of learning occurs out of class. Thus, effective and efficient teaching is only part of the story. A large portion of our efforts should focus on shaping the environment to improve student learning (Menges, 1990). In this chapter, I explore general issues of learning and teaching. Chapter 5 focuses on lecture courses in which students learn from the professor. In Chapter 6, I examine problem-oriented courses, in which students to a large extent learn from each other. In Chapter 7, I consider developing rapport with students. Chapter 8 focuses on improving the learning that students do alone.

4.1. Good Teaching

Definitions of good teaching have been given by Brown and Atkins (1988, 4–5), Lowman (1985, 1995, chapter 1), McKeachie (1994, 315–316), Ramsden (1992, 89–90, 96–102), and Schmier (1995, 58, 140–147, 152, 240, 265–268). The definition given here, which follows that given by Wankat and Oreovicz (1998a), does not totally agree with any of these authors.

Good teaching achieves:

- High amounts of student learning—this is most important
- Coverage of the right content at the right depth
- Good student attitudes
- High ratios of both student learning to instructor time and student learning to student time
- Opportunities for students to learn how to learn
- Learning appropriate to the context
- Authentic interactions between the professor and the students

Teaching methods that encourage the students to become involved and actively engage with the material increase student learning (Astin, 1975, 1993). These methods include cooperative groups, role plays, debates, simulations, real projects, and brain-storming.

Knowledge of the subject is consistently associated with good teaching (Boyer, 1990; Cross, 1993). Subject knowledge is almost a given for college professors, except that continuing trends to hire professors on contract, part-time professors, and those without Ph.D.s (Wilson, 1998) could lead to the hiring of teachers who do not know the material. Most professors know their subjects but lack a practical understanding of pedagogy.

Although professors know their subjects, selecting the right content without overloading the course is difficult. The phrase "right content" can lead to many argu-ments. Students also need practice in discipline-specific critical thinking, problem solving, communication, and interpersonal skills. Selecting content and controlling content tyranny are explored in section 5.1.

The course context influences the pedagogies used (McKeachie, 1994, 18, 144; Ramsden, 1992; Weimer, 1990, xiv). A focus on learning instead of teaching often leads to a mix of methods and may increase productivity (Barr & Tagg, 1995; Layzell, 1999). Courses intended to convey the basics of the field may require teaching methods different from those required for courses intended to prepare students for professional practice. Different methods may be used in electives than in core courses. Since mature students can benefit from less structure and more freedom, teaching styles appropriate for gradu-ate students and seniors are different from those required for first-year students.

Authenticity, which involves being what the professor *is,* is discussed at length by Palmer (1983, 1998) and Wilshire (1990). This dimension is evident in many former students' recollections of great teachers (Carson, 1996; Epstein, 1981; Peterson, 1946). Consider Professor Jenkins, one of my professors when I was an undergraduate. He was a brilliant and somewhat arrogant scientist who was not fond of students who did not try to think. The one characteristic he valued most highly was the ability to think. When he wasn't lecturing, he used a Socratic approach. He could be sharp and merci-less, but whenever a student made halting progress toward independent thinking, Pro-fessor Jenkins became encouraging and supportive. His eyes twinkled as he cajoled the student into thinking. Many students learned for the first time that they could think independently. His former students remember and tell stories about him. Although he was not loved, he had a great impact on many of his students. He was authentic.

The quality of teaching and learning needs to be assessed, but the assessment needs to do more than evaluate performance in lectures (Kennedy, 1997). Reflection by the professor on all aspects of the course should be the first step. After every class, take a few minutes to reflect on the class and write a few comments on possible changes. Formative feedback on student understanding can be obtained by using "one-minute quizzes" (Angelo & Cross, 1993). After the first test, I give my students a three-by-five-inch card and ask them to answer the question, "What can the professor and the TA do to help you learn?" Most of the students' comments are thoughtful. I then make appropriate midterm changes in the course.

Students' attitudes and the appropriateness of the teaching method can be gauged with student evaluations, which are both reliable and valid if properly designed and administered (Centra, 1993; Marsh, 1984). Unfortunately, many student evaluation forms in use were designed for lecture-style courses and are inappropriate for other teaching methods. Peer evaluations can be used to determine correct content coverage (Centra, 1993, 118–119). Peer visits or videotaping can be used to help improve teaching methods. Although scary (what if I'm terrible?), both methods are helpful. Finally, some means need to be developed to determine whether the students have learned.

A generally underexplored item in books on teaching is how to be efficient while retaining effectiveness. New professors often spend too much time preparing for class (Boice, 1992, 2000). Even if this results in effective teaching—and it usually doesn't—it is not sustainable, since it reduces the time they can spend on other aspects of their jobs. Fortunately, many teaching methods, such as solving test and homework problems before using them, are both effective and efficient. These methods are interspersed throughout Chapters 4 to 8. Paying attention to efficiency does not need to interfere with one's passion for the subject or for students.

4.2. Increasing Student Learning: What Works

A three-word summary of all the research on student learning is: *Involved students learn* (Astin, 1975, 1993; Pascarella & Terenzini, 1991, 50–51, 610, 611, 616–626, 648–650). If this doesn't ring true to you, watch a teenager learning how to play a new video or computer game. The question for teachers is how to get students involved in the course material, not video games.

Many researchers, including Dewey and Piaget, have contributed to the current understanding of knowledge structures (e.g., Flavell et al., 1993; Kurfiss, 1988, 25–28, 34–37; McKeachie, 1994, chapter 27; Pintrich, 1992; Ryan, 1995, 82, 127). It is now clear that *people construct their own knowledge structures*. The brain does not photograph a beautifully constructed lecture and then hang this photograph in a hall of knowledge. Instead, each person constructs his or her own structure, which may have little resemblance to what the professor presented. The more people know about a subject, the easier it is for them to learn additional material that fits into their existing knowledge structure. However, it becomes harder to fit in new facts that do not fit. People tend to ignore these facts, which means they are not learned. This is one reason professors may have more difficulty than students in learning new ways to look at their subject.

The research on how people learn helps explain why particular teaching approaches are effective. Here are some procedures and actions that are known to work:

1. *Involve* the students (Astin, 1975, 1993). Many of the following items are methods for involving students.

Student Actions:
2. Ensure that the students are *actively processing* material (Bonwell & Eison, 1991; Chickering & Gamson, 1987; Ramsden, 1992, 100–102). This helps ensure involvement. Students discussing a topic in a small group may be quite obviously

active. A solitary student reflecting on the material is also active, but this activity is not as obvious. Processing requires time.

3. Give the students some *control* over what and how they learn (Freire, 1993; Ramsden, 1992, 100–102). Students learn more and enjoy learning more if they have some control over the process. In choosing which elective courses to enroll in, students exercise control over what they learn. In core courses, projects can provide students some of this control.

4. Require student *practice* (Angelo, 1993; U.S. Department of Education, 1986, 41–42), including homework, papers, oral presentations, projects, and tests. Practice strengthens the neural pathways that make up the knowledge structure in the brain.

5. Encourage and aid student *reflection* (Ehrlich, 1995, 84–85; Kolb, 1984). When there is no direct feedback, students need to reflect on the experience to learn. This can be done privately in a journal, one-on-one with a knowledgeable person, or in a small-group discussion. Reflection is an important component of service learning (see section 6.3).

6. Provide ways for students to be *challenged yet often successful* (Angelo, 1993; Ramsden, 1992, 100–101). Unchallenged students become bored and perhaps disruptive. Students who are never successful become frustrated and perhaps disruptive. Disruption is a symptom that something is wrong.

7. *Encourage students to teach other students* (McKeachie, 1994, 144–146; U.S. Department of Education, 1986, 36). The old cliché is that the teacher learns more than the students. Usually the teacher is more involved with the material than the students. Students who tutor others either individually or in small groups learn more, and they are more likely to go on to graduate school. Since the students being tutored also learn more, this is a win–win situation. Interaction among students is a powerful factor in learning (Angelo, 1993).

8. Encourage focused *time on task* (Chickering & Gamson, 1987; McKeachie, 1994, 157; U.S. Department of Education, 1986, 34, 41). As time on task, increases students learn more. This appears to be a major reason why teaching techniques such as computer simulations and the personalized system of instruction increase student learning.

9. Have the students *come to class prepared* (Uri Treisman cited by O'Brien, 1998, 102). Only prepared students can intelligently discuss the material, and the students will learn more if they are prepared. To encourage preparation, require them to turn in a short assignment or a question before class, or give a very short quiz at the beginning of the period.

Teacher Actions:
10. Have *positive expectations* of the students (Carson, 1996; Chickering & Gamson, 1987; Ramsden, 1992, 100; U.S. Department of Education, 1986, 32).

Research has repeatedly shown that students learn a lot more when teachers expect them to learn more. I started to do well in grade school after obtaining a high score on an IQ test in third grade. The results went into my file, and the teachers started expecting me to do well. The same principle works in college. It is easier to have positive expectations if one believes that talent and ability are abundant rather than scarce (Barr & Tagg, 1995).

11. *Be enthusiastic* and demonstrate the joy of learning (Bonwell & Eison, 1991, 21–22; Cross, 1993; McKeachie, 1994, 25). Students will like the class more, have better attitudes, and probably study more. The professor's love of the subject is contagious (Carson, 1996). Professors who are introverted need to make an effort to show this love.

12. *Guide* the learner (J. R. Davis, 1993, 141; Ramsden, 1992, 99–100; U.S. Department of Education, 1986, 35). It is easier to learn when a trusted guide points out the key concepts and best resources and informs one of potential difficulties. Set clear objectives for the students (McKeachie, 1994, 328). Show the students the content's underlying structure. It is easier for students to form new knowledge structures from well-structured material. Emphasize concepts instead of facts.

13. For new material, use an *inductive approach* starting with specifics and proceeding to general rules (Felder & Silverman, 1988). Deductive approaches can be efficient if students are studying the material for the second time. There is a trap here. When professors select textbooks, they already know the material. Textbooks using deductive approaches may look very attractive, but for introductory courses they are generally a disaster. A related idea is to start with concrete experiences and lead to abstract ideas (U.S. Department of Education, 1986, 29).

14. *Depth* works better than shallow breadth (McKeachie, 1994, 61; Ramsden, 1992, 75, 79–81). Looking at many variations of a single example is more effective than looking at many unrelated examples. It is also an efficient use of class time, since the context of only one example needs to be explained.

15. *Clear presentation* styles are essential (Angelo, 1993; Ramsden, 1992, 96–97). Use analogies and metaphors to relate the material to what students already know. Note that analogies and metaphors must relate to what the students know, not what you knew at the same age. As professors age, they need to change their analogies and metaphors.

16. Use *images and visuals* (Bonwell & Eison, 1991). Most students are visual learners and learn more and faster when visual images are presented. Apparently, visual images are often easier to incorporate into the knowledge structure, but the visual material should be used with an interactive, active teaching method. Incorporating visual images is difficult for professors who are mainly oral learners and prefer, for example, reading and listening.

17. *Separate instruction and assessment of student learning* (Kennedy, 1997, 78–79). Ideally, instructors help students learn the material. Unfortunately, students tend to believe the instructor is a hindrance instead of a help when the instructor first teaches and then evaluates the performance of students. Outside examiners or another professor in the department can help by doing summative evaluations. Supplemental instruction (see section 8.5) is effective partially because it follows this principle. If an evaluator is not available, make most of the evaluations formative and give the students an opportunity to correct their mistakes.

18. Provide *rapid feedback* (Chickering & Gamson, 1987; Ramsden, 1992, 99; U.S. Department of Education, 1986, 43). Reinforce correct knowledge structures and modify incorrect ones. Be sure that the students use the feedback. Make students turn in a corrected paper, problem, or test after they have received feedback

19. Ask *thought-provoking questions* (U.S. Department of Education, 1986, 38). This involves students in actively modifying their knowledge structures. Try posing "challenge problems" that are not answered until later.

20. Make the class more *cooperative* (Bonwell & Eison, 1991, 44–45; Chickering & Gamson, 1987; Johnson et al., 1991a, chapter 2, 1991b, 1998). Most students learn more in a cooperative class. Competitive classes have losers. Use a standard grading scale (see section 5.7) to reduce competition. Cooperative group techniques (see section 6.1) are effective at increasing cooperation.

21. *Individualize* the teaching style (Ramsden, 1992, 101–102). Students have a wide variety of learning styles. Varying your teaching style helps students learn. For example, an occasional brainstorming session will engage students who enjoy developing new ideas. Individualizing instruction is difficult in large classes, however.

22. *Be accessible* to students both in and out of class (Carson, 1996; Chickering & Gamson, 1987; McKeachie, 1994, 26; Ramsden, 1992, 97–99). Signal this accessibility in class. Be sure to be present during your office hours and be friendly when students drop by (see section 7.2). Students who interact with their teachers learn more (Angelo, 1993).

23. *Develop rapport* with students (Bonwell & Eison, 1991, 22–23; McKeachie, 1994, 328; Ramsden, 1992, 76, 97–99). Perhaps the most important factor in developing rapport is a real interest in and liking of students. At a minimum, learn and use students' names. Be friendly and smile. Chat with students. Make them laugh. Chapter 7 addresses developing rapport in detail.

24. "The absence of threat is utterly essential to effective instruction" (Leslie Hart quoted by J. R. Davis, 1993, 314). When threatened, students often freeze and the cerebral brain shuts down. The student literally cannot think. This most often occurs during tests. The Socratic method can also be perceived as threatening.

One way to summarize this list is to quote Pascarella and Terenzini (1991, 619), "Student learning is unambiguously linked to effective teaching." There is nothing magical about these two dozen items. The list could be one or three dozen. (Note that this list is neutral about technology. The use of technology in teaching is discussed in section 4.5.)

> TIP: Start incorporating changes into your work patterns now. Choose a few of the teaching methods that are known to work and incorporate them into your daily teaching. It often works well to select one for preparation, one for in class, and one for out-of-class activities. It is natural to feel awkward using new procedures at first. If you persist throughout the term with just one of the principles, you will have developed a new habit.

Experienced teachers use certain tools to incorporate learning principles into their courses. In the next two sections, I discuss four of these tools—behavioral objectives, a syllabus, a course outline, and a textbook. In section 4.5, the potential of new technological tools to satisfy learning principles is explored. In section 4.6, I compare different pedagogical styles and how they satisfy learning principles.

4.3. Behavioral Objectives in Course Development

A behavioral objective is what the student will do—that is, the behavior that can be observed—to complete the course satisfactorily (Bloom et al., 1956; Gronlund, 1991; Kibler et al., 1970; Mager, 1962; McKeachie, 1994, 9–11). Although it is challenging and time-consuming to develop and use behavioral objectives, they are ultimately effective (more student learning) and efficient (less professor and student time) because they help you satisfy learning principles.

In traditional courses, objectives connect lecture content and activities, outside readings, homework, examinations, and, ultimately, final course grades. In project courses, objectives help relate projects to course goals. In both types of courses, objectives help the professor and students stay focused on what is important. They help the professor decide what to include in the course and on tests.

The most important work on objectives was the development of what is now known as "Bloom's taxonomy" (Bloom et al., 1956). Benjamin Bloom chaired a committee that worked for years to formulate a taxonomy of cognitive objectives. Their book on the taxonomy has become almost a bible of teaching. Bloom's taxonomy classifies objectives into a hierarchy with six major levels:

1. *Knowledge:* Retaining facts, definitions, jargon, and so forth. These items can be memorized without understanding.
2. *Comprehension:* Understanding the material. Students can explain the material in simple terms with no jargon.
3. *Application:* Using abstract ideas in concrete situations. Students can solve simple problems within the discipline.
4. *Analysis:* Breaking down an idea or problem into its components. Critical thinking or problem solving is often required.

5. *Synthesis:* Putting together component pieces or parts to create a new whole. This leads students to multiple correct solutions and allows for creativity.
6. *Evaluation:* Making a judgment about a solution, thesis, paper, process, or other work. Judgment may include internal and external evidence and values.

Objectives, questions, and problems that rank higher in the taxonomy usually include the lower levels. For example, an analysis objective usually inherently requires the ability to satisfy application, comprehension, and knowledge objectives. Unfortunately, in science and engineering, students can often bypass the comprehension step and still do problems that require application or analysis (Mazur, 1997, 4–7).

Most professors want to develop their students' critical thinking, creative problem-solving, and judgment capabilities. This requires inclusion of the three higher order objectives in lectures, assignments, and tests. But the three lowest levels of objectives are the easiest to test for, particularly in multiple-choice exams. Using Bloom's taxonomy forces one to consider the level of the course objectives, lecture presentations, assignments, and test problems. An unexamined course may well be focusing on the lowest levels and thus be relatively ineffective (Stice, 1976). Using objectives can help you tie together the parts of the course while maintaining focus on what is important. Share the objectives with the students, perhaps in the syllabus, and periodically remind students of them.

Develop objectives for every topic in the course. If you cannot develop a good cognitive objective, consider dropping the topic. Focus most of your attention on writing objectives at the analysis, synthesis, and evaluation levels, since the lower three levels are usually included automatically. When you write your objectives, use action words such as *calculate, choose, compare, derive, describe, estimate, identify, paraphrase, predict, select, solve,* and *write.* Objectives with action words direct the students to produce a product that you can examine to see if they have met the objective. Avoid using *know, learn,* and *understand,* since you cannot tell directly whether the students satisfy these directions (Felder & Brent, 1997).

A word of caution. My experience in teaching Bloom's taxonomy is that using the taxonomy is much more subtle than it appears at first. Read a book on objectives (Gronlund, 1991; Kibler et al., 1970; Mager, 1962). Start by writing a set of objectives for one part of your course. Ask someone knowledgeable about Bloom's taxonomy to evaluate the level of your objectives.

Professors also have noncognitive (affective) objectives for their courses. They want their students to appreciate the power or beauty of the subject. They want them to become self-motivated learners. They want them to be honest, hardworking, and ethical. It is appropriate to share these objectives in a positive way in the course syllabus and sporadically throughout the semester. A taxonomy in the affective domain is available (Krathwohl et al., 1964).

When Professor Harvey Jones analyzed his old tests, he was chagrined to find that almost all of the questions were in the first three levels of Bloom's taxonomy. He had thought he was testing for critical thinking. For his new tests he reduced the number of questions, aligned the questions with the objectives, and made sure he was testing at higher levels of the taxonomy. Since he was aware that many students used files extensively, he informed them that from now on tests would consist of new questions covering the course objectives. His students didn't believe him until they took the test.

4.4. The Syllabus, Course Outline, and Textbook

After several years of teaching graduate courses, Professor Sally Crabtree was assigned a large lecture course for first-year students. Sally prepared as she always did, giving the students a brief outline of the territory she expected to explore with them and a detailed list of resources on reserve in the library. She realized within a few weeks that the course was not progressing well. The students were obviously unprepared for classes, had no idea how to do the assignments, and complained that Sally was not telling them what to do; a few had become disruptive during her lectures.

This represents an extreme case of a mismatch between teaching style and student needs. This example sounds far-fetched but is based on a real situation. First-year students want and need guidance. They benefit from a detailed syllabus, course outline, and a quality textbook. All students benefit from a syllabus and course outline, which tell them what to expect in the course.

The Syllabus

The course syllabus is both a guide for students and an agreement with them (B. G. Davis, 1993, chapter 2; Duffy & Jones, 1995, 55–119; Lewis, 1994, 323–326; Matejka & Kurke, 1994; Weimer, 1993, 29–44). The purpose of the syllabus is to tell students where they will end up when the semester is over and how they will get there. It also indicates the professor's philosophy and style. A thorough syllabus reduces the number of student questions and challenges to course policies during the term.

The syllabus should include your name, office number, office telephone number, e-mail address, and office hours. Including your home phone number is optional, but is appreciated by students. If you do include your home phone number, be sure to tell students what hours are acceptable (e.g., "Call anytime before 10:00 P.M."). If you have a teaching assistant (TA), give the TA's name, office hours, and e-mail address. I protect the TA from excessive interruptions and do not list his or her office address or phone numbers.

Delineate the formal course prerequisites and the skills students are expected to possess (e.g., "Students are expected to be skilled in searching the World Wide Web and the library for information"). After checking that the textbook you intend to use is still in print, list it and supplemental references. Check with the library that books and other resources are on reserve. Check e-mail addresses, since they change frequently. Include the course mission, learning goals, or a complete list of course objectives.

Inform students in the syllabus why you will be using active learning. Giving a short explanation of why you are doing anything often reduces student resistance (Sorcinelli, 1994a, 367). It is useful to discuss briefly any teaching method that is different from what the students are familiar with. The syllabus is the first indicator of how power will be distributed between the professor and students (Baecker, 1998). In a traditional lecture course, the professor retains the power, whereas in student- or problem-oriented teaching the power is shared. Thoroughly explain any power-sharing procedure.

We all expect our students to be honest and not cheat. This expectation should be specified on the syllabus with the positive rationale that they will be expected to follow the ethics of the discipline once they graduate, and now is the time to learn and practice them. Explain the procedure for taking tests. For example, if you expect the students to sit in alternate seats or use blue books, state this. If you don't want the students to do something, such as eat in class, be sure to state that with a reason. However, don't turn the syllabus into a rule book.

Since learning is ultimately the students' responsibility, include a short section on student responsibilities. This could include items such as attending class, reading the assignments, doing the homework, and asking for help when necessary. Students pay particular attention to tips from other students (Quiddus & Bussing-Burks, 1998).

Explain the grading procedure, as well as the types of graded assignments, such as homework, oral reports, projects, and tests, and the percentage of the final grade that each type contributes. If the students can negotiate percentages, explain the procedure that will be used and the ranges they may choose for each item. Clearly state your policies on late assignments, makeup tests, extra credit, regrades, and so forth. If you use a standard scale for grading, list the scores required for each grade. If you use a curved grading scale, give the students some idea of the quantity and quality of work required.

Be careful in explaining your grading procedure, since the entire section will be scrutinized if there is a grade appeal. In our litigious society the syllabus may be treated as a legal document; craft it carefully. Clearly list expectations and penalties for failure to comply with these expectations (Kibler et al., 1988, 23). Spending the time to make the syllabus complete and accurate will improve the course and reduce the number of grade appeals. And *if there is a grade appeal, following your own written rules is your most powerful defense.* I prefer to make the syllabus and course outline separate documents. This tends to remove the outline from legalistic interpretations.

If it fits your style, the syllabus can also contain personal information about you. This is a good way to start developing rapport with the students. However, you have to follow through and be open and friendly.

The syllabus includes silent messages that tell the students a lot about the professor (Baecker, 1998; Weimer, 1993, 41–43). A syllabus that contradicts itself sends a mixed message. A professor who acts contrary to the syllabus can destroy his or her credibility. For example, if the syllabus states that no food or drink is to be brought into class and the professor walks in with a cup of coffee, the students wonder why they should follow the rules.

TIP: Once a satisfactory syllabus has been crafted, it can be reused with little revision and can serve as a template for other courses. But be sure to proofread the new syllabus to check that you have changed all references to the correct course. During the term, note on the course outline and syllabus any changes you might make the next time you teach the course.

The Course Outline

The course outline tells students the approximate pace at which they will progress through the material and when tests and important assignments are due. How much detail to offer beyond this is debatable. Felder and Brent (1995) recommend handing out an outline listing all assignments and tests, since that will reduce the number of complaints about time conflicts. Lewis (1994, 324) suggests at least a week-by-week outline for the entire term. McKeachie (1994, 16–17) advises that the course outline not be detailed and include only assignments for the semester and possibly examination and laboratory dates. Weimer (1993, 32–33) suggests that professors privately keep a calendar that tentatively schedules every class period. For the students she suggests a list of topics in the order in which they will be covered. What you do depends on the context of your course. However, since you do want students to plan ahead, list at least the dates of tests and when major projects are due. The students appreciate having this information in advance.

With a new course, develop the schedule a month or so at a time. This makes it easier to adjust the course during the term. Professors are usually overoptimistic about the amount that students will learn. If you find yourself unable to cover everything you planned, develop a new schedule for the remainder of the term and cover less. Needless to say, students have no problem accepting changes that reduce their workloads.

Pay attention to the overall term calendar as you prepare the course outline (Brinkley et al., 1999, 13–15, 88–89; Davidson & Ambrose, 1994, 29). Avoid scheduling major tests or assignments immediately after big college weekends or before vacations. Students will learn significantly more if the workload is spread out throughout the term. Talk to other instructors to try to avoid having the students take clusters of tests at the same time. Avoid clusters of assignments within your own course.

Since dates during the term always change, the course outline needs to be revised every term. Including the word "tentative" on the course outline gives you permission to change the schedule. Before I started to call my outlines tentative, I always had student complaints if I changed the schedule for any reason. Be flexible during the term. If a number of students inform you in advance that you have inadvertently selected a bad date for a test or assignment, search for a more acceptable alternative. Students will appreciate this effort, and it will provide a more reliable assessment.

I include reading assignments in the course outline, but some professors prefer to do this separately. If the edition of the textbook has changed or you are changing textbooks, considerable time will be needed to develop new reading assignments. *Always read new editions of textbooks.* Failure to do this invariably leads to nasty surprises. Reading assignments for lower level courses need to be detailed, specifying, for example, the pages to read and the pages to skip. I list homework assignments on separate sheets that are given to the students after each test. The reading assignments are repeated on these sheets.

Plan to spend some time during the first class period discussing the syllabus and course outline with the students. This encourages the students to read these materials and not just tuck them away unread in a notebook. It is also helpful to take the time to describe useful features of the textbook, such as the appendices.

Courses improve when the instructor develops clear objectives, ensures they are understood by the students, covers the objectives in class, and tests on the objectives. The course outline should follow from the important objectives. The syllabus tells the students what to expect in your course and helps set the tone of the course. However, students are not going to comment on what great objectives, course outline, or syllabus the course had. Instead they will note that the course was well organized and the tests were fair.

Textbook Selection

First, decide whether to use a textbook. In upper division and graduate courses, particularly research seminars, the original literature may be preferable. In required undergraduate courses, a good textbook helps students learn and reduces the professor's workload. A bad textbook alienates the students and increases your workload. Making the effort to pick a good textbook in the planning stage will save you grief later.

Robinson (1994) presents a short but useful chapter on textbook selection, and Johnson (1990, chapter 2) gives a useful checklist. Content coverage is relatively easy to judge. A good textbook must cover the content of the course at the appropriate level, but missing a few topics you want to cover is not a fatal flaw. It is much more challenging to determine whether the book is written at the appropriate level. Since there is seldom time to evaluate several books completely, do an evaluation of one chapter. Pick a chapter that covers a topic familiar to you. Check that the content is correct and the writing clear. Is the organization of material appropriate for students? Textbooks for introductory courses should use an inductive approach. (Cahn [1986, p. 15] rejects this approach, asserting that "instructors should never adopt a text they have not themselves read.")

Work your way very carefully through a few examples. Numerical errors will confuse students who use examples as a template to solve problems. If you intend to assign problems from the book, look at the quality of the solution manual. The absence of a solution manual is often a sign that homework problems were a low priority for the authors. Homework problems with mistakes and vague questions will take up a lot of your and your students' time.

Try to select a student-friendly, considerate textbook (Robinson, 1994). A considerate textbook has:

- *Directives* such as objectives and questions for the students
- *Transitions* that show the relationships among topics
- *Signals* of important material, such as changes in type font, underlining, and centering
- *Advance organizers,* such as an *outline* or *graphical organizers,* that show the global picture

If you have the time, ask a few typical students, not just A students, to review the book. Always adopt a textbook tentatively so that if students dislike it, you can use another book next term.

If you end up using a bad textbook, do not disparage the book to the students. If you do, they are even less likely to read it and will wonder why you had them buy a bad book. Do the best you can and start looking for a better textbook.

TIP: Take a look at your textbook and determine whether it is mainly inductive or deductive. Using a textbook the students like and learn from is obviously effective—it is also efficient, since the text will do some of the teaching.

4.5. Teaching with Technology

Almost all teaching is done with technology. Some of the technology, such as print and the blackboard, is so familiar that we forget these are forms of technology (Landow, 1996; Laurillard, 1993). *Thus the question is not whether we will use technology to teach, but which technologies we will use.* Currently, the technology of interest is the computer and its applications, particularly the Internet and World Wide Web. In this section, which complements section 3.2, I consider specific applications of technology in teaching.

Student Learning with Technology

Use technology when it is appropriate—that is, when it aids student learning and is efficient. It is important to avoid "an almost Luddite hostility to the introduction and adaptation of new technologies to the teaching process" (Pelikan, 1992, 186). On the other hand, believing that the computer or other advanced technology will automatically improve student learning is naive. There are a number of reports on the unsuccessful use of computer technology in teaching (e.g., Jacobson, 1993; Oppenheimer, 1997). Many successes have also been reported (e.g., Dede, 1999; Finlayson, 1996; Kadiyala & Crynes, 2000; Laurillard, 1993; Moore, 1999).

Technology is appropriate in a course if:

1. The task done by technology is essential to the course.
2. The task cannot be done as well—if at all—without technology.
3. The use of technology is efficient. That is, the added cost of both capital and labor using the technology is reasonable (Carnegie Commission on Higher Education, 1972; Kussmaul et al., 1996).

Technological teaching methods are appropriate when nothing else will do. An example is the development of Braille pictures to help blind students learn inherently visual material, such as anatomy or organic chemical structures <http://www.taevision-line.purdue.edu> (Rawls, 1999). Technological teaching methods may also be used when they are more effective than but not as efficient as nontechnological methods (e.g., videotape feedback of student presentations) or when they are more efficient and equally effective (e.g., TV, videotape, and streaming video for distance education). I believe technological methods will continue to develop *niches* in education where they meet these criteria. Change in the use of technology will probably continue for many years (J. Leslie, 1998).

Technology that helps professors satisfy the principles of student learning (section 4.2) will be effective. For example, in our department we videotape all students during their laboratory oral presentations. The feedback the student gets from watching the tape is much more compelling than listening to a professor give feedback. Technology can also be used to improve written communication. Students will improve their writing if they do extensive rewriting. The use of word processing programs has helped to improve writing because professors are willing to require and the students are willing to do extensive rewriting when they have word processors.

Commercial computer software can engage students, increase their time on task, and increase their learning. For example, in many fields, such as statistics and engineering, practitioners routinely use complicated software. My experience, which is corroborated by Moore (1999), is that students learn how to use this software much faster if they are taught it in a computer laboratory instead of in a lecture hall. A form of problem-based learning (see section 6.2) works well in computer laboratories. The immediate feedback provided in the laboratory prevents tiny errors from derailing student progress. A drawback is that the laboratory is much more expensive than a lecture class because of the cost of the computers and the small class size.

The Internet provides new methods to communicate with students. E-mail can improve two-way communication (see section 7.2). A course homepage allows professors to post information such as the syllabus and notices (Brinkley et al., 1999, 149–152). Some students will never log in, but the homepage does provide another communication venue. It's also a place to post student questions and lecture notes. Of course, the same communication can be achieved with handouts. The web has an advantage in distance education since it is cheaper and faster than mailing handouts. If you need to advertise your course (either locally or for distance education), a course homepage with suitable links is an effective supplement to traditional advertising.

New technology can be misused, however. For example, lecture notes inscribed by a paid student have been posted on a commercial web site without the professor's permission (Blumenstyk, 1999). Eventually the courts will decide whether this is legal. In the meantime, make sure that coming to class is useful to students in ways that cannot be duplicated by student notes.

One advantage of computerized instruction is that it may help students follow good learning principles, which may be more difficult to do with normal instruction. Mastery learning techniques such as the "personalized system of instruction" (Keller, 1968), in which the material is divided into small modules and the students are required to master each module before progressing to the next, show significant learning advantages in controlled studies (Kulik et al., 1979; Pascarella & Terenzini, 1991, 646). Unfortunately, these methods require both significant startup effort to construct study guides and tests and significant effort every time the course is taught. Much of the continuing effort, particularly the record keeping, can be computerized. Then the daily effort, once the course is set up, is no more than that for a lecture course, and most of this effort is focused directly on student contact. Since the basic pedagogical method is effective, this is a prime area for applying computer technology. A recent analysis of the literature showed that computer-based individualized instruction improved both examination performance and retention in dental education (Kadiyala & Crynes, 2000).

Another example of the use of technology to incorporate good learning principles is the use of computerized tutoring programs to individualize instruction (Kadiyala & Crynes, 2000; Suppes, 1996). The best the programs can do is duplicate what a patient instructor does, but programs can be cloned indefinitely and thus handle large groups of students with 24-hour availability. By incorporating cognitive learning models into the software, the tutoring program can use diagnostics to guide the student to the best path to learn.

After using computers to present lectures for six years, Nantz and Lundgren (1998, 53–54) found that "using the computer as the course presentation vehicle is not the panacea we originally thought it to be. . . . The key is that technology is subservient to teaching." Use of the computer will be efficient if you can simultaneously do two jobs. For example, if you routinely give students partial class notes, computer lecture presentations will be efficient, since the class notes and the lecture can be developed simultaneously. However, you need to be sure that the class is interactive, and not let the computer dictate a lecture with no breaks.

Many successful educational technologies are relatively low tech and simple. Perhaps relatively simple technology, such as overhead projectors, e-mail, and word processors, has had more impact because professors know how to use it. Technology that is spontaneously adopted by many professors will have more immediate impact than technology that has to be force-fed. Professor Robert Jensen's web site <http://www.trinity.edu/~rjensen> provides links to tutorials on using new technology and links to educational technology resources (Floyd, 1998).

One of the disadvantages of computer technology is the need for an extensive support system (Van Dusen, 1997; Inglis et al., 1999). Many institutions have this support system in place for common audiovisual equipment and computers—most professors have ready access to overhead projectors, e-mail, and the World Wide Web. What is needed is easy access to experts who can help a professor develop a homepage for a course on the web, develop animations, or computerize an entire course (Brinkley et al., 1999, 146–148; Inglis et al., 1999, chapter 7). Any institution serious about using higher technology must make these services readily and freely available to professors. Most professors do not have the time to learn to use new technology without help. The amount of money necessary to hire experts in computer technology is often modest, since students are often those experts.

TIP: When you decide to use technology in a course, ask for assistance.

Distance Learning

Distance learning was introduced in the United States more than 130 years ago as correspondence courses delivered on print media through the postal service (MacKenzie et al., 1968) and usually offered by for-profit companies. Such courses have been useful because students who cannot attend school can take them, and this rationale remains a strong impetus for distance education. One of the major problems in correspondence courses, however, has been obtaining sufficient, timely student–instructor interaction. Because modern computer communication techniques have the potential to reduce this problem, new technologies have stiffened competition that traditional colleges and universities face from correspondence courses (Layzell, 1999).

The older technology for distance education used TV or videotapes. This relatively expensive technology is slowly being replaced by teleconferencing and streaming video ("Mechanical Engineering," 2000). Fortunately, this transition will be easy for professors who have taught on TV, since the teaching techniques required are similar (e.g., Cyrs & Smith, 1990). In this discussion, I will refer to all of these courses as "TV courses." Many of my comments are based on my experience in teaching a course on TV and directing a continuing education unit.

Although many students prefer live presentations if they are convenient, TV versions rapidly become preferable if live presentations are not convenient. Even a 15-minute drive may be enough to make distance education preferable for many students. In my experience, *most students prefer asynchronous instruction,* which means they can watch the lesson at a time convenient to them, not when it is offered on campus. With asynchronous instruction, it is impossible to use modern communications technologies (Arreola, 1995) that allow live interaction with the remote students during class. Contact between students can be developed through telephone, e-mail, and chat rooms.

The increased availability and convenience of TV courses balance their negative aspects. Compared to live instruction, the students tend to be more passive, and it is more difficult to provide individual attention and instruction. However, asynchronous instruction has the advantage that students can watch the class at a convenient time, go at their own pace, and replay parts when necessary. Many studies have found no significant difference in test scores between on-campus and remote students (Gibbons et al., 1977; Russell, 1999).

Since audiences at many locations can be taught simultaneously, TV courses can be efficient, but they are not cheap. At Purdue University, the local students are taught live in the television studio, giving the professor a live audience. Our remote students want these students to ask questions. Arreola (1995), on the other hand, recommends that local students use a classroom separate from the studio so that all students have identical classroom experiences.

It is more difficult to develop rapport with the students in a TV course than in a normal course. Communication with students at remote locations can be enhanced by e-mail and the web. If monitored regularly, e-mail is very useful. A web homepage for the TV course disseminates information such as assignments, class notes, or problem solutions faster than normal mail. Telephone office hours allow students to talk to the professor or TA. I felt that it was easier to develop rapport with students after I visited them at the major remote site or they sent me a photograph (either electronically or by mail). The personal aspect of face-to-face contact is difficult to replace electronically.

Web-based courses are the latest distance education method (Inglis et al., 1999; Petre et al., 1998; Sanoff, 1999). These courses can incorporate multimedia and may have the "canned" portion of the course delivered on a CD or DVD. When the new streaming video technology (essentially TV on a computer monitor) is used, a web course can include the advantages of both TV and computer instruction ("Mechanical Engineering," 2000). Although few well-controlled experiments have been done, entirely web-based courses have been shown to be effective with older, mature students, particularly graduate students, and less effective with younger undergraduates (Sanoff, 1999). One advantage of using the Internet is that the *students are in control* of when and how long they watch, the order they use to study the material, the number of times they repeat a sequence, and so forth. Students are also encouraged to be active and interactive. But adults who are technologically challenged (Wagschal & Wagschal, 1995) will be hesitant to take Internet courses, and there is considerable concern about fair access for underrepresented students (Gladieux & Swail, 1999).

Britain's Open University has offered web classes with enrollments of up to 5,000 students (Inglis et al., 1999; Petre et al., 1998). The multimedia web "lectures" require several years of extensive development, testing, and revision. An infrastructure was developed to support these courses. Fast network connections with high bandwidths are used to deliver the web lectures, but it has been essential to make sure that students with rather simple computers can still receive a suitable version. At first, technical problems were frequent. If they were addressed rapidly, the students soon forgot about these initial problems.

Most important, *students still require individual attention*. In Britain's Open University, one tutor is hired for every 25 students (Petre et al., 1998). The tutors mark all papers and provide copious written feedback. Electronic submission, marking, and return of assignments has significantly reduced turnaround time for feedback. Electronic submission has also reduced tutors' time requirements, since it is much easier for them to reuse comments. Face-to-face or electronic tutorials have been important to combat the students' commonly reported feelings of isolation. Many students prefer asynchronous, electronic tutorials because of the scheduling flexibility they offer. Tutors are also responsible for answering students' questions either electronically or by telephone. Quick response to questions has been critical to student satisfaction.

Lectures need to be extensively reformatted for web delivery unless streaming video is used. Interactive lessons and lessons using animations are effective. Merely transcribing lecture notes onto the web invariably leads to failure. Good distance education instruction includes a knowledgeable professor who interacts with students, a learning-centered approach, and the development of a sense of community (Carnevale, 2000). Currently, preparing interactive web lectures is reported to be a tremendous time sink for professors (Eberts, 1998; Inglis et al., 1999). Estimates of thirty hours to prepare a single one-hour interactive web lecture are common (Eberts, 1998). Streaming video converts the web-based course to a TV/video course, and the time needed for preparation plummets; however, students' learning may also drop if they become passive.

Although distance education and virtual universities will fill a useful niche in higher education, I believe their potential has been oversold. *If undergraduate education is to be more than information dissemination, there must be personal contact between students and instructors and among students.* Some contacts can be efficiently managed electronically, but someone needs to respond to them. And some face-to-face contact is essential for motivation (Dede, 1999). When students have questions, they want to contact a real person, not an automated answering system. This requires time from the professor, TAs, or tutors.

Effective rapport with students is difficult to maintain when the class size becomes too large. This will minimize some of the supposed economic advantages of distance education and virtual universities (Tucker, 1995). Online and TV courses often cost about the same as or more than on-campus courses and can be very expensive because they do not take advantage of economies of scale (Inglis et al., 1999).

Web-based courses (probably with "lectures" delivered by CD, DVD, streaming video, or the next technology) will have an economic advantage for very large courses if the Open University model (Petre et al., 1998) is used. A detailed economic analysis showed that U.S. universities *can* reduce the cost per student significantly by switching from the current remote classroom model to a resource-based delivery model (Inglis et al., 1999, chapters 4 and 5). Since part-time tutors take over many of the functions of professors, widespread application of this model will have major implications for professors.

The potential of distance education for specialized advanced study has been barely tapped (Suppes, 1996, 157). Distance education, perhaps by TV or video but more likely as a web-supported seminar, does have an economic advantage for very specialized courses for which the audience is small.

To end this section on a positive note, there is preliminary evidence that technology can improve instruction by allowing a variety of teaching modes to be used in the same course (Carnevale, 1999; Dede, 1999). Previous studies comparing one mode to another typically showed no significant difference among modes. However, if a number of technological methods—such as streaming video, interactive web instruction, synchronous interactive virtual conference center, asynchronous conferencing, and electronic collaborative learning—and face-to-face instruction are used in the same course, learning increases, since almost all students find a pedagogical approach that appeals to them. The face-to-face portion is critical since it motivates students, even though they may learn more with one of the other methods. The "Emerging Educational Technologies" course web site <http://www.virtual.gmu.edu/EDIT750/syllabus. htm#Table of Contents> has more details.

TIP: If you are assigned to teach a distance education class, try to arrange for at least a little face-to-face instruction.

4.6. Contrasting Pedagogical Paradigms

Teaching methods in higher education can be classified by comparing active versus passive students, teacher versus student control of learning, and knowledge transfer versus fostering of student growth or individualization of learning. These are not independent constructs. The professor who believes that the purpose of education is information transfer is likely to believe in teacher control and may have passive students in the classroom. Each of these pairs represents a continuum.

Figure 4.1 synthesizes these ideas into a map of different teaching methods. The abscissa is the level of student involvement in the classroom, which varies from passive

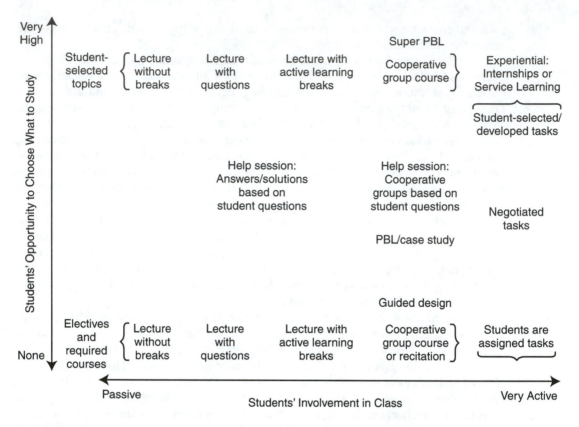

FIGURE 4.1.   Interaction of students' classroom involvement and their opportunity to choose topics for study. PBL = problem-based learning.

to very active. This dimension is concerned with the teaching methods used in the course. Active students learn more, and certain types of activities foster student growth in critical thinking, problem solving, communication, and teamwork. Students may also learn a modest amount about how to learn. Courses in which students are active (right side) result in more student learning than do courses in which students are passive (left side). The teaching methods at the bottom right of the figure conceptualize teaching "as organizing student activity" (Ramsden, 1992, 113–114); this is an advance over conceptualizing teaching "as information transfer" (Ramsden, 1992, 111–112), which is at the bottom left of the figure.

However, *students* also need practice in deciding what should be learned, why it should be learned, and how it should be learned. The ordinate in Figure 4.1 represents students' opportunity to choose what to learn, which ranges from none to complete control of topics. This dimension is concerned with who selects course topics and develops the course outline. Note that experiential courses, which tend to have very involved students, can have a tremendous range of student involvement in planning the learning experiences. Teaching methods that will maximize student growth in higher order cognitive and affective dimensions will have active students who make educational decisions about their learning (the upper right of the figure). Ramsden (1992, 114–116) calls this conceptualizing teaching "as making learning possible."

Note that the two axes are semi-independent. A professor can believe students should be very active in class, yet not give them the opportunity to choose topics. Alternatively, the professor could let the students choose topics but teach in a way that produces passive students. Or the professor could use the "super problem-based learning" technique (see section 6.2) to maximize both students' involvement and their choice of topic.

To explore how different teaching methods help students learn, it is useful to contrast extreme positions. I will start by presenting caricatures of traditional and student-centered pedagogies.

Traditional Pedagogy

The extreme of traditional pedagogy has the goal of information and attitude transfer with total teacher control and passive students. Freire (1993, 52–55) states that in this caricature of traditional pedagogy, professors

1. Use the "*banking theory*" of education. Deposits are made by the teacher into the depositories (students). The students receive, memorize, and recite the deposits. This type of education has a narrative character and is nothing but information and attitude transfer.
2. Expect students to record their pronouncements passively.
3. See no need to explain to students why they are to learn the material.
4. Establish all the objectives.
5. Believe that the function of professors is to teach and the function of students is to learn what is taught without question.
6. Believe that students should be taught as they themselves were.
7. Retain all power in the course.
8. Do not foster student growth.
9. Prepare course plans, lessons, and objectives without student input.
10. Prepare monologues and stop dialogues whenever they threaten to erupt.
11. Expect automatic respect.
12. Control the evaluation and grading methods.
13. Control entry into the profession.
14. Have no faith or trust in students.

Probably subconsciously, this pedagogy is meant to retain the professor's position of privilege, authority, and power. Freire (1993, 54–59) claims that this method of teaching is a tool of the ruling class used to oppress students, although many well-intentioned teachers do not realize this. His claim may be true in underdeveloped countries, but does not appear to be valid for many developed countries. When this extreme form of traditional pedagogy is used, student learning is stunted, because many key learning principles are ignored. Students are uninvolved, and they do not develop rapport with the professor. The professor has negative expectations of the students and does not individualize instruction, encourage cooperation, or show the joy of learning.

Fortunately, there is a range of styles within the traditional mode (Duffy & Jones, 1995, 5–8). Less extreme forms can satisfy most learning principles if the professor has a positive attitude, involves the students, and encourages them to be active learners. Traditional methods are familiar, and everyone's roles are well defined. Since the professor retains control, many professors are comfortable with the more humane traditional models (Palmer, 1983, 39). The trap for professors in this method is the "Atlas complex," wherein the entire weight of learning is on their shoulders (Moore, 1994, 56). Unfortunately, many students are comfortable in the traditional model, since it allows them to hide and quiet their fears (Palmer, 1998, 37). Barr and Tagg (1995) note that the trap for institutions using this "instructional paradigm" is that improvements invariably require more resources.

Even relatively effective applications of the traditional model do not encourage students to ask questions such as, Why are we learning this material instead of other material? Why are we solving these particular problems or doing these analyses instead of alternatives? How does one choose the material to learn and the best ways to learn it? When the instructor makes the pedagogical decisions, students usually do not learn to be independent learners. This point is important, since "a teacher's best contribution to a student's education is to help him [or her] learn how to learn independently" (Ericksen, 1974, 11).

Appropriate teaching methods depend on the *context* of the course (McKeachie, 1994, 18, 144; Weimer, 1990, xiv). Perry's theory (see section 6.2) also implies that education depends on context (Moore, 1994, 60). If students must assimilate large quantities of knowledge, solve well-defined problems, or both, the traditional lecture methods explored in Chapter 5 supplemented by the methods of Chapter 7 may be appropriate teaching procedures. Lecture methods may also be appropriate for less mature students who will benefit from highly structured courses.

Student-Centered Pedagogy

Student-centered pedagogy attempts to address the shortcomings of the traditional approach. Unfortunately, the professor who takes the extreme approach to student-centered pedagogy goes too far toward giving students total control. This professor

1. Asks the students, without guidance, to select topics.
2. Expects the students, without guidance, to choose appropriate teaching/learning methods.
3. Refuses to lecture or provide resources. Does not try to transfer any knowledge to the students.
4. Abdicates power to the students.
5. Expects the students to decide how to evaluate and grade their work.
6. Believes everyone's opinions should have the same respect regardless of the knowledge or logic or lack thereof behind them.

This description of the extreme of student-centered pedagogy is based loosely on Palmer's (1998, 116, 119) description of the degeneration of student-centered classes. In its extreme form, this pedagogy abandons and rejects all of the professor's privilege, authority, power, and responsibility. This pedagogy has limited effectiveness. Learning principles are not satisfied, since the students have no guidance and there is no structured hierarchy of content, no structured logic, no assurance that the students will spend time on task and look at issues in depth, no clear presentations, and no feedback.

Student-centered teaching can be effective if the teacher avoids the sins of the extreme position. Again, there are a range of effective styles (Duffy & Jones, 1995, 5–8). The teacher needs to provide some guidance and structure and ensure that students spend time on task. It is possible for teachers to guide without controlling everything in the classroom (Wilshire, 1990, 264).

The foregoing descriptions are caricatures, but as a student I had professors who were close to each. Neither the extremely traditional nor the extremely student-centered approach to pedagogy satisfies the definition of good teaching developed in section 4.1.

Problem-Posing or Subject-Centered Pedagogy

If the students are relatively mature and the course goals include fostering critical thinking, higher level reasoning, and the ability to solve ill-posed or value-laden problems and having students learn how to learn, methods that move away from the two axes of Figure 4.1 are appropriate. The more important it is that students learn how to define problems or define what is to be learned, the further we need to move from traditional pedagogy. For these goals we can use a pedagogy that is based on student growth and problem posing and is subject centered (Barr & Tagg, 1995; Freire, 1993, 60–67; Palmer, 1998, 116–120; Stage et al., 1998, 51–64;). This pedagogy

1. Poses problems. Problem posing consists of acts of cognition, not transfers of information. The problem or subject is central to the education and mediates between teacher and student.
2. Requires both faith in students and the development of mutual trust.
3. Involves mutual learning and mutual teaching.
4. Involves joint development of objectives, lessons, and teaching.
5. Requires dialogue.
6. Expects students to think and, as appropriate, disagree with the professor.
7. Believes respect must be earned.
8. Believes that all have the potential to grow and that education is a process of growth that is never complete.
9. Believes in searching for different teaching methods to improve education.
10. Requires initially guiding students in how to learn in this new educational environment.

Problem-posing pedagogy does *not* rule out the use of lecture or other traditional teaching methods for part of the course (Barr & Tagg, 1995; Freire, 1993, 103–104). If one of the agreed-on objectives is acquisition of knowledge, lecture could be appropriate. In fact, students often demand lectures when they need information (Tobias, 1992, 88). But it would be a lecture in which the students can question the assumptions and conclusions of the lecturer. For different objectives, other teaching methods could be used (Palmer, 1998, 118–119).

Since the roles of students and professors in problem-posing classes are different from their roles in traditional classes, the method may arouse fear in students and faculty. And it is not universally applicable. Even when this pedagogy is applicable, it may fail. Since the professor's efforts will not be understood by tradition-minded peers and students, a failure can be spectacular. The students will believe the professor was not teaching—a common complaint from students in problem-posing classes is, "I had to learn everything by myself." They may rate the class low in their student evaluations. This problem is magnified by student evaluation forms that include inappropriate questions for problem-posing classes. Few of the professor's colleagues will be supportive, because they do not understand what the professor was trying to accomplish.

Problem-posing pedagogy is liberating for students since it allows them to develop their potential. It is also liberating for professors, since it removes many of their burdens. The professor is no longer solely responsible for the students' learning—this responsibility is shared with the students. The professor can also share the responsibility for setting objectives, teaching the class, deciding what to learn, assessing learning, and so forth. Lifting these burdens can reduce the professor's workload considerably and make the course a joy. Problem-posing methods are discussed in Chapter 6.

4.7. Summary

At one time, teaching was totally an art form, and good teachers could not explain what they did. Enough research has now accumulated that we know many actions that good teachers take to help students learn. These learning principles can help professors improve their teaching. They also are helpful in evaluating technological teaching methods. I believe that the two most important actions for students are to become involved and spend time on task. The most important actions for teachers are any actions that involve students and encourage them to spend more time on task.

Although much is known, much remains unknown about why some teachers are great while others are merely competent. Words such as *authenticity, caring,* and *context* still contain mystery. These concepts go beyond formulas. The same action can be effective in one context and ineffective in another. Reflecting on both good and bad teaching moments can often help us identify the subtleties.

Behavioral objectives, the syllabus, and the course outline are all meant to guide students. Objectives tell students what they are expected to learn. The syllabus and course outlines are also guides. The syllabus is a guide to the conditions of teaching and learning that will be used in the course. The course outline is a guide to when material is to be learned and when important assignments and tests are due. These tools are appropriate in all courses.

Textbooks are appropriate for lower level classes where the material has been codified. Select a textbook that covers the important material for your course and is considerate of student learning. For beginning courses, look for a book with an inductive style that incorporates a number of examples. The book should have objectives and questions for students, transitions that show the relationships among topics, and some method to show the global picture. Signals such as italic or bold print that indicate the most important material should not be overused.

There is increasing pressure on institutions and professors to use technology in teaching. We need to keep open minds and explore when technology will significantly improve student learning, make education more accessible, or reduce the cost of education. Although the killer application that will do all three may never appear, technology will continue to affect higher education. Distance education and the Internet are not fads. They will play roles in higher education, but the size of those roles is unclear. The exciting role that technology can play is making it possible to deliver instruction that satisfies learning principles even without the luxury of small classes and low teaching loads. The scary part of the scenario is that application of technology will affect the structure of higher education. In the past, most technological innovations have made some jobs obsolete while creating new types of jobs. The widespread introduction of technology in teaching will probably do the same.

Since no teaching method is best under all circumstances, consider the course context. Autonomous teachers teach in the way they believe will lead to the most student learning (Walker & Hale, 1999). Thus, you have to decide which teaching methods to use in each of your courses. Since students and professors are familiar with traditional methods, these methods are predictable and few students will actively fight the teacher. In most disciplines, one's colleagues will be familiar with traditional methods and will support your efforts. Traditional methods work well for the traditional objective, that is, dissemination of instructor-chosen knowledge in an orderly classroom. If this is a major goal in your course, you may choose traditional methods for part or all of the course. I teach the lecture portion of my junior course in a traditional fashion. Many technological teaching methods are designed to supplement traditional methods and can be used to supplement traditional teaching if they enhance learning.

With problem-posing methods, students may be asked to decide what should be learned and how it should be learned. Since most students and professors have little or no experience with these approaches, they are likely to be hesitant to try them. Switching to a problem-posing method from a traditional approach requires a leap of faith that the method will work. Yet problem-posing methods are appealing because of the promise of greater student learning and development. I have been successful using problem-posing methods in a computer laboratory with juniors and in an entire course with graduate students.

Fortunately, both styles can be used in a single class. For example, the majority of the class can be taught traditionally, but a substantial portion may be set aside for course projects that use problem-posing methods. This approach has been successful in classes ranging from sophomore to graduate level. Problem-posing techniques are somewhat familiar for projects, and students are more willing to try new approaches when they will not be tested on the material.

Teaching is normally considered to be labor-intensive (Fairweather, 1996, 96–97, 114), since traditional methods are the standard for comparison. With traditional methods, increasing the number of students requires more teachers if the amount of attention that students receive is to be kept constant. Thus it is difficult to find ways to save significant amounts of money with the traditional model. However, if learning is emphasized and many of the teaching functions are delegated to the students, significant savings are possible. Thus, the use of a *learning paradigm,* instead of a teaching paradigm, can lead to efficiencies (Barr & Tagg, 1995). Problem-posing methods are more compatible with a learning paradigm than are traditional pedagogies.

5 Lecture-Style Classes

Professor Harvey Jones likes to lecture. There is something about organizing his thoughts and determining the best way to verbalize them that is deeply satisfying to him. He works hard to weave together all the fascinating details of his subject to give the big picture. He loves his subject, often spending almost an entire day developing and writing a single lecture. His colleagues tell him he should be writing a book. Harvey is proud of his lectures.

Unfortunately, the students don't have the same opinion of his lectures. "He's boring." "If you can stay awake, you might learn something." Several students regularly doze through the lectures. Even the "good" students become restless. And they all complain when Harvey talks on past the end of class as he tries to finish the last page of his lecture notes. They complain among themselves and on their course evaluations that Professor Jones doesn't like student interruptions for questions and is never available outside of class. One student threw a paper airplane last week. When the students take Harvey's tests, it appears that they have not even seen much of the material, let alone learned it.

Harvey feels he has tried everything. He has spent more time preparing. He tried reading his lectures to the class, but that was a worse disaster. He blames the students. "They're lazy and they don't care about learning." He complains about teaching a sophomore core course with large classes. How can the department chair expect him to do a good job with eighty students? These complaints have not impressed the department chair.

Harvey needs to accept some responsibility for his difficulties. He is stuck using a lecturing style that is ineffective and inefficient. He can learn to reduce his enormous preparation time and engage the students' attention more. And he needs to look at the other responsibilities of teaching, including developing rapport with students, helping the students, and writing tests that correspond to the course objectives.

Lecturing is the traditional form of teaching in higher education. It was used extensively by 47.2 percent of professors responding to the 1998–99 University of California, Los Angeles, survey (Magner, 1999b). Only class discussion was reported by more professors. Whether lecturing is an appropriate teaching style depends on the goals of the course, the students' maturity level, and the teacher's capabilities. When lecturing is an appropriate teaching method, it can often be improved. In this chapter I explore improving lectures, involving students in lecture classes, testing, and grading. Sections 7.1 to 7.3, on rapport, complement this chapter.

5.1. Content Tyranny and Content Selection

The most important part of a lecture is its content. A lecture's effectiveness is reduced if too much material is included, so selectivity is needed. Lecturers also need to connect with students (see sections 5.5 and 7.1).

Content Tyranny

When the need to cover content dictates how to teach the course, the teacher is suffering from content tyranny (Palmer, 1998, 120–121; Svinicki, 1994, 6; Tobias, 1992, 58; Wankat & Oreovicz, 1998b; Weimer, 1993, 86–96). Student learning, not covering content, should be the paramount concern. It is easy to cover content without student learning—lecture to an empty room. However, it is the interaction between students and the professor that can make outstanding lectures very motivating. Content tyranny leads to many pedagogical sins, including talking for the entire period, discouraging students' questions, ignoring students' reactions, regularly continuing past the end of class, and writing tests that are too long.

When content tyranny is controlled, there is time to have the students practice communication and critical-thinking skills. Professors can relax in class when they don't feel pressure to cover everything. Relaxed professors enjoy teaching more and find it easier to develop rapport with students (Boice, 1992, 139–143, 283, 2000).

We feel pressure to cover content for a number of reasons:

- Our professional ethics requires us to cover everything.
- Knowledge is expanding.
- We want to add our own bits of knowledge to the course.
- Adding new material is easier than removing it.
- Covering more content will satisfy all possible teachers of follow-up courses.
- We believe more content leads to a rigorous course.
- We have never learned alternatives to lecturing.
- We are afraid of running out of material (Weimer, 1993, 86–96).

Ever expanding content is the academic form of Parkinson's law: "Work expands to fill the time available."

Content tyranny can be controlled. In electives there is no reason to let content take over. Since students who do not enroll in the elective cover none of the material, it is impossible to argue that it is all absolutely necessary. Even in highly structured disciplines, courses contain excess material. In one experiment, four experienced engineering professors at very different institutions shared their detailed course outlines for several courses (Wankat et al., 1994; Wankat & Oreovicz, 1998b). An analysis of the time spent on each topic showed that for four courses using three different textbooks, the overlap in number of class periods spent on the same topics (including examination time) was 61 percent. For two courses, one required and one elective, using the same textbook, the overlap was 65 percent. For two required courses using the same textbook, the overlap was 72 percent. The courses in each of these three groups were equivalent for transferring credit. Even for the two closest courses, the two professors disagreed about 28 percent of the coverage. Certainly some of the material that professors disagree on could be removed. In other disciplines, the overlap may be more or less. For example, there was about a 50 percent overlap in the content of Biology 14 at Duke University among the three instructors teaching the course (Christensen, 1988). No difference in student performance was seen in upper division courses.

> TIP: Have several professors independently analyze the content of a course and decide which items they would not include. This material is probably optional.

Content Selection

Learning is the students' responsibility, and most learning will and should occur outside of class. In class, cover the following content:

1. Key points and general themes. Use these to develop a structured hierarchy or an argument. Be sure that the number is limited—one per mini-lecture (a 10- to 15-minute lecture) is sufficient. All of the remaining content suggestions serve to explain the key points and general themes.
2. Connections. The lecture should connect with previous lectures and with the readings and assignments.
3. Especially difficult material or material that is poorly explained in the textbook.
4. Hints on learning traps to avoid. Guide the students past these pitfalls.
5. Material not covered elsewhere. Lectures can be as up-to-date as the morning newscast (McKeachie, 1986).
6. Material of high interest to students. Life is short. Take advantage of course content that is very interesting to students.
7. Examples and illustrations. "Illustrations, anecdotes, specific instances, and practical applications all add to the effectiveness of a lecture" (Reid, 1948, 106). They are essential for an inductive approach. When the lecture bogs down, it is time for a concrete example or a break (Brinkley et al., 1999, 53–56; Lowman, 1995, 136–139; Ramsden, 1992, 135–138; Reid, 1948).

It may be useful to cover details once in an example, but details can be skipped in later examples. Unless the course is in your area of research, don't include your research, no matter how fascinating it is to you. Cover less material, but cover it deeply (Boice, 2000, 21, 57–58; Davidson & Ambrose, 1994, 54; Palmer, 1998, 121, 135; Ramsden, 1992).

Cull obsolete material from your lecture notes. Tradition is not an excuse for retaining this material, but removing any traditional material will be controversial. I have been berated for suggesting that an obsolete but beloved part of the chemical engineering canon be eliminated. Stress covering less material but in more depth.

Consider delegating to the students the responsibility of learning material that is explained well in the textbook or other sources. But be sure to include these topics in the objectives, the practice sessions or projects, and the examinations. As a rule of thumb, plan so that 15 to 20 percent of the material on tests is covered only in the lecture, another 15 to 20 percent of the test material is covered only in the reading assignments, and the remaining 60 to 70 percent of the test is covered in both the lecture and readings. This gives students incentive to attend lectures and read the assignments.

Textbook authors often include any content that a potential adopter of the text might want. This causes megatexts. You cannot use the content in textbooks as a reliable guide of what to cover in lecture.

Harvey's course will benefit from his attempt to control content tyranny. After analyzing his coverage, he realizes that he includes many items that are tangential to major course goals. He decides to emphasize the key points and illustrate them with examples. Harvey writes objectives for the first month of the course and finds they help him keep his lectures on track. Covering less material allows him to relax in class, and for the first time in his life he actually starts to enjoy teaching.

5.2. Improving Lectures

Attention Span

Harvey ignores the attention span of his students. McKeachie (1994, 6) notes that students' attention is highest the first 10 and the last 10 minutes of a lecture. Gibbs (1992, 13–14) states, "After 15 minutes or so of a lecture, students will be performing much less well than at the start." Centra (1993, 23) agrees. Bonwell and Eison (1991, 8) state, "Ten to twenty minutes into the lecture . . . confusion and boredom set in and assimilation fell off rapidly." B. G. Davis (1993, 99) cites research showing that the attention span is 10 to 20 minutes, and she recommends 15 minutes. Mazur (1997, 25) suggests a mini-lecture of 7 to 10 minutes. Boice (2000, 45) recommends 8 to 12 minutes. Middendorf and Kalish (1996, 3) suggest a "20 minute attention span as a rule of thumb." Wankat and Oreovicz (1993, 93) stated that students have a 20- to 30-minute attention span, but they were being generous. You can take your choice, but the message is clear: *Fifty minutes of straight lecturing does not work.*

After approximately 15 minutes of lecture, most students need a short break. If the teacher does not provide this break, the students take it anyway. Watch students in a lecture or seminar. Around 15 minutes into the lecture you will see their eyes glaze over as their attention shifts elsewhere for a few minutes. Or monitor yourself while attending a seminar. Even if I am interested, I cannot keep my focus for longer than 15 to 20 minutes. The rare exception occurs when the lecturer is very enthusiastic and achieves a high level of audience involvement throughout.

Lectures are more effective when they consist of mini-lectures separated by activity breaks. The mini-lectures should probably be at most 15 minutes. The activity or involvement breaks, discussed in section 5.3, should relate to the lecture objectives.

Very long lecture periods (e.g., three hours) are difficult, because although there is recovery, the falloff after each break is faster (Gibbs, 1992, 14).

One method to obtain better student attention during lectures is to administer a short quiz immediately after the lecture. The students should be told in advance that there will be a quiz. This method almost doubles the amount students remember after eight weeks (Cross, 1990, 131). Quizzes focus students' attention even more if they are told the topic that will be covered. This method also greatly increases students' questions.

Explaining Content

Student learning increases when the lecturer follows a logical, inductive sequence and the presentation is adapted to the students (Hativa, 1995). If there is a hierarchy, showing it helps students see how the pieces fit together. Think of the presentation as a spiral with increased depth in each pass through the content. *Simplify the initial pass* by presenting one of the following (Duffy & Jones, 1995, 47–48):

- An anecdote
- A concrete example
- An analogy
- The core notion
- A rough idea
- A visual or intuitive presentation
- A presentation without math
- A presentation with math only

The second pass should contain more depth and fill out the details. Give specific instances and work toward general theory. Encourage students to build their knowledge structures as you give them more depth and details.

To increase learning, *link the material to the students* (Duffy & Jones, 1995, 49–50; Hativa, 1995). Relate it to their life experiences, their prior learning, and their senses. Use analogies that relate to their experiences. One can relate historical events, political theories, and economics to current events or to the students' family histories. For example, the electoral college comes alive every four years as the United States prepares for a national election. With a little ingenuity, many phenomena studied in science and engineering classes can be related to ordinary life. For example, a host of physical and chemical changes occur during cooking. Check students' understanding by asking them to explain these phenomena based on the course material. Be creative in linking material to the students.

Reduce distractions. "Noise" interferes with learning. Lecture classes held outdoors may be ineffective because there are too many distractions. Avoid excessive detail, especially in the initial presentation. Clearly explain jargon and introduce it into the course slowly.

In later passes though the material, *sharpen the students' understanding*. Consider additional analogies, including false ones. Briefly apply the material to other fields. Explore the limits of validity. Consider special cases that either are very easy to solve or have different solutions. Provide a global picture and, if appropriate, illustrate deductive logic. Small-group discussions can help students increase their understanding. Summarize with a phrase or sound bite that students will remember.

Performance Aspects

Performing is a key part of lecturing. Be enthusiastic—it helps keep students awake. Think of yourself and the students as a team and make eye contact with many students (Ekeler, 1994). Whatever you do, DO NOT READ to students, and remember to SPEAK LOUD ENOUGH (Reid, 1948). Many aspects of performance, such as voice, gestures, the use of props, and responsiveness to the audience, are explained in detail by Lowman (1995).

The completeness of lecture notes is clearly a personal preference. Some professors write a full text of the lecture (Brinkley et al., 1999, 56–57) while others prefer shorter notes (Boice, 2000, 25). When I started teaching, I wrote complete texts as lecture notes, but as I became more experienced, I became comfortable with less detailed notes. Boice (2000) emphasizes that shorter notes are more efficient and, he believes, more effective. In any case, include visual aids, questions to ask the students, and plans for the involvement breaks (discussed in section 5.3). Script some of your dramatic movements as stage directions. Choreograph the lecture. Remember that you are preparing for a dramatic performance, but lectures should be more spontaneous and involve more audience participation than plays. Experiment until you find what works for you.

If you write a great deal of material on the board during lectures, your presentation will probably improve if you switch to an overhead projector. It is easier to write clearly on an overhead projector and much easier to maintain eye contact. In large lecture halls, overhead transparencies are easier to see than the blackboard (Davidson & Ambrose, 1994, 58). Moreover, overhead transparencies can be prepared in advance, which is particularly useful for complicated figures, such as those needed in anatomy. Although word processing programs are sufficient, computer presentation software such as PowerPoint produces better transparencies. However, if transparencies are prepared in advance it is tempting to lecture much too quickly (Davidson & Ambrose, 1994, 59) unless you give the students partial lecture notes. Except for fairly complicated figures and diagrams (e.g., the circulation system in the body), the use of color seldom helps clarify content, and using color makes copying much more expensive.

> TIP: If you will reuse a transparency often, place a clear plastic sheet over it or slide it under the plastic from a roll. This allows you to add details and keep your original (B. G. Davis, 1993, 324).

Lecturing Less and Student Preparation

For professors who normally lecture, the best advice is, *lecture less*. Cover less material and involve the audience more (Eble, 1988, chapter 6; Weimer, 1993, chapter 6). Don't lecture every class period (Ekeler, 1994). Of course, lecturing less works only if you have content tyranny under control and are selective in your choice of material to cover. Since most learning in college does not occur in the classroom, less lecturing may have little effect on learning or may actually increase learning (Ramsden, 1992, 154). If the students have clear objectives, they can learn most of the material on their own.

Make sure students are prepared for class (O'Brien, 1998, 102). If students come prepared, you can minimize the lecture portion to cover only the key points and material that is not in the textbook. For the remainder of the class, you can focus on student discussion (in small groups or the entire class) and student presentations. Students are likely to become involved and grapple with the material during lively discussions.

Making sure students come prepared is difficult, however. You can encourage student preparation. Inform the students in the syllabus that you expect them to be prepared for class. Short, simple multiple-choice quizzes at the beginning of class will encourage more students to read the material (Mazur, 1997). Or require students to hand in a card before class with a question about the reading assignment or a comment about the personal applicability of the reading. If you allow students to come in unprepared and then lecture on everything, most students will see no reason to prepare ahead of time.

Large Classes

There is no pedagogical advantage to large classes (B. G. Davis, 1993, chapters 12 and 15; Centra, 1993, 66–67; McKeachie, 1994, chapter 20), and from a pedagogical viewpoint, large is more than 15 to 20 students. In small classes, it is much easier for professors to develop rapport with students and for students to ask questions and become involved. Of course, in academe a contrary view can always be found, and Solomon and Solomon (1993, 119) argue that "big classes are OK"—but they qualify this by requiring that students be actively involved.

If you are assigned a large class, expect to do more preparation, impose more rules, and work harder to develop rapport with students. Lecture handouts, which are valuable in any lecture class, are even more valuable in large lectures. The syllabus needs to be detailed and clear. As the number of students increases, students are more likely to miss tests or fail to turn in assignments on time. Learning students' names becomes more difficult, but the students appreciate it more.

It is important to provide opportunities for individual attention. Come early and stay late. Get a cordless microphone and wander up the aisle into the audience as you lecture (Ekeler, 1994). Institute office hours and help sessions before tests. Consider breaking the class into smaller recitation sections that use a participative teaching procedure (see Chapter 6). Help the students get to know other students in the class and to form study groups. Give students frequent feedback and a chance to provide you with feedback. Act on some of the feedback.

Whereas small classes are often fun, large classes are work. The good news is you are more likely to be assigned a teaching assistant (TA; see section 9.3).

Swallowing his pride, Harvey admits that since his students are not learning and have poor attitudes, his teaching needs to improve. He develops a list of the most important objectives and focuses his lectures on them. All the other fascinating material is either ruthlessly removed or relegated to examples and illustrations. This surgery gives Harvey less to prepare and more time in class. He can now relax in class, cover the important items, and still have time for student questions and one student activity. He tries to never talk for longer than twenty minutes at a stretch. Students' interest in the class increases, and students start to stay after class to ask him questions. Most important, the students learn more and perform better on exams, and Harvey is able to accomplish this while spending less time on the course than previously.

5.3. Increasing Student Involvement

Involvement is the single best predictor of student learning and success in college (Astin, 1975, 1993). "Involvement breaks"—activities that involve students—are an excellent way to break up long lectures.

Most lecturers are comfortable filling the entire lecture hour with words. Once they realize that this is relatively ineffective, they do not know how to structure breaks. Breaks and mini-lectures should build on and reinforce each other (Eble, 1988, 80; Gibbs, 1992, 13, 21–23; Johnson et al., 1991a, chapter 5; McKeachie, 1994, 58; Osterman et al., 1985). Successful breaks do not occur spontaneously—they must be planned and scripted. Breaks should clearly shift gears from the lecture to revive student attention for the next mini-lecture. Breaks are also more effective when they are varied. The students' response to the fifteenth time in the semester they are asked to take a one-minute quiz will be a collective groan. Here are some ideas for lecture breaks:

■ Divide the class into small, informal cooperative groups. This can be done by asking students to talk to their neighbors, by counting off one, two, three, four, and so on, or with permanent groups. Three or four is a good group size. One exercise is to ask each group to come to consensus about one good question. Ask them to neatly print the question on a three-by-five-inch index card or a piece of paper and turn it in to you. Then read and answer some of these questions. You will be surprised by the quality of the questions. This is a form of one-minute quiz, but it actually takes three or four minutes. I have found that this procedure elicits questions about assignments that are due in a few days.

■ Give a one-minute quiz that asks the groups to summarize the two or three most important parts of the lecture. Different forms of the one-minute quiz provide useful feedback about what the students are learning (Angelo & Cross, 1993).

■ Run a brainstorming exercise either in small groups or with the entire class. Follow the rules of brainstorming: no criticizing, build on others' responses, record all responses on the blackboard or overhead projector. Brainstorming works well on questions that do not have a single correct answer such as, "What were the causes of World War I?"

■ Pose questions either to small cooperative groups or to the class as a whole.

■ Provide a one-minute stretch break. Students appreciate this in long class periods, but you will have to be assertive to restart the class.

■ Provide rest room breaks in classes and workshops that last several hours.

■ Have a few students introduce themselves to the class. Repeat this procedure in other class sessions until all students have participated.

■ Play a few minutes of music that is related to the class. For example, you might play Spanish music in a Spanish class and period music in a history class.

■ Have student groups present brief role plays. Students often become very enthusiastic while developing small dramas.

■ Show or pass around props such as tools or kitchen utensils that relate to the content (Duffy & Jones, 1995, 45–47).

■ Give a pop quiz. Be sure the students are warned in the syllabus, make the quiz very easy, and either don't count it heavily or use it for bonus points. Otherwise, you can ruin your rapport with the class.

■ Have a brief, prescheduled student presentation. For example, a student could report on a relevant news item. This activity provides an opportunity for students to practice presentation skills.

■ Allow students a few minutes for reflection or to catch up on their lecture notes (Boice, 2000, 27, 45). Let them ask their neighbors for clarification. This is particularly useful if the lecture has been fast paced.

■ Ask a challenge question. If nobody volunteers an answer, assign it for the next period or use a Socratic approach to tease out an answer.

■ Present a problem to the students and ask them to work it out individually or in small groups. Participation will be increased if students are asked at random to present their results.

At first it will be more difficult to plan involvement breaks, but using them increases student attention and learning. Switching lecture topics is *not* an involvement break. Be creative and use variety. Students tend to interpret experimentation by the professor as interest in teaching. This "Hawthorne effect" (Peters & Waterman, 1982, 5–6) implies that most new teaching activities will be interpreted positively unless the students feel threatened. As long as the breaks are not graded, students are unlikely to feel threatened.

Most students are comfortable sitting passively during a lecture. Many are not learning, but they are comfortable. When you first introduce activity breaks in your lectures, students are likely to be uncertain that you really want them to do this, and there may be some resistance. Spend a few minutes at the beginning of the first lecture to explain to them why you will be using activity breaks (they will learn more). Tell them you expect them to become involved. Immediately before the break, give them a warning (e.g., "OK, listen up. I have some instructions for you"). Then give clear instructions as to what they will do (Gibbs, 1992, 17–21). And tell them to start. When the break is done, use a consistent signal such as turning the lights off and on or hitting a pen against the overhead projector to get their attention. Students are slow to start activities and slow to end them. Their attention span is much longer for activities they are involved in than it is for a lecture. As the semester continues and they become trained in doing activities, they will start and stop faster.

Cooperative groups are a useful teaching method (Johnson & Johnson, 1975; Johnson et al., 1991a, 1991b, 1998; McKeachie, 1994, chapter 13; Michaelsen, 1994) that is discussed in detail in section 6.1. Successful use of informal cooperative groups during activity breaks is relatively easy. Since students do a new activity more willingly when the rationale for it is explained to them, before using groups the first time, give a reason. I explain that they will be expected to work in groups when they graduate, and now is a good time to learn how. The membership of these spur-of-the-moment groups can be informally assigned every class period. Early in the semester the students appreciate an opportunity to introduce themselves within their groups.

Give the groups a clear task and request a deliverable, that is, what they will have to produce. Merely saying "discuss this issue" usually doesn't work. Instead, ask them to form a consensus on a possible solution, to come up with a good question, to determine a good first approach to solve a problem, and so forth. Tasks should be interesting, challenging but doable, and open ended and should allow all group members to participate. Deliverables keep the students focused on the task at hand and prevent them from straying into tangents. The deliverable could be the index card used in the one-minute quiz or a brief oral report to the entire class.

I have been successful in using informal groups during breaks. Early in the semester I encourage participation, but once students have been exposed to the technique they need no encouragement. Most students enjoy the opportunity to work with other students, particularly when there is no grade pressure involved. Students who do not talk in class often open up in small groups (Brinkley et al., 1999, 26, 44).

Varying your teaching methods keeps the students' interest high. Substitute other teaching methods for a few lectures (B. G. Davis, 1993, chapter 16; Ekeler, 1994, 96). For example, if the topic doesn't have a single correct answer, a panel discussion can be entertaining and informative. Arrange for panelists, provide them with ground rules (e.g., a five-minute opening statement), and remind them the morning of the class.

TIP: Keep the number of panelists small. This reduces the time required to arrange for the panel and provides more time for students' questions.

Short field trips that can be taken during a normal class period can often be arranged on or very close to campus (B. G. Davis, 1993, 166–172; Wankat & Oreovicz, 1993, 138–139). Visit a library, museum, computer resource room, store, construction site, bank, courtroom, power plant, research laboratory, hospital, day care facility, school, or another class. These trips will be the highlight of the semester for some students. You need to formulate goals for the trip and make phone calls to arrange it.

You can also show an appropriate video or movie during part of the class. Be sure to check out the TV or projector ahead of time and make sure the tape or film is at the appropriate starting point. To increase student learning, introduce the film or video and tell students what to look for. Asking for a deliverable, such as a paragraph about the movie or a small-group discussion, will help keep the students focused.

Spending a class period or two on a computer simulation can also spark considerable student interest. However, be sure a bug-free simulation is available. It is much more efficient to use an existing simulation than to develop a simulation specifically for the course.

Professor Harvey Jones has started incorporating an activity break into his lectures. About halfway through a lecture, he introduces a small, preprepared group activity. He likes one-minute quizzes since they require almost no preparation time, but he is careful to use this method once a week at most. Students also appreciate a few minutes to get their notes in order, and this break requires no preparation time. He has prepared some more elaborate small group exercises that have worked reasonably well and has planned a field trip to the library when the class discusses the required paper.

> TIP: If you have never used involvement breaks, start slowly. Pick a few lectures in which you have content tyranny under control and intersperse breaks in them. If you do not feel relaxed in class and are worried about losing control, pick a structured break, such as a one-minute quiz. If the students do not normally ask questions, the one-minute quiz with student groups developing questions works well. If you are worried about student participation, be sure to pass out one three-by-five-inch index card to each group. The card reinforces that it is a group effort, limits the question length, keeps students from shuffling off to find a piece of paper, and helps maintain control since you "own" the index cards. In your lecture notes write the instructions for the break in the same amount of detail you normally use for content. If you routinely use the overhead projector, prepare an overhead in advance that gives the instructions and the question the students are to answer. Watch the student groups. When more than half of them are done, start collecting cards. Then read the questions to the entire class and answer them. Once you feel comfortable with these breaks, try others for variety.

5.4. Professor Preparation for Class

To reduce the time required to prepare for class, arrange with your department chair to teach the same class several times. Clark (1987, 230–231) notes that professors at community colleges are able to cope with heavy teaching loads (15–20 hours per week) by teaching the same courses over and over. Their total preparation time is about the same (75 percent prepare less than 10 hours per week) as at research universities.

Preparation Time

New professors often spend too much time preparing for each class (Boice, 1992, 2000), while experienced professors may err on the other side. A total preparation time from a half-hour to an hour will normally allow you to prepare and modestly modify an existing lecture. Assuming that you know the material, a total preparation time of two hours spread out over two or more work sessions is usually sufficient to prepare a new lecture (Boice, 1992, 136; Wankat & Oreovicz, 1993, 22). However, plan to finish preparation well before it is needed so that interruptions and surprises do not force you to walk into class only half prepared.

It is easy to spend days preparing. The 80:20, or Pareto, principle should be followed (see Table 3.4). Eighty or even 90 percent of the benefit of lecture preparation appears to occur in the first 10 or 20 percent of the preparation time. If you are spending too much time preparing, force yourself to prepare new lectures in two hours, with an absolute maximum of three hours. The students probably will not be able to tell any difference, or they will prefer the lecture you spent less time on. It is easier to control content tyranny and present material spontaneously when you spend less time preparing.

Boice (2000, 19–38) recommends the following procedure to prevent overpreparation. At least a day before the lecture, do a brief prepreparation to familiarize yourself with the material and write down the key points. Conceptual outlines for a lecture can be developed in 15 minutes or less. With later reflection and some filling in of missing points, the conceptual outline becomes your lecture notes.

Figures 5.1A and B illustrate the impact of professorial effort on course effectiveness (Wankat & Oreovicz, 1993, 22). New professors and, to a lesser extent, experienced professors in a new course follow the learning curve shown in Figure 5.1A. Quite a bit of effort is required before course effectiveness significantly increases. Then effectiveness levels off. At high amounts of effort, the professor becomes over prepared and course effectiveness may decrease. We would expect a much steeper learning curve for experienced professors. As shown in Figure 5.1B, they can achieve high effectiveness in much less time. This is particularly true when the professor has taught the course before.

It is efficient but dangerous to spend the minimum amount of time necessary to be effective. If the effort drops below the critical point (labeled C in Figure 5.1B) for any reason, such as excessive travel, course effectiveness will plummet, and it probably cannot be recovered that semester. This "falling off the cliff" is one reason professors can have good student ratings one term and terrible ratings the next. A slow decline in teaching effectiveness occurs if one becomes bored. Then it is time to move on to new teaching methods or new courses.

On rare occasions, such as important seminar presentations, it may be useful to spend twenty to thirty hours to attempt to prepare the "ultimate" lecture. Start preplanning the talk at least a month before the presentation. Think about key points to emphasize and how to involve the audience. Prepare a conceptual outline and then flesh it out to develop the presentation. Prepare a draft of the visual aids and then make color transparencies or a PowerPoint presentation. Look for special effects that will enhance audience involvement and understanding. Practice to get your timing and words just right. Read some of the excellent commentaries on improving lectures. Watch excellent and poor lecturers at meetings and during seminars. Make notes on what they do, and practice emulating the excellent lecturers. Improving the ultimate lecture will tend to improve your daily lectures.

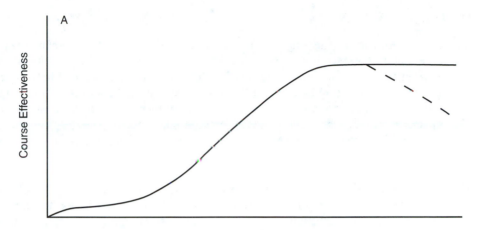

Time required for new professors or experienced professors with a new course

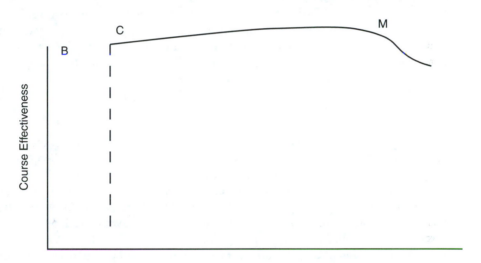

Time required for experienced professors with an established course

FIGURE 5.1. Course effectiveness. A. New professors or experienced professors teaching a new course. B. Experienced professors with established material. C = critical point at which course effectiveness plummets; M = point of maximum effectiveness. Reprinted with permission from Phillip C. Wankat and Frank S. Oreovicz, *Teaching Engineering* (New York: McGraw-Hill, 1993), p. 21.

Handouts

If transparencies for the entire lecture are prepared in advance, you can cover much more material. In fact, it is easy to cover too much material for the students to comprehend unless you hand out lecture notes in advance. "Handouts are almost *de rigueur* for large lectures" (Gibbs, 1992, 28–29). However, if the handouts are too complete, students may see no reason to pay attention during lectures. Partial lecture notes and transparencies that have blank spaces force you and the students to fill in the blanks while the lecture proceeds (Ekeler, 1994). This helps keep the students active and ensures that most students will have a good set of notes.

You need to obtain permission to use copyrighted material in lecture handouts, whereas it is unlikely that this permission is required for a lecture without handouts. Avoid including copyrighted material unless it is critical and is not available in the assigned textbook. Goldstein (1995) reviews the history of copyright law. If the material is from a U.S. Government publication, you can use it and simply cite the source without obtaining permission.

Preparing lecture handouts for an entire term for a new course is a daunting task. It is OK to work in spurts and prepare handouts for only parts of the course. If you and the students like using partial lecture notes, you can complete the task the second or third time you teach the course. Some schools will not appreciate the cost of distributing copious notes to students. It may be necessary to prepare the notes ahead of time and sell them to the students through the campus bookstore.

Preparing for the Presentation

Usually, you will have prepared the lecture a few hours or days in advance. Immediately before class, prepare for the presentation. Quickly skim your notes to refresh your memory and make sure nothing is missing. Review the names of the students. Collect all the items you might need: lecture notes, textbook, handouts, props, chalk, Magic Markers, spare clean transparencies, whatever. Check your appearance in a mirror. It doesn't do to walk into class with a ketchup stain on your cheek or spinach stuck between your teeth. Prepare psychologically for the class. Get into the mood of the subject and the mood of a performer. Five or ten minutes to a half-hour is sufficient (Boice, 2000, 52; Ekeler, 1994, 95; Lowman, 1995, 123). At the very least, spend the five minutes walking to the classroom preparing yourself psychologically. Don't answer the telephone if it rings just as you're leaving for class.

Plan to arrive at the classroom at least five minutes early. This will prevent last-minute problems such as a dirty blackboard or misaligned chairs from causing you to start late. Early arrival also gives you time to write a lecture outline on the board and chat with students. Doing these activities before the start of class helps the students prepare psychologically for the class and settle in quickly. Finally, early arrival sends the psychological message that you are ready and eagerly looking forward to this class. If you don't normally come to class early, try it. Staying late has similar benefits.

Shortly after presenting a lecture, debrief yourself (Eble, 1988, 72). What worked, and what didn't? What parts did the students have difficulty understanding?

How far did you progress in the lecture? Were there any insightful student questions that you could use in the lecture? On the spur of the moment did you think of a particularly insightful or humorous way to present something? If so, record this in your notes. The most efficient time to fix or fine-tune a lecture is immediately after giving it.

Harvey found it psychologically difficult to reduce his preparation time. When he actually forced himself to prepare a lecture in two hours, the presentation went more smoothly than his previous lectures. Including a prearranged involvement break in his lecture notes was the only way Harvey ever remembered to stop talking. Including even one activity break in the lecture required time, but Harvey gained back much of that time by coming early instead of a few minutes late. He knew he was on the right track when a student asked him to repeat the exercise with the index cards, since she thought Harvey's spontaneous answers were easier to understand than his prepared lectures. Harvey laughed. This was the first time any student could remember Harvey laughing.

5.5. Lowman's Two-Dimensional Model of College Teaching

Lowman's (1985, 1995) two-dimensional model of effective college teaching is useful for analyzing teaching in lecture classes. The combination of presentation style and content makes up the dimension that Lowman calls *intellectual excitement*. Meticulous organization of content is not sufficient for high intellectual excitement. The professor also needs to consider presentation skills, such as voice, timing, and involving the audience. In content-oriented courses, this is the most important dimension. The exception to this is when a professor is rude or does something that is interpreted as racist, harassing, or sexist (Wankat & Oreovicz, 1993). A single such incident can overshadow the good teaching during the remainder of the term.

Lowman's second dimension is *rapport with students,* which is discussed in sections 7.1 to 7.3. Although less important than intellectual excitement in content-oriented courses, without rapport most professors will not be effective teachers. Excellence requires a high level in one of these dimensions and at least a moderate level in the other.

A modified form of Lowman's model appropriate for content-oriented courses is shown in Figure 5.2. The vertical axis is the level of intellectual excitement, and the horizontal axis is the level of rapport with students. Although these two axes represent continua, for simplicity Lowman divided them into three levels: low, moderate, and high. Likewise, the nine cells are not distinct but blend together. Movement from left to right represents increasing rapport with students, while movement upward represents increasing intellectual excitement. Cells with higher numbers represent better teaching in terms of both student learning and student ratings. The cells are labeled for courses in which intellectual excitement is the more important dimension. Increasing intellectual excitement by one level (vertical arrows) results in a greater teaching improvement than does increasing student rapport by one level (horizontal arrows). The diagonal arrows indicate increases level by level.

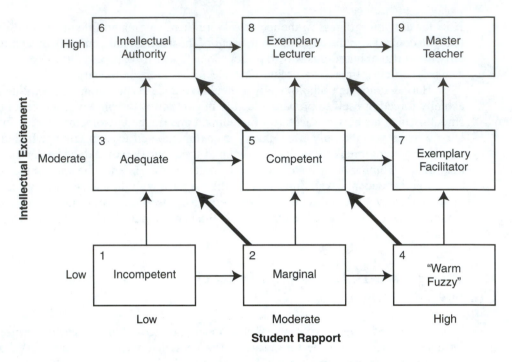

FIGURE 5.2.   Modified version of Lowman's (1985, 1995) two-dimensional model of teacher effectiveness for content-oriented courses.

Professors who teach at low levels in both dimensions are incompetent (cell 1). Increasing rapport to the moderate level (cell 2, "marginal") will greatly reduce students' complaints, but they probably will not be well prepared for subsequent courses. A further increase in rapport to the high level (cell 4, "warm fuzzy") results in a lovable but fuzzy-minded teacher. Returning to cell 1, increasing intellectual excitement from low to moderate (cell 3, "adequate") results in teachers who achieve sufficient student learning, but the students' attitudes may suffer. Students probably grumble about these teachers. If these teachers are able to increase rapport to the moderate level, the result (cell 5) is a truly competent teacher. Another increase in rapport creates the exemplary facilitator (cell 7). This teacher is especially skilled in small classes and will be an award-winning teacher if assigned to small classes. Returning to cell 3 and increasing intellectual excitement to the high level, the teacher becomes an intellectual authority (cell 6), which is the stereotype of the brilliant but aloof professor of science or engineering. Increasing rapport to moderate results in another type of award-winning teacher (cell 8, "exemplary lecturer") who excels in large, relatively formal classes. Finally, the rare master teacher (cell 9) is highly capable in all teaching situations.

This definition of a master teacher is not the same as the common use of the terms "great" and "master teacher." From stories of great teachers it is clear that most have a passion for their subject, some for their students, and some for both (Epstein,

1981; Peterson, 1946). Many are not outstanding lecturers, and some are austere. They are great teachers because they inspire their students, initiate a spirit of inquiry, show students how to think, and act authentically. None of these qualities is easy to impart in professors who would be great.

All professors can improve from low to moderate levels. Cell 5, which represents a fully competent teacher, is within reach of everyone. Improvement from moderate to high levels on either dimension requires either a strong inherent ability or significant effort. Reaching the high levels for intellectual excitement or rapport requires passion for content or students, respectively. Since passion cannot be taught, the usual goal of development programs for professors is competence. Many professors have the skills and passion to reach the high level in either intellectual excitement or rapport. If they achieve their natural potential in one dimension and raise the level of the other dimension to moderate, they will become award-winning teachers.

Some writers, such as Hanna and McGill (1985), Palmer (1983, 1998), and Wilshire (1990), contend that the affective aspects of teaching are more important than the cognitive aspects. An adaptation of Lowman's model for that case is shown in Figure 7.1.

5.6. Assignments and Tests

Assignments and tests improve student learning by giving students opportunities to practice and receive feedback. Students think of tests and grades as the most important parts of the course. And they are quick to take umbrage at professors who they feel are unfair in these matters.

Establishing a clear connection among course objectives, lectures, reading, assignments, and tests increases student learning and helps prevent charges of unfairness (Clegg, 1994, 425–426; B. G. Davis, 1993, 240; Eble, 1988, 45; McKeachie, 1994, 72). This connection also helps motivate students to pay attention in lectures and do the reading and assignments. Students are not motivated to attend lectures if the professor always lectures on theory but gives problems for assignments and tests. Unfortunately, this is often done in technical subjects. If theory is important, there must be objectives, assignments, and test questions that focus on theory. If theory is not important, spend little lecture time on it. If the professor tells students to read the book but always gives tests based on lecture notes, most students will quickly stop reading. If the book is important, it must relate to the assignments and test questions.

Assignments

"Assignments are ways of getting students to do things" (Eble, 1988, 141). If you want to have students write, they need writing assignments. Writing samples do not have to be long, and a series of short writing assignments throughout the semester will probably help improve writing more than a single long assignment. Since good writing requires rewriting, make sure that students rewrite (Palmer, 1998, 138). Students will rewrite if they can improve their preliminary grade. Rewriting is important even for relatively short assignments.

If you want students to be able to solve problems, they need problems on assignments. Since success is motivating, start with relatively easy problems. But if all the problems in assignments are easier than the test problems, the students will complain bitterly. Thus, at least a few of these problems should be quite challenging and more difficult than the test problems.

Not all assignments need to be graded, but it *is* necessary to provide feedback. Feedback can be provided for ungraded assignments by posting solutions on a bulletin board and/or on the web. Most students will at least try these "for yourself" problems if they can see a clear connection between them and tests. Since there is no grade, you can reuse problems even if files exist.

Randomly grading a subset of the turned-in problems and checking that the others were attempted will encourage most students to do the turn-in problems. When returning problems, be sure to let students know which problems were not graded, since they may assume that an absence of marks means their solution was correct. It is wise to place a sentence in the syllabus stating that not all problems will be graded. If an assignment or project extends over several weeks, suggesting when the students should complete various parts will help limit, but not eliminate, student procrastination.

TIP: Not all assignments need to be handed in, and not all problems that are handed in need to be graded.

An excellent generic assignment is to have student groups develop an original homework or test question and its solution (Felder, 1985). This assignment requires students to function at the higher levels of Bloom's taxonomy, and rewards for creativity can be built into the assignment. Grade both the question and the solution. If the assignment is to develop an original test question, it serves as a bridge to testing. In my graduate class on educational methods I ask the students to develop a test for the course. The students are told they can share their assignments before handing them in. The actual test for the course consists of questions I select from the student's tests. Course projects are discussed in more detail in section 6.2.

Developing Tests

In the minds of students, tests are important—often too important. But they do have the effect of motivating most students to study, which is desirable. Therefore one method to increase student time on task, which will increase student learning, is to give more quizzes and tests (Eble, 1988, 144–145; Ericksen, 1974, 196; Johnson, 1988; Lowman, 1995, 253–256, 260–261; McKeachie, 1994, 73–74). Figure 5.3 illustrates the effect of giving more tests and assignments. When there are few tests or major assignments (Figure 5.3A), many students coast until the week before a major assignment or test. When there are many assignments, quizzes, and tests (Figure 5.3B), the coasting periods are much shorter. The net result is that students spend more time studying and learn more. Frequent testing also reduces student anxiety, since each test or quiz is worth a smaller percentage of the course grade. Frequent testing requires more test preparation and grading but does allow some reduction in turn-in assignments.

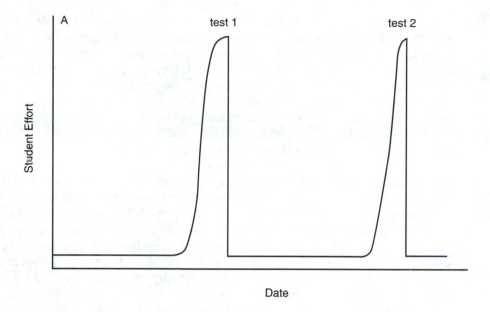

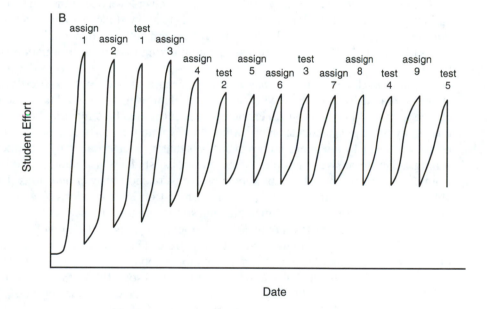

FIGURE 5.3.   Schematic representations of student effort in courses. A. Few tests and assignments. B. Many tests and assignments.

But *you* believe you can't give frequent tests because you have to cover the content. Don't let content tyranny prevent you from using teaching methods that will increase student learning! Frequent testing increases your workload, and it does not encourage students to become self-directed learners. Test first-year students and sophomores frequently and reduce the frequency progressively for juniors and seniors.

Write new tests every semester. If you use the same test, students with files will circumvent the learning process, and students without easy access to files will believe that the tests, and hence you, are unfair. Since students appreciate access to old tests, use previous tests as ungraded assignments. If it is clear that these are old tests, students will attempt them even if they are not handed in. But remember that feedback has to be available. This procedure is fair since it gives all students the same access to previous tests. Brinkley et al. (1999, 87) allow that there may be good reasons to reuse test questions and suggest that if you do this, use questions that are several years old.

The hardest part in writing tests is to generate new ideas for questions and problems that test the objectives but can be done in the time allotted. *Keep a file of ideas for test questions*. Every time a new idea comes—say, after a lecture or a student question—jot it down and put it in the file. Before actually writing the test, take the course outline and privately brainstorm ideas for test questions for each major topic. These two methods will usually give you good ideas with which to start constructing the test.

Open- and closed-book exams both have advantages and disadvantages. One advantage of open-book tests is they tend to force the professor to write questions at the higher levels of the taxonomy, since answers to lower level questions can be looked up in the book. A useful intermediate procedure is to allow students to bring a *key relations card,* that is, a three-inch-by-five-inch index card with any information they want on it (Mettes et al., 1981). The process of summarizing their own information is very beneficial.

Multiple-choice tests are easy to score because they do not require decisions about partial credit and can be computer graded. However, I'm not a fan of multiple-choice tests, except as pretests to encourage students to read the material before a lecture. They don't give students an opportunity to explain their answers, and credit may be given for a lucky guess or for correct answers that were determined by incorrect reasoning. Also, to answer multiple-choice questions, students use strategies different from those they use to find the answers to problems or short-answer questions (Hilton, 1993). Although multiple-choice questions can test on higher order objectives, they (and their cousins true/false and matching questions) are usually ineffective for testing at the higher levels of the taxonomy. For higher level objectives, it is appropriate to use tests that display the reasoning used but are more difficult to score. Frequent use of multiple-choice exams leads to "communication atrophy" (Kennedy, 1997, 81) and does not increase students' academic development (Astin, 1993, 282). Pope (1995, 102) goes even further: "Multiple-choice exams . . . are easy-to-grade cop-outs."

Always, always solve the test before finalizing it (Clegg, 1994, 427–431). This rule applies even to essay questions. By solving the test first, you will find questions that are ambiguous, cannot be solved, are too long or too hard, or are trivial. Including an unsolvable or poorly written question on a test can lead to a grading disaster. Straightforward grading is one characteristic of a good test (Davidson & Ambrose,

1994, 70), and solving the test before using it allows you to adjust it to simplify grading. The time it takes you to solve the test can be used to estimate the time it will take students to solve the test. As a rule of thumb, try multiplying your solution time by five for first-year students, four for juniors, and three for graduate students. Adjust these factors until you obtain good predictions. One-hour (fifty-minute) tests must be fairly short to allow most students to finish them.

Once you have constructed the preliminary test, analyze it to check that important objectives are included at appropriate levels in Bloom's taxonomy (Svinicki, 1976; Wankat & Oreovicz, 1993, 216–217). Since the taxonomy is a hierarchy, lower levels can normally be assumed to be present when the question tests at a higher level. It is not necessary to cover all levels on each test, as long as they are included on some of the tests and assignments during the term. Failure to check the level of test questions often results in a test that is overloaded with questions at the lowest three levels of the taxonomy (Stice, 1976). This is particularly troublesome with multiple-choice tests, including those supplied in publisher's test banks (Gardiner, 1994, 60–64). This analysis also helps ensure that questions are fairly distributed among topics.

I want my tests to discriminate between students who know the material and those who don't. There should be sufficient time on tests for students who know the material to finish and earn a high grade, perhaps even 100. If there are no 100s or 90s, the test was too long, too hard, or both. I want some high scores because they convince everyone the test is reasonable. When there are some 100s, students with low grades complain less, apparently because they cannot rationalize their failure as the professor's fault. I expect that students who have not learned the material will earn low scores. If there are no low scores (below 50) in a medium-sized undergraduate class, the test may have been too easy or the professor did a great job motivating the students.

If the test discriminates on the basis of knowledge, the resulting distribution will *not* be normal, and may be bimodal. Writing tests that discriminate on the basis of student knowledge is a challenge but can be learned with practice. Note that the difficulty of problems and questions increases geometrically as the number of logical steps increases (Strandberg, 1958). Thus, it is much more difficult to solve a long, multiple-part problem or write a long essay than it is to answer a short problem or write a few sentences. Giving hints to the students on the appropriate order of steps makes problems and essay questions easier.

Giving students sufficient time on tests is absolutely necessary. Tests that are speed races discriminate on the basis of a combination of speed and knowledge, as shown in Figure 5.4. In this hypothetical example, students are divided into fast, average, and slow workers on the ordinate and into high, average, and low knowledge levels on the abscissa. I have arbitrarily assumed that fast workers can finish all the test questions, average workers can do three-fourths of the questions, and slow workers can finish half. Students with a high knowledge level will get all the test questions they try correct, those with average knowledge will get two-thirds of the questions correct, and those with a low knowledge level will get one-third correct. The resulting test scores will be the fraction attempted multiplied by the fraction correct. These scores, along with letter grades awarded by a generous grading scheme, are shown inside the grid. Each box in the grid contains 11.1 percent of the students. Since the two axes are not

	Low (1/3)	Average (2/3)	High (1)
Fast (1)	33.3% D	66.6% B	100% A
Average (3/4)	25% F	50% C	75% B
Slow (1/2)	12.5% F	33.3% D	50% C

Speed

Knowledge Level

FIGURE 5.4. Hypothetical distribution of test scores showing interaction of speed and knowledge. Speed represents the fraction of questions students have time to answer. Knowledge level is the fraction of questions students could answer correctly if they had sufficient time. The percentage in each cell represents the students' final scores. Each cell contains 11.1 percent of the students.

necessarily related, the distribution spreads out and looks like a skewed normal distribution. This often fools professors into thinking that a test is good. Unfortunately, speed is often more important than knowledge in determining grades. In this example, fast students with average knowledge earned higher grades than did slow students with high knowledge. Clearly, timed tests that become a race do not discriminate cleanly on the basis of students' knowledge.

Put the test together and proofread it. Proofread it after every change. After copies have been made, check that the tests have all the pages. Take reasonable but not paranoid precautions to prevent cheating. For instance, don't leave a copy of the test or solution lying open on your desk. Don't throw away rough drafts. Students have been known to search wastebaskets. Lock the test up overnight or take it home with you. The temptation of an open test on your desk or in the copy room may be too much for even honest students.

Administering Tests

Before the test date, discuss the test in class (B. G. Davis, 1993, 253–254; Lowman, 1995, 262–263; McKeachie, 1994, 81–84). Be clear which lectures and reading assignments are included and what items will not be tested on. A short review of important topics can help overcome the tendency of students to focus on recent topics. Discuss the testing procedure. Tell the students whether the test is open or closed book. Tell them what items, such as pencil and calculator, to bring to class to take the test. If you want them to sit in alternate seats, tell them this in advance. Preparation will make test days smoother and help reduce student anxiety.

Many professors schedule tests when they will be out of town. It is much better to *be there* (Clegg, 1994, 431; B. G. Davis, 1993, 254; Lowman, 1995, 264). The test is important to the students, and you signal that it is important to you by being there. If any typographical errors are found, the author of the test is the person who can do the best quick fix. And if you have developed rapport with the students, there will be less cheating if you are present.

Take care in administering the test (Clegg, 1994, 431–433; B. G. Davis, 1993, 254–257; Lowman, 1995, 264; McKeachie, 1994, 84–85). Every student should have the same amount of time to do the test. The exception is students who have been legally classified as disabled. By law, these students must be accommodated, which may mean additional time (B. G. Davis, 1993, chapter 4). Develop a procedure to rapidly pass out the tests. Start passing out the tests or have the students turn them over at the start of class. Tell the students to examine their tests. Say, for example, "Look at your tests. You should have three pages with ten questions. If you don't, raise your hand. Write your names on your tests now." As soon as the students start, record the number of students taking the test. Unless your school has a functioning honor code, a proctor should be in the exam room during the test. The best proctor is the professor. For small classes, the proctor can sit at the front of the room. In large classes, I use this time to look at my photographs of students and try to match students to their photographs. I do this to learn names, but my wandering around also strongly deters certain forms of cheating. The circulating proctor can also answer student questions. Periodically write down the time remaining on the board or overhead projector. Warn the students when there are two minutes left. When time is up, stop all the students and collect the tests. In large classes, it is essential to have help at this time to make sure that all students stop on time, do not change answers after seeing someone else's solution, and turn in their tests. After the test is over, count the tests and perhaps log them in.

Students will appreciate the use of some method to help them relax before or during the test. Duffy and Jones (1995, 233) recommend taking a bowl of wrapped candy or dried fruit around the room during the middle of the test. This quietly encourages students, and gives the students who want it a sugar boost. I have found cookies to be equally effective—homemade are preferred, but store-bought will do.

Many authors devote an entire chapter to cheating (B. G. Davis, 1993, chapter 34; Eble, 1988, chapter 14; McKeachie, 1994, chapter 7; Wankat & Oreovicz, 1993, chapter 12), and Kibler et al. (1988) essentially devote their entire book to it. Cheating is not a new phenomenon. C. J. Lucas (1994, 315) notes, "Dishonesty and cheating on tests are nothing new either; efforts to keep assessment and evaluation efforts honest by all parties involved extend back many centuries and probably always have enjoyed about the same degree of mixed success." Professors who develop good rapport with students and give tests that the students think are fair will have only a small amount of cheating in their classes. More details on preventing cheating are given in section 7.1.

Scoring Tests

Learning is increased if students receive prompt feedback (Clegg, 1994, 434–436; B. G. Davis, 1993, chapter 32; Lowman, 1995, 265–267; McKeachie, 1994, 85–88; Wankat & Oreovicz, 1993, 221–224). An effective way to do this without requiring speed grading is to have student groups re-solve the test in a recitation section. The recitation instructor can briefly quiz each group orally when they are finished, to be sure that each group member now understands how to do the test. Under no circumstances should scoring of the tests be unduly delayed. There is no advantage and many disadvantages to procrastinating on scoring. Ericksen (1984, 119) presents a contrary view, arguing that it is better to take the time to be thorough in providing feedback.

Hilton (1993) and I have opposing views on whether to award partial credit. I am in favor of partial credit, since it seems unfair to give students a zero when they do 80 to 90 percent of a problem correctly. Use a scoring template to award partial credit fairly. For problems, the template shows points for each step in a standard solution. For an essay, the template could be a list of items that would be included in a good answer. A scoring template is essential if TAs will grade the test. Even if the professor will grade the test, a scoring template helps make scoring consistent and fair. Templates are efficient, since many of the judgments about how to score an answer need to be made only once, when the template is produced. After developing the template, check it with a few selected tests and adjust the scoring if necessary. The few answers that do not fit into the scoring scheme will require separate judgments. When students earn very high scores or significantly higher scores than they have previously scored, write a few words of praise on the test (e.g., "Great Job!"). Grading tests is difficult work. Take frequent breaks and reward yourself when finished.

Since scoring homework and tests is subject to human error, particularly in large classes, it is reasonable to allow and, to some extent, encourage regrades. However, regrade requests should be written (Christensen, 1988; Wankat, 1983a). This prevents your having a cluster of students surrounding you after class, demanding points. Requiring that the written regrade request and the test be returned within one week helps to prevent end-of-term efforts to raise grades. In their request, students must explain why they believe there is a mistake in grading and why they deserve more credit. It is *not* a plea for more points. Regrade the entire problem, but not the entire test. Written regrade requests give the professor time to ponder the grading and consider each case individually. This makes it less likely that the professor will be perceived as arbitrary—a behavior deeply resented by students (Kennedy, 1997, 83). Written requests require students to practice rationally requesting a change from an authority figure, and they reduce frivolous requests.

5.7. Grading

Grading is controversial. Eble (1988, chapter 13), Elbow (1986), and Smith (1986a) suggest choosing grading methods that subvert the grading system, while B. G. Davis (1993), Johnson (1988), Lowman (1995), McKeachie (1994), Ory and Ryan (1993), and Wright (1994) moderately defend the grading system. I am in the latter category, but find myself leaning more and more toward the former.

Course grades and grade point averages (GPAs) have assumed an importance totally out of line with their predictive ability. Most evidence indicates that above a certain rather low break point (about 2.4 or 2.5 on a 4-point scale), GPAs do not correlate with later success in life (Eble, 1988, chapter 13; Ericksen, 1974, 212–213; Gardiner,

1994, 67; Milton et al., 1986; Stice, 1979), and studies that show a positive effect of grades have typically shown that it is weak (Pascarella & Terenzini, 1991, 624, 626–627). On the other hand, Bowen and Bok (1998, 140–142, 165, 184–185, 201–202, 261) found that rank in class in college correlated strongly and positively with compensation level, satisfaction with life, and satisfaction with college 19 years after matriculation. Leadership in civic organizations did not correlate with rank in class. Their study was restricted to 28 highly selective colleges and universities.

Grades are reasonable predictors of future grades, and little else. Yet many companies use GPAs as a screen for hiring and often set standards so high that many current employees, including the CEO, would not be hired. And of course, GPAs control admission to graduate and professional schools (Pascarella & Terenzini, 1991, 629). Excessive grade inflation has caused saturation at the high end that makes discrimination among students difficult (Kennedy, 1997, 80). Perhaps a partial solution is to award pluses and minuses, which at least would reduce the number of students with perfect 4.0 grades. Deemphasizing grades would be helpful, but is unlikely to happen.

Because of the supreme importance students attach to final course grades, awarding them probably causes professors more grief than any other part of teaching. A consistent philosophy of grading helps minimize this grief. I believe that grades, inaccurate as they may be, should be a measure primarily of the student's learning, not the student's ability to follow arbitrary rules. Thus, when there is good cause, I am lenient about accepting late work and allowing makeup tests. The work must be done—the leniency is on the due date. I don't want to give an A student a B or C in the course because she had a family emergency that prevented her from taking a test at the prescribed time. Yes, I have been burned, but only once by any one student.

Generally speaking, the more scores you have, the more accurately the final grade will reflect student learning. Plus a large number of grades allows you the luxury of dropping everyone's lowest grade (a zero if they miss a test without an excuse), which can be a boon to students who are inconsistent. But I found from sad experience that dropping too many grades encourages sloth (Wankat, 1999a).

Ultimately, *all grading schemes are subjective* (Wankat & Oreovicz, 1999; Wright, 1994). Many professors believe that standard (criterion) scales are not subjective. But it was professors who set the scale—there is nothing sacred about "90 or above is an A." And professors write the tests, which means they subjectively cover the material. With essay questions, or if partial credit is awarded, scoring is also subjective.

Curves have arbitrary, subjective grade levels and encourage competition. McKeachie (1994, 88–89, 109–110) is uncharacteristically strongly negative about grading on the curve. B. G. Davis (1993, 292), Ory and Ryan (1993, 127–128), and Wright (1994, 444–445) castigate both the common method of using gaps in the curve to determine borders between grades and grading on the curve with a predetermined quota for each grade. Svinicki (1998), on the other hand, defends the use of gaps in grading, since gaps often indicate a performance difference. If the gap does show a performance difference, I find Svinicki's argument the most convincing, but I still prefer a criterion grading system.

T scores are a statistically manipulated curve. The professor sets the grade level for the mean score (and it does not have to be a C) and the break points (which do not have to be one standard deviation). Since the statistical assumptions necessary to use T scores are often not met, T scores can result in unfair grades. They also encourage competition. However, Wright (1994, 445) accepts the use of T scores.

I currently use a form of criterion grading for my sophomore and junior courses. I list the scores in the syllabus that will *guarantee* the students As, Bs, and so forth. For example, a score of 85 to 100 guarantees an A; 75 to 85, a B; 65 to 75, a C; and 55 to 65, a D. If half the class gets above 85 percent, those students have all earned As. This reduces competition and allows students to work together and help each other. The standard scale also gives the students something to aim for and tells them exactly what their grade is at any time. When deciding on the final course grades, the TA (if I have one) and I discuss all students whose net scores are close to the borders (e.g., between 83 and 85). We recheck the computations for these students. We look at other factors, such as attendance and the student's understanding of material when he or she is not taking a test. We often decide to award the higher grade. Thus, in effect, I use slightly lower standards than the published values at the end of the semester. I have seldom regretted being generous to students on a border between two grades. Some students may be unhappy about their performances, but there have been only a small number of complaints about the grading.

In graduate-level classes in which group projects are a major part of the grade, I use a procedure closer to a contract grading system. I make it clear that all groups *will* turn in a professional-quality project. Then I make sure groups have feedback throughout the course of the project and an opportunity to use the feedback to improve their papers or web pages to a professional level. Almost all groups rise to the challenge and produce A or at least A– quality work. The final grades become distributed when other grades earned during the semester are included.

Don't automatically follow what I or any experts recommend. Develop your own philosophy of grading. Develop a picture in your mind of the performance of typical A students, B students, and so on. Try different grading methods until you find one that fits your philosophy and is reasonably fair. Always look closely at the students on the borders. In small classes, it may be possible to take into account personal factors. If you have a TA, talk to the TA about student performance. Seriously consider raising some of the students who are just below the border, but don't play favorites. Be consistent with or slightly more generous than the procedure outlined in your syllabus. Record a grade in pencil and sleep on it before awarding the final grade.

Harvey has always had low test averages and many student complaints. Although he worries about loosening standards and grade inflation, he attempts to align his tests with course objectives and provide sufficient time. The scores of the better students increase, but those of the poorer students hardly change. On his third try with this new philosophy, three students earn 100s, but again the poorer students' scores remain low. Much to Harvey's surprise, nobody complains about the test or the grading. At the end of the term, Harvey finds that his new testing procedure spreads the final scores significantly. He continues to grade "on the curve" as usual, but the break points are significantly larger than previously, which makes grading easier. Perhaps next year he will be able to try using a standard scale. Finally, Harvey realizes that regardless of what he does, some students will be unhappy.

5.8. Summary

Professors routinely use the need to cover content as an excuse for not involving students. Content tyranny can be overcome, but is often so ingrained in our teaching styles that change is difficult. Since the content in courses naturally increases, we must periodically clean house and throw out unessential items. Reducing the content coverage will help you relax and enjoy class, and it provides time to involve the students.

Lectures can be improved by first focusing on the constraints imposed by the audience's attention span. Any lecture that continues for more than twenty minutes without student involvement has run too long. You can increase students' understanding of the lecture material by simplifying the initial presentation, linking the material to what the students know, reducing distractions, and then sharpening the students' understanding. Although performance is important in lecturing, the two most important points are simple: Do not read to the students, and speak loud enough. Students' understanding will also increase if they come to class prepared.

Involved students learn more. Use the breaks between the mini-lectures to involve the students. Thus, the breaks, which are forced by the students' relatively short attention span, can be used to satisfy positive learning principles. Since breaks are novel for both professors and students, there will be some initial discomfort. This discomfort will dissipate as the professor continues to use them. Small-group activities are particularly good for breaks, since they involve many students in active learning.

The perhaps surprising advice for many new professors is, *spend less time preparing*. It is easier to control content tyranny and be spontaneous when preparation is not excessive. But do preparation in at least two sessions, since it gives you time to reflect and change the presentation. Experienced professors need to be sure to spend enough time preparing. All professors will benefit from setting aside at least five minutes immediately before class to become psychologically prepared.

Teaching involves both intellectual excitement—content and presentation—and rapport with students. Lowman's two-dimensional model is a useful compromise between models that are too simple to be useful and those that are so complicated they're not practical. All professors have the capability of becoming competent teachers in Lowman's scheme.

For many students, tests are the course. Although we can lament students' lack of commitment to learning, we can also use their concern about testing to increase their learning. Students study more when there are frequent tests. Professors can improve their tests by analyzing them from the perspective of Bloom's taxonomy and being sure to give students sufficient time. Problems during the administration of tests will be reduced if the testing procedures are discussed in class ahead of time and the professor is present for the test. Reasonable precautions to prevent cheating are usually effective and not resented. Although cogent arguments can be made against them, I am in favor of awarding partial credit and allowing written requests for regrades.

Grades clearly have been given more importance than they would in a rational world. But since students consider grades to be important, professors need to be accurate and fair in grading. Having tried both criterion and normative grading schemes, I am convinced that the former are superior. They decrease grade competition, making it easier for students to cooperate and learn from each other, and they give the students targets to strive for. But criterion grading works only when the professor has control of test length and difficulty.

Will all the changes that Professor Harvey Jones makes in his teaching win him teaching awards? Considering how poor his teaching was originally, the answer is probably no. However, his teaching has improved significantly, and he is no longer a departmental embarrassment. Plus, he has developed a foundation of good practices on which to build further improvements. He will become a more complete teacher when he improves his rapport with students.

CHAPTER

6 Problem-Oriented Learning

Professor Sarah Appleton was incredibly busy. She was a department chair charged with a major recruiting effort for her college, she had numerous administrative duties, her five graduate students deserved attention, and she was going to teach a graduate-level elective. How could she possibly find the time to be a good teacher?

Sarah decided that the only possible way was to *delegate* most of the intellectual work to the students (Wankat, 1993b). The course would consist of completing a single large project. Student groups would select a topic and write a professional-quality book chapter. The week before the semester started, Sarah wrote a short syllabus, developed the course outline, listed fifty potential topics, and arranged for guest lecturers. During the semester, Sarah gave three lectures. A librarian gladly gave three lecture/demonstrations on computerized literature searches, and a communications specialist lectured on writing and oral presentations. The student groups turned in periodic progress reports throughout the semester. A month before the semester's end they turned in a content outline, which allowed Sarah to check that their papers were focused and had not left out any important items. Two weeks before the end, the groups turned in rough drafts. These drafts were critiqued by another group, and Sarah graded the critiques. She also commented on the rough drafts, but without grading them. During finals, the class met for oral presentations and turned in their final papers.

What did Sarah do doing the semester? She organized the course, picked topics, invited guest speakers, presented a few lectures, and graded the final book chapters. During most of the semester she provided significant individual attention by meeting individually with each group during the scheduled class period for 15 minutes twice a week. During these meetings, she served as a resource person, the group conscience, and a cheerleader when the students doubted their ability to finish. These frequent meetings limited procrastination. Sarah estimated that she spent an average of four hours per week on the course, *including* the three hours of class time per week. The exceptions were the first, twelfth, and last weeks of the semester, when she presented lectures, read critiques and rough drafts, and graded the final reports, respectively.

The students worked much harder than they expected, learned how to do a literature review and how to complete a substantial writing project. Sarah's student evaluations were the highest she ever received. Later, many of the students thanked Sarah since their experience in the course made it much easier for them to write their theses.

This chapter focuses on problem-oriented courses, in which much of the learning occurs by students teaching students. These courses can be structured so that the student groups receive individual attention. A variety of teaching methods, including cooperative groups, case studies, problem-based learning, experiential learning, and student learning without courses, are explored. This variety allows one to select a course structure that matches the course goals and the students' maturity level.

6.1. Cooperative Student Groups

Cooperative student groups are not only the critical component of cooperative and collaborative learning, but also an essential building block of other teaching methods. Thirty-seven percent of respondents to the 1998–99 University of California, Los Angeles (UCLA), survey of professors reported using cooperative learning in most or all undergraduate classes (Magner, 1999b). In section 5.3, I touched on the subject of informal cooperative groups, which are often used to provide activity breaks in lecture classes. They have a short duration, do not affect students' grades, and need not be carefully constituted. Although informal groups can fail, the failure lasts only a short time and is seldom serious.

Formal Student Groups

Formal cooperative student groups are "permanent" groups that last either the entire term or a substantial portion of it, affect the students' grades, and need to be carefully constituted. They can be used in the recitation sections of lecture classes, to teach content in a group setting, in guided design, in problem-based learning, in service learning, in laboratories, and in a variety of other settings.

Cooperative group techniques, collaborative groups, peer learning, and syndicate-based learning (British) are similar teaching techniques that I will lump together. Cooperative group teaching methods can be both efficient and effective. Research shows many advantages of these methods (Astin, 1993, 234, 423–424; Bonwell & Eison, 1991, 45; Felder et al., 1998; Gardiner, 1994, 20–22; Johnson & Johnson, 1975; Johnson et al., 1991a, chapter 2; 1991b, 1998; Light, 1990, 70–73; McKeachie, 1994, 145–146; Michaelsen, 1994, 149–151; Pascarella & Terenzini, 1991, 616–619; Stage et al., 1998, 79, 85–86). Although instructors worry that less content will be covered, what is included is covered in more depth. Exam grades are usually the same or better than in lecture classes. The average student in a cooperative group environment performs about two-thirds of a standard deviation above the average student in both competitive and individualistic environments. Introverts often do about as well on tests when they study alone, although their grades do not suffer from the group experience. Extroverts usually do better on tests when group teaching methods are used. These methods often produce significant increases in student learning of the higher order items in Bloom's taxonomy. There is growth in both the Piagetian stage of cognitive development (see section 8.2) and in moral reasoning. When students do peer tutoring in groups, both the tutee and the tutor benefit. The method helps students make intellectual connections and increases their self-confidence and self-esteem. The students value different viewpoints more, increase their empathy, improve their attitudes toward other races, and are more willing to cooperate in general. When small groups first discuss material and then share it with the entire class, the quantity and quality of the discussion improve. The students' oral communication skills improve. The absentee rate goes down, sometimes dramatically, when cooperative learning methods are used. The students learn group processing skills, such as how to make disagreements constructive and how to keep a group focused. The more they are involved in small groups, the more their leadership and interpersonal skills improve. The effects of taking courses taught by cooperative group techniques appear to be cumulative. A series of such courses increases retention and graduation rates dramatically.

One reason cooperative groups produce these results is that adolescents are very people oriented. Group activities pull adolescents into participating in academics (Brufee, 1993, 5). Second, time on task is necessary for learning, and groups encourage students to spend more time on task. Third, reflection is important in learning. Introverts tend to reflect on their own, but extraverts' reflection appears to be greatly aided by the continuing conversation about the academic subject in groups (Brufee, 1993, 26). Fourth, teaching others, which aids learning, occurs naturally in groups. Finally, group methods almost invariably involve active learning instead of passive.

To avoid failure with cooperative group methods, pay attention to the pedagogical details (Bonwell & Eison, 1991, 59–72). Professors who start slowly with elements that are least likely to fail and then move on to riskier applications of groups are less likely to experience a catastrophic failure. Try informal groups as lecture breaks. Once you are comfortable with this, try formal groups in a recitation section or for a portion of the course. Eventually, you may be ready to convert the entire course to this teaching method. A step-by-step procedure exposes professors to a new teaching method in small increments and helps to overcome their natural resistance to change. Innovating in small steps makes you more confident as you approach the bigger steps. The difference between success and failure of a teaching innovation may depend on the confidence of the professor.

Setting Up Effective Groups

The professor's role in cooperative group teaching is quite different than in lectures. The professor *structures* the assignments and the groups and, most important, the professor *sets a tone* of cooperation and learning together. Instead of lecturing on the material, the professor *facilitates* the learning of the groups and helps the students learn how to interact to achieve the purpose of the group. The professor *evaluates* the work, the processing of the groups, and individual learning. Structuring and evaluating are similar to the processes used in lecture classes, but facilitating is much closer to the advising skills discussed in section 7.4.

Getting off to a good start using groups early in the term will help ensure success. The following seven-step procedure works (Smith, 1986b; Wankat & Oreovicz, 1993, 122–124):

1. The professor needs clear objectives for the group portion of the course and a plan for how to achieve them. There is no substitute for carefully determining your course goals and cognitive and affective objectives. Know why you intend to use cooperative groups. Then develop the tasks that the students will do. Good tasks for small groups

- Have several possible solutions or at least several possible solution paths. Individuals are often faster than groups in solving single-answer problems.
- Are clearly related to the course. "Mickey Mouse" projects will cause students to conclude that group work is a waste of time.
- Are interesting. Routine drills will be divided among the group members, and they will work on them individually, not as a team. Tasks that allow for friendly competition among groups often increase students' interest level.
- Are challenging but can be done. Maintaining this balance is the biggest challenge for the professor. If there are a series of tasks, arrange them in order of increasing difficulty.
- Require many skills. This helps ensure that a single member could not do better than the group, which reinforces the reasons for group learning. Also, tasks that require many skills are more likely to have a part at which each member can excel.
- Encourage all group members to contribute. Tasks that cannot be done by more than one student, such as operating a scientific instrument, can push some members to the sidelines.
- Have a clear deliverable. Groups must produce something at the end of the task. This helps the group stay on task and focuses their efforts to finish. It also provides for easier evaluation (Brufee, 1993, 41–43; B. G. Davis, 1993, 150; Hamelink et al., 1989; Michaelsen, 1994, 148).

Use highly structured assignments with first-year students and any students who are unfamiliar with cooperative group techniques. As the students become adept in group work, the assignments can become progressively less structured. Groups of seniors and graduate students should be capable of assignments that require them to choose an appropriate problem and then solve it. The first time students do this they will need help and encouragement. In all cases, there needs to be a deliverable. Advanced students can be given considerable latitude in choosing the exact form of the deliverable.

2. Group formation needs to be done with care. The professor should choose the groups and consider a variety of factors. (B. G. Davis, 1993, 151; Hunkeler & Sharp, 1997; Johnson et al., 1991a, 1991b, 1998; Lowman, 1995, 209; Michaelsen, 1994, 143; Miller et al., 1994, 35–38; Schmier, 1995, 27–29; Stage et al., 1998, 45; Wankat, 1999a; Weimer, 1993, 64; Wilde, 1997). The students will accept the rationale that the professor does this to ensure that the groups are roughly equal in ability and to help train the students for teamwork in industry. Smith (1986b) suggests random assignment of group members, however. Group sizes from two to around eight have been used; having three to five students per group seems to work well. Groups with an odd number of students are less likely to become deadlocked on an issue, since they can vote. Aim for groups that are diverse in a variety of ways. Although initially there will probably be more conflict, diverse groups tend to be better at solving difficult problems and are usually more innovative. Working in diverse groups also helps the students learn much more about group processes and interpersonal skills. The following measures can be useful in assigning groups larger than two:

- Scholastic competency. Put at least one high achiever and one low achiever in each group. The usual measures are grades in the current course or the grade point average. Both good and poor students will benefit from working with each other. The poor students benefit from watching the problem-solving and study habits of the good students. The informal tutoring that occurs can be helpful to both tutor and tutee. This procedure also helps to level the playing field if groups compete with each other.
- Extraverts and introverts. Extraverts are often much better at performing the maintenance functions necessary for smooth long-term operation of the group. Make sure each group has at least one extravert.
- Intuitive versus sensing. Since intuitive students are often better at creating ideas, groups with at least one intuitive student will probably have more creative solutions. If the group will build something, place one or more sensing students in each group. This dichotomy can be determined with the Myers-Briggs Type Indicator (MBTI). If MBTI results are not available, spread out the students who appear to be creative (Wilde, 1997).
- Perceptive versus judging. If MBTI results are available, placing one judging student in each group will help ensure that assignments are done on time. If the groups will have to adjust to unforeseen circumstances, it is an advantage to have one perceptive student per group. If MBTI results are not available, spread out the students who always get assignments done on time.
- Other learning styles. If the results of any test that determines learning styles are available, aim for groups with a mix of learning styles.
- Practical experience. Students with industrial, cooperative education, or internship experience often have experience working in groups. Spread these students among as many groups as possible.
- Majors versus nonmajors. If there are a minority of nonmajors taking the class along with students who are majoring in the discipline, spread out the nonmajors among the groups. If there are students from a variety of majors, groups will be more diverse if they contain students from a mix of majors; however, for some projects there may be good reasons to keep students from the same major together.
- Age. Mix the ages of group members.
- Gender. Suggestions in the literature are contradictory; however, it is clear that group dynamics are different in same-sex groups (Rosser, 1998; Tannen, 1991). In majors such as engineering and science, where women are a minority, place either no women or at least two women in a group. This will help

ensure that the women are heard and reduce the likelihood that a woman will automatically be assigned "a woman's job," such as being group secretary.

- Minorities. Again, the literature suggestions are often contradictory (Rosser, 1998). Some authors favor clustering underrepresented minorities in groups, but my experience, which may be unique to engineering students, is that groups work well if they have at least two members who are minorities (not necessarily from the same minority group) or international students. This appears to help prevent the potential dominance of the majority students.
- International students. One reason international students come to the United States is to learn about American culture. Spread them out to make them mix with American students. If the number of international students forces you to put two in the same group, make sure their native languages are different.
- Friends, roommates, fraternity brothers, sorority sisters, and so forth. Place these students in different groups. Their presence in the same group may prevent the group from gelling. Students who are dating each other should *not* be put in the same group. Their closeness—or their breakup—can cause other group members to be uncomfortable. Of course, if students start dating after you assign groups, the group may have to cope with any problems that arise.
- Student choice. Although I will not let students choose another group member, I have on occasion let students privately inform me of one student they do *not* want. Few students take advantage of this opportunity.
- No-shows. Place students who are likely to drop the course or stop coming to class in different groups. This information may be available later in the semester.
- Miscellaneous factors. Any grouping that clearly gives one group a major advantage or disadvantage should not be used.

Following these suggestions for group formation is time-consuming, particularly in large classes. And professors rarely have information about all of these factors. Use the information that you have to make the groups as diverse as possible. When no information is available, assign the groups randomly (Brinkley et al., 1999, 45–46). Prevention of potential group problems is preferable to trying to cure problems after they occur. Time spent on assignment of groups is repaid several times over during the term.

3. Clearly explain the task to the groups. This can be done in writing or verbally. Clearly explain what the deliverable is—a paper to hand in, a presentation to the class, a model to build, etc.—and when it is due. When students are first learning to function in groups, this step is important. If possible, before teaching, ask another professor or teaching assistant (TA) to read the directions and explain his or her understanding of the assignment. Use this feedback to improve the description before handing it to students. One trick to help new groups work together is to give each group only one copy of the assignment.

4. Help the students learn how to function in groups. Give them clear norms for group behavior, such as the following: Everyone in the group has something to contribute, and everyone will be given an opportunity to contribute. Educational groups are embedded within a community of scholars and should maintain scholarly standards. Logical arguments should be used, and students need to control their emotions. It is OK to disagree with another person's arguments, but one should never attack the person. Group conflicts are part of the learning experience. Through conflict, the students learn more about functioning in groups and develop skills that will be useful after graduation.

Since many of these norms are relatively obvious to most students, it is not necessary to make a big deal of them. However, it is useful to give students a background sheet on behavior in groups. For example, the five elements for group success (discussed in the next section) plus a list of dos and don'ts of group behavior may be useful background information. This sheet can be referred to if a group starts to malfunction. Gibbs's (1994) student manual has useful ideas on training students to work in groups. Independent learners may resist learning how to work in groups. Seat and Lord (1999) found that a directive approach that included didactic material was effective with independent learners. The material on improving committees presented in section 11.2 may also be useful for students.

Students will be better processors if they understand how they and other people interact. The MBTI has proven useful in this regard, although be careful that students do not use their type to excuse their behavior. The Blake and Mouton conflict model (K. A. Smith, 1999) is useful for understanding interactions in groups and helping students become better group members. Be sure students realize that this experience is just the start of learning to work in groups. The processing of group behavior should continue throughout the project.

5. Monitor the groups. Early in the session, check that each group understands the assignment. Later, listen to different groups to ensure they are remaining on task. Your presence and perhaps a few words will normally get straying groups back on track. Listen and watch the discussion to be sure that everyone is contributing. Early in the term, assigning roles, such as facilitator and reporter, to different group members may involve more group members. Struggling groups may benefit from a quick pep talk. Diverse groups often are much more capable than they think. A professor who believes the groups can succeed can often infect the groups with this belief. The best role for the professor may be respectful silence followed by a few complimentary words ("Keep up the good work") upon leaving the group.

Ensure that the environment is safe. The time to intervene is early, before anything occurs that will fester in a student's mind. The sudden presence of the instructor in the group may be sufficient to calm students. Mentioning the norms for behavior or calling a student aside for a discussion of interpersonal dynamics also helps. A few students may have major deficiencies in this area and will benefit from personal counseling with a professional counselor (see section 7.4). One of the arts of using cooperative group teaching methods is to know when to intervene and at what level.

6. Provide closure to the session. If the task is finished, groups can achieve closure by making presentations to the entire class or by turning in papers. Everyone in the group should have a chance to do presentations during the term. Early in the semester, name the student who will be the presenter when you assign the problem. Later in the semester, either let the groups choose the presenter, being sure it is not always the same person, or choose the presenter randomly yourself toward the end of the period. Encourage the groups to be innovative in their presentations (e.g., group presentations, role plays, or skits).

For continuing tasks, close the session by hearing brief progress reports from the groups, which will help keep them focused during the period, and spend a minute or two reminding the groups where they are headed with the task, what will be done next class period, and what work needs to be done outside class. A common mistake is to give the groups as much time as possible for their work and not have sufficient time for the wrap-up.

7. Evaluate the groups' deliverables and functioning. The grading procedure needs to be determined in advance and should be shared with the students. Even if the formal group work is a relatively small part of the course, such as in recitation sections, there needs to be a grade. Many students believe that only graded parts of the course are important. If there is no grade for the group work, some students will not take it seriously and either not work or not show up. Unfortunately, it is usually the students who most need to come who will be absent. Assigning a small portion of the course grade (5 to 10 percent) will ensure that most students will come and work in their group. This grade can be based on attendance. Although the oral presentations or written reports do need to be graded, having the students turn in group assignments significantly reduces the number of grades to assign.

Effectively assigning grades is one of the most difficult aspects of cooperative group teaching (B. G. Davis, 1993, 152–153; Johnson et al., 1991a, 1991b; 1998; Michaelsen, 1994, 143–144). If the groups work together for only a small portion of the course grade, everyone in the group who attends and pays a nominal amount of attention (at least they were not sleeping or reading the newspaper) can receive the same grade. Grading projects that are a substantial portion of the course grade is more challenging and can result in vehement student complaints. A number of methods have been developed, all of which have potential drawbacks.

The professor can grade the deliverable and make this the highest grade on the group project any group member can receive. Whether an individual gets this grade or a lower one depends on his or her contributions. The easiest method of allocating individual grades, although probably not the fairest, is to give each group member the same grade. A second procedure is for the professor to decide how much of the maximum each group member deserves. If work is done outside class, this is difficult to do fairly unless the professor meets with groups regularly or requests individual progress reports. A third approach is to ask the students in the group to allocate a portion of a total number of points to each group member. If students are given a matrix with columns listing each student in the group and rows for the total number of points to allocate, you can force them to decide how to allocate the points for a number of scenarios. This will give you a good picture of the students' views on how much each student contributed to the group. You may want to require students to justify their allocations in writing. A fourth procedure is to have both students and the professor allocate fractions of the individual's grades (Wankat, 1999a), as illustrated in the following example:

The professor grades the project and assigns a grade of, say, 80. This raw score is divided into two parts. The first fraction (say, 0.6) is assigned to the member by the other students in the group, and the second fraction (say, 0.4) is assigned to the group member by the professor. The students and the professor can assign fractional scores ranging from zero (appropriate for no-shows) to one (appropriate for students who contribute significantly to the project). The individual scores are then calculated as:

Individual's grade = (fractional score assigned by students) × (0.6) × (80) + (fractional score assigned by professor) × (0.4) × (80)

A student who makes significant contributions to the group will be assigned fractional scores of 1.0 by the other students and the professor and would receive a grade of 80. A student who did nothing would earn fractional scores of zero and a grade of zero. All students in the group would have scores within this range. The professor can assign the fractions in each category in advance or can negotiate these fractions with the entire class or individual groups.

Give the students at least minimal guidelines on how to grade the members of their group. Requiring students to grade their peers gives them recourse if one student is freeloading. This greatly reduces student complaints about other group members. It also gives students a method to let overly dominating members know that their tactics are not appreciated. Even a small grade adjustment can have more impact than any other type of feedback. Since the entire grade is not at jeopardy, major injustices will be avoided. Requiring the students to assign part of the grade has the added advantage of giving them practice in the highest level of Bloom's taxonomy—evaluation. Many students become more discriminating in their assignment of grades as they become more experienced in evaluating the work of their peers.

Elements for Group Success

Getting a diverse group to work together is challenging. The number of failures can be reduced by carefully assigning groups, by teaching the students interpersonal and group processing skills, and by monitoring the groups on a regular basis. When group failure appears eminent, step in and work with the group to get them back on track. Five elements for group success have been identified (Johnson et al., 1991a,b; 1998).

Positive Interdependence. Students must believe that their success depends on the group's succeeding. This can be fostered by proper grading procedures. If the project grade sets the highest grade that can be achieved by any student in the group, they soon realize that group success is necessary. Do not undermine this by making private deals with students. Positive interdependence can also be fostered by encouraging the groups to involve all members and determine the best way to use each member's talents. This implies that there will be some division of labor in groups working on long projects.

Often, introverted students who have earned good grades on their own will resist working in groups. One option is to let them be a "group" of one. If projects are difficult, they may soon recant and want to join a group. I prefer to use the following arguments to convince these students that they will benefit from group work. First, work, particularly in industry, has become to a large degree team oriented (Gardiner, 1994, 19–21; Stage et al., 1998, 85). Group work in college will help them obtain and retain a job after college. This argument is particularly effective with engineering students. Second, research shows that most students learn more in groups and even those who don't are not penalized by the group work. Third, groups can complete more realistic assignments than individuals can.

Cooperative group courses can effectively use the motivation developed by competition, but it must be competition between, not within, groups. The groups need to be supportive of their members. If the competition is handled in a spirit of fun so that there are really no losers, it is even more effective. An example is to have a "quiz bowl" with questions submitted by students and the professor (McKeachie, 1994, 356).

Face-to-Face Promotive Interaction.   The students must work together, talk and listen to each other, and respect each other. It is helpful if the group can meet together for face-to-face discussions; however, this is clearly not necessary, since successful groups can function entirely by e-mail or telephone without ever meeting. Thus, distance education is not an insurmountable barrier to cooperative group efforts.

Individual Accountability and Personal Responsibility.   Group members must do their share of the work (Bonwell & Eison, 1991, 44; B. G. Davis, 1993, 152; Johnson et al., 1991a, 3.7–3.8; Michaelsen, 1994, 144–148). At its simplest, this means coming to meetings prepared and on time. If everyone in the group does slightly more than his or her share of the work, the group will probably function fairly smoothly. However, a student may unknowingly sabotage the group by preparing everything alone and then showing up expecting the group to adopt his or her solution (Eaves, 1996).

One of the main mechanisms to ensure individual accountability is individual tests. If the course does not have tests, the instructor can informally ask various students in the group to explain different concepts. An alternative is to require each student to turn in a weekly individual progress report.

Encouraging both individual accountability and positive interdependence can be difficult. Students must work alone and together to learn the material. The grading scheme cannot undermine cooperation by penalizing a student if other students improve. Some form of absolute scale grading is appropriate. One way to encourage all students to learn is to offer a group award for individual achievement (Bonwell & Eison, 1991, 44). For example, every student in a group can receive bonus points on a test if the group average beats a specified score. This will be seen as fair if all the groups are roughly equal in ability.

Interpersonal and Group Skills.   Students need to develop certain social graces if they are to work well as a group. Many of these requirements (e.g., good personal hygiene and being courteous to nonsmokers in the group) may not be obvious to all students. One way professors can focus on these social skills without embarrassing anyone is to hand out a sheet with common dos and don'ts for getting along with others.

Many students are unaware of how their behavior affects others. There can be clashes between students who "tell it like it is" and those who have been schooled to be polite and diplomatic at all times. The group interactions can be helpful to both types of individuals *if* they recognize that both approaches have some validity. Conflicts are normal in diverse groups. Groups often do quite well initially and then deteriorate (Miller et al., 1994, 40–42). Most will recover if given the time and responsibility to do so. Make the groups work out their problems. They won't learn how if you interfere or dissolve the group. Training in listening and other communication skills will be beneficial.

Although some students will be experienced in group dynamics, many will not be. If they are to function well in teams in and after college, they need to learn the principles of leadership, decision making, trust building, interpersonal communication, and conflict resolution (K. A. Smith, 1999). They need practice the more the better. Formal courses are the appropriate place to learn some of the theory and practice it in a safe environment.

All this extra training is too much to add to a single course that also has to cover disciplinary content (Seat & Lord, 1999). However, it is certainly not too much to add to a coordinated curriculum. Ideally, every course would reinforce the previous courses and add new skills to the students' repertoires. However, it is difficult for students to obtain enough practice. Encourage students to become *involved* in one extracurricular student activity that would let them practice these skills (see section 6.4).

Group Processing. Groups need to set aside maintenance time to help themselves function smoothly. The students should explicitly discuss what each member has done that was helpful to the group and what each member can do in the next group meeting. This discussion provides feedback—it needs to be basically positive—to the members and focuses on the importance of collaboration. Groups will not automatically process. The professor needs to demonstrate processing early in the semester and remind the groups to process in subsequent meetings. Later in the term they can be expected to process without a daily reminder.

Continue to monitor groups while they are processing. The students will pay more attention to processing if they are required to write about it in their journals. An even more forceful method is to have every student turn in a weekly summary of the processing.

Efficiency

Cooperative group teaching can increase the professor's efficiency (Johnson et al., 1991b; Wankat, 1999a). First, putting students into groups reduces the number of entities the professor needs to deal with, and the number of papers to grade. Since the professor answers the questions of a group, there is less repetition of questions and answers. Students also tend to come in groups to ask questions during office hours, which reduces the number of individual visits. To some extent, interaction among students in groups compensates for the reduced opportunity for faculty-student interaction in large classes (O'Brien, 1998, 99). Second, with cooperative group teaching, it is easier to develop rapport with the students, particularly in large classes, since this method provides significantly more time to interact with students. It is easier to learn student names, since they are clustered into groups. The students often interpret attention to their group as individual attention. Third, the students tend to spend more time on task. Since attendance is better and the students are more focused, more learning occurs without increased effort by the teacher. Fourth, the students are able to help each other. Groups can often finish assignments that none of the students could do individually. Since the students are doing some of the teaching, there is less for the professor to do. When a group gets stuck, the students are often much more aware of exactly what is causing them problems. This makes their questions more to the point. Fewer students get far into the semester without a clue of what is happening. Fifth, preparation time is often significantly less. The professor spends much of the time in class helping groups get past difficulties in assignments. Experts do not have to prepare in order to do this. Preparing group assignments does take time, but less time than preparing a good lecture. Sixth, a small class, special equipment, or a special classroom is not needed (Felder et al., 1998). This reduces struggling with scheduling or trying to be sure equipment is available and working properly. Finally, once the teacher relaxes, this form of teaching is fun, which is motivating and makes it easier to prepare psychologically for the class.

On the negative side, effective use of formal cooperative groups requires professors to learn about group processing, conflict resolution, facilitation, and so forth. Fortunately, you can use groups effectively before you are an expert. Much of the know-how needed can be obtained by trying group teaching and reflecting on the results. Knowledge and understanding can be obtained by reading and attending workshops.

6.2. Teaching with Problems: From Guided Design to Problem-Based Learning

A variety of teaching methods use realistic problems or situations to help students learn. (I use "problems" in a broad sense and do not mean only those with a mathematical solution.) Although these methods are a routine part of professional education, they can be used at other educational levels. The basic idea is to ask students to solve a realistic problem that requires the application of fundamental principles. Once the students discover that certain principles are applicable, they will be highly motivated to learn to apply them. In other applications of the method, the students are expected to learn material for the first time as they apply it. The students usually work in groups to obtain the benefits of cooperative group learning. Both oral and written communications are natural deliverables and help the students hone their communication skills in a professional context.

Guided Design and Case Studies

Case studies are relatively detailed descriptions of real or realistic situations that require a problem resolution (B. G. Davis, 1993, 159, 161–164; Hutchings, 1993; Naumes & Naumes, 2000; Weaver et al., 1994). *Guided design* is a structured method to have student groups work through a case study (Duffy & Jones, 1995, 215–219; Stager & Wales, 1972; Wales & Nardi, 1982; Wales & Stager, 1977; Wales et al., 1974). Since guided design is a step-by-step procedure, and neophytes are guided through the steps, failure is unlikely. Thus, guided design is excellent preparation for case studies and problem-based learning (discussed in the next three sections).

To prepare a guided-design project, the instructor starts with a case study. The procedure to resolve the case study is broken into steps. If a problem-solving strategy is being used in the class, this strategy can be applied to defining the steps. The instructor then writes a question or direction for each step (e.g., "Define the problem. What needs to be done?") The instructor also prepares written feedback on what was actually done for each step and why. For open-ended problems, emphasize that the feedback represents one possible solution, not necessarily the best solution.

Groups are normally given the scenario before class. Either before or during class they are given the first question or direction and told to develop a group response. They prepare oral or written responses (the deliverables) and present them to the class. The instructor hands out the written feedback and leads a discussion comparing and contrasting the various responses. The class is told to use the written feedback as the basis for the next direction. The use of written feedback forces all groups to move in the direction of a reasonable solution. However, individual groups cannot explore their own ideas, and that can be frustrating. The entire exercise can take anywhere from 2 to 15 hours.

Since much of the feedback is written, guided design works well with large classes. It was originally developed for first-year students, who need considerable guidance. Guided design serves as a bridge from academic problems with a single solution to applied, open-ended problems. It prepares students to tackle less structured case studies or problem-based learning. I have used guided design successfully with Ph.D. students. Since these mature students can quickly become frustrated with the fetters of the written feedback, the guided-design project should be short, a small fraction of their grades, and probably used only once during the term.

Professors can use guided design to teach applications after students have studied the basics or to help students learn basics and applications simultaneously. For the latter, students must study on their own before the class, and there must be tests or other means to ensure individual accountability.

Guided design is an effective teaching strategy when used in moderation. If it is used repeatedly, some students will make it a game to guess what is on the feedback sheets. With younger students, it is less likely to fail than a case study. However, since students have less freedom, there is less potential for growth. Developing guided-design projects is even more work than developing case studies, although the workload can be reduced by modifying a published case study. Preparing guided-design projects will be efficient if they can also be published or reused several times. Reuse has not caused me difficulties when the projects were used mainly to generate discussion and were a small part of the students' grades. When the projects are a major part of the students' grades, reuse will lead to excessive student use of files.

Case Studies

Case studies are most commonly used in education for the law, business (Naumes & Naumes, 2000), and academic professions (Bennett, 1983; Hutchings, 1993). Cases are an excellent method to teach students how to apply principles they have already studied. There are a number of published cases available in case libraries in different disciplines (B. G. Davis, 1993, 162).

The best case problems or situations do not have one right answer and require economic, political, and aesthetic analyses for decision (Eaves, 1996; Weaver et al., 1994, 172–174). Where should the new landfill (or airport or university) be located? What can students at this college do to ensure racial harmony? What should be done about the old plant, which although a valued employer in town, is also a major polluter? How can the teacher best help a class of fourth-graders learn? The cases should have sufficient detail to distinguish the characters and allow a resolution (e.g., if politics is important in the choice of an airport site, it should be included in the case details). For advanced students, cases should also contain extraneous information, since in real situations which details are important is not always clear. It may also be appropriate to have some of the characters provide misinformation or downright lies, since this also occurs in real life. Advanced cases should have a number of ancillary issues in addition to the main theme.

The application of knowledge in the real world almost always involves emotions as well as facts and logic, and the emotions are often more important. (Teaching follows life in this respect.) Good cases often evoke emotional responses from the students (Eaves, 1996; Weaver et al., 1994, 172–174). For example, it is one thing to study automation and quite another to become involved in a case in which five people you work with every day are laid off because you automated part of the plant. Professionals need to learn to cope with their own emotions and those of others.

The cases need to be at a level that will challenge but not overwhelm students. Good cases can be analyzed at a variety of levels. By focusing on different aspects of the case and using different teaching methods, it is possible to use the same case with different classes.

The simplest use of case studies is to have students read the case and the resolution. This method shows students that factors that are normally not considered in theoretical classes may be important. For example, a family may decide to forego a medical procedure because of their religious convictions, or a town may receive a new branch campus of the state university because of political considerations. However, since the students just read about the case and someone else's resolution of it, their education is vicarious. They learn less using case studies this way than when they become involved with the case and grapple with the issues. The advantages in using cases as reading assignments are that it doesn't take much time, several cases can be reviewed, the students are less likely to become emotionally distraught, and complex cases are less likely to overwhelm the students. Students who cannot resolve a complex case can nevertheless understand it when they read about it. This is a moderately effective teaching procedure that is efficient for the professor if published cases are used. It works well for first- and second-year students.

The most common use of the case study is to have small groups of students analyze it and determine an appropriate resolution. The case could last anywhere from one class period to the entire term. For longer cases, the students can be expected to determine facts or do field studies on their own. Thus, students doing a case study on the site of a new airport could visit potential sites to see whether they are physically appropriate and interview residents to determine the political climate. Different groups can compete with each other to determine the best solution. Each group would prepare oral and written presentations. Long cases should have intermediate assignments to prevent excessive procrastination. Through their interactions while solving the problem, the students have an experience similar to that of professionals.

The case is not over after the students have finished their reports. Each group should compare their solution with other solutions, including the actual resolution of the case. They need to reflect on how their individual strengths and weaknesses affected their solutions. Groups should process how well they worked together (see section 6.1) and how to improve in the future.

If the cases are chosen wisely and students are guided in their use, case studies are an effective method to teach students to apply their knowledge. They are also an efficient method for the professor, if published cases are available that can be adapted with little or no revision. On the other hand, writing a good case study takes time, and cases always need to be revised after they are tested (Naumes & Naumes, 2000). Writing cases is efficient only if synergism between teaching and the scholarship of teaching is planned. If you write cases, publish them.

Of course, the case study approach can fail. Students who have little experience with the method and little or no practical experience are likely to be overwhelmed if they are asked to resolve a complicated case study. If they get off track, they may never get back on unless the professor intervenes. It helps to have the students first read a case study, including the resolution, since this gives them an idea of what is being asked for.

Problem-Based Learning

Problem-based learning (PBL) is a third method for teaching with problems (Boud & Feletti, 1991; Hendley & staff, 1996; Nooman et al, 1990; Palmer, 1998, 125–127; Ramsden, 1992; Woods, 1994a, 1994b; Woods et al., 1997). PBL is based on the approach developed at the McMaster University medical school in the late 1960s. It has been extensively used in professional programs such as medicine and other health care fields, veterinary medicine, business, and, to a less extent, engineering and science. The medical model of PBL assigns a tutor to each group (Boud & Feletti, 1991; Nooman et al., 1990). Here I emphasize nonmedical applications that are much less staff intensive. Allen (1997), Groh et al. (1997), and Williams and Duch (1997) discuss the experience at the University of Delaware in a variety of classes. Web sites concerned with PBL are available at the University of Delaware <http://www.physics.udel.edu/~pbl/>, Samford University <http://www.samford.edu/pbl>, and San Diego State University <http://edweb.sdsu.edu/clrit/home.html> and at <http://www.beconline.ctc.edu/premises.html>.

Unlike case studies, PBL is used to teach fundamentals and application simultaneously. There is much less guidance than in guided design. Because of their many advantages, cooperative groups are almost invariably used. The basic principles of cooperative group teaching need to be followed, particularly group formation, positive interdependence, and individual accountability. Grades should depend on both group effort on projects and individual effort on tests and group projects. Tests should emphasize deep understanding, not surface knowledge.

The class periods are used for reporting deliverables, monitoring the groups and providing feedback, teaching a modest amount of material, taking quizzes and tests, checking that the problems are understood, questioning, encouraging discouraged groups, and helping the students develop their agendas for group meetings outside of class. The groups must meet outside class. Expect students to study to prepare for class and group meetings. Because many students find real problems motivating and others get the support they need from the cooperative groups, most students work more in a PBL course than in a lecture course. This extra time on task is one of the main reasons for PBL's effectiveness.

The key to PBL is the *problems* posed by the instructor. The problems need to have many of the characteristics of good case studies. They should be realistic. At least at the beginning of the term, they need to be relatively short (about one per week) so that turnaround time is short. Otherwise, the students tend to slack off until something is due. Short problems also reduce the period of floundering if a group gets off track. The problems need to expand the students' thinking and require them to learn new material, but they have to be related to what students already know so they can see an initial path.

Problems from professional practice are often appropriate. In medicine, psychology, and social work, PBL problems can be introduced by having student groups meet and examine a patient or client. In veterinary school, the student groups can examine a sick animal. In business and engineering, the students can meet with a company representative who outlines the problem or can be given a product and be told to improve it or market it (e.g., "This toaster often fails. Build a better toaster"). If there are too many students to actually interview the patient, examine the animal, or question the representative, videotapes can be used to introduce the problem. Of course, at some point in their education the students must actually see the patient or animal or client. One advantage of PBL is that real problems can be incorporated into classes on fundamentals. PBL problems should include messy details such as politics, suffering, economics, and ethics. These issues should play a small role in the problems at the beginning of the course and become more important to the problems as the course proceeds and the students become adept. One difficulty is that real-world problems don't fit the artificial boundaries of our courses (Allen, 1997, 261).

Each group must determine what they need to know. To help them, first ask them to try to solve the problem with what they already know. This helps clarify what other knowledge is needed. Since each student group will identify only about 60 to at most 80 percent of what they need to know, feedback to the groups is necessary. One way to do this is to have groups present their objectives to the entire class while the instructor records them on the board. The entire class will discover a higher percentage of the necessary objectives. When all objectives are listed, the instructor can comment on them and add any needed. Since the students should own the process, they should determine most of the objectives and preferably all of them. If an objective is important, be sure it is part of one of the problems. Avoid the tendency to sneak in extra objectives for "enrichment." On longer projects, students often cannot see everything that they will need to know at the beginning. Consider holding a second meeting on objectives later, so that groups can adjust their objectives.

Students need to learn the material. Ask the groups to prioritize their learning objectives. Have the students immerse themselves individually in learning. When the groups reconvene, students should teach the other students in their groups. The professor and TAs should monitor this activity to be sure the students are actually teaching, not just reporting, and that what is taught is correct. If only the "teacher" in the group is active, the other students are not learning much.

Anything the professor can do to make the students' work visible helps maintain accountability. For example, have the students fill out feedback forms after group meetings, keep student journals, provide evidence that their groups are processing their functioning, and take individual quizzes and tests. Without this feedback, some groups will start going through the motions, stop teaching each other, and stop growing as a group.

A modest amount of lecturing by the professor is appropriate and appreciated by the students (Williams & Duch, 1997, 456–459). They appreciate the professor's assuming authority and doing traditional "teaching." However, don't lecture to passive students for six weeks and then switch to PBL. If PBL will be used for only part of the course, involve the students in group activities throughout the lecture portion of the course. If PBL will be used for the entire course, immerse the students in solving a problem during the first week.

Be sure the students determine the objectives for the problem *before* you start teaching. If they have uncovered the need for the knowledge before you begin lecturing, they will be motivated and pay attention during the lectures. And be sure the lectures force the students to be active. Use other teaching methods for disseminating knowledge—demonstrations, guest lectures, videotapes, field trips, individual reading, multimedia, and tutorials. Less than a third of class time should be spent with the instructor or other experts disseminating information. After the material is taught, student groups need to be sure that every group member understands. Quizzes and tests that offer bonus points if every group member scores above a minimum encourage members to teach each other.

Problems must have deliverables such as oral reports, written reports, diagnoses, designs, or models. A good evaluation exercise is to require each group to critique another group's deliverable before it is turned in for a grade. Grade the critiques but don't use the critiques to determine the other group's grade. After the critiques, groups need time to revise, rewrite, or rebuild their deliverables. Students are often very proud of their results. Let them have an opportunity to show off. Put the models or reports on display.

To avoid failure, pay attention to process. Introduce the teaching method carefully and identify course objectives, such as learning to work in groups, learning how to learn, effective time management, and ethics. Develop a course environment that ensures that the students control most of the learning. Avoid the easy way out by lecturing on everything. The first exercise can be done as a tutored dry run or as a guided-design project for a small percentage of the course grade. Later projects can reduce

successively the amount of guidance, until by the end of the term the students are completely in charge of their learning and own the process.

Monitor the groups, ask leading and open-ended questions, encourage the students, raise issues that have been overlooked, help a group get back on track if it has
gone astray, and encourage the groups to process. Professors need "to stifle the instinct
to share their own hard-won knowledge, so that their students may win their own"
(Groh et al., 1997, 89). However, less mature students benefit from some preparation
before engaging in the problem. One of the professor's goals in teaching a PBL course
is to almost disappear and have the students take over. When PBL succeeds, less reflective students are unaware of the professor's contribution and think they did all the
learning themselves. Because of this characteristic, standard student evaluation forms
are often inappropriate for PBL courses.

Help students learn to be effective in groups and encourage groups to resolve
their own conflicts (see section 6.1). Students will try to dump the responsibility of
resolving group conflicts on the professor. Refuse. Groups with conflict learn more
about group behavior than those without conflict. The grading scheme should require
students to evaluate the performance of other group members. Since inexperienced students often struggle with PBL, the teacher needs to keep the faith that the method
works. Point out to the students that getting experience addressing interpersonal difficulties now will help them in the working world later.

PBL can be very effective (Palmer, 1998, 125–127; Ramsden, 1992, 81, 141,
148, 255; Williams & Duch, 1997, 468–470). It has the advantage of using cooperative
groups and keeping students active. It leads to deeper learning than results from studying the academic discipline separately from professional applications. Although only
about 80 percent as much material is covered, on identical tests the students do as well
as or better than students in traditional courses. Their learning of higher order tasks is
significantly better. PBL motivates students to become involved with the content. The
students become better problem solvers, learn how to learn, and learn how to evaluate
better. The interaction between teachers and students is usually friendlier than in a traditional course. The students act more professionally, and the amount of cheating and
sabotage of others' work drops dramatically.

PBL is demanding of students, however. They are expected to act in a mature,
professional manner. They need to be responsible for their own learning, manage their
time, and work hard. They need to set goals and meet them in a timely fashion. They
critique their own work and that of others, and they need to redo their own work to satisfy these critiques. They face real issues involved in their discipline and need to learn
to work in a group that may have conflicts. Students may be overwhelmed with work if
they are taking several PBL courses simultaneously.

Many younger students are not ready for the rigors of PBL. With first- and second-
year honors students, either provide a large amount of assistance to the groups with
faculty, graduate, or undergraduate tutors (Allen, 1997, 267, 271–272; Nooman et al.,
1990) or modify PBL to be similar to guided design. Include mini-lectures and use
PBL for only part of the semester. Even seniors and first year graduate students are
likely to rebel unless PBL is introduced carefully and slowly. Full immersion without
warning invariably results in howls of fear and anger (Woods, 1997). Unless the shock

of full immersion is part of a strategy to prepare the students for professional practice, it is better to ease them into the process. PBL can fail, and when it does the students are likely to be particularly irate, since they don't see the professor doing much "teaching."

PBL and related methods are reported to require more professorial time than traditional courses (Fairweather, 1996, 99; Hendley and staff, 1996; Woods, 1997). Preparing the problems can be time-consuming, although adapting existing case studies should save time. Using PBL during part of the semester reduces the number of problems to prepare. The need for personal attention may require somewhat more personnel, such as undergraduate tutors (Allen, 1997, 267, 271–272), although some teachers are able to use PBL in classes of ninety students without additional help (Woods, 1997). Class size would not normally be a problem in graduate school. If the PBL class is required to experiment or build their designs, there are the expected extra costs of laboratory classes. A method to drastically reduce the professor's time is explored next.

Super Problem-Based Learning

One way to drastically reduce the professor's time is, for lack of a better name, "super PBL." I described this technique at the start of this chapter. Reread the introduction to see how Professor Sarah Appleton's course fits into a PBL framework. This is not a new idea (Palmer, 1998, 117–119; Rogers, 1969) and is sometimes considered a form of student-centered teaching. Thinking of the course as a PBL class places the problem posed at the center, gives the professor a clearer role, and helps prevent some of the excesses that may occur in student-centered courses.

Professor Appleton was able to reduce her workload in her elective class by *delegating* to the students the tasks of developing the problem and specifying the content to learn. However, she did establish the *boundaries* for the projects by giving the students an acceptable list of topics (Ericksen, 1974, 41). Super PBL is probably appropriate for seniors in honors programs, for graduate students in electives or research seminars, and for a core class for graduate students in any discipline to teach the *processes* of literature searches and writing.

Of all the classes I have taught, the super PBL class (Wankat, 1993b) is the one that stands out as the most fun to teach and the one in which each student grew the most. The students also received much more individual attention than in any other class. And all this was done with significantly less professorial work than in a lecture class. This is the only class I can remember in which every student worked harder than I did. Super PBL classes are firmly within Barr and Tagg's (1995) learning paradigm, instead of the standard instruction paradigm. This switch allows major increases in the professor's productivity.

Since the professor does not control the content in a super PBL class, it is even more important that he or she be a content expert than in a lecture class. The professor needs to have faith in the students, since they will control their learning. But the teacher can guide without having to control everything (Wilshire, 1990, 264). Setting a professional tone for the course is critical. The skills the professor needs for most of the classes are facilitation skills. The students should see the professor as someone who is there to help them learn and succeed.

There is a limit on class size. By meeting with three groups of 3 every other class period, one professor could handle a class of 18 students. If group size were increased to 4 students, 24 students could take the class. Of course, increasing the number of groups increases the end-of-term grading.

Group Projects in Lecture Courses

Many of the ideas in this and section 6.1 can be used in lecture courses for projects, particularly if class time is devoted to the project. The 1998–99 UCLA survey of faculty found that 23.4 percent of faculty used group projects in most or all undergraduate classes, while 33.1 percent used independent projects (Magner, 1999b). National merit scholars reported that a required project was one characteristic of their most stimulating courses (McKeachie, 1994, 154).

Most students prefer group course projects to individual efforts. Groups usually produce significantly better deliverables, it is easier to have oral presentations, and there are fewer projects to grade. Assign groups after the class enrollment has stabilized. Use the last ten minutes of the class period to allow groups to exchange phone numbers and e-mail addresses.

Give the groups considerable latitude in picking projects and setting objectives. Ideally, the projects require the groups to do something they really enjoy. Set firm dates for titles, goals, intermediate progress reports of increasing formality, rough drafts that will be critiqued by another group, and final written and oral reports. If the class is small enough to allow the professor to meet with groups every week or every other week, procrastination will be minimized. This works best if the normal classes are canceled and the students are given that time for the group project. Projects can become quite professional when a significant amount of class and student time is devoted to them. It is important to provide feedback during the course of the project so that students can incorporate it in their final project. Providing feedback on preliminary reports and expecting students to use this feedback in their final reports can greatly improve the quality of the writing. Encourage groups to involve everyone in original oral presentations such as a drama, TV show, or panel. The grading procedure can require students to rate their other group members. I have had good results with group projects lasting from two weeks to two months.

6.3. Experiential Learning

A logical next step is to have students tackle real problems outside the classroom. Nineteen percent of professors who responded to the 1998–99 UCLA survey of faculty reported using experiential learning or field studies in most or all undergraduate classes (Magner, 1999b). One compelling reason for involving the students in different forms of experience- or field-based education is the students *do* the discipline (Jim Ostrow, quoted by Morton, 1996, 278). Experiential courses almost automatically involve students (the right-hand side of Figure 4.1) and thus result in more learning (Race, 1998). Sociology students working with the homeless in a service-learning course do sociology. Engineering students on a cooperative education assignment or in an engineering clinic practice engineering. Students in law school practice law in clinics. Education students teach during internships and counseling students counsel in practica. A second compelling reason is that if the experience included reflection, students learn better after returning to the university (Ehrlich, 1996; J. R. Davis, 1993, 316–317). A third important reason is that students learn communication, interpersonal, and leadership skills that they report using after they graduate (Wankat et al., 2000).

There are a variety of experiential education methods (B. G. Davis, 1993, 166–172; J. R. Davis, 1993, 299–341). Jacoby and associates (1996) and Fyler and Giles (1999) focus on service learning, Edward (1998) discusses work-based learning, Houze and Simon (1981) explore cooperative education in the United States, Smithers (1976) compares cooperative education in the United States with sandwich programs in Great Britain, Bright and Phillips (1999) describe the Harvey-Mudd engineering clinic, Underwood (1997) profiles clinics in law school, and Eaves (1996) discusses a field project course. Although some authors differentiate among experiential learning, experienced-based learning, and field-based learning, I use these terms interchangeably in this chapter.

Ehrlich (1995, 42–44) postulates that there are seven personal qualities we want our students to develop: (1) enlightened self-esteem, (2) a desire to serve others, (3) appreciation of diversity, (4) dedication to the larger goals of society, (5) strong motivation, (6) lifelong curiosity, and (7) belief that an individual can make a difference. Experiential-learning courses can have an impact on all of these qualities. The educational advantages of cooperative education include the integration of theory and practice, increased student motivation, increased student maturity, and a greater understanding of other people, with a resulting greater skill in human relations (Smithers, 1976, 20–21). The graduates of professional schools commonly state that their field experiences were the most valuable components of their education (Ehrlich, 1995, 78–79; Ericksen, 1974, 53).

Kolb's Theory of Experiential Learning

A practical experience does not ensure that learning will occur. David Kolb's theory of experiential learning is useful to understanding how experiential education can be improved (Kolb, 1984, 1998, 1999; McCarthy, 1987; Smith & Kolb, 1986). Kolb developed two dichotomies to help explain learning preferences. First, the individual must take in or grasp the information. Some people prefer to do this by concrete experience (CE), or "learning by feeling," including personal involvement, particularly with people, in the learning activity. Others prefer abstract conceptualization (AC), or "learning by thinking," involving logical analysis and planning. Once people have taken in the information, they process it by either active experimentation (AE)—"learning by doing"—or by reflective observation (RO)—"learning by watching and listening." People who prefer AE want to try the activity and learn while they do it. People who prefer RO want to process the information internally, ponder it, and examine it from many angles.

Everyone can do all four functions, but people tend to favor one method for grasping information and one method for processing information. Kolb developed the following four learning styles based on the combination of preferred styles:

Convergers prefer AC and AE. They like to apply ideas to practical problems, particularly problems with a clear correct answer. They are more comfortable working with things than with people. Convergers are commonsense learners. Their basic question is, How do I do it? In McCarthy's (1987, 80–81) study of K-12 teachers and administrators, 14.8 percent of women and 23.5 percent of men were convergers.

Divergers prefer CE and RO. They view concrete situations from many perspectives and enjoy developing a coherent global picture. They tend to be comfortable working with people. Divergers are imaginative learners. Their basic question is, Why do I want to do it? In McCarthy's study, 25.0 percent of women and 19.4 percent of men were divergers.

Assimilators prefer AC and RO. They use inductive reasoning to create theoretical models and an integrated explanation. They are interested more in abstract concepts than in people. Assimilators are analytical learners. Their basic question is, What should I do? In McCarthy's study, 27.5 percent of women and 37.5 percent of men were assimilators.

Accommodators prefer CE and AE. They use trial-and-error problem solving and prefer to rely on people instead of analytical analysis. Like convergers, they act and get things done. Accommodators are dynamic learners. Their basic question is, What if we did this? In McCarthy's study, 32.7 percent of women and 19.6 percent of men were accommodators.

Preferences may differ in other professions, but the relative preference of men for abstract methods and of women for concrete (people-oriented) methods shown in McCarthy's study appears to be general.

In a longitudinal study of the Kolb learning styles of veterinary students and practicing veterinarians, Stickle et al. (1999) found that learning styles were not stable over a 13- to 14-year period and the learning style preferred during college did not predict the success of graduates. The majority of respondents changed their preferences, sometimes drastically. Perhaps this indicates that the environment and needs of practicing veterinarians are different from those of students. Veterinarians who were divergers in college were most likely to change their style.

Divergers and convergers form complementary pairs who are likely to conflict but can accomplish complicated tasks together if they resolve the conflict. For example, as a diverger, I often see many possibilities that my wife, a converger, does not see. She can then help me converge on a choice and move on to action. Together we come up with better decisions. Assimilators and accommodators also form complementary pairs.

Kolb (1984) hypothesized that learning would improve if all four functions—CE, RO, AC, and AE—were used in a spiral learning cycle. Although schematics of the learning cycle such as that shown in Figure 6.1 are typically drawn in two dimensions,

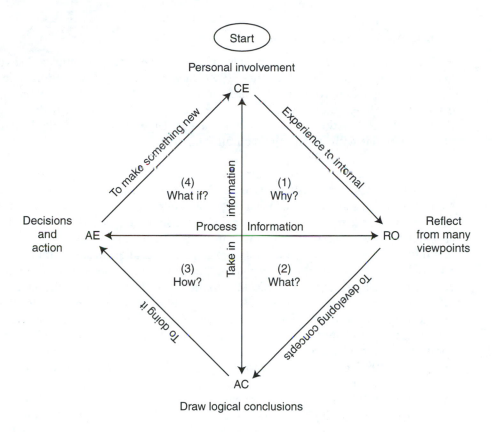

FIGURE 6.1.   Modified Kolb's (1984) learning cycle. Quadrant 1 = divergers, quadrant 2 = assimilators, quadrant 3 = convergers, quadrant 4 = accommodators, CE = concrete experience, RO = reflective observation, AC = abstract concep-tualization, AE = active experimentation. Reprinted with permission from Phillip C. Wankat and Frank S. Oreovicz, *Teaching Engineering* (New York: McGraw-Hill, 1993), p. 293.

the learning cycle should be thought of as a three-dimensional spiral. If students short-circuit the learning cycle and use only their favorite learning methods, they learn signif-icantly less. Since teachers tend to teach using their favorite learning styles, it takes considerable effort to teach around the cycle and use all four functions. Traditional lec-ture courses, which typically go back and forth between AC and RO, are really comfort-able only for assimilators and are very uncomfortable for accommodators (McCarthy, 1987). Stickle et al. (1999) found that students classified as accommodators were more likely to fail a veterinary medicine course. The courses probably used a traditional lec-ture style. Traditional laboratory courses tend to swing between AC and AE and are comfortable for convergers and uncomfortable for divergers. Case studies and PBL can use the entire cycle, but the professor needs to be careful to include all steps.

Application of Kolb's Theory

Reflection is a particularly important step in Kolb's cycle for experiential courses (J. R. Davis, 1993, 299–341; Eyler & Giles, 1999; Jacoby & associates, 1996). Reflection can be done individually through journals or logs, papers, and portfolios. Small-group discussions among course participants encourage reflection while providing support (B. G. Davis, 1993, 166–172; Jacoby & associates, 1996). If time is available, individual consultations with students are helpful. This form of teaching is close to advising (J. R. Davis, 1993, 322–327).

In practice, many cooperative education, internship, and student organization activities (see Section 6.4) emphasize personal involvement (CE) and actively doing something (AE), and do not include a significant, ongoing reflection component (RO). This pendulum pattern is most comfortable for accommodators and uncomfortable for assimilators. Everyone will learn more from experience-based courses if the entire learning cycle in Figure 6.1 is used. For example, have students start with the experience (CE) to generate emotional responses, then reflect on that experience (RO) to analyze what occurred and determine the implications. Next, require the students to integrate their observations with existing knowledge to develop new understanding and ideas of what will work (AC). These new concepts are then tried and tested (AE). This leads the students back to the feelings caused by the experience (CE) to start another loop of the learning cycle spiral.

Kolb (1984) notes that the learning cycle can be entered anywhere. Convergers and assimilators are more comfortable and benefit more if there is an extensive orientation program that uses a logical presentation and careful planning (AC) before the start of the experience. During the course, these students should be required through meetings and assignments to try something (AE), experience their feelings (CE), and reflect on the experience (RO). Convergers need more encouragement to do the CE and RO steps, whereas assimilators need encouragement for the AE and CE steps. Accommodators in experiential programs learn more if there are regular exercises and meetings that force them to reflect and abstractly conceptualize. Divergers benefit from abstract conceptualization (AC) and doing something different (AE).

McCarthy (1987) relates Kolb's theory to other learning theories, such as right/left brain theories (Herrmann, 1990; Lumsdaine & Lumsdaine, 1993). Svinicki and Dixon (1987) suggest ways to modify Kolb's model for classroom use. Exactly which theory is used by practicing teachers appears to be much less important than the fact that a theory is used.

Teaching Experiential Courses

If there is academic credit for the experiential activities, there should be academic control over them (Mintz & Hesser, 1996; Morton, 1996). The experience needs to be related to learning objectives and content (Morton, 1996). The degree of faculty involvement in experience-based courses varies significantly. For example, some institutions help students find internships and cooperative education positions and then essentially ignore them until they return to the university. Work supervisors are expected to provide feedback in the interim. These programs would certainly benefit from the model commonly used in service learning, in which student groups meet fairly often with the instructor and have regular assignments. Communication could be maintained through e-mail.

Experiential opportunities, particularly co-op and internships, should always have a course number, even if they are not for credit. The advantages for the students are that they remain a college student: Insurance does not change, loans do not become due, international students do not have to change their visas, and so forth.

The experiential-learning experience can be done as part of a class (Brennan, 1998; Deans & Meyer-Goncalves, 1998; Jacoby, 1996, 6; Morton, 1996, 283–284), making it easier to relate the experience to learning objectives. Examples include students in an environmental chemistry course who measure pollutant levels in a river, graphics arts students who work with a business to redesign brochures, and writing students who work with service agencies to write fund-raising literature. It is important to relate the practical experience to the remainder of the course and use the entire learning cycle. However, this procedure may increase the professor's workload (Morton, 1996, 283–284).

Most students will benefit if they are assigned to a student group for experiential activities. Groups of students can be assigned to work together with an agency or business. If the group contains all classes, experienced students can be assigned to leadership positions (Coyle & Jamieson, 1999; Tally, 1997; <http://purcell.ecn.purdue.edu/~epics>). This reduces the probability that the first-year students will be overwhelmed by the experience, provides an excellent leadership experience for the seniors, and reduces the professor's direct supervision. The professor supervises the experienced undergraduates, who serve as the direct supervisors of other students. Since the students in leadership roles usually start to affect the assignments of the group, they can move up the "choosing" scale in Figure 4.1. This increases their investment in learning and helps them learn how to learn. To retain quality control, the professor and the students need to meet periodically to process the experience. Not only are groups likely to produce a better product, but the students will support each other and learn more. Groups reduce the time professors need to spend facilitating and evaluating. If group efforts on the project are not possible, group meetings outside the work environment are useful for reflection, support, and planning. At remote sites, a part-time tutor could be hired to facilitate the group and provide support.

Evaluation should focus on the student's learning. Learning can be evaluated on the basis of journals, consultations, and an academic paper. However, the evaluation must also ensure that the service or work was done properly (B. G. Davis, 1993, 170; Morton, 1996, 287–288). Thus a fraction of the grade needs to be based on attendance, the field supervisor's feedback, or both. There are students who present a good academic face but are unable to perform the work on the job. For example, a student who was placed as an intern wrote good reports and had excellent rapport with her professor, but she was unreliable and disliked on the job. The professor ignored the unanimous negative reports of the field supervisors and gave her an A. The supervisors resented this and stopped accepting student interns.

When experience-based learning is successful, the students do better when they return to the university (J. R. Davis, 1993, 301, 307, 315; Edward, 1998; Morton, 1996, 280). The experience can stimulate curiosity and deep learning. Students develop professional knowledge rather than academic knowledge, and often "develop such skills as the ability to synthesize information, creative problem solving, constructive teamwork, effective communication, well-reasoned decision making, and negotiation and compromise." They can also develop "initiative, flexibility and adaptability, openness, and empathy" and "an increased sense of social responsibility" (Jacoby, 1996, 21). These skills appear to be transferable to other situations. The students become better prepared for the transition to life after graduation when they will be expected to be on time, get the job done right without a grade, dress to a higher standard, and function well in teams.

Unfortunately, administrators may see experience-based courses as a cheap way to educate students (Gose, 1997). Quality experience-based learning is not cheap, because these courses often demand a lot of the professor's time. These demands will be reduced if there is sufficient staff support for scheduling and routine matters (Morton, 1996). Developing new contacts for placement of students is much more time-consuming than maintaining existing contacts. Continuity of effort will reduce the overall workload. Since the effort required to get an organization to place ten students is little more than that needed to get an organization to place one student, try to place a number of students or student groups with each organization. Good field supervisors are important to the success of the student experience—be appropriately appreciative (Bellack & King, 2000). Perhaps you can show your appreciation by doing small favors for the supervisor, such as cutting red tape or providing free access to continuing education courses. Another form of appreciation, particularly if the supervisor has just dealt with a difficult student, is to send excellent students.

Some high schools, colleges, and universities are requiring that students perform a specified number of "volunteer" service hours to graduate (Barber, 1992, 253–261; Ehrlich, 1995, 79). The arguments for this are threefold (Barber, 1992, 251–252): First, the students who most need the experience of service learning are least likely to volunteer for it. Second, education regularly requires students to take courses and do assignments. Third, the goal of education is to empower students, and service learning can do this. Require experience, but let's drop the word "volunteer." Although service learning is the current hot method, I am unaware of any studies that compared different types of experiential learning. Thus, there is no evidence that one form of experiential learning is preferable to another.

The professor's workload for students taking three credits of an experiential-learning class is practically the same as that for students taking one credit. However, since the time required of students for individual and group meetings is about the same, the amount of useful service or work they can perform is more than three times greater in the three-credit class. Require students who want to take an experience-based course to take a minimum number of credits.

Faculty effort will be reduced further if service projects are created within existing student organizations. This is the topic of the next section.

6.4. Student Learning without Courses

Students believe that much of their learning in college occurs outside class (Moffatt, 1989). Learning how to get along with others, how to manage one's time, how to lead, how to integrate knowledge, and so forth often occurs more outside the classroom than within. In this section, I discuss the learning that occurs in organized activities such as student clubs. This section naturally leads into Chapter 8, which explores student growth and learning.

"The only factor predictive of adult success—however defined, and including post-college income—is participation in out-of-class activities" (Kuh et al., 1991, 9). Student organizations and clubs, in which the students, not faculty, organize activities, have tremendous potential as practical learning experiences (Pascarella & Terenzini, 1991, 624). For these activities to be effective, the students must become *involved* in them. Passive members do not learn much. Students enhance their leadership and inter-personal skills when they actively work in student organizations and become officers (Astin, 1993, 233–234). A survey of chemical engineering alumni showed that they rated extracurricular activities as the most important source of learning leadership skills while they were undergraduates (Wankat et al., 2000). Their work experiences while they were undergraduates were a close second. High school students who were involved in extracurricular activities did better in college as long as involvement was not excessive (U. S. Department of Education, 1986, 61). My personal experience as both a student and a faculty advisor corroborates the benefits of being involved in student organizations.

National student service organizations such as Alpha Phi Omega and Circle K provide their members many opportunities to practice leadership of projects. Social fraternities and sororities also do service projects. Students can find opportunities to practice what they have learned in class in any student organization. The accounting student who becomes the treasurer of the Rugby Club will practice accounting. Psychology students who volunteer at the local crisis center learn practical psychology. Both the sociology student and the building construction student who work with Habitat for Humanity will practice what they have learned. Joining the student chapter of a professional organization is useful *if* the student becomes involved. Merely joining to put the name of the organization on one's resume is not helpful.

The potential of student organizations to foster learning is shown by the critical importance of the Whig and Clio Societies at the College of New Jersey (now Princeton University) in the 1800s. "In his society he could exercise his own judgment, have a part in making regulations and shaping policies, strive for honors without the interference of the faculty, express his opinions from the floor, sharpen his wit by debates with other members, learn to cooperate for the good of the society, to feel the stimulus which comes from rivalry. In comparison with the intellectual life in Whig and Clio, regular college courses seemed dull and uninspiring" (Wertenbaker, 1996, 203). Some students still feel the same intellectual stimulation when they are involved in student organizations. However, it is unlikely that extracurricular activities will again become the central organizing theme of college life (Moffatt, 1989, 37–38, 64–65).

Professors can take two roles in student organizations. First, they can encourage students to become involved. This encouragement can be given in feedback (e.g., "You would benefit from frequent opportunities to speak. Have you ever considered joining Toastmasters?") or in professional development seminars. Simply encouraging students to get involved doesn't require much time and can lead to unexpected dividends. The suggestions are more likely to have an effect if they are offered in a personal way.

The second role is to be a faculty sponsor or advisor. At many institutions, particularly research universities, student organizations are desperate to find faculty advisors. The more involved the advisor, the more the organization and the advisor benefit. Since turnover is high in student organizations, a major role of the faculty advisor is to provide continuity. Serving as a faculty advisor provides an opportunity to interact with students in a relatively unstructured environment. If the organization is not the student chapter of a professional society, faculty advisors may have their only opportunity to get to know students outside their discipline.

It may come as a surprise, but involvement in student organizations often satisfies many of the learning principles discussed in section 4.2. In the best of experiences, this involvement is equivalent to a student-run service-learning course, but without credit. Faculty advisors can guide the student leaders using the PARE model (Jacoby, 2000) to be sure that the students' experiences lead to learning. There are four steps in the PARE model:

1. **Preparation.** Be sure the members are prepared for the service experience.
2. **Action.** Meaningful action is critical. Students want to feel they have made a difference, even if it is small.
3. **Reflection.** Reflection distinguishes a service-*learning* experience from volunteer activities.
4. **Evaluation.** Did the project succeed? Can it be improved?

Students may ask if they can get credit for voluntary service activities they are involved in. The advantages of allowing this are (Morton, 1996, 277) as follows:

- The students can be required to do reflective journals and a paper.
- They can reflect in group meetings.
- Individual meetings with the professor can be required.
- The students do the planning and organizing. Involvement in leadership positions has a positive impact on students' careers.
- Faculty control is retained in the evaluation.
- Faculty time is significantly reduced.

The main disadvantages are a lack of faculty control and the lack of official credit for the faculty for overseeing these activities. Although some projects will fail, these projects may result in more learning than successful ones.

Where does one find the time to become involved as an advisor? Spending valuable time working informally with students is one way professors can contribute their fair share to the "commons" of unassigned service (see section 11.1). Of course, the only external rewards will be from the students. They appreciate the attention and contact from professors, and they clearly benefit from it (Pascarella & Terenzini, 1991, 620–624). The human contact provides internal rewards for faculty. The key is to not overdo it. Choose one organization or activity to become involved in.

One of the major problems in higher education is that commuting students often do not participate in opportunities available outside of class. And the longer the commute, the less likely they are to be involved or to graduate (Astin, 1993, 390–391). Professors can help by explaining the importance of doing something other than just taking classes. Students will listen to advice about obtaining better jobs after graduation. Spend a few minutes in or out of class to discuss the importance of outside activities with students. Obviously, these discussions must occur early in their programs. It doesn't do any good to tell a graduating senior who has trouble finding a job that he or she should have been involved in activities.

6.5. Summary

At some point in the careers of students, professors should require them to take charge of their own learning in a supportive environment that encourages success. Since most first year students are not ready for self-directed learning, lead the students to it gradually. Individual mentoring or tutoring is an effective but expensive method to help students become self-directed learners. The use of small cooperative groups is an affordable alternative. Groups provide a structure that allows professors to reduce control while retaining support. Cooperative groups can be used with a variety of other teaching methods, such as case studies or PBL. These methods focus the class on the problem, not on the professor or the student. Technology can be included as needed, but it is not necessary for the success of these techniques. Although some of these methods may require extra work, others reduce the professor's workload.

Teaching with cooperative groups is different from lecturing or leading a discussion. The professor becomes a trainer/facilitator by setting up the conditions for learning to occur. Although the students help teach each other and the professor works with groups, not individuals, the students feel they receive more individual attention. Successful small-group instruction requires planning and preparation. Careful development of group tasks and assignment of members to groups will get the groups off to a good start. Most students will benefit from instruction in becoming more effective team members. Grading needs to both encourage cooperation and require that everyone do his or her share. Obtaining feedback from the students on the performance of group members can help ensure fair grading.

Guided design, case studies, PBL, and super PBL all use problems as the center of instruction, but they differ with regard to the guidance provided the learners. Start with structured problems. Then lead the students to make the problem-solving decisions and eventually educational decisions on their own. Professional programs, in particular, need to use techniques that allow the students to practice applications in an atmosphere relatively close to that of professional practice.

A natural next step is experiential learning. Existing experiential-learning programs will probably benefit from developing a structure that requires the student to reflect on his or her experience, as is done in service learning. Extracurricular activities can also be important sources of learning interpersonal and leadership skills.

Faculty can change individual courses to be problem oriented and have a large impact on students. A faculty group can work together to change a number of courses in the curriculum. By starting with first- or second-year students and gradually increasing the students' responsibilities, a group of faculty can have significantly more impact on a larger number of students. The more mature students who will come out of these courses will probably affect teaching by the remainder of the faculty, since they will accept and perhaps demand a more active role in the classroom. Large government grants, although helpful, are not needed to introduce these techniques and reform education.

7 Rapport with Students and Advising

Professor Jim Lin was concerned. He had always had good relationships with his students, but his latest set of student evaluations was quite negative. The students said he was cold and unapproachable. They criticized him for never being available outside of class. Jim argued to himself that his course syllabus had encouraged them to see him, and he had set his normal number of office hours. He liked students and was hurt by their criticism. After calming down, he admitted to himself that he had been busy last semester. Chairing the meeting of his professional society had been exciting but much more time-consuming than he had expected. He had not been available outside of office hours, as he normally was, and had skipped office hours fairly regularly the month before the meeting. Maybe he had unconsciously sent signals to the students that he was too busy to talk to them. Perhaps the student criticisms weren't unfair last semester, and none of these students had known him before last semester.

The day after receiving his student evaluations, Jim saw an announcement for a workshop titled "Increasing Rapport with Students." The timing couldn't have been better. Although Jim had never bothered to go to a teaching improvement workshop before, he decided to make time for this one.

The workshop surprised Jim. It started with an exercise on the professor's attitude, not the students' attitudes. Next on the agenda was a panel of students who talked about how they saw professors. Some of their comments made Jim feel a little uncomfortable. He resolved to remold his attitude and not let being busy become a barrier between him and his students. Later in the workshop he picked up several hints that he was sure would help him regain his lost rapport. Now he couldn't wait for the semester to start.

One of the reasons for doing routine tasks efficiently is to free up more of your time for students. Students want, and often deserve, more time from professors. *Student* learning is absolutely necessary for an effective course, and good student attitudes are part of the definition of an effective, efficient course. Individual attention often provides an opportunity to influence student motivation, and motivated students invariably learn more.

What if you love your discipline but don't particularly like students? It is more important to be authentic and share who you are with the students than to try to fake something that does not exist. Some famous, influential teachers, such as Professor

Woodrow Wilson, were noticeably aloof (Peterson, 1946, 131–152). However, rudeness and punitive behavior are never justified in the name of authenticity.

7.1. Developing Rapport with Students: In-Class Behavior

Why Have Rapport with Students?

Rapport with students is the second dimension in Lowman's (1985, 1995) model of effective teaching (see Figure 5.2). Even when intellectual excitement is the most important dimension, outstanding teaching requires at least a moderate level of rapport with students. However, there are courses in which content is *not* king and rapport with students is the key dimension. Figure 7.1. shows my modification of Lowman's model for situations when rapport is more important than content. The greatest improvement in teaching quality now occurs for increases in rapport with students. Figures 5.2 and 7.1 are in accord with Murray et al. (1990)'s observation that professors who are very good teachers in some types of classes may not be nearly as competent in other types of classes.

Rapport is easier to develop in small classes than in large ones. Unfortunately, public institutions, which enroll more than 80 percent of students, rarely believe they have the faculty resources to provide small classes (Benjamin, 1998). Between 1949 and 1992 the average student-faculty ratio at all institutions increased from 11:1 to about 17:1, and the ratios are larger at public universities and community colleges. Conditions are not likely to improve. For professors at large institutions who want to develop rapport, it is important to achieve a sense of smallness *within* the large institution (Schumacher, 1973, 242).

A second problem is that developing rapport takes time. Fortunately, much can be done to develop rapport in class. The professor's attitude is critical (Eble, 1988; Hanna & McGill, 1985; Lowman, 1995, chapter 1, 97–98; Schmier, 1995). It helps to really *like* students (Carson, 1996: Highet, 1976; Peters & Austin, 1985, 343). For high ratings in rapport, passion for students is necessary. It also helps to have a positive outlook on your profession, your course, and life in general. Sharing this outlook will help students see that you are enthusiastic. Even moderate levels of rapport require some interpersonal skills or emotional intelligence (Gardner, 1983, 1993; Goleman, 1995). Older professors may find it more difficult to develop rapport with students because of the age difference (Kennedy, 1997, 42), and so need to work harder at it. If you always meet what Bogue (1994, 17) calls a "dignity test"—treating students with dignity, courtesy, and competence—you will enjoy the respect of students, and that is a good building block for rapport. All professors can reach at least the moderate level of rapport.

As soon as they punish or demean students, professors will lose whatever rapport they have built during the semester (Pelikan, 1992, 54; Wankat & Oreovicz, 1993, 5). In extreme cases, rapport with students will fall to negative levels. Although students may learn, they do so in a climate of fear and end up hating the class. Since the students have bad attitudes, this is not good teaching. Punitive behavior is not justified in higher education.

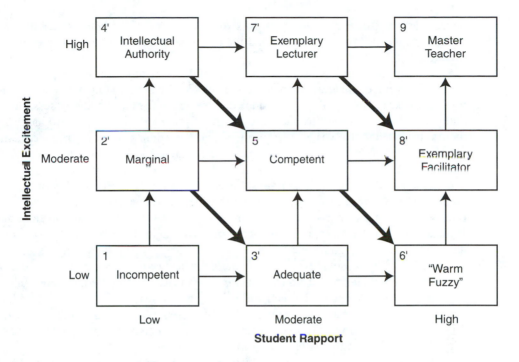

FIGURE 7.1. A modified version of Lowman's (1995) two-dimensional model of teaching effectiveness when rapport with students is the most important dimension. Primes indicate cells that are rated differently than in Figure 5.2.

Learning Names

The most important single activity you can do to show students that you are interested in them is to learn and use their names (Brinkley et al., 1999, 23–24; Chism, 1994; Duffy & Jones, 1995, 141–143; Lowman, 1995; McKeachie, 1994; Sorcinelli, 1994a, 368). If you don't know their names, the students believe they are just numbers in your grade book. Since numbers are less accountable for their actions, discipline problems and cheating are worse when professors do not know their students. These statements are true whether you have three or three hundred students in your class, but there is a difference in degree. A class of three students will expect you to know their names. With three hundred in the class, students will be surprised and pleased if you know who they are.

In classes of modest size (say, fewer than 30 or 40) it is possible to learn all the students' names by using informal methods. Come early and look over the class list as students enter. Ask students who they are and, if necessary, how to pronounce their names. Write down the pronunciation phonetically on the class list if this will help you remember. Practice using their names. If a student comes to your office hours and you can't remember his or her name, ask. Students appreciate a professor's efforts to learn their names and do not mind the professor's asking. Of course, if a professor never learns a student's name and asks over and over, the student's reaction may become negative. Most professors find they become better at learning names as they practice.

At large institutions or with first-year students at any institution, the students appreciate methods that help them learn the names of the other students in class. Some professors have a few students introduce themselves to the class at every session until the entire class has been introduced. A variant of this method is to pair students, have them introduce themselves to their partners, and have their partners introduce them to the class. The "name game" is also useful for learning a number of names quickly. The students and the professor stand in a circle. First the professor says his or her name. The person next to the professor says the professor's name and then his or her own name. The next person says the professor's name, the name of the person next to the professor, and his or her own name. This procedure is continued around the circle. When it gets back to the professor, the professor should then try to say everyone's name in order. This game generates a lot of joking and good feeling as students struggle their way through the names. It starts the class with everyone in a good mood and shows the students that you are trying. If you use this procedure, you will not remember everyone's name, but you will have a good base to build on. Duffy and Jones (1995, 142–143) and McKeachie (1994, 22–23) present other forms of the name game. Be creative in developing a procedure that meets your needs. Use the students' names when you see them in the hall or on campus.

Large classes often require more formal procedures. Some professors assign students to seats, and then memorize the locations in the seating chart. They then call students by name in class and relate names to faces. The alternative I use is to photograph all the students in the class and before class and during tests study the photographs. Departments could photograph their students with a digital camera, store the images in a computer, and print the photographs for each class using the class lists. Delegating this task to an administrative assistant or secretary saves professors considerable time but still helps them get to know their students.

> TIP: Come to class early and stay late. Coming to class early and staying late helps you learn names and provides time to mingle with students. Just chatting with students can be a useful method for developing rapport. Being there also makes you accessible to students for questions and special concerns. If a student brings up something that should be confidential, ask him or her to see you during office hours or make an appointment to discuss it.

Increasing Rapport

There are many other things you can do to increase rapport with students during class. Be friendly and smile. Moffatt (1989, 44) found that "friendliness was the fundamental code of etiquette among the students." Brusque behavior is often interpreted as impersonalness and unfriendliness, particularly by groups of students who have a history of being discriminated against. Sincere praise is always appreciated. Maintaining eye contact helps students in the United States feel you are talking to them, but the suitability of eye contact is culture dependent. In large lecture halls, walking up and down the aisle to be closer to the students in the middle and back rows is helpful and helps reduce discipline problems. If you need a microphone, ask for a portable one. Use methods such as one-minute quizzes to obtain feedback from the students, and then act on that feedback.

> TIP: Pick one item—say, smiling or calling students by name—to work on in class. Ask the teaching assistant (TA) or another professor to count the number of times you do this behavior in class. A refinement is to have the observer record your responses to men, women, and minorities.

In interactions with students, always be polite and civil. Be polite and compassionate even when refusing a student's request. Although flexibility in dealing with student requests is important, there will always be requests that must be turned down. An effective method for handling special requests is to tell the student you will think about it (Sarkisian, 1990, 21). This delay gives you time to search for wisdom while you ponder the case, and sometimes the problem disappears by itself.

Inappropriate Faculty Behavior

Rudeness or putting students down is always inappropriate. Even a single incident of rudeness will destroy rapport and will be the one thing that many students remember about you. Watch your language in and out of class. An inadvertent comment or attempt at humor that is interpreted as racist or sexist will destroy rapport (Bowser et al., 1993; Chism, 1994).

It used to be that you could pat a student on the back or squeeze his or her shoulder to show support, but now this gesture must be used with extreme caution. It is too easy for a student to misinterpret touch as sexual. Charges of sexual harassment are so upsetting to everyone involved that it is essential to make sure that your behavior *cannot* be interpreted this way. Probably the best advice is to avoid all actions that could be misconstrued as sexual harassment, such as

- Staring, leering, or ogling;
- Frequent commenting on physical appearance;
- Touching out of context;
- Excessive flattery and praise;
- Changing behavior with student when observed;
- Injecting male versus female comments;
- Emphasizing sexuality in all contexts (Dziech & Weiner, 1984, 119).

Of course, sexual harassment can be much more subtle and complicated than this (Sandler, 1988). Professors are professionals who have the knowledge and ability to avoid these problems.

Unfortunately, overattention to the possibility that actions might be interpreted as sexual harassment will diminish the effectiveness of some professors. Bemoaning political correctness will not change the situation, however. Instead of touching, one can use words and actions to indicate caring and support. For example, if a student has a death in his or her family, giving the student extra time on assignments, delaying a test for that student, and providing extra help all speak loudly that you understand.

Research on student reactions to faculty behavior has revealed four behavior patterns that students consider improper (Centra, 1993, 34–36):

- Moral turpitude
- Particularistic grading
- Interpersonal disregard
- Inadequate planning

The first two are unethical, and the third may stem from arrogance, which Kennedy (1997, 71) notes is a persistent characteristic flaw of some professors. Only the last item is related to content.

Romantic entanglement with a student can easily lead to moral turpitude, sexual harassment, or preferential treatment or at least the appearance of it. The actual behavior is unethical, and the appearance of it will drastically affect the professor's rapport with other students (Rosovsky, 1990, 290–292). Refuse all invitations for romantic entanglements with your students (Cahn, 1986, 35–36). If the romance is real, it will still be there when the student graduates.

Discipline and Cheating

This section should not be interpreted as being soft on discipline or letting anything go. Professors should explain the rules for conduct in class to students in positive ways (e.g., "Avoid talking during the lecture since many students want to hear the lecture"), and the rules should have clear pedagogical or safety justification. Students are much more likely to rebel against arbitrary rules, such as "No baseball caps in class." A professor who has developed rapport with students and has reasonable rules will have relatively few problems.

One effective method for dealing with some problems is to ask the class for feedback (Angelo & Cross, 1993, 148–153; Sorcinelli, 1994b, 369). In a one-minute quiz, ask the students, "What can the professor (and TAs) do to help you learn?" Collate the responses and present them to the class. If behavior such as excessive talking is a problem, this will appear on some of the responses (e.g., "Tell people to shut up"). This gives you the backing of the class to ask students to be quiet. Use of properly channeled peer pressure is often effective in controlling undesired behavior. This use of a one-minute quiz increases rapport, *assuming* you are willing to make changes in the course based on the feedback.

TIP: Use a one-minute quiz for feedback after your first test in the course.

Cheating is one behavior that must not be tolerated. Tolerating cheating tends to make it worse. And students who are observed cheating may be tolerated in course after course. Prevention of cheating is much more effective and efficient than trying to cure it once it has occurred. Sorcinelli's (1994b, 9) assertion that "students don't basically want to cheat" is an optimistic view of the situation, while Gardiner's (1994, 68) view that "grades provide for many students a rationale to engage in unethical behavior" is too pessimistic. I've observed that a form of the Pareto principle is followed. Approximately 20 percent of the professors have 80 percent of the cheating incidents and other discipline problems.

Fortunately, if a professor knows student names, has rapport with students, and has the reputation for giving fair tests, there will be little cheating (Kibler et al., 1988, 19–20, 23–24; Sorcinelli, 1994a, 1994b). Taking reasonable precautions in writing and administering tests (see section 5.6) reduces cheating even further. The fewer excuses professors give students to cheat, the less cheating there will be. Certain forms of cheating, such as plagiarism, can be reduced by educating the students on what the standards are (McCabe & Trevino, 1996). However, the rise of the Internet has led to new types of cheating. McCollum (1999) reported on a recent survey by Timothy Rumbough in which 15 percent of students admitted using the Internet to cheat. Care must be taken that students are not buying term papers. One method to reduce this is to require periodic progress reports and an outline of the paper before it is written.

Institutions with functioning honor codes also tend to have less cheating (Kennedy, 1997, 85–88; McCabe & Trevino, 1996). At Stanford University, which has an honor code, 6 to 15 percent of the students admitted to some form of academic dishonesty on anonymous questionnaires (Kennedy, 1997, 85). Professors can reduce cheating by discussing honesty and responsibility. In teaching engineering students, I have found it effective to frame the discussion around the engineer's code of ethics. This strategy can be applied in any professional program.

I try to trust all students until there is some evidence that they are untrustworthy. If you suspect cheating but can't prove it, photocopy everything before returning the test to the student. If you suspect a student of changing his or her test before a regrade request, after the next exam, copy that student's test before returning it.

When a cheating incident occurs, decide whether to use an informal or formal resolution. Informal procedures, if available at your school, usually require much less time. However, *it is absolutely necessary to provide for due process* even for informal resolutions (Kibler et al., 1988, 42–63; Stevens, 1996). Fortunately, due process can be fairly simple if the potential penalties are not harsh. U.S. Supreme Court rulings authorize the following steps for due process for informal resolution of cheating and discipline cases (Stevens, 1996):

1. *Preliminary.* Calm down. Review the evidence. Check your school's rules to be sure informal resolutions are allowed. If they are not allowed, go through the formal procedures. Decide on rational steps.

2. *Give notice.* Present the student with a clear oral statement of "charges" and consequences. Explain appeal procedures and rights. Remain calm and be polite. Notice can be given privately if the potential penalties are not harsh.

3. *Individual, investigative hearing.* If the potential penalties are relatively light (e.g., losing points or receiving an F on this test, repeating work, or failing the course), an immediate cursory hearing conducted by the professor satisfies due process. This hearing has no attorney, no oaths, no opportunity to confront witnesses, and no written record. The professor can decide on the penalty, even if the student maintains his or her innocence. However, the penalty must be decided on a case-by-case basis. A blanket rule (e.g., "F in this course for any cheating") does *not* satisfy due process. Stevens (1996) recommends relying on memory for minor cases, since incomplete notes are often worse than memory if there is an appeal. Record the grade and the date of the hearing and keep a copy of the disputed test or paper. If there is no appeal, the results of the hearing can remain private, and Stevens (1996) suggests they usually should.

4. *Appeal procedure.* If the student appeals, follow your institution's formal procedures. Note that there must be an appeal procedure for due process. Since the appeal is no longer completely private, the student may decide to accept the penalty as long as it is not too harsh.

Administrators need to back up professors in cheating cases (Schneider, 1999).

Jim has made a concerted effort to develop rapport with his students. Although he does not know the names of all 92 students in his class, he knows most of their names and recognizes the rest. His syllabus is more complete. The rules look forbidding, but he interprets them flexibly. Small talk is not one of his strengths, but he makes an effort to chat with the students before class. He has noticed that discipline problems are fewer and tests seem calmer, with many fewer cases of suspected cheating. When he overheard some of the students talking about how nice Professor Lin was, he smiled to himself. His efforts were working.

Burnout

A professor who is burned out or bitter is rarely a good teacher. Attitude invariably infects teaching. From the students' viewpoint, good teaching always depends on "What have you done for me lately?" Winning a teaching award ten years ago does not necessarily mean that one is still a good teacher. If you are in the category of burned out or bitter, first try to change your behavior. Teach in a positive way. Often behavioral changes result in an attitudinal change. Professors who are burned out may find it useful to consult a book on this phenomenon, such as Freudenberger (1980). Reread Chapter 2 of this book and generate new goals for yourself. If you are seriously contemplating a new career, Bolles (1981) has suggestions for changing your views of school, work, and retirement, and Rosen and Paul (1998) emphasize self-assessment before job hunting. The classic book on job hunting is *What Color Is Your Parachute?* (Bolles, 2000). If a deep malaise persists for longer than a year, perhaps personal counseling is appropriate.

7.2. Developing Rapport with Students: Activities Outside of Class

Availability and Office Hours

Students are concerned about their professor's availability outside of class (Carson, 1996). Although they may not take advantage of it, they want to make sure the opportunity to visit exists. Students interpret availability as a sign that the professor cares. It is helpful to go beyond being approachable, and "actually do some approaching" (Eble, 1988, 183). Invite specific students to come and talk to you.

Professors need to have office hours (Lowman, 1995, 71). Check class schedules and select times when the majority of students are free. List your office hours in the syllabus and post them on your office door. Make it clear that you are also available by appointment. Office hours are useful for students who take advantage of them. Be there for office hours or inform the students in advance if you will be absent. For many students coming to a professor's office is an act of courage. If they make the effort and the professor is out, they may never try again. Part-time and adjunct professors need access to an office to provide office hours.

When a student does come to office hours, be welcoming, or the student may never return. Avoid sitting behind your desk, and consider offering the student a snack (Hanna et al., 1999). I keep a jar of Hershey kisses on my table for visitors. Humor and laughing at yourself will also help you break the ice and develop rapport with students (Hanna et al., 1999).

Since many students who will benefit from office hours do not use them, it may be appropriate to stongly encourage attendance (e.g., by requiring them to come in to pick up a test) or require them to come for an interview. I have required students in a small senior seminar and in a graduate elective to come in for a fifteen-minute to half-hour chat. The chats were informal and not graded. I enjoyed the individual discussions, and several of the students said they thought they were a good idea. At least at the end of the chat, the students felt comfortable about coming in to talk to me again.

Students like professors who have open-door policies and are in their offices most of the time (Carson, 1996). If you decide to have an open-door policy, you should still specify office hours, because they are guaranteed times of availability.

What if you decide to not have an open-door policy and set office hours, but students come at another time? When a student who has never come before does this, you can be very helpful and encourage him or her to come back at office hours. If a student does this and has done this before, offer quick help and politely encourage the student to come during office hours or make an appointment. If a student abuses your hospitality, become firmer. If a student drops by at a very inopportune time, explain that you can't talk now and ask the student to come back later (e.g., "I have a lecture in half an hour and it isn't ready. Are you free at 2:30 this afternoon?"). Setting a definite appointment removes the sting of rejection and signals that you really do want to talk to the student. Students are prone to ask, "Professor, are you busy?" Restrain your urge to be sarcastic or to strangle the student. A response that students appreciate is "I always have time for students, if only a minute to make an appointment." If there are too many interruptions to get anything else done in your office, consider working else-where part of the day (see section 3.5).

Many students who will never come privately to a professor's office will attend voluntary group help sessions held in a classroom. These sessions are effective because students control the questions and thus their own learning, and they can hear other students' questions and the answers to them. They are also efficient, since many students simultaneously can receive what's close to individual attention. Students interpret help sessions as the professor's attempting to be accessible and help them learn. It is helpful to clearly explain the ground rules for a help session when you announce it in class (e.g., "I will only answer student questions. When there are no more student questions, the help session is over").

E-Mail

E-mail is a useful method for communicating with students. Some students who would never ask questions in person use e-mail. It is also less intrusive than office visits or phone calls. However, e-mail can be interpreted as impersonal; it is easier to misinterpret e-mail than face-to-face communication, since there is (currently) no body language or vocal intonation; and some students do not have easy access to e-mail (Kussmaul et al., 1996). Atamian and DeMoville (1998) did an experiment in which e-mail was the only method students were allowed for out-of-class communication. They guaranteed the students faster than 24-hour turnaround on any e-mail question. Although the experiment appeared to be successful and most students thought the professors were more accessible than normal, the authors cautioned that this would not work in all situations. I prefer to use e-mail as an additional way for students to have access.

Professors can use e-mail to contact individual students or the entire class when other communication methods would be difficult (e.g., "There is a typographical error in problem 2 on the homework. The question should be . . ."). Aliases allow the professor to contact the entire class easily. Class pages on the web are also useful to make information available to students, but they are not as direct as e-mail when there is a specific problem to be addressed.

Attention to Students

Extensive surveys of undergraduates show that retention is positively correlated with their overall satisfaction. Two factors that boost students' satisfaction are talking to faculty outside of class and visiting a professor's home (Astin, 1993, 278–279; Light, 1992; Smith, 1989; Tinto, 1993). The first is clearly part of professors' jobs. The second is voluntary, but has a big effect. Any activity that involves professors in students' academic or social lives can have a big impact. This includes eating meals with them, becoming involved in student organizations, attending parties (even short visits are effective), going to award banquets, and volunteering to work on service projects with them.

Faculty who act interested in students are often asked to write letters of reference even if they don't know the students well. This is particularly true in large departments with large classes. When this happens, ask the student to write down for you the name and address of the person to send it to, and the deadline. I always ask for a current copy of the student's resume, and spend a few minutes asking about the job or scholarship the student is applying for. I spend extra time composing the first letter on my word processor. For other requests I modify the letter as appropriate. This is efficient and results in an improved letter by the second or third revision. Because candor and privacy laws don't always mix well, giving the reference in a telephone call is often preferable (Kennedy, 1997, 91–93).

Controlling Students' Desire for Attention

At many universities, students are desperate for attention from professors. Professors who pay attention may be inundated with requests for more attention and can spend a lot of their time interacting with students. How much is appropriate depends on your job assignment, goals, personal preferences, and position. Tenured full professors can probably decide to focus much of their time on students, but this might be dangerous for the careers of untenured assistant professors at research universities. If you decide that excessive student demands need to be controlled, learn to say no politely but firmly, and without feeling excessive guilt (a little guilt is OK). Students are often understanding if they are told reasons for the refusal. For example, if you are already an advisor for one student organization and students ask you to advise another, they usually understand when you tell them that one is all you can do effectively.

Occasionally, a student will become overly dependent on a professor. When this happens, do not ignore the situation and let it become worse. Privately discuss the situation with the student. Frame the discussion positively by basing it on your goals for students. Thus, if one of your goals is for students to become self-directed learners, you can express regret that this does not appear to be occurring. If the student doesn't take the hint, become more directive. In extreme cases, limit the student's access to a specified number of minutes every week.

Students also develop romantic fantasies about professors. Most students who develop a crush on a professor will not push the borders of good taste if the professor acts in a professional manner. Hanna et al. (1999) suggest that counselors give attention to adolescents who seek it, and the same advice is probably appropriate for professors. However, Nathans (1988, 163–164) adds this caveat: "Avoid absolutely situations where you meet behind closed doors!" If the student becomes aggressive, procedures similar to those suggested for overly dependent students will usually be effective.

Jim sets his normal office hours for the semester and makes sure he is available. He encourages students to drop in anytime. His office door is propped open, and he is warm and inviting when a student stops by. He encourages students to e-mail him with questions and guarantees quick responses during the week. He obtains e-mail addresses for all the students and occasionally uses e-mail to contact them. Student evaluations at the end of the semester show that he has not only regained his former level of approval, but also improved it in several areas. More important, Jim feels better about his teaching and knows he has done a better job.

7.3. Student Motivation

In this section I discuss a theory of how interactions affect undergraduates' motivation (in section 8.3, I discuss Maslow's theory of motivation). People are intrinsically motivated to learn. Babies always try to understand objects, and one way they do this is to put the object in their mouth. This action is potentially dangerous, but it helps learning and is universal. There must be a very high evolutionary advantage to learning. Although some people retain their curiosity throughout life, many of our students have lost or buried their inherent drive to learn. Helping students rekindle this drive is exceptional teaching.

Motivational Interaction Theory

The major unspoken question of many professors regarding undergraduates' motivation is, Why aren't they as motivated as we were? Professors with this attitude believe that when they were students they were motivated in all classes and conveniently ignore the attitudes they had toward certain required classes. They also conveniently forget that most professors were very good students, and very good students are equally motivated today.

Motivated students learn more, are more fun to teach, rate the professor higher, and in general make the professor look and feel good. Anything you can do to motivate students will pay high dividends. Demotivation is the opposite of motivation. Anything you do to demotivate students can result in extensive damage.

There are three major difficulties in controlling motivation/demotivation (Pintrich, 1994). First, motivation is hidden. We must use observable behaviors to hypothesize that a student is motivated or demotivated. Second, there is no universal motivator, not even money. What motivates one student (e.g., grades) may not motivate or may even demotivate another. Third, interactions have an indirect effect on motivation. We can never be sure ahead of time that our behavior will have the desired motivating effect. A theory of motivational interaction is useful for understanding these difficulties and deciding what methods to try to motivate individuals.

A naive view of motivational interaction is illustrated in Figure 7.2. In this view, the professor's activities and those the professor has the student do directly motivate the student. The student is motivated to focus on study and work persistently on projects for the course. The feedback to the professor shows that the student is studying and learning the material. The student's expression, body language, and verbal messages are all congruent and indicate that the student is happy with the course. The professor concludes that he or she has motivated the student. Unfortunately, this model is invalid. If it were valid, all students in a course would become motivated, and that does not happen.

The actual interaction process is significantly more complicated, as Figure 7.3 shows (Ellis, 1973; Gazzaniga, 1998; Pintrich, 1994). All messages from the professor, including the syllabus, assignments, tests, words, and actions, must first be observed by the student. The observed parts of these messages are sent to the student's left brain, where they are interpreted (Gazzaniga, 1998). Interpretation depends on cultural clues,

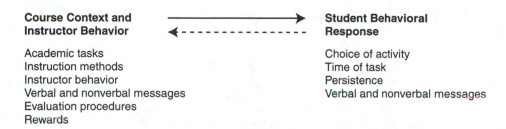

Course Context and Instructor Behavior		Student Behavioral Response
Academic tasks		Choice of activity
Instruction methods		Time of task
Instructor behavior		Persistence
Verbal and nonverbal messages		Verbal and nonverbal messages
Evaluation procedures		
Rewards		

FIGURE 7.2. A naive and invalid view of how interaction affects motivation.

the student's beliefs about the class and the professor, and the student's physical and emotional states (e.g., the interpretation is likely to be different if the student is sick or just received bad news). Unfortunately, the left brain is good at generating plausible but not necessarily valid interpretations. "He's scowling! He must be angry with me" might be the interpretation, when in fact the professor's stomach is upset. Since being suspicious probably led to longer lives for our ancestors, the left brain is predisposed toward negative interpretations. The clearer the message, the more likely it is to be correctly interpreted.

After interpretation, the message goes to the student's belief system. Expectancy is student's' belief that they can do the task and have control over it. A clear syllabus with well-explained course objectives and a clearly described grading scheme help students believe they can succeed. Comments from former students who have succeeded also help. The belief system questions the value of academic tasks. Do they meet the student's goals or are they valuable for other reasons? Showing students how this course fits into their plans of study and discussing the power that mastery of the material will provide can be motivating. The student may be motivated by intrinsic reward (e.g., mastery of new knowledge) or extrinsic reward (e.g., the potential for a high or low grade). Affective processes such as anxiety or self-esteem can change the students' beliefs. The belief system then translates these beliefs into behavior. For example, the student may study alone or in small groups and may work on assignments diligently or halfheartedly.

Students send messages to professors all the time. Attending class and paying attention send one message, while coming in late and sleeping in class send another. The quality and quantity of their work send another message. Attending or not attending help sessions and office hours is another message. First the professor observes or fails to observe these messages, and then his or her left brain interprets them. This interpretation varies, depending on the professor's emotional and physical states. The professor's belief system then determines the actions to take. Even if the professor does absolutely nothing, this is a message that, if students observe it, will activate the cycle again.

Considering the complexity of this process, it is surprising that any extrinsic motivation occurs at all. First, many actions are not observed or are only partly observed. Even when the entire action is observed, the left brain can interpret the

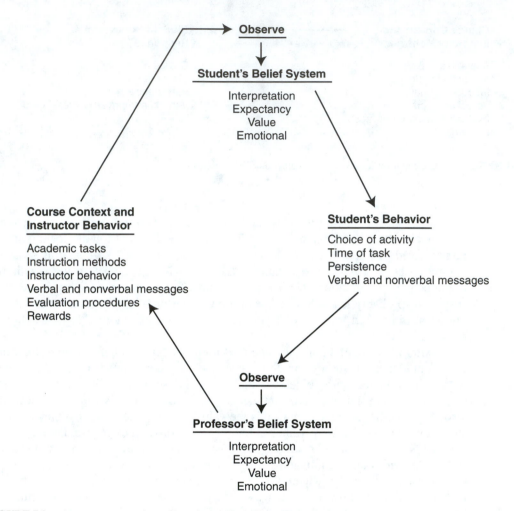

FIGURE 7.3.   A more accurate view of how interaction affects motivation.

message in a way that is totally different from what's intended. Of course, in some cases misinterpretation may result in motivation! Even if a message is correctly interpreted, the student's belief system can decide to ignore it. I have seen many students enter engineering because their parents are excited by the potential salary. Some of these students decide they are *not* going to be engineers and flunk out to "prove" they can't do it. They are strongly intrinsically demotivated. Other students are so intrinsically motivated that they overcome all obstacles, such as discrimination, physical disability, lack of money, or uncaring professors, to obtain the education they want.

Methods for Motivating Students

When there is competition between strong intrinsic and extrinsic motivations, the strong intrinsic motivation (or demotivation) usually wins. However, since students often have neutral, nonexistent, or weak beliefs (Fazey & Fazey, 1998), extrinsic motivators can influence them. Money is motivating to many students. Unfortunately, the promise of money in four or five years is not immediate enough. A paycheck next semester from a cooperative education program or in the summer from an internship often has more impact. Immediacy is also a plus for students who are motivated by the chance to help people. Service learning and volunteer work can be very motivating for these students.

Despite the difficulties, professors can help motivate students (Brown et al., 1998; Cashin, 1979; B. G. Davis, 1993, chapter 23; Ericksen, 1974; McKeachie, 1994, chapter 31; Pintrich, 1994). First, be sure they observe the actions you take to motivate them. Go over the syllabus *in class*. If it is handed out and not discussed, most students will not read it. If a student does well on the test write, "Great job, Sherri!" in big letters next to the grade. If a student's test score is mediocre but shows significant improvement, acknowledge this: "Keep working, you can do this!" Making a positive comment in passing ("Ed, really good comment in class today!") can also boost students. Anything you can do to make a student feel special will be motivating. After you learn students' names, be sure to use them. Otherwise, the motivational impact of your learning their names will be lost.

Success is very motivating, and the lack of it, such as repeated low grades, is demotivating (Tobias, 1990, 78). At the same time there may be considerable pressure to control grade inflation and "maintain standards." This pressure certainly conflicts with a professor's desire to motivate students and have them succeed. Although this quandary will always exist, since students may decide to fail, it is significantly reduced if we focus on student learning. Follow the principles of what works (see section 4.2) and encourage students to learn and use good learning principles. Many students do not know how to learn effectively and efficiently and will benefit from this instruction (see section 8.6). Use of a criterion-referenced grading system (see section 5.7) will help you maintain standards while encouraging students to help each other.

To help students believe they can do the required tasks, start slowly and make sure that all students can do simple problems. Mastery learning is effective at this aspect of motivation. You'll enhance the value of the task if you explain why it is important and how it fits into the students' studies (Race, 1998). Anxiety tends to lessen if students believe they can do the course work. However, test anxiety can cause students to perform poorly on tests or even freeze. I have had good success referring anxious students to the university's psychology clinic. These students talk to an empathic counselor and learn some simple exercises to help control anxiety. Visiting the clinic a few times usually helps them perform during the stress of tests.

TIP: Make sure that students have enough time on tests. Allowing insufficient time on tests is demotivating.

As much as possible professors should observe but not interpret student behavior. Remember that the left brain will generate plausible, but often wrong, interpretations. Suppose a student stops coming to class in the middle of the term. One plausible interpretation is that she has lost interest, but there are many other possibilities, such as illness or family problems. Before assuming the worst, try to contact the student or ask the departmental advisor to contact her. Most students will interpret this contact as concern.

A professor's responses may not meet students' expectations. For example, many first-year students expect the same degree of interaction they had from high school teachers and interpret a lack of interaction with their college professors as a lack of interest. Since many students will interpret your silence as indifference, try to be responsive. Also, professors often have higher expectations of students than the students have for themselves. Some students interpret this as trust in their abilities and are motivated. Others assume the professor is never satisfied and give up.

Demotivators

Herzberg showed that people are affected by two sets of factors (Herzberg, 1966; Herzberg et al., 1959; Uris, 1968, 41–42): *motivators* and *demotivators*. Ensuring that demotivators are absent may prevent demotivation but does not necessarily motivate. Strauss and Sayles (1980, 34–36) and Ullrich (1981, 96–101) discuss flaws in the data, but note that the theory empirically works for some people. When interacting with students, avoid the following demotivating behaviors ("Managing People," 1996):

- Silence
- Glaring
- Abruptness
- Ignoring
- Put-downs
- Disrespect
- Blaming
- Controlling
- Threats
- Yelling
- Loss of control
- Harsh grading procedures

Institutions need to avoid the following demotivators:

- Poor registration procedures
- Slow processing of bills
- An unresponsive financial aid department
- Sidewalks that are snowy or icy
- Poor lighting of streets at night
- Poor housekeeping in buildings

- Poor or unimaginative food in residence halls
- Heavy-handed responses to student demonstrations

Professors need to eliminate demotivators and work to motivate students. Fortunately, students usually interpret any special effort as a sign that the professor cares (Ericksen, 1974, 22). This perception is usually motivating. The students' perception of the professor's attitude is often more important than what the professor actually does.

7.4. Advising Students

Although professors are often assigned the role of academic advisor, much of the advising done by faculty is more informal. Once students have rapport with a professor, it is relatively easy for them to drop by the professor's office for informal advising. Advising and out-of-class teaching blend together. Although advising skills are not taught in graduate school, professors need to develop a basic competence in advising skills (Eble, 1988, 107). The interpersonal skills (Gardner, 1983, 1993; Goleman, 1995) involved in effective undergraduate advising are also useful for facilitating student learning during interactive teaching.

Academic Advising

Academic advising is the duty of professors at 80 percent of institutions (Gardiner, 1994, 91), but there is confusion whether advising is a service function or part of teaching. Since advising interacts significantly with teaching, I classify it as a form of teaching.

Few schools are proud of their academic advising, and students routinely rate the quality of advising and career guidance as poor (Eble, 1988, 107; Edgerton, 1993; Feagin et al., 1996, 116–121; Gardiner, 1994, 91; Moffatt, 1989, 316; Wankat, 1986). In Astin's (1993, 274–276, 310) national survey, only 44 percent of the students were satisfied or very satisfied with academic advising and only 42 percent were satisfied or very satisfied with career counseling. This is important, since students who are more satisfied are more likely to stay in college (Astin, 1993, 278–279). High-quality advising increases student retention and graduation rates (Gardiner, 1994, 88–90). Feagin et al. (1996, 116–121) note that advising is critically important to African American students, but is usually poor.

Unfortunately, professors widely believe that advising counts little in promotion and tenure decisions. In a Carnegie Foundation survey, only 5 percent of respondents reported that academic advisement was very important for granting tenure and 20 percent reported it was fairly important (Boyer, 1990, table A-18). Only 24 percent of respondents reported that student evaluations of advising were used for promotion and tenure decisions (Glassick et al., 1997, tables 3.1 and 22 in the appendix). Schwehn (1993, 11) comments, "Few believe that academic advising should be rewarded; it seems to almost all faculty an irksome task at best." This view certainly does not apply to students and parents who believe that academic advising is important and needs to have more emphasis (Boyer, 1987, 289; Gardiner, 1994, 88). Students are required to visit their academic advisor frequently at institutions that guarantee graduation in four years (Woodhams, 1998).

Many large schools have delegated academic advising to professionals who have advising degrees (Plater, 1998, 707). Professional counselors with master's degrees are less expensive than professors, enjoy advising, and want to help students grow (Gordon, 1992). The faculty are expected to mentor students, but the boundaries are fuzzy. This approach can work if the professional academic advisor is socialized in the discipline. Ideally, the advisor has an undergraduate degree in the discipline. When the advisor's undergraduate degree is in another area, the advisor should study the discipline; talk to students, alumni, and professors; sit in on a variety of classes; and audit the introductory course in the discipline.

Most faculty are not trained for either academic advising (Berquist & Phillips, 1977) or more serious student problems, such as medical emergencies or suicide (Horning, 1998). Unlike teaching, few faculty have had good faculty role models for academic advising.

Good academic advising depends on the individual student. Students want different things from advisors. In one survey, 61 percent of the male students at Harvard University said they wanted advisors to make concrete suggestions, while only 23 percent of the female students did (Light, 1990, 17, 18, 21). Most (64 percent) of the men wanted advisors to know facts about the courses, while this was important for 43 percent of the women. Many women wanted an advisor who had similar interests (58 percent) and who would take the time to get to know them personally (72 percent). Only 31 percent and 30 percent of the men wanted advisors to behave in these ways, respectively. These differences agree with well-known differences in how men and women communicate (Tannen, 1990, 1994). Good advisors avoid prejudging students on the basis of stereotypes and determine what each student wants and needs.

Academic advising can be thought of as a specialized form of teaching. If facts are most important, then Figure 5.2 is the appropriate model for improvements. If rapport with the student is most important, Figure 7.1 applies. However, there is one major difference between advising and normal teaching. In academic advising, the student decides daily whether content or relationship development is more important. If the student wants to develop a relationship and the advisor gives the facts, the student will become frustrated. The student will also become frustrated if he or she wants the facts and the advisor insists on trying to develop a relationship. Even worse, a student may want facts one day and a relationship the next. Start with methods to gain rapport. Then adjust as necessary on the basis of the student's behavior.

Methods for Academic Advising

Good academic advising requires confidentiality, availability, correct information, active listening, and a counseling theory (Grites, 1980; Wankat & Oreovicz, 1993, 201–203).

Confidentiality.   With the exception of emergencies (see section 7.5), everything the student tells you during advising should be confidential. Confidentiality is discussed at length in the education of professional counselors and is the subject of an entire section in the code of ethics of the American Counseling Association (1995, section B; Hackney & Cormier, 1996, appendix).

Availability.   Advising takes time. Although occasionally a student needs only the answer to a simple question (e.g., "Will English 304 count as an elective in my program?"), usually considerably more time is needed. This time requirement makes advising appear to be inefficient, but compared to bad advising, which can easily cost a student an extra term at school, it isn't.

Correct information.   Since the majority of students want facts, advisors need to have *correct information* (B. G. Davis, 1993, 376–377; Nathans, 1988). Dedicate a small part of one book shelf to necessary information: school catalogs, course schedule, student handouts, and three file folders. One folder should contain more or less permanent information, such as degree requirements, registration requirements, the term calendar, phone numbers of referrals and resource people, and so forth. The second folder can include course advertisements and miscellaneous sheets for the next semester. The third folder contains your notes on previous sessions with students. If in doubt about a student's question, look up the answer. A corollary to this is that professors need to make sure advisers have correct course descriptions (McKeachie, 1994, 267). Use sound bites, not paragraphs, when imparting information to students (Hanna et al., 1999). Many students will not listen to a long explanation.

Part of the information faculty advisors need is a list of phone numbers and contacts for appropriate referrals. This could include the university counseling center, local crisis center, student health center, police department, writing clinic, and so forth. Since faculty should *not* do professional counseling (American Counseling Association, 1995), they need to be able to refer students to the proper place. Professors should, at most, see a student once plus a follow-up for a given concern (Lowman, 1995, 94).

Active listening.   *Active listening skills* separate good advising from mere dispensing of facts. Active listening skills are discussed in a variety of counseling sources, such as Cormier and Hackney (1999), D'Andrea and Salovey (1983, 17–34), Egan (1998), and Hackney and Cormier (1996). Other sources on active listening from a variety of disciplines include Bolton (1979, 27–114), Gordon (1974, 80–155, Gordon 1975, 29–94), Harrisberger (1994, 190–191), Larson (1978), Sloan (1994), and Wankat (1979, 1980). Empathy is discussed in detail in many of these sources and by Goleman (1995, chapter 7).

Most professors like to talk and explain. This behavior is the opposite of what is needed most often in advising, however. Listen actively and direct all your attention to the student. Outstanding counselors have a remarkable ability to focus their entire being on the client. This is difficult for professors, since we routinely juggle a variety of tasks. Concentrate on both the verbal and the nonverbal messages of the student. Follow your intuition as to how the student is feeling. Face the student and make eye contact. Be inviting.

"John, what can I do for you today?"
"Susan, you mentioned on the phone you need to drop and add some courses?"

Note that the second question is asked through intonation and inflection. Use the non-verbal behavior you normally use to encourage someone to talk (e.g., lean toward the student, nod your head, and encourage with your hands). Use minimal verbal responses ("uh-huh, go on") to encourage the speaker and indicate you are listening.

Verbal and nonverbal responses need to be *nonjudgmental*. Now is not the time to tell the student that his or her behavior is stupid. If it is, the student probably already knows that, and you don't want to sound parental. Thus, do not emphasize your role as an authority while advising students. Nonjudgmental means suspending judgment, being neutral and accepting. It does not mean agreeing with the person. Here are examples of nonjudgmental responses:

"Tell me more."
"That does sound serious."
"I can see that you became angry."
"You're scared?"

The last two responses also illustrate a *focus on feelings*. Most professors are cognitively oriented, and focusing on feelings is awkward for them at first, but it is necessary for developing empathy with students. For example, even if you never faced failing a class, you have been afraid and frustrated. Thus you can empathize, even though the situation of failing a class is novel to you.

Don't interrupt needlessly, but when appropriate, ask the student open-ended questions (questions that can't be answered with a yes or no).

"How does that make you feel?"
"What are you scared of?"
"What happened then?"
"How will that course fit in your plan of study?"
"I'm confused. Can you go over what happened again?"

Open-ended questions keep the conversation going without overly directing the student. Do not ask questions that lead the student to what you think is the "correct" answer.

It is better to ask what and how than to ask why. Asking why may lead some students into tangents on their pasts and digressions into pop psychology, which are not fruitful directions. Stick with the present concern and, for problem solving, the future. Clarify your understanding and show students that you understand by reflecting (throwing phrases back to them) and paraphrasing what they have said. Summarizing is useful when students come to a stopping point. They will correct you if you have missed some subtlety.

Don't fake caring or listening. Unless you're a wonderful actor or actress, your nonverbal cues will give you away.

> TIP: Since active listening is a critically important skill in interacting with people, take a workshop on active listening.

Counseling Theory. Finally, it is helpful to use a simple *counseling theory* that helps you to conceptualize the situation and guides you while advising. Professional counselors use a variety of theories in their work. Professors have neither the time nor the need to learn complicated theories. I have found that modification of a method developed for crisis intervention is simple to use but robust enough to handle most situations, including the emergencies discussed in the next section. Edwards (1977) developed an ABC model of crisis intervention that Wankat and Oreovicz (1993, 203–205) modified to ABCF, the F being an optional follow-up. D'Andrea and Salovey (1983, 37–100), Egan (1998), and Hackney and Cormier (1996) discuss related but more detailed theories.

The basic assumption of crisis intervention is that students are functioning adults who are capable of coping with their situations and can make good decisions once they have explored the alternatives. The professor's goal is to help the students in the process, not decide for them or manipulate them to a "correct" solution. The ABCF steps in the crisis intervention model (Edwards, 1977; Wankat, 1980; Wankat & Oreovicz, 1993, 203–205) are as follows:

A. *Acquiring Information and Rapport.* First, the helper actively listens and guides the conversation with open-ended questions to simultaneously determine the information and develop rapport. Depending on the complexity of the problem and the individual student, this step can take from 30 seconds to 30 minutes. Emotional students need time to vent and become rational before possible solutions can be explored. Students may start with a "presenting problem," which although real, is not the problem that is bothering them the most. The presenting problem gives them an opportunity to feel you out and see if you can be trusted. By going slowly you gain trust and get past the presenting problem to the most important problem. Advisors need to make a judgment call regarding when a student needs only a quick resolution and when more time is needed.

Helpers often err in one of two ways. "Problem solvers" tend to rush step A to try to get to step B too quickly. We need patience. This is a common difficulty because professors want to "fix" students' problem and get on with other business. *Often people do not want solutions.* They want to be heard and understood. The opposite of problem solvers are "empathics," who want to develop empathy and actively listen. Empathics often never get to step B, although staying in the Acquiring step too long is rarely a serious problem. Effective advising requires a balance between these two extremes.

B. *Boiling Down the Problem.* Students do not always know what their problems are. Once you have conceptualized what the problem is, as perceived by the student, and the student is ready to hear it, you need to clearly state it.

> "The problem is that you don't like pharmacy, but you're feeling a lot of pressure from your parents to become a pharmacist?"

Adding some uncertainty to your voice gives students permission to disagree. If you hit the nail on the head, this step is short and you move on to step C. If you miss, return to step A. If you hurried through step A, it is easy to jump to an incorrect conclusion. And students who have not finished venting or don't quite trust you may deny a problem statement that ten minutes later they will agree with.

C. *Coping Plan or Decision.* Help students decide what to do or set up a plan to cope with the situation. This is *not* giving advice. Students are functional and can cope for themselves. This step may be quite straightforward.

"OK, which of these three electives do you want to take?"

Developing a coping plan may be somewhat more difficult, but it certainly lies within the province of academic advising.

"What steps do you plan on taking to study more effectively?"

An even more open-ended way to start the discussion of the coping plan is to ask,

"What is your plan?"

This question implies that the student should have a plan but leaves the delineation of the plan to the student (Glasser, 1965, 37). Since students are notorious for seeing only one possibility, ask them to generate alternatives.

"Good, that should help. What other things can you try?"

You may be able to suggest additional alternatives to consider. Then explore the probable consequences of different decisions.

"Will delaying math delay your graduation date?"

This is a leading question, and the advisor may already know the answer. At this point in the counseling process the advisor often needs to be more directive than during the Acquiring stage. Although some consequences may not be important to students (e.g., many students are in no hurry to graduate), be sure they are considered.

There are important academic factors that students forget or are unaware of (B. G. Davis, 1993, 377–378; Light, 1992, 43, 49–58). For example, they should consider class size when developing a class schedule. Encourage them to register for at least one small class each semester. Encourage students, particularly first-year students and transfer students, to join a small study group. Isolation and lack of involvement put a student at risk for dropping out. Encourage them to develop time management strategies (see section 8.6). This is also the appropriate time to be directive and make referrals.

"Are you familiar with the Study Skills Center? They have helped other students."

Although it is the student's responsibility to decide what action to take, the advisor can make it easier for the student to take action.

"Here's the phone number for the Women's Resource Center."

When the student has been quite upset, I may ask for his or her permission to call to make an appointment.

"Should I call and make an appointment for you?"

I then call and briefly explain the situation. When it comes time to set the appointment, I hand the phone to the student. If the student needs to discuss private information on the phone, I leave him or her alone in my office. Note that the ultimate responsibility still resides with the student, since a substantial percentage of counseling appointments are no-shows.

Usually the goal of the Coping step is for the student to develop an action plan. The more specific the plan, the more likely the student is to do it. Finally, summarize the student's action plan.

"OK, you plan to . . . and then . . . Does that include everything?"

F. *Follow-up.* Occasionally it is appropriate to informally or formally schedule *one* follow-up to see how the student is doing.

"After you check with the professor about the course prerequisites, call me and I can sign you up."
"Let me know how this works out."

If the student is in my class, I will sometimes catch him or her after class and do an informal follow-up.

After the advising session, make a few notes and store them in your advising folder. These notes are valuable if the student is a regular advisee or if you plan on a follow-up. They are also helpful when you reflect on which advising procedures appeared to work and which did not. While reflecting, note that it is the student, not you, who is ultimately responsible for the outcome (Dyer & Vriend, 1988, chapter 1). As Foster (1996) states, "Perhaps the most important characteristic of an effective helper is the ability to be freeing rather than controlling."

Improving Academic Advising

Active listening and advising skills are difficult to learn from books or lectures, although worksheets can be helpful (Cormier & Hackney (1999). The training of faculty advisors is discussed by Gordon (1992, 145–146), who states, "The lecture method is probably the least desirable method." Workshops that include role plays are clearly preferable. If not available on campus, a local crisis center may offer crisis intervention workshops for volunteers. Arranging to observe a skilled advisor in action, discussing cases with an advisor, and asking students for feedback on your advising can also be helpful.

Advising is time-consuming, but it can be made more efficient (B. G. Davis, 1993, 376–379; Goodman, 1992; Keegan, 1986; Wankat & Oreovicz, 1993, 202–203). Use referrals for counseling tasks that cannot be accomplished in at most two brief sessions with the student. Require students to come in for regular checkups on progress toward their degrees. Routine registration matters can often be handled efficiently by requiring students to come to a group meeting. It may be useful to distribute forms to the students ahead of time to start them thinking about what courses they want to take. If the program of study is tightly structured, many students will have almost identical plans of study. Perhaps 70 to 80 percent of the students can have their questions answered and complete their registration in a group meeting. Invite the other students to drop in for an individual meeting or, even better, set up an appointment.

Trained and supervised peer counselors (undergraduates or graduate students) can be effective academic advisors. (Cranshaw & Hughart, 1985; D'Andrea & Salovey, 1983; Gordon, 1992, 32–33, 151–152). Peer counselors who attended a half-day training program followed by a half-day of shadowing an experienced advisor greatly increased their skill levels and confidence and decreased errors (Wankat & Gaunt, 1994).

Computers are obviously appropriate for keeping student records. Delegate data entry to a secretary or work study student. Students appreciate computer programs that allow them access to their schedules and academic records, and this reduces some of the routine visits to advisors. Some computer programs for career advising are also excellent, but an advisor needs to be available for consultation.

The relationship between teaching and advising is used to improve advising in the voluntary Freshman Advisor Seminars at the Massachusetts Institute of Technology (MIT) (Merritt et al., 1997). Groups of eight first-year students are matched with a professor (the advisor) and an upper-class student in a seminar of great interest to the students. The interests may be vocational or avocational and may involve hands-on learning. The students receive modest credit and a pass/fail grade that ensures they will attend and prepare. The seminars provide for one-and-a-half hours of relaxed weekly contact with the professor, and students who need to talk individually with their advisor can do so at the end of the seminar. This method improved the rating of advising and essentially replaced the usual advising procedure. To a large extent, the seminars depend on faculty volunteers, but after ten years, finding interested faculty has not been a major problem at MIT. The very small class sizes used in this program may not be necessary—at Purdue University, orientation courses with forty students in a section also showed a significant increase in first-year student satisfaction with academic advising (Hatton et al., 1998).

Summary of Advising Techniques

The eight commandments of advising (D'Andrea & Salovey, 1983, p. 4) are as follows:

1. Be nonjudgmental.
2. Be empathic.
3. Don't give personal advice.

4. Avoid "why" questions.
5. Don't take responsibility for the student's problems.
6. Paraphrase instead of interpreting.
7. Stay in the here and now.
8. Put feelings first.

7.5. Crisis Intervention: What to Do When Students Have Severe Problems

College students have become more diverse, and the problems we read about in newspapers have invaded college campuses (Horning, 1998). Severe family problems such as a death in the family or divorce disrupt a student's ability to focus on studies. More students who are likely to have medical emergencies are attending classes. Even in relatively rural settings, students are beaten, robbed, and raped.

This section is *not* about playing psychologist. Even if they are trained as professional counselors or clinical psychologists, professors should *not* engage in personal counseling with their students. The American Counseling Assocation's professional code of ethics for counselors states, "Counselor educators do not serve as counselor to students or supervisees over whom they hold administrative, teaching, or evaluative roles unless this is a brief role associated with a training experience" (1995, section F.3.c). What all professors can do is handle emergencies and make appropriate referrals, and this is the focus of this section.

One of the paradoxes of counseling is that the more serious a crisis, the less formal training a person needs to be helpful (Edwards, 1977, 3–7). The disruption of normal coping mechanisms during a crisis makes people much more willing to accept help. Once they are helped past the crisis, their normally effective coping mechanisms reengage. Chronic problems are a signal that normal coping mechanisms are inadequate. Helping dysfunctional people requires professional intervention. The professor's role in chronic problems is limited to making appropriate referrals and, in a few specific incidents, notifying the authorities.

Crisis centers across the country use volunteers who are trained in crisis intervention techniques. The ABC and ABCF models discussed in the previous section were originally developed from crisis intervention experience (Edwards, 1977; Wankat, 1980) and, with the major modification of taking charge, are very effective for emergencies. Other crisis intervention models are similar (Hackney & Cormier, 1996, 308–314). Some experience with crisis intervention techniques will make you more prepared and confident to handle students with crises ranging from a death in the family, to a medical emergency, to extreme anger about a grade.

Crisis intervention training typically involves role plays and shadowing experienced volunteers (D'Andrea & Salovey, 1983; Delworth et al., 1972; Edwards, 1977). Only a modest amount of lectures and reading is used. O'Donnell and George (1977) found no significant differences in effectiveness ratings between trained volunteers and professionals. Both these groups scored significantly higher than untrained nonvolunteer controls. However, there is a need for in-service training or volunteers relapse into giving advice (D'Augelli et al., 1978). Everstine and Everstine (1983, 10–11) disagree with the use of volunteers and state that crisis intervention should use highly trained professionals.

A Death in the Family

A death or a very severe illness in the family is among the more common severe crises in students' lives. Professors become involved because the student misses a series of classes, perhaps a test, and does not hand in assignments on time. There are two tasks the student needs to deal with. The simplest is what to do about classes. You can help by being flexible on due dates for assignments and by giving makeup tests when necessary. Discuss other possibilities with the student, such as receiving an incomplete in the course and finishing the work before the next term starts. Students generally prefer to avoid incompletes, but the availability of this option may remove some of their time pressure. There is never any question that the work has to be done to receive the grade. The flexibility is on when it must be done. Be warm and supporting with these students. Later in the term, check informally on how they are doing.

The second major task is to deal with their grief. For a variety of reasons, they may not want to talk to you about it. Respect this wish. If a student does want to talk about death or dying, don't ignore it. Ignoring it tends to make it taboo, which does not help the student adjust. Listen to the student and use the ABCF counseling method discussed earlier. The goal of the Coping step is to see if he or she wants a referral to a professional counselor.

It is helpful to know a little about the stages of grief. Kubler-Ross (1969) identified the following five stages of grief that people go through when a loved one is dying:

1. Denial. It can't be happening. It's a mistake.
2. Anger. Why me? Anger at doctors for doing nothing. Anger at the universe.
3. Bargaining. Perhaps being good will change things. (This stage is brief.)
4. Depression. A sense of great loss.
5. Acceptance. Life goes on.

The entire recovery process can last a year or longer. However, most college students are relatively young and resilient. People recovering from a divorce go through similar stages (Fisher, 1981).

Emergencies

You may not want to deal with a medical emergency or a suicidal student. Why not let the professionals deal with it? You will, *once* the professionals are on the scene. Until then, it is better to know what to do. The helper must take charge and be directive during emergencies until any immediate danger is past. Taking over and becoming directive is the modification required in the counseling model. First, determine if 911 works on your campus. Locate the phone and fire exit closest to your classroom. After the immediate danger is past, the helper should revert to the crisis ABCF counseling model, which is much less directive.

Suppose you're teaching class as usual when a student slumps to the floor and lies unconscious. This is an obvious medical emergency (Horning, 1998). If you are trained in first aid/CPR, stay in the room and assist the student. Send a reliable student to call 911 or the medical emergency number. Tell that student to report to you after making the call or if unable to make the call. Ask this student to meet the emergency personnel at the building entrance and lead them to the classroom. If the student on the floor is cold or clammy, cover him or her with a blanket or coat (this treats shock). Authorities recommend that you ask the other students to leave the room (Horning, 1998).

If you aren't trained in first aid/CPR, ask if any of the students are trained. Assign a trained student to help the victim. If there are no trained people in the room, ask a reliable student or friend of the victim to stay with the victim. Go to the nearest phone and call 911. When you get back, ask one student to meet the emergency personnel at the building entrance. Ask the other students to leave the room.

After the incident is over, a short follow-up (the F step in the ABCF model) is appropriate. Visiting the student in the hospital has a very positive impact. Express your concern and find out if the student is OK. Since the medical emergency was public, ask the student if he or she wants to say a few words to the class thanking them for their concern. Realize that the student may be embarrassed by the incident.

Sometimes it's difficult to recognize that a medical problem is an emergency. It is better to err on the safe side. For example, if a colleague has chest pains, don't let him or her drive to the hospital. Call 911 or an ambulance, or drive the colleague to the emergency room.

Always treat fire alarms as real. If a fire alarm occurs while teaching, stop the lecture, calmly ask the students to gather their things, and march the class to the nearest exit. Although many campuses have a number of false alarms, treat fire alarms as real unless you are told that it is only a test.

Suicidal Students

Students (and faculty) commit suicide. A graduate student in my dorm hung himself. This is a somewhat unusual circumstance, but it had a big effect on me and the other graduate students. In the United States the annual suicide rate for college students (7.5 per 100,000) is half that for the age group overall (15.0 per 100,000) (Brennan, 1999). Reisberg's (1998) statistics are similar. This number is undoubtedly low, since many suicides are classified as accidents. Students age 25 or older, including graduate students, are at higher risk than younger students (Brennan, 1999).

Most people who try to commit suicide drop hints or leave clues ahead of time. If you have developed rapport with students, a student who becomes suicidal may drop hints to you. If the suicidal thoughts are a crisis and not chronic, you can often get the student past the crisis without the need for professional intervention. As a student I was twice able to talk fellow students out of suicide. For chronic conditions such as severe depression, amateurs (and professors are amateurs when it comes to crisis intervention) can help the person past a suicidal crisis, but long-term recovery requires professional intervention. The following discussion on suicide is based on my experience as a crisis center volunteer and on Brennan (1999), D'Andrea and Salovey (1983), Delfin

and Hartsough (1976), Edwards (1977), Everstine and Everstine (1983), and Shneidman (1996).

Suicidal people are often in extreme psychological pain. Use the Acquiring
step of the ABCF counseling model to explore this. It is helpful to identify this pain
and do what you can to reduce it. When a student gives hints of suicide, switch to
the Boiling Down step. Be blunt and firm when talking to suicidal people. Use the
"s" word. Ask, "Are you thinking of committing *suicide*?" If they aren't, your question will not start them thinking about it. Use other shock words, such as "die" or "kill
yourself."

Take charge and set clear boundaries for acceptable behavior (Hanna et al., 1999)
Do not allow students to do anything violent to themselves while you are talking to
them. If they show you a gun, say something such as, "That gun is making me nervous.
Please put it away." Note that this is directive but polite. "Please" is a magic word that
works even with highly agitated people (Everstine & Everstine, 1983, 26). I've never
had anyone show me a gun. However, I have asked crisis center callers to put a gun or
pills away. I know talking about death is gruesome, but it has shock value. The more
definite and lethal the plans, the more dangerous the situation. Guns and carbon
monoxide are the most dangerous; cutting one's wrist is the least dangerous.

With people who are considering suicide because of a crisis, time is your ally.
The longer they talk, the less likely suicide becomes. Talking helps most people reduce
their psychological pain. Use your active listening skills and have them talk about
what caused the crisis. Explore reasons to live. People are often suicidal because
they can think of no other alternatives. Finding options may end the suicidal crisis.
Talking about suicide is a clear sign that the student is at least ambivalent and maybe
really wants to be talked out of it. Try to reengage the student's support system, and
provide additional short-term support. For example, give the student the number of
the local crisis center or make an emergency appointment at the health center with a
psychologist. Before the student leaves, ask for a short-term promise. "Look, I want
you to do something for me. Promise that you won't kill yourself until after you have
called the crisis center [or visited the psychologist]." A suicidal person will make
and honor these short-term promises. Global promises, such as a promise to never
commit suicide, are not effective. A short-term promise leaves ultimate control in the
person's hands.

Professional counselors are expected to follow the code of ethics of the American
Counseling Association (1995, section B) that provides for exceptions to confidentiality in the case of "clear and imminent danger to the client or others or when legal
requirements demand." This brings up a dilemma. Should you respect or violate confidentiality? Edwards (1977, chapter 10) notes that confidentiality needs to be broken
when human life is endangered. She writes (p. 63), "When suicide or homicide are
imminent, the police should and must be brought in." If in doubt, consult with the university's psychologist or professional counselor, who is responsible for treatment of
suicidal students.

When the suicidal incident is over, talk to someone about it. Crisis intervention
with suicidal people is draining.

Rape and Child Abuse

Suppose you're working in your office in the evening and one of your students bursts in. She is crying and somewhat hysterical. You give her a tissue and help her to calm down. She then mumbles that she has been raped. At this point, I don't want to be there, either. But this emergency needs to be dealt with. In a calm voice, confirm that you heard correctly. "You were raped?" Once this is confirmed, ask her if she is scared that the rapist has followed her. If this is a possibility, lock the door and call 911 or the police immediately. Otherwise, insist that she receive prompt medical attention (Delfin & Hartsough, 1976; Everstine & Everstine, 1983). Either call 911 or take her to the emergency room. If she decides to prosecute, obtaining immediate medical attention is a good first step, since the medical authorities can witness any injuries and verify that intercourse occurred. Before you leave, make sure that she is in good hands and has support available.

Afterwards, do not avoid the student. Rape victims may feel soiled and be afraid that everyone else looks at them that way. Be friendly and say something inviting but not embarrassing, such as, "I know some people who can help if you want to talk." If she does come in, refer her to the appropriate professionals. Be directive. Ask for her permission and then call the number for her. Rape victims may develop chronic problems that require professional attention.

A second type of rape incident can occur. In this case the rape (or incest) is not recent. Once this has been determined, the goal of the Coping step is to have her obtain professional help for the chronic problem caused by the rape. Again, be directive and get help. Schmier (1995, 152–157) emotionally discusses his personal encounter with a survivor of incest. He referred her to professional help.

Child abuse causes grave responsibilities for anyone who listens. State laws require helping professionals to report cases of child abuse or suspected child abuse to the proper authorities. Are professors "helping professionals"? This is not always clear. If you know that child abuse is occurring or strongly suspect it, report it. To whom? Call your university's staff psychologist or a professional counselor. He or she can help you report it through professional channels. Proper reporting of death threats to the authorities and to the potential victim is also the law.

These traumas in students' lives will be traumatic for you also. Talking to someone after dealing with a traumatic situation is standard operating procedure at crisis centers. Talk to someone and vent some of your pent-up emotions. Respect confidentiality and do not reveal the student's name. Although these events are traumatic, there can also be a tremendous sense of satisfaction in knowing that you have truly helped someone in a crisis.

TIP: When you check out the classroom before the start of the term, spend a few minutes to plan what you would do in case of an emergency. Look for the exits and other ways out of the building. Determine where the nearest available phone is located. Finding a phone after normal working hours can be a challenge. Determine how to describe the location of the classroom to a 911 dispatcher.

Professor Lin didn't believe he would ever have to deal with an emergency, but he prepared just in case. Then one day the classroom became unusually warm. He was wondering why when the fire alarm went off. He felt the door with his hand and found that the door was very hot. Since he had already examined the room, he had a plan. He had two of the taller students climb out of one window and drop down to the ground. Then one-by-one the other students climbed out the window and were helped down. He even had the foresight to gather up all the books and coats in the room and toss them out another window. Jim was the last one out. Although the building was destroyed, no one was hurt. That was his most memorable class period and the class that he grew closest to.

7.6. Summary

Rapport with students can be developed in and out of class. Professors need to care for students and believe they are important. Learn and use students' names. Come to class early and stay late to answer questions and chat with students. Try to be friendly at all times, even when denying a student's request. Be available to students outside of class. Keep your office hours. Experiment with other means of communicating with students, such as e-mail and the World Wide Web. Volunteer to spend time with students in nonacademic settings. Avoid actions that can be misinterpreted, such as touching students or particularistic grading. Develop a course environment that minimizes cheating. If you suspect cheating, follow a procedure that is simple but provides for due process.

Motivating students is difficult because motivation is hidden, there are no universal motivators, the interaction process is complicated, and intrinsic motivation ultimately controls. Work to understand interactions with specific students. Then try to meet some of their needs. Avoid demotivating behaviors such as yelling and blaming.

Advising students on academic, professional, and career matters is important but often neglected. Advising is difficult since good advisors must be confidential and available, have up-to-date information, and tailor their advising style to what the student needs. Develop your listening skills and learn simple counseling procedures.

You can prepare for emergencies by mentally rehearsing what you would do in various emergencies, such as a fire, potential suicide, or medical emergency. Take charge, since the students consider you to be an authority figure and you probably know more about local facilities than the students. Once the immediate emergency is over, revert to a mode of operation that puts the student in charge of his or her life.

8 Undergraduates

Professor Sarah Appleton liked students, but now that she was busier, she found that she preferred students who already knew how to study and think critically, valued intellectual pursuits, and were well motivated. In other words, she liked the students who least needed to be taught, were intellectually similar to her, and made the least demands on her time. She wished all her students were intellectually mature and well motivated.

Most institutions have many students who are not in Sarah's preferred category. Only 5 percent of higher education institutions are highly selective, and most of the remaining institutions' students are not highly motivated intellectually (Matthews, 1997, 22; Pope, 1995, chapter 2). In the mid-1990s 63 percent of all high school graduates eventually went on to some form of higher education, and 33 percent of all high school graduates earned a four-year degree (Lucas, 1996, 103). Almost all high school graduates are admissible at some institution.

Demographic trends predict increasing enrollments. The number of 18- to 24-year-olds started to climb in 1998 after a 16-year decline. By 2010, this number is expected to reach the 1981 peak of 30.2 million. Traditional 18- to 24-year-old students are likely to primarily account for the growth in college students (Frances et al., 1999). One effect of this prolonged increase in the number of high school graduates will probably be an increase in the selectivity of many institutions (Frances et al., 1999).

A survey of faculty by the Higher Education Research Institute at the University of California, Los Angeles (UCLA), shows that most faculty are not thrilled by the quality of their students (Almanac, 1998, 32). Only 12 percent of the respondents thought that "most of the students are very bright" was a very descriptive attribute of their institution, and 48 percent thought that the quality of their students was satisfactory or very satisfactory. In a later survey, only 28.8 percent of faculty agreed strongly or somewhat that at their institution, "most students are well-prepared academically" (Magner, 1999b). The results from a survey on professors' views of the quality of students done by the Carnegie Foundation in 1984 (Boyer, 1987, 75) are in good agreement with the UCLA surveys, which shows that faculty have been unhappy about student quality for years.

Why don't all students enter college intellectually ready for college? Blaming everything on high schools misses the point. Students develop at different rates, depending on a mix of genetics and environment. If a student does not develop intellectually in high school, the development process needs to occur in college, or the student will be unsuccessful. Understanding the development of college students will help professors when confronted with these students.

Fortunately, most students are at developmental levels where they can understand, perhaps with difficulty, if they will but try. But they do not all try. Understanding a student's lack of motivation, at least in a general sense, may be the first step in reaching that student. However, motivating the unmotivated remains difficult.

There are students at the proper stage of development who are motivated but don't know how they learn best, don't know how to study effectively, don't manage their time well, and are ineffective and inefficient writers. Professors can help them learn how to learn. Students can learn effective study methods and how to cope with test anxiety. Spending a small part of class time on exploring the process of learning can have a major impact on students (Zinatelli & Dubé, 1999).

8.1. A Portrait of College Students

Most faculty had a reasonable understanding of students when they were students, but memories dim and students change. Moffatt (1989, 26) found that many faculty at Rutgers University did not know their students.

Statistical Characteristics of Students

The annual surveys of first-year college students done by the Higher Education Research Institute at UCLA present a changing picture of entering college students. The 1998 snapshot shows students who see themselves as middle-of-the-road and not overly interested in their studies (Reisberg, 1999a). The vast majority of these students were 18 (67 percent) or 19 (26 percent) and had just graduated from high school (94.5 percent). Physical disabilities were reported by 4 percent and learning disabilities by 3.5 percent. Thirty-seven percent of students said that neither of their parents had a higher education, and 30 percent had only one parent living at home. During the fall term 61 percent planned to live in a college dormitory, while 31 percent planned to live with parents or relatives. After the first year, only 15 percent will live in dorms (Matthews, 1997, 67).

Only 35 percent of the students had no concerns about financing college. Fourteen percent had major concerns and were not sure they would have the funds to complete college (Reisberg, 1999a). The numbers of students who selected college because it "offered financial assistance" (32 percent) or had "low tuition" (29 percent) were near all-time highs. Astin's (1998) review of the first 31 UCLA surveys found a significant increase in concern about paying for college from 1987 to 1996. That concern remains high. Professor Dalton Conley found that families without significant assets have difficulty affording a college education despite what appears to be an adequate income (see Miller, 1999). Many poor students struggle to pay for college, and lack of money is the number one reason students drop out (Levine and Nidiffer, 1996).

The students listed the following objectives as essential or very important (Reisberg, 1999a): "becoming very well-off financially" (74 percent); "raising a family" (73 percent); "becoming an authority in my field" (60 percent), and "helping others who are in difficulty" (60 percent). "Developing a meaningful philosophy of life" was chosen by 41 percent, down from greater than 80 percent in the late 1960s. These data paint the picture of a cadre of vocation-oriented students.

Fifty-seven percent of the students—a 14-year high—rated themselves as middle-of-the-road politically, while 21 percent were liberal and 19 percent were conservative (Reisberg, 1999a). Support for legal abortion dropped to 51 percent from 65 percent in 1990 (Astin, 1998). Agreement that casual sex is acceptable dropped to a record low 40 percent from the high of 52 percent in 1987. This question showed the largest gender-based difference: 54 percent of men agreed, compared with 28 percent of women (Reisberg, 1999a). The highest agreement (87 percent) was for the statement "Just because a man thinks that a woman has 'led him on' does not entitle him to have sex with her." First-year students were also generally in favor of federal control of handgun sales (83 percent), allowing employer drug testing (79 percent), prohibiting racist/sexist speech on campus (62 percent), and requiring wealthy people to pay a larger share of taxes (59 percent). They also thought there was too much concern for the rights of criminals (73 percent).

Continuing the high school grade inflation that started in the late 1960s, most entering students had good high school grades, with 32 percent receiving A+, A or A– grades (Reisberg, 1999a). Most were attending the college that was their first (72 percent) or second (20 percent) choice. The students were not overly interested in studying: A record 38 percent reported they had been bored in class during the last year, and only 33 percent (compared to 42 percent in 1989) reported studying six or more hours per week in high school. In contrast, 65 percent worked for pay and 78 percent socialized with friends six or more hours per week. Eighty percent had used the Internet for school projects, and almost two-thirds used e-mail.

Although the entering students were not engaged in studying hard to obtain an education, they had high educational aspirations (Reisberg, 1999a). Only 28 percent expected that their highest degree would be a bachelor's degree, while 39 percent expected a master's degree; 14 percent, a Ph.D. or Ed.D.; 7 percent, a medical, dental, or veterinary medicine degree; and 3 percent, a law degree.

In 1993, 40 percent of all undergraduates were 25 or older, and about 27 percent were 30 or older (Pascarella & Terenzini, 1998). In 1996, about 43 percent of all undergraduates attended school part-time. Approximately 28 percent of all U.S. colleges and universities are two-year institutions, and they enroll about 37 percent of all students (Pascarella & Terenzini, 1991, 613). These institutions have a much higher percentage of commuters and part-time students than do four-year institutions. More than half of all students commute to school, and more than one-third of campuses have no residential facilities. Contrast these numbers with the 93 percent of first-year students who were 18 or 19 and the 61 percent who planned to live in a college dormitory. The apparent contradictions in these two sets of numbers are explained by the nearly 70 percent of students who transfer, drop out, or flunk out. The United States has a traditional class of first-year students but a nontraditional group of students finishing or returning to college.

Most students do not finish at the college they start at, because many students make bad initial choices and some large schools practice "freshmanicide" (Pope, 1995, 1–2, 175). Attrition of first-year students ranges from 8.8 percent at highly selective institutions to 46.2 percent at open-admission institutions (Reisberg, 1999c). The percentages of students who complete college within five years of entering ranged from 82 percent at highly selective private institutions to 38 percent at open-admission public institutions (Tinto, 1993, 19).

Astin (1998) hypothesizes that the women's movement has had a major impact on women's college aspirations and attendance. There are now more women than men in college. The percentage of women entering college went from 46 percent in 1966 to 55 percent in 1996 (Astin, 1998). Women earn better grades, are less likely to cheat, and are more likely to go to graduate school than men (Page, 1997, 5). Despite earning higher grades in college, women average 4 points lower in the verbal and 35 points lower in math sections of the SAT and 0.2 points lower on the ACT (equivalent to 8 or 9 points on the SAT) (Page, 1997, 199). There has been a convergence of the educational aspirations of men and women, and, with few exceptions, such as engineering, women are majoring in what formerly were considered "male" careers. There has also been a convergence in male and female attitudes about values. One downside is that the attitudes toward smoking of women and men entering college crossed, with the percentage of women who are heavy smokers (16 percent) greater than the percentage of men who are (13 percent) in 1996. This compares to 13 percent and 19 percent, respectively, in 1966 and 17 percent and 11 percent, respectively, in 1978 (Astin, 1998).

Only a third of the entering students were in favor of laws prohibiting homosexual relationships (Reisberg, 1999a). Colleges are often relatively more tolerant than students' hometowns, and 6 percent of students identified themselves as gay, lesbian, or bisexual (Sherrill & Hardesty, 1994, 7).

From 1984 to 1994 there was a 5 percent increase in white students and a 61 percent increase in nonwhite students in college (Pascarella & Terenzini, 1998). The actual percentage of nonwhite students in college went from 18 percent in 1984 to 26 percent in 1994. Significantly more college students are female and nonwhite than most professors remember.

Six-year graduation rates were 56 percent for whites and 32 percent for African American students (Feagin et al., 1996, 136). Only 3 to 6 percent of students who have not earned a degree within six years will eventually do so ("Scholarships," 1999). Retention rates for black students are significantly higher at predominately black schools. Although only 27 percent of black students and 34 percent of black graduates attended predominately black schools, the overwhelming percentage of black professionals did (Lang, 1994). The majority of African American students at a predominately white campus said they had been mistreated by a white professor and a white administrator or clerk because of race at least once (Feagin et al., 1996, 84, 116). Bowen and Bok (1998), Feagin et al. (1996), Sidel (1994), and Singham (1998) offer thoughtful studies of racial issues in college. The good news is that previous discrimination against Catholic and Jewish people has largely disappeared (Altbach [1995] refers to professors, but this is probably true of students also). Professors need to remember that gender, sexual preference, and racial inequalities remain.

Students generally find that college is more difficult than high school. About half of students get lower grades in college than in high school, about 30 percent get the same grades, and 20 percent earn higher grades (Astin, 1993, 188).

Moffatt's Anthropological Analysis of Students

Although different institutions have different climates and students, a detailed study of one university is useful. Michael Moffatt (1989) studied students at Rutgers University in the 1970s and 1980s by living with them in their dormitories and extensively questioning students in his anthropology classes. Rutgers University appears to be relatively typical of large, research-oriented state universities. The dorms were heavily populated by first-year students. Although the students have changed somewhat since his studies, the picture he painted remains valuable.

The goals of students at Rutgers were to do well in class and have fun (make friends) (Moffatt, 1989, 34, 54, 58, 274). Balancing these two goals was important. Half the students said academic learning (credentials) and extracurricular activities were of equal influence, 40 percent said extracurricular activities were more important, and only 10 percent said academics had more influence. Most students felt they learned intellectually both in and out of class. Although students wanted to broaden their intellectual horizons, most thought college should have a useful vocational outcome.

Moffatt (1989, 34, 54, 58, 274, 301, 322) asked students to fill out extensive time logs. About one-sixth studied outside of class four to five hours per day, five days per week. This was considered hard studying. Many of these students were included in the 20 percent of students considered to be "brains." In the dorms the hard studiers were mocked mildly and sometimes affectionately. Apparently, other students respected their commitment. About half the students studied one to three hours a day, three or four days a week, for eleven weeks of the semester and studied hard during the remaining three weeks, when there were tests. About a quarter of the students were "blow-it-offs" who never studied until exams, when they crammed extensively. About two-thirds of students who tried all-nighters said they did more harm than good. Overall, the "average" student studied about two hours per day, four days per week. This contrasts sharply with the official Rutger's advice of 33 hours per week. Moffatt (1989, 321–322) notes that despite individual recollections to the contrary, most students did not study too hard in the past, either.

What did the students do with their time? Most left the campus on weekends. During the week, their days broke down as follows (Moffatt, 1989, 32–33):

Sleep	8 hours per day or more
Friendly fun	4 to 10 hours
Class and commuting to class	4 hours
Study	0 to 7 hours, average about 2
Organized extracurricular activity	1 to 2 hours (about 1/4 of the students)
Work	1 to 4 hours (about 1/8 of the students)

In addition, about 10 percent did some type of intramural or personal athletics (the intercollegiate athletes were sequestered in separate dorms) and 40 percent watched a modest amount of TV. Students partied on average 11.5 hours per week, and parties usually meant alcohol (Moffatt, 1989, 50). Time for eating and personal hygiene is not mentioned by Moffatt.

Moffatt's results show that for most students "college was about fun" (29) and friendship was "the core relationship in undergraduate culture" (41). Students expected everyone to be friendly and call others by their first name. They were relieved at the friendliness of the dorms but unhappy with what they perceived as the unfriendliness of bureaucrats and some professors. For first-year students, the dorms were the central place to spend time on campus. For noncommuters, 68 percent of college friends were made in the dorms. Commuters had far less access to college fun (62). Further investigation showed that not just fun but sexual fun was "at the very core of college life" (48). Moffatt devotes two chapters to this aspect of college life. According to the freshman survey data discussed earlier, sexual fun may be somewhat less important now.

Most of the students were proud to be in college (Moffatt, 1989, 50), and 90 percent of the students were satisfied with their education (272). Nationally, 83 percent of students at schools with more than 10,000 students were satisfied (Moffatt, 1989, 311). Unfortunately, the students' definition of academic satisfaction was "making the grade" (287), not substantial learning of the material. They compared Rutgers to life before college, not to an idealized picture of how college should be. In general, learning was passive and mechanistic, and most of the teaching was indifferent at best. The students clearly disliked large classes and "the herd approach to higher education" (292). Although 82 percent of the seniors said there was at least one professor who made a difference in their lives, only a few professors called students by name (291, 292). The students had little idea of what professors did with most of their time, and perhaps 99 percent of the professors were "virtually faceless" (290). Students could slide through Rutgers with little work if they stayed away from the hard majors. This picture of students complements the faculty survey discussed at the beginning of this chapter.

Contemporary Student Behaviors

Moffatt's results can be updated and completed in several ways. First, his data on study hours appears to be accurate. Flacks and Thomas (1998) suggest an average study time of fewer than 10 hours per week. Matthews (1997, 103) lists a 29-hour workweek, including classes, and states (48), "Many, many undergraduates never speak to a senior professor from one year to the next, or ever." Second, students, particularly affluent ones, are more cynical and often feel they are entitled to good grades whether or not they study (Matthews, 1997; Sacks, 1996). Third, drinking appears to be, if anything, more important now (Flacks & Thomas, 1998; Matthews, 1997, 82–85; Wechsler, 1996). Astin's (1998) data also showed an increase in drinking beer, particularly among women. Binge drinking and alcohol abuse not only are major problems for the abusers, but also produce a culture of disengagement rather than involvement. However, the good news is that although most students drink, they don't drink all the time and seldom get drunk (Reisberg, 1999b). The average A student consumes significantly fewer drinks per week than the average D or F student. Fourth, many students continue to struggle to pay for college (Levine & Nidiffer, 1996). Fifth, most of the older students who have returned to college and are commuting do not fit into any of these neat categories. Finally, every student deserves to be treated as an individual.

Although there are certainly institutions where students are much more intellectual and more involved than the picture painted here (Kuh et al., 1991; Pope, 1995), for most professors this is a reasonable representation of their residential students. The percentages of intellectual students and blow-it-offs vary from school to school and even within schools. Departments with reputations for being difficult have more students who are willing to study. Since the intellectual climate that undergraduates perceive depends more on their peers than on the faculty, it is important to have a critical mass of intellectual students. If there are too many blow-it-offs, the climate will deteriorate. Since grading practices vary significantly between departments at the same institution, departments do have some say in their intellectual climates. Most state universities are dominated by the middle-of-the-road students who do enough work to get by. How much work is enough is clearly influenced by the institution.

If we include graduate students, the majority of students in the United States are not 18 to 22 but over 25. Many of these older students attend part-time, commute to school, are wage earners, and have a family (Ehrlich, 1995, 41, 112–118; Wagschal & Wagschal, 1995). More than half are women, most of whom returned to school because of a life transition such as divorce or the children's leaving home. Male adult learners often return to school because of work transitions. All adult learners tend to be vocation oriented. They are usually motivated to succeed, are very grade conscious, and are anxious about failure. Unlike traditional students, who organize their lives around school, most adult students organize their lives around work, family, or something else. Thus they want class schedules different from those that traditional students want.

Professors who teach adults need to adapt their teaching (Wagschal & Wagschal, 1995). Since adult learners want to relate their life experiences to what they are learning, professors need to validate their experiential learning in addition to their learning from books. Adult learners usually want to talk about their experiences, not sit passively; thus, professors need to use interactive teaching methods such as cooperative groups, student presentations, and debates. Professors also need to listen, since many of the adult students are used to being listened to.

8.2. Cognitive Student Development

Developmental theories can help professors diagnose learning problems and sometimes find cures. I say "sometimes" because students always control their own learning. The development theories can be classified as cognitive theories such as those of Kitchener and King, Kohlberg, Perry, and Piaget, with numerous modifications of each; psychosocial theories such as those of Chickering, Erikson, and Loevinger; typological models such as the Myers-Briggs Type Indicator; and sociological theories of college impact, such as those by Astin and Tinto (Pascarella & Terenzini, 1991, 15–61; J. R. Davis, 1993, 60–93).

Piaget's Theory

Cognitive theory started with Jean Piaget, a Swiss psychologist-epistemologist-philosopher who was originally trained as a zoologist. He founded the study of the development of cognition in children. He was incredibly prolific—he published 20 papers on mollusks by the time he was 21 and more than 40 books before he died. Since Piaget is noted for being a difficult and obscure writer, I have used secondary sources. Phillips (1981) and Singer and Revenson (1997) are primers, Phillips (1975) is at an intermediate level, while Flavell et al. (1993) is advanced. Singer and Revenson (1997) are unique in using excerpts from children's books and cartoons to illustrate Piaget's theories. The danger in discussing Piaget is that his "ideas are particularly prone to distortion, oversimplification, and general misunderstanding" (Flavell et al., 1993, 4).

Piaget discovered that children go through four periods in their cognitive development. These periods and their approximate ages are as follows:

Sensorimotor	0 to 2 years
Preoperational	2 to 7 years
Concrete operational	7 to 11 years
Formal operational	11+ years

The transition ages are the earliest ages the transition can occur. The first two periods are of great importance in child development. In the sensorimotor period, very young children explore to learn about objects and their relationship to them. In the preoperational period, children first use and master language and then start to draw conclusions based on their perceptions. Their conclusions are often rigid, even though from the adult viewpoint they are erroneous.

Around age 7 or later children enter the concrete operational period, when they can do mental operations tied to real (concrete) objects. Thus, grade school teachers often have children manipulate objects when they learn arithmetic. Children in this period can understand conservation of amounts. In one famous Piagetian experiment, children are shown a glass containing a liquid. They watch as all the liquid is poured into a taller glass. When asked which glass holds more water, children in the preoperational period point to the taller one. Children in the concrete operational period can answer this and other conservation questions correctly. Human thinking in the concrete operational period is much more advanced than that of any other species, but it falls "far short of the intellectual accomplishments of an intelligent human adult" (Phillips, 1975, 120).

If all individuals made the transition to the next period, formal operations, before they were 18, the concrete operational period would be of little interest to college professors. Although some children make this transition as young as 11, many people never make the transition. Current estimates are that from 40 to 70 percent of adults in the United States routinely use formal operational thinking (Pintrich, 1992, 830). Thus, many college students are concrete operational thinkers or in a transitional phase between the two operational periods. Piaget's theories apply to a narrow type of logical, scientific thinking that is valued much more in the modern world than in previous eras. Concrete operational thinkers can be good workers who are valued in many occupations. However, since they don't know how to do abstract thinking, they will have great difficulty in many college classes.

Formal operational thinkers can generalize from one type of real object to another and to abstract notions. They consider what is logically possible, whether or not it is practical. They think about the future and about hypothetical things. They reason about relationships between real objects and between abstract ideas. They use scientific thinking (Flavell et al., 1993, 161). When people first start to use formal operations, they often believe their own cerebration is omnipotent, and they develop a number of idealistic schemes (Phillips, 1975, 132). Concrete operational thinkers cannot perform any of these operations.

Students in a transitional phase learn to apply formal operational thought in subjects that require it. These students may survive in college classes, although they encounter frequent difficulties. Concrete operational thinkers will be unable to perform if a course requires formal operational thought. They will not follow arguments and proofs in lectures and are likely to become frustrated. They may try to cope by memorizing everything. What they will not do is learn the material in the way the professor wants them to, because developmentally they *cannot*. Students who can do formal operations have higher success rates in college courses (Gardiner, 1994, 11).

Unfortunately, the transition to formal operational thinking appears to be extremely difficult if it occurs after age 18. Development of formal reasoning during college is erratic and slow (Gardiner, 1994, 12). Use of a learning cycle, such as Kolb's cycle (section 6.3), or an inquiry approach, which stresses inductive reasoning with concrete activities, can help students in transitional and concrete operational phases develop abstract reasoning skills (Pascarella & Terenzini, 1991, 628). It is important not to dispense "the truth" of logical-mathematical skills to such students. Instead they must be guided in seeing how to think from another point of view. Interacting with other students and peer tutoring can be helpful, since the relationship is more egalitarian and the students are more likely to try to reason things out for themselves (Phillips, 1975, 145). Piaget's theory is useful for understanding why some students are totally lost, but I am pessimistic about the ability of colleges to help students make the transition from concrete to formal operational thought.

Perry's Model of College Student Development

The theories of cognitive college student development by Perry (1970, 1981), Kitchener and King (1981, 1990), Baxter Magolda (1992), and Belenky et al. (1986) chronologically, but not in other ways, take up where Piaget left off. Although they differ in details, these studies found similar developmental paths. William G. Perry Jr., a Harvard psychologist, developed the prototype theory. Perry's theory is the best known and has had the most impact. Kurfiss (1988, 51–67), Moore (1994), and Wankat and Oreovicz (1993, 269–280) present fairly extensive reviews of Perry's model, and Schwehn (1993, 97–102) traces Perry's thought patterns to Henry Adams. To thoroughly understand this area, study Perry (1970) modified by Belenky et al. (1986).

Perry's investigators conducted open-ended interviews of men toward the end of each year of their four years at Harvard University. The interviews were taped and analyzed. The analysis of this very rich data set uncovered a pattern that was then used to rate another cadre of Harvard men. The results were reproducible. Perry included only a very small number of women from Radcliffe College in his study and has been criticized for having a sample that was overwhelmingly young men from privileged backgrounds. Other studies have now essentially duplicated most of Perry's scheme, except that (1) modifications need to be made for the development of many women (Baxter Magolda, 1992; Belenky et al., 1986), and (2) his sample rated significantly higher on Perry's scale than the average U.S. college student.

Perry found seven different positions (belief and thought patterns) and hypothesized two other positions at the ends of his continuum. These positions are generally seen as four major categories: dualism, multiplicity, relativism, and commitment within relativism. Students do not go from position to position uniformly. They may move to the next position in a few areas and remain stuck in a position in other areas.

Dualism.   In *dualism,* positions 1 and 2, students believe that there is a right and a wrong. Studying hard and following the rules will be rewarded with good grades. Perry did not observe any students in position 1, but hypothesized its existence from students' reports of how they had thought in high school. In position 2, students can dimly perceive that multiplicity exists but still believe the world is dualistic. Gray areas are an indication that the authorities are wrong or are playing games. Many professors are perceived as playing games at this stage. Students in position 2 want the professor to give *the* answer, and they become frustrated with professors who refuse to do this. Confrontation in class and particularly in the residence halls moves students from position 1 to 2. Perry found only a few freshmen at Harvard in position 2, but later studies at other institutions have found a much higher percentage of entering students in position 2 and a few in position 1. All studies have shown that college attendance reduces authoritarianism.

Multiplicity.   In *multiplicity,* positions 3 and 4, students start to see that there can be more than one answer to questions. In position 3, students believe that there is still a right answer although authorities may not be smart enough to know it. Eventually, the truth will be known. One major question students ask is, "How will my work be evaluated?" The students' certainty that hard work will lead to good grades erodes, and they believe they must convince professors with elegance or good expression.

In the latter half of the multiplicity category, position 4, students realize that there are areas where there are no clear right answers. Answers depend on context and there can be legitimate differences of opinion. Students are willing to look for multiple answers, yet, deep in their hearts, still believe that the world is basically dualistic and think it is partly their own limitations that prevent them from seeing the truth. Students can respond to the multiplicity required in courses in one of two ways. They may conform and produce "independent-like" thought to earn good grades. This transition is often triggered by getting low grades despite hard work. Fortunately, independent-like thought often leads to independent thought. The alternative response is to fight authority and believe that everyone has a right to his or her own opinion, since there is no way to determine that one opinion is better than another. These students believe that grading is totally arbitrary.

Men and women often make the transition into positions 3 and 4 differently. For most men, education plays a major role. Men in the humanities and social sciences usually make this transition as undergraduates. However, in business, engineering, and the physical sciences, most undergraduate courses are taught in a dualistic mode. It isn't until their senior case study, design, or research experiences that these students are exposed to multiplicity in their major. Thus men in these areas often graduate when they are at the transition between positions 2 and 3 or in position 3. These students are confronted with multiplicity in graduate school or on the job.

For most women, education in the classroom is less important for the transition to multiplicity ("subjective knowledge" and "transitional knowledge" are the terms used by Belenky et al., 1986, and Baxter Magolda, 1992, respectively). This shift tends to occur for women "after some crisis of trust in male authority in their daily lives, coupled with some confirmatory experience that they, too, could know something for sure" (Belenky et al., 1986, 58). The timing of this shift is quite variable.

Relativism. The transition to *relativism* ("procedural knowledge" and "independent knowing" in the schemes of Belenky et al., 1986, and Baxter Magolda, 1992, respectively) is the most profound in Perry's scheme, although it is a quiet revolution when it occurs. In position 5, the person sees the world as relative with dualism as a special case, instead of the other way around. The student's view of the world reverses. Position 5 is powerful, because students can be detached and objective. They can use various types of evidence to develop better or more likely answers. They no longer expect the professor to have the right answers, but instead see the professor as a source of expertise. Evaluation is no longer traumatic, since the detached students realize that the professor is evaluating their work, not them. The danger in position 5 is that decisions made earlier are now reexamined. "Values" that might have been used earlier are called into question, and there often does not appear to be a way to decide what is important. Thus, position 5 can be a period of crisis when career decisions and marriages falter. Although Perry saw many undergraduates in this position, that appears to be a unique characteristic of his sample. At most institutions, there are few students higher than position 4 under the age of 24. Position 5 may occur in graduate school or much later in life, when it is triggered by a crisis. Many college-educated people live their entire lives and never get past position 3 or 4.

Once again, men and women often differ. The majority of men and some women use objective knowledge or separate knowledge, that is, the traditional knowledge structure, to form opinions in position 5. This type of argument purposely removes the person's feelings. This is the traditional approach of higher education that has been most successful in the physical sciences and engineering. The opposite approach, connected knowledge, is favored by the majority of women and some men (Belenky et al., 1986; McEwen, 1996, 61–62; Palmer, 1983). In this case, the purpose of argument is to empathically understand others' views, not to win logical arguments. This approach is more contextual and allows both people to be right from their viewpoint.

In position 6, people start to see a way out of the quagmire of not having any values. They realize that they can, if they choose, make firm new commitments within a relativistic world. These new commitments may or may not confirm the old ones they made when the world appeared dualistic. Although they realize that they can make commitments, they are not ready to do so yet. Position 6 can be a relief, since people realize that there is a way out of their uncertainty and old commitments can be kept if they still make sense. Few undergraduates in the United States go through this transition, although it is not unusual for graduate students.

Commitment within Relativism.   The fourth category, *commitment within relativism* ("constructed knowledge" and "contextual knowledge," according to Belenky et al., 1986, and Baxter Magolda, 1992, respectively), was originally divided into three positions, although Perry did not observe any students in position 9, the highest level. These positions were not clearly delineated and now are usually treated as one. People first test the waters in relatively safe areas to be sure that making commitments really does work. As people find that commitments do work, they make them in more and more areas. At most institutions there are few undergraduates in this position, although advanced graduate students may be. The instructor needs to provide students in this position the freedom to learn what they need to learn. These students are certainly ready for independent research, a super problem-based learning course (see section 6.2), or experiential learning (see section 6.3.).

Growth versus No Growth.   Perry came to believe that movement to higher positions is *growth;* thus his model has an implicit value system. This value system may conflict with other value systems, such as fundamentalist religions. Growth is not inevitable; the alternatives are temporizing, retreat, and escape.

   Temporizing is a holding pattern or pause that lasts longer than a year. Students often appear to be resting and waiting for the energy to move on, or they may drift and wait for fate to decide. *Retreat* involves regression into lower level positions. Students may react to the stresses of multiplicity by retreating into position 1 and dropping out of college. Retreat may also occur from the uncertainties of relativism, position 5, or from the need to eventually make commitments, position 6, into the comfort of "everyone has the right to their own opinion," position 4. In *escape,* people avoid the need for commitment by staying detached in position 5 or 4. They can avoid questions of meaning, since they are very good at the technical aspects of their studies or careers. This is a position adopted by some professors. Neither retreat nor escape need be permanent. People are resilient and often find ways to continue growth after years of stagnation.

Applications of Perry's Model to Teaching

Professors can usually identify dualistic students by listening to their comments. Dualistic students have an absolutist view of the world and do not see shades of gray. Unfortunately, there is no simple way to quickly determine a person's level in Perry's model past position 3 or 4. This difficulty has inhibited the routine use of these models in the classroom, although teaching applications of Perry's theory and the related theories have been widely studied (Baxter Magolda, 1992; B. G. Davis, 1993, 177–180; J. R.

Davis, 1993, 71–72; Duffy & Jones, 1995, 61–67; Finster, 1991; Fitch & Culver, 1984; Kloss, 1994; Kurfiss, 1988, 63–67; McEwen, 1996, 60–65; Moore, 1994, 53–56; Schwehn, 1993, 98–99; Wankat & Oreovicz, 1993, 276–280).

Perry's model is useful for understanding the sometimes confusing behavior of students. Beyond this, professors need to make a value judgment. Should students be pushed to higher levels in Perry's scheme? Some colleges have clearly chosen not to, but most try. Some departments have implicitly decided to push students past duality, and to be hands off after this. This compromise often appears reasonable to practically oriented departments, since students will have trouble functioning from a dualistic position in an America that is clearly multiplistic. It is also much easier to nudge students to position 3 than it is to push them to position 6 or higher. Different disciplines and different departments vary widely in their effects on students' cognitive development (Pascarella & Terenzini, 1991, 592). Many could do much more if they chose to.

If they decide to foster development, colleges should encourage students to live on campus during the first year. Dormitory living appears to be one of the best methods to move students away from position 1 (Perry, 1970). It is probably impossible to live in a dorm at any reasonably diverse institution and stay in position 1. Once they start to pay attention to cognitive development, most college professors will be surprised at how *low* most college students' cognitive development is (J. R. Davis, 1993, 70). *Most college instructors, except for those in physical sciences and engineering, target instruction at levels that are too high*. This leads to mutual frustration. Students probably cannot understand questions that are two or more levels above their level. They can understand and are challenged by questions one level above theirs.

Highly structured courses with right or wrong answers, particularly those presented in a multiple-choice format, reinforce the lower levels. Although appropriate for many first-year students, these courses will not foster growth past position 2. Physical sciences, business, and engineering tend to teach undergraduate courses dualistically, and there is often little growth on Perry's scale of the students in these disciplines (Finster, 1989; Fitch & Culver, 1984). Fitch and Culver (1984) found that the mean position for engineering students is 2.8.

Growth is induced by courses that expose students to multiple points of view. Problems that require synthesis of several possible answers are useful, particularly if the context needs to be taken into account. Problems with partial credit challenge a strictly dualistic view. Writing and essay questions can lead to growth. Journals requiring reflection are useful. Experiential learning is useful when the students are developmentally ready for it. Other teaching methods that tend to induce growth include requiring students to take the opposite view, study it, and defend it in a paper or debate; having students do the highest level in Bloom's taxonomy, evaluation, for situations that require value judgments; and asking students for their evidence when they make statements. Model the appropriate behaviors and reward students who show growth. Encourage discussion among the whole class or in small groups, since it decreases students' perception of you as an authority figure. Use silence to encourage discussion. Finally, expect that students can grow and understand higher level reasoning.

Generalizations

An overview of cognitive development models shows that they have the following traits in common (Pascarella & Terenzini, 1991, 43–44):

1. Development depends on the individual.
2. Development is not in stages, but is continuous. The positions are plateaus. Most developmental effort occurs between positions.
3. Development is cumulative.
4. Behavior goes from simple to complex.
5. Development tends to be relatively orderly and follow a pattern from position to position.
6. The level of development is reflected in the tasks that need to be done.
7. Being ready is a necessary, but not sufficient condition for further development.
8. People recognize complexity before higher level changes actually occur.
9. Challenge to the current state is needed for further development to occur.
10. Detachment from self and empathy are needed for higher level development.

Perry's model also applies to the development of professors. Personal observation tells me that in disciplines that tend to be taught in a dualistic mode, such as engineering and physical sciences, it is perfectly possible and perhaps common to earn a Ph.D. and be no higher cognitively than position 4. Professors may escape and stay in position 4 for years or even their entire lives. I have also met people who retreated to position 1 after earning a Ph.D. Further development may occur when the person's comfortable lifestyle is interrupted by a severe challenge, such as denial of tenure, divorce, or the death of a parent. The latter two trials had a big effect on me. The pain of my divorce wrenched me out of position 4, leading to a six-year journey through positions 5 and 6 to commitment. Transition into position 5 led to somewhat unusual behavior and questioning of previous choices of lifestyle, which some friends interpreted as a midlife crisis. Continued growth into positions 6 and 7 eventually made me a more integrated person who was a more effective professor in both teaching and research.

8.3. Student Motivation: Maslow's Theory

"Unfortunately, there is no single magical formula for motivating students" (B. G. Davis, 1993, 193). Although there is no formula, a good theory can help one develop alternatives. In section 7.3, I analyzed the communication transactions involved in motivation. In this section I focus on Abraham Maslow's theory of motivation.

Most students attend college because they are vocation oriented. A survey of first-year students by the Higher Education Research Institute at UCLA (Reisberg, 1999a) reported that they come to college because their parents want them to come (40 percent), all their friends are coming (5 percent), they can't find a job (7 percent), or someone important to them encouraged them (16 percent) or because they want to find a better job (77 percent) and make more money (75 percent), prepare for a profession

(49 percent), gain a general education and appreciation of ideas (62 percent), get away from home (17 percent), improve reading and study skills (42 percent), or prove they can succeed (37 percent). We can probably add that they come because they couldn't think of anything else they would rather do.

The good news is that in a well-planned elective (student-selected) course with an enthusiastic instructor who cares for students, motivation is seldom a problem (Ericksen, 1974, 78), although the professor still needs to avoid demotivating behavior (see section 7.3). The bad news is that many students do not want to take required courses and so are initially unmotivated. It is up to the instructor to reach out to them.

Maslow's theory helps to explain students' behavior (Hoffman, 1988; Maslow, 1970). The vast majority of people follow a hierarchy of needs, as shown in Figure 8.1 (Wankat & Oreovicz, 1993, 299). At the bottom are physiological needs, such as air, water, food, and shelter. Once these needs are satisfied, students move to higher order needs. If one of these physiological needs is suddenly not satisfied, the higher order needs are temporarily forgotten as the student returns to the basics. For example, an evicted student will have a very difficult time focusing on classes until shelter is found. Financial aid is critically important because it helps provide for these most fundamental needs. The majority of students are worried at least to some extent about paying for college (Reisberg, 1999a). Professors can help by encouraging individual students to apply for the aid they are eligible for and helping students find appropriate part-time and summer jobs.

The next level in the hierarchy is the need for safety. Students who feel unsafe at night may not attend an optional help session, even though they would like to. Institutions can help by ensuring that all parts of campus are well lighted and frequently

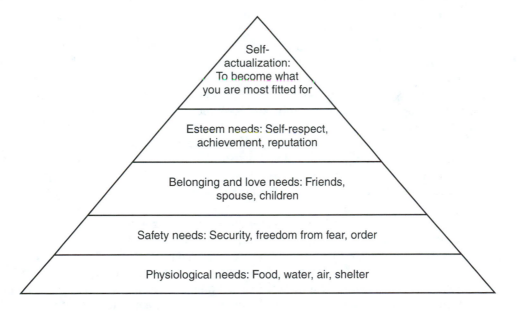

FIGURE 8.1. Maslow's (1970) hierarchy of needs. Reprinted with permission from Phillip C. Wankat and Frank S. Oreovicz, *Teaching Engineering* (New York: McGraw-Hill, 1993), p. 299.

patrolled. Professors can encourage a buddy system and allow a few minutes during the help session for students to arrange for rides and escorts. Students may prefer help sessions during the day. An incident on campus or even something that is scary although innocent can bring safety needs to the forefront and distract students' attention.

New students often have problems with the middle level of Maslow's hierarchy: belonging and love needs. First-year students and new graduate students have left their support systems at their high schools or undergraduate colleges. Within the first few weeks of the term they must start to develop a new support system. This transition is more difficult for first-year students, who are usually leaving home for the first time, but the transition can be difficult for new graduate students also. However, graduate students usually have a "home" department, a luxury most new undergraduates don't have yet. Orientation programs help new students adjust and feel they belong. Students who fail to adjust within about ten weeks often decide to leave the institution, although they may wait until the end of the term or school year to actually leave (Tinto, 1998). If you meet with prospective students, encourage them to live in the dorms and attend orientation.

The failure to satisfy belonging and love needs can occur at any time. When these needs are not met, they will take precedence over higher order needs. Students whose love interests turn sour, who have an ill parent or sibling, or who face the death of a parent or grandparent will be spending more energy coping with this problem than studying for class.

Students who feel they belong in a department or academic area satisfy part of their belonging needs within their department. This tends to be particularly true of graduate students and seniors. Studying with study groups or within their research team helps these students feel they belong. Thus they may react to a loss of belonging or love by studying more and working harder. Students who don't feel they belong to a department are likely to reduce time on academics when they have a loss of belonging or love. Students can also help to satisfy their belonging needs by joining a student club, fraternity, or sorority. Unfortunately, these organizations are often neutral or hostile toward academics.

Professor Jim Lin found he could help students feel they belong in his course. He learned their names, was friendly, and took the time to chat before or after class. In small classes he learned something personal about everyone, and he used some type of name game (see section 7.1) to help students learn one another's names early in the term. He also assigned students to permanent small groups to help develop intellectual communities. Being greeted by name helps his students feel they belong. Even his megalecture became more inviting after he asked students to introduce themselves to their neighbors in class.

Academics becomes very important in helping students satisfy esteem needs: self-respect, achievement, and reputation. It is important for students to have some successes, often signaled by good grades, in their courses. They also need some challenges, or they will not value their successes. Simultaneously challenging the better students while ensuring that the average and poorer students can have some success is difficult. "Challenge problems" that are not turned in are a way to motivate the best students. Frequent assignments, quizzes, and tests encourage students to spend more time on task, which results in more learning and more success. Students' GPAs are positively correlated with the number of hours per week spent studying (Astin, 1993, 190). Unfortunately, not all students believe this connection between the amount they study and the amount they learn, and many students who realize study is necessary do not have the self-control to study unless prodded by the instructor. However, the negative side to frequent assignments and tests is that students are less likely to grow into self-motivated learners. Perhaps other encouragement, such as question sheets and small-group assignments, can promote both student development and good study habits. Since a test grade of 30 percent is demotivating even if it is an above-average grade, sufficient time needs to be available on tests. Mastery learning is an effective motivational tool, since any student who is willing to work can be successful.

Achievement is motivating. Projects motivate students if they feel they have accomplished something. Local and national student competitions such as building a solar car, designing a paper airplane, or publishing a poem can build a sense of achievement. These contests should be devised in such a way that a large number of students feel they have accomplished something worthwhile. Students who have the opportunity to present a paper or poster at a meeting are motivated to finish. Professors can use this motivation by offering students such an opportunity. Extracurricular activities can also motivate and help students feel connected to the institution.

Money may have little or no motivating effect for students who have enough and believe they will always have enough. However, the potential to make money is motivating for approximately three-fourths of today's students. The desire to make money can act as a motivator at any of the four lower levels of Maslow's hierarchy. Poor students may be motivated to make money so they will never need to worry about food or shelter again or so they can move out of a dangerous neighborhood. Students may want money so they can buy things for loved ones. Money may also satisfy esteem needs, since making a large amount of money is widely considered to be a sign of success in America. Since the skills learned in some courses are readily marketable for internships and part-time and summer jobs, professors can use the potential for making money to motivate many students. The marketability of computer, laboratory, writing, and oral communication skills may not be obvious to students. Telling a few anecdotes of former and current students who parlayed these skills into lucrative jobs while they were students can help motivate. Relatively immediate gratification—a job and money in two to four months—is usually a more powerful motivator than a job in three or four years.

Maslow discovered the highest level of his hierarchy—self-actualization—by studying very high performing individuals. Self-actualization is the "full use and exploitation of talents, capacities, potentialities, etc. Such people seem to be fulfilling themselves and to be doing the best that they are capable of doing" (Maslow, 1970, 150). The self-actualized individual is also free of neurosis, psychosis, psychosomatic illness, or strong tendencies toward these. They are accepting of themselves, count their blessings, and don't see the need for much self-introspection. They usually invest much of their energy in their life's mission. Although they often win honors, these are less important to them than personal growth and satisfaction. They often have peak experiences. Self-actualized people can indeed be great "creators, seers, sages, saints, shakers, and movers. This can certainly give us hope for the future of the species even if they *are* uncommon. . . . And yet these very same people can at times be boring, irritating, petulant, selfish, angry, or depressed" (Maslow, 1970, 176).

Since people first need to satisfy their lower level needs, they are more likely to become self-actualized as they grow older. However, self-actualization is rare. Few undergraduates or graduate students are self-actualized—Maslow (1970, 150) found one student in 3,000. Most students are working mainly at the belonging or esteem levels. A minority of professors are self-actualized. The best thing an instructor or administrator can do for self-actualized people is to serve as a resource when asked and other than that stay out of their way.

Since few people reach self-actualization, one of the conclusions that can be drawn from Maslow's hierarchical theory is most people are never satisfied. Once they satisfy needs at one level, they become dissatisfied as higher level needs become apparent. This dissatisfaction can spur further growth.

Curiosity and cognitive needs do not neatly fit into Maslow's structure. These needs are present at all five levels, although they are relatively weak except in self-actualized people. Although it is hard work and often frustrating, the joy of learning is motivating. The joy of learning and curiosity are most evident in young children and self-actualized people. Both curiosity and the joy of learning are useful motivators.

Motivation of students can be highly effective and efficient. Sometimes a few carefully chosen words will unleash a student's intrinsic motivation. Enthusiastic, student-centered teaching often develops a classroom climate that encourages intrinsic motivation to learn (Fazey & Fazey, 1998). Involving the students in doing something increases learning, and success at learning is motivating (Race, 1998). Professors need to be creative to find the switch that turns on a student's motivation.

8.4. Learning Styles

Several different aspects of student learning styles have already been discussed. A major difference in how people learn, sensing versus intuition, was discussed in section 1.4. All things being equal, intuitive students have an advantage on timed tests (Felder & Silverman, 1988; Schroeder, 1993). At many less selective higher education institutions, approximately 75 percent of the faculty and 40 percent of the students are intuitive (Schroeder, 1993). This mismatch in teaching and learning styles will make learning more difficult for the majority of students. The differences between extraverts and introverts help to explain whether students want to work and study in groups or alone. The differences between thinking and feeling students in making decisions can lead to conflict in groups. Judging students want to control time and hence tend to do work ahead of time. Perceptive students, on the other hand, continue gathering information and wait until the last minute to finish. Higher education has traditionally valued the introverted-intuitive-thinking-judging style, although with the recent increase in group work extraverts are increasingly valued. One of the goals of individualization of teaching is to change teaching methods during a course so that all styles are valued (Fairhurst & Fairhurst, 1995).

Inductive versus deductive approaches were mentioned in sections 4.2 and 4.4. For most people, inductive approaches, which start with a number of specific cases and then induce the general rules, are the natural way to learn new material (Felder & Silverman, 1988). This is the way babies and children learn, and most people do not change as they mature. Inductive approaches work well because the knowledge structure can be constructed piece by piece. In beginning courses an inductive presentation is more effective than a deductive one. The deductive approach superficially seems more efficient, but it isn't, because most students won't learn with it. Deductive teaching styles can work well once the students have learned a rudimentary knowledge structure. Since professors already know the material, deductive approaches are seductive, and there is a tendency to use deductive textbooks and lectures where they are inappropriate.

Another important difference is the use of *visual and verbal learning modes* (Barbe & Milone, 1981; Dale, 1969; Felder & Silverman, 1988). People can also learn through the senses of touch, smell, and taste. The preferred mode for most people is visual, but attention span, learning, and memory are all improved when multiple modes are used. Learning and memory are weakest when purely verbal or purely visual information is received passively. Reading is considered a verbal mode of communication, since the information is encoded in words. Most people remember more of what they see than what they hear or read. Memory improves if they both hear and see something, as in watching a movie, looking at an exhibit, or watching a demonstration. Actively participating in a discussion or talk increases memory. Actively saying and doing something with both visual and verbal components usually results in the longest memory of events (Dale, 1969). Examples include being part of a dramatic presentation, simulating the real thing, and doing the real thing. The unfortunate conclusion is that students will automatically have relatively low recall in many lecture classes. Teaching and learning will improve if multiple modes are used.

The Kolb learning style model was discussed in section 6.3. Perhaps the most valuable idea from Kolb, which is applicable to all teaching, is *teaching around the cycle*. Teaching around the cycle purposely uses all four functions and goes around the circle in Figure 6.1. When this is done, all students can use their learning strengths during part of the cycle. Other learning style models also advocate teaching around a cycle. "Which model educators choose is almost immaterial; the instructional approaches that teach around the cycle for each of the models are essentially identical" (Felder, 1996, 22).

There has been a significant amount of research on *deep versus shallow approaches to learning*. This research reinforces the suggestion in section 4.2 to focus on depth. In deep approaches to learning, students focus on determining the meaning of what they are learning and making connections to what they already know (Claxton & Murrell, 1987, 24–25; Marton, 1988; Marton & Saljo, 1984; McKeachie, 1994, 289–290; McLeod, 1996; Ramsden, 1992, 38–84). Students using a deep approach to learning are likely to understand "*because they intended to understand and organized the information they read to that end*" (Ramsden, 1992, 42). Deep approaches to learning cause increased biochemical changes in the brain and can result in lasting changes in cognition and attitude (McLeod, 1996). Like many other "modern" ideas, deep approaches to learning can be traced to John Dewey (Ryan, 1995).

Students who use shallow approaches to learning focus on learning isolated tasks, often by memorization. Their goal is to reproduce the information and pass the course. They do not use understanding to determine meaning but instead depend on superficial form. In subjects such as physics and engineering, in which a number of equations have to be manipulated, students often use a particular type of shallow learning. They believe that if they find what appears to be the right equation, insert numbers, and calculate, they will get credit even if they have no understanding of the problem. A slightly more sophisticated version of this approach is to make sure the units are dimensionally correct. Unfortunately, shallow learning is an *imitation* of the discipline (Ramsden, 1992, 37). Students may survive and earn satisfactory grades, but they do not learn to reason or learn how to learn.

Although students generally prefer either deep or shallow approaches to learning, they can choose to do either. There are times when a shallow approach to learning is appropriate (e.g., memorizing a telephone number), but most college professors want their students to use a deep approach. Students who prefer a shallow approach are likely to find it difficult to use a deep approach. They have to learn how to think. Students who prefer a deep approach are likely to be unsatisfied and frustrated if forced to use a shallow approach.

Since most students attempt to do whatever the grading systems requires, the instructor can influence their approach to learning. Examinations that require memorization or can be answered from memory encourage a shallow approach to learning. Excessive workload and a rapid pace encourage a shallow approach, since the students will not have time to think, and thinking is required for a deep approach. Thus, examinations that are speed races encourage a shallow approach. To encourage a deep approach, it is essential to control content tyranny (see section 5.2). Students need practice on assignments that require understanding and cannot be completed by regurgitating the textbook or lectures. Tests need to be written in the same fashion, and there must be sufficient time for relatively slow students to finish. Either reduce the number of questions on the test or schedule more time.

Understanding learning styles in general and one's own learning style in particular is useful. Most professors assume that learning strategies that work for them work for everyone (Lenze & Dinham, 1999). Understanding the differences can help professors plan more effective teaching strategies and help students become more effective learners. Since students are interested in anything about themselves, they find inventories of learning styles interesting. I have successfully administered a learning style inventory in a required seminar and had students score their own inventories in class. The entire class of 120 students discussed the implications of different learning styles and the advantages of diversity in study groups. Several learning style inventories are available (Duffy & Jones, 1995, 171), and at least one is currently available free. Try the URL <http://www2.ncsu.edu/unity/lockers/user/f/felder/public/> and then click on "Index of Learning Styles."

8.5. Involving Students in the Academic and Social Life of the Institution

Students who become involved academically and socially in their college or university are much more likely to stay and graduate than those who do not (Astin, 1993; Pascarella & Terenzini, 1991; Pope, 1995; Tinto, 1993, 1998). Since most student attrition occurs during the first year of college, it is important to ensure that students become involved quickly. Contrary to the opinion of many professors, the majority of the students who leave have the capability to do college-level work, although they may not be performing at this level. The loss of these students is a considerable expense for the institution and the students. Institutions may try to compensate for early attrition by overpopulating the first-year class. This can lead to a downward spiral. The entering students take large, impersonal first-year classes that fail to involve them. Capable students earn poor grades because they aren't motivated and leave the institution because they are unhappy.

The downward attrition spiral continues in introductory classes in the disciplines, usually in the sophomore year, which are also often large, impersonal, and uninvolving. Many students transfer to another discipline or leave the university. Professors may find it difficult to develop rapport with students in large classes, particularly when they know that many of the students will not continue in the discipline.

Institutional Responsibilities

Although it is the students who must get involved, institutions can make it easier for them. First, most institutions strongly encourage first-year and transfer students to live in the dorms (Astin, 1993, 194, 367; Landis, 1995, 74–76; Pascarella & Terenzini, 1991, 611–613; Pope, 1995, 70). Living in an apartment off campus or commuting from home is isolating. Students make friends in the dorms (see section 8.1) and are more likely to stay at the university. Second, since large institutions tend to have lower retention rates than small ones, many larger institutions try to develop smaller, self-contained entities. One effective but expensive method to do this is an honors college (Astin, 1993, 379; Pascarella & Terenzini, 1991, 388). An inexpensive approach is the development of special-interest floors in the dorms (Moffatt, 1989). For example, floors for women in engineering have been successful in involving and retaining women in this discipline.

Third, extensive orientation programs either before classes start or throughout the first term can increase retention (Kuh et al., 1991, 8). Many textbooks are available for these programs (see section 8.6). Orientation programs help students meet other students and provide them with guidance for navigating the complex university bureaucracy. Since excessive red tape and rude staff are strong demotivators, institutions need to reduce these problems as much as possible. A fourth approach is to encourage the formation of student clubs, intramural athletics, and organizations. Students who become involved in a student organization are more likely to stay, and they benefit in other ways (see section 6.4). Of course, they need to balance social involvement and academics. A fifth approach is to encourage learning communities by registering students together as a block in the same sections of three or more large courses (Tinto, 1998). This helps students make friends in classes and facilitates the formation of study groups. Finally, the Posse Foundation has been successful in increasing the retention of urban, mainly minority students on campuses with few minority students (Pulley, 2000). The foundation's approach is to send a "posse" of about ten carefully selected students to the campus as a team.

Students need informal places on campus to meet (Pope, 1995, 69; Solomon & Solomon, 1993, 43–45). Students living in dorms have lounges in their buildings, but commuting students need a place to meet on campus, preferably a place with lockers. The biggest step to satisfy commuting students would be to solve the parking problem. (This would also make faculty happy.) Commuters, including those at community colleges, are much less likely to become involved (Astin, 1993, 366, 391; Pascarella & Terenzini, 1991, 590, 611, 641; Pope, 1995, 69–70). This, plus the difficulty in transferring to four-year colleges, translates into significantly lower rates of completion of the bachelor's degree for students who start at community colleges. The tragedy is that *if* these students had earned bachelor's degrees, where they entered college would not have made much difference (Pascarella & Terenzini, 1991, 590, 597, 641–642).

Faculty Responsibilities

Professors also have a role to play in involving students in the life at the institution. First, there is attitude. Supporting the aforementioned institutional efforts helps students, doesn't require much effort, and is in everybody's best interest. A slightly higher level of support is to encourage students to become involved. For example, encourage upper division students with good attitudes to become involved (often for pay) with the orientation and special-interest programs. Encourage the housing office to develop a special interest floor for your discipline. Encourage the registrar's office to routinely create learning communities by block registration instead of randomizing class assignments. Since these matters affect academics, professors, particularly an organization of professors such as the faculty senate, should be listened to.

Although the social involvement that these changes foster is important, academic involvement is more important (Tinto, 1998). Professors have a primary role in increasing their students' academic involvement. This is particularly important with first-year students and students who are just starting in their major.

Students want four basic things from professors and their classes (Chism, 1994, 225):

1. To feel welcome.
2. To be treated as individuals.
3. To feel they can fully participate.
4. To be treated fairly.

The lack of any one of these four tends to inhibit involvement and reduce student satisfaction and retention. Beyond these four basic desires, students want to learn in class and they appreciate becoming friends with the professor.

Increasing interaction between students and faculty and between students and other students increases retention (Astin, 1993, 196; Chism, 1994, 227; Pascarella & Terenzini, 1991, 620–623). Increasing class size tends to reduce retention, because it reduces the opportunities for participation. Informal out-of-class interactions between faculty and students seem to have the greatest impact, perhaps because they are relatively rare. Kuh and Vesper (1997) found that at baccalaureate colleges student–faculty interaction increased between 1990 and 1994 and the use of active learning remained constant. Unfortunately, at doctorate-granting universities both of these factors decreased. Interacting with a professor is particularly important for students with a learning disability, since they are much more likely to overcome their problems if they collaborate with individual faculty members (Pope, 1995, 29).

Teaching strategies such as peer teaching, collaborative learning, and individualized learning increase student involvement (Pascarella & Terenzini, 1991, 616, 619; Pope, 1995, 62–64; Tinto, 1998). Thus students learn more and are more likely to be retained. Encourage study groups, which increase student involvement, by encouraging collaboration on homework. Since this requires only adjusting your attitude, it is an efficient strategy. Some professors spend class time to set up study groups (Light, 1992, 21). Another effective method is to involve undergraduates in your research (Astin, 1993, 199; Landis, 1995, 177–178; Pope, 1995, 118; Tobias, 1992, 126, 162). Undergraduates who do research with a professor are more likely to go on to graduate school (Tobias, 1992). However, it is important to really involve the students in the research. Washing dishes in a laboratory or being a gofer doesn't have the same impact. Including undergraduates in research is time-consuming and should be counted as part of the professor's teaching load.

Supplemental Instruction

Although remedial education has had notable successes (e.g., at the Community College of Denver, Hebel, 1999), in general it has been under attack for doing what high schools should do. An alternative for struggling students is supplemental instruction (SI). Unlike students in remedial education, SI students take regular classes, but they receive supplemental instruction in the skills needed for the specific classes they are enrolled in. SI can be on a voluntary, no-credit basis (Martin & Arendale, 1994) or in a voluntary SI class for credit with required attendance (Tobias, 1992, 36–37). A required SI course is likely to be sabotaged by students who do not want to be there. Although usually done administratively, SI can also be set up by an individual faculty member.

It is important to clarify what happens and what does not happen in SI classes (Ainsworth et al., 1994; Arendale, 1994). The SI class is led by an instructor or trained undergraduate who is *not* involved in the grading of the course the SI class is attached to. This helps students see the instructor as a resource person whose mission is to help them. The SI leader neither lectures nor answers questions. These methods of learning are available in the regular course, but have not been sufficient for the students in the SI class. Instead, the SI leader monitors the students as they work in cooperative groups. The groups explore and discuss both the material and study skills, develop the specialized vocabulary needed for the course, solve problems, take practice tests, and so forth. The leader circulates among the groups to ensure that they stay on track and help those that become stuck. The SI leader can also act as a model student in the course by attending, taking good notes, and sharing how he or she learned the material. This description can also serve as a guide for an excellent recitation section.

Since the course instructor cannot also be the SI instructor, there is an additional expense. However, numerous studies show that SI helps the students who most need help (Kenney & Kallison, 1994; Widmar, 1994). Freshman engineering at Purdue University has used an essentially identical method called "counselor-tutorial instruction" since the early 1970s. Most students who are predicted to fail the required mathematics, chemistry, or physics courses on the basis of their high school grades and SAT scores pass these courses if they voluntarily take a one-credit SI course connected to the required course. If the cost of student attrition is included, SI produces a very high return on the modest investment required to hire SI instructors.

Departments

The student's department is a major subenvironment (Gardiner, 1994, 130; Pascarella & Terenzini, 1991, 613–614). Unfortunately, professors and staff in some departments are hostile to undergraduates. Improving the departmental environment is primarily an attitude factor. Being friendly and calling students by name help generate a more positive environment that will increase retention. Professors need to change their attitudes first, since staff and teaching assistants take their cues from professors.

Many of the things professors can do that involve students require little time. The most important factor is that we care about students. Since students who become more involved are more satisfied, learn more, and are more likely to graduate, a small amount of effort at critical moments can pay large dividends. Professors who become involved are also more likely to be satisfied.

8.6. Student Study Skills and Time Management

Students need to become academically involved. Unfortunately, as the data presented in section 8.1 make clear, most students are not studying enough. The most important issue—how to motivate the students to become more involved and study more—was discussed in sections 8.3 and 8.5. In this section I focus on how professors can help students be more effective and efficient in the time they do spend in class and studying.

There are a number of popular books written for new college students on how to adjust to and succeed in all aspects of college (e.g., Chickering & Schlossberg, 1995; Di Yanni, 1997; Farrar, 1988; Gardner & Jewler, 1995; Gerow & Gerow, 1997; Higgins et al., 1994; Landis, 1995; Van Blerkom, 1995). Books that focus more on the academic experience include Kahn (1992), Lenier and Maker (1998), and Robinson (1993). Any of these books will be useful *if* the students will read them. Professors will probably benefit from spending an hour skimming a few of these books (try your college library).

Many new students do not have a clue on how to take notes, study, prepare for and take tests, and manage their time. Professors can help students become better learners (Zinatelli & Dubé, 1999). Give advice. Hand out lists of good study practices such as those presented in Tables 8.1 to 8.4 and discuss these techniques. Help students set goals. Explain the consequences of poor study habits. Encourage students to use study groups. Spending class time on study methods is efficient if even a fraction of the class spends more time on out-of-class assignments every week. Tables 8.1 to 8.4 may be photocopied and passed out to students as long as the source is properly identified.

TABLE 8.1. Effective Student Use of Class Time

1. Motivate yourself:	Calculate the cost of each hour of instruction.
	Determine to get your money's worth. Don't skip class.
2. Come prepared:	Stay caught up on assignments.
	Review notes from the previous class.
	Quickly read the assignment before class.
	Warm up psychologically.
3. Appear interested:	Come a few minutes early.
	Pay attention and listen. Search for structure in the lecture.
	Take notes.
	Ask intelligent questions.
4. Note taking:	Paper is cheap. Don't try to save paper.
	Leave room on the page for later editing and additions.
	Date and number every page of your notes.
	Speed write and use abbreviations.
	Don't try to write everything.
	Start writing immediately, and don't stop before the professor does.
	Write the notes for yourself—experiment to find what works.
	Include key items, anything written on the board or overhead, all items in lists, anything the professor stresses or notes as important, answers to student questions, anything the professor seems to spend too much time on, and drawings.
	Pay particular attention to material that is not in the text, since the notes will be your only source.
	Include questions the teacher assigns or poses without answering.
	Add your own ideas to your notes, but initial them so that it is clear they are your ideas and not the professor's.
5. After Class:	Review and edit your notes.
	Add missed material.
	Complete words and ideas that are incomplete.
	Convert your notes to visual notes if you remember these better.
	Spell out abbreviations that may be forgotten later.
	Compare your notes with another student's.
	Highlight issues in the textbook that were discussed in class.
	Selectively mark key items with an asterisk (*) or a highlighter.
	Look up any jargon words you do not understand.
	Do *not* recopy your notes.
	Use e-mail to ask the professor or teaching assistant questions.

TABLE 8.2.   Effective Study Methods

1. Goal:	To understand the material.
2. When:	Think of going to college as an alternative to a job. If you weren't in college, you would be working 40 to 50 hours per week. Class plus study time should be at least the same amount.
	Study is most effective if done on a daily basis.
	Graduates with poor or average grades regret not studying more.
	Study after each class and before the next.
	Use odd moments: Don't go back to your room between classes—study instead.
	Study until the parties start after 9:00 P.M. Study during the day when you are alert. Don't wait until evening to get started.
	Don't let yourself get behind.
3. Where:	Find places where you can concentrate without being interrupted: library, empty classroom, study lounge, coffee shop, your room.
4. Reading:	Buy a copy of the textbook and other assigned materials.
	Skim the entire book, including preface, appendices, and index.
	Read the text using one of the standard reading procedures:
	P2R: Preview, Read, Review.
	SQ3R: Survey, Question, Read, Recite, Review.
	PQ4R: Preview, Question, Read, Write, Recall, Review.
	Include diagrams, figures, and tables in your reading.
	Adjust your reading rate to the difficulty of the material.
	Take notes in the text instead of highlighting or underlining.
	Reflect on your reading a day or two later.
	Develop and use flash cards to memorize material.
	Skim another text in addition to the required one.
5. Pattern:	Study for 50 minutes—break for 10. Repeat. Repeat again.
	If something in your life is distracting, write down your thoughts and feelings as they occur. Think about them during breaks.
	Do not study seven days a week. Take one day off.
6. Assignments:	Do the reading.
	Try the assignment by yourself first (50 to 75 percent of your study time).
	Then work on the assignment with your study group.
	If the group cannot do the assignment, see the professor or a teaching assistant.
	Turn assignments in on time.
7. Feedback:	Always read the comments on returned assignments.
	Determine what you did wrong to avoid repeating the mistakes.
	Consult with the professor, particularly if invited.

Methods for students' effective use of class time are summarized in Table 8.1 (Buxton, 1994; Di Yanni, 1997, chapters 3 and 6; Farrar, 1988, chapter 3; Gardner & Jewler, 1995, chapter 7; Gerow & Gerow, 1997, chapter 3; Kahn, 1992, 12–19; Landis, 1995, 90–91; Lenier & Maker, 1998, chapter 7; Robinson, 1993, 57, 86–87; Van Blerkom, 1995, chapter 5). You will help students take good notes if you logically organize the lecture and provide advance organizers or, in other words, give the students a brief outline and tell them how the lecture fits together. It also helps to give students time to think and reflect during a lecture (B. G. Davis, 1993, 182). If the class is small enough, collect and comment on their notes early in the semester. I find it useful to have a teaching assistant take notes during each lecture and then deposit them in a notebook in the reserve section of the library. This serves as a model of good notes and provides a resource for students who miss class.

Effective study methods are outlined in Table 8.2 (Buxton, 1994; Gerow & Gerow, 1997, chapter 4; Kahn, 1992, 20–38; Landis, 1995, 79–84; Lenier & Maker, 1998, chapters 4 to 6; Robinson, 1993, 83–86; Van Blerkom, 1995, chapter 6; Weinstein, 1994). Bowen and Bok (1998, 208) found that almost half of the graduates in the middle third and more than two-thirds of those in the bottom third of their classes regretted not studying more. Discuss the importance of study—note that coming to class is necessary but not sufficient. A small amount of credit will encourage more students to do the reading and assignments. Short, easy multiple-choice quizzes at the beginning of class encourage students to read the assignments. An alternative is to hand out question sheets that are to be turned in at the beginning of class. These and similar methods increase the students' comprehension of material during class and allow the professor to conduct a discussion or other activity that requires student understanding. Since learning-to-learn courses improve students' average GPAs by about 0.5 points on a four-point scale, suggest such a class for students who are trying but struggling (Polansky et al., 1993; Weinstein, 1994).

Students who work, particularly those with young families, may not have enough time and energy for studying. Students who work 10 or fewer hours per week are usually able to take a full course load without affecting their grades. Students who work around 20 hours per week should be advised to take no more than 12 credit hours, while those working 40 hours a week should take at most 8 (Landis, 1995, 74). Students who insist on working full-time and taking a full load are likely to flunk out. Advise them to restructure their timetable so that they will eventually graduate.

Methods to help students prepare for and take tests are outlined in Table 8.3 (Di Yanni, 1997, chapter 7; Gerow & Gerow, 1997, chapter 5; Kahn, 1992, 90–106; Landis, 1995, 94–95; Lenier & Maker, 1998, chapter 9; Robinson, 1993, 186–189; Van Blerkom, 1995, chapter 6). Discuss tests ahead of time and give the students previous tests as samples. The extent of the material to be covered on the test should be clear. The number of points for each question should be identified on the test. Students should have enough time to finish the test if they know the material and avoid mistakes.

Test anxiety is a major problem for many students. When professors are clear about what is to be learned and what will be on the test, students have more control, tend to study more, and are less anxious (Whitman et al., 1986, 23–28). Develop and use objectives. During tests, professors can help students who appear to be severely

TABLE 8.3.   Preparing for and Taking Tests

1. Goal:	Deep understanding of material.
2. Ahead of time:	Set your goals for the course.
	Study regularly. Students who study more get better grades.
	Review the text and your notes regularly. Find relations between topics.
3. Studying for the test:	Review material you have already read. Recite it to yourself.
	Summarize concisely. Develop a key relations chart.
	Teach material to others in your study group.
	Develop your own test by yourself or in your study group. Take this test with a time limit and an alarm clock.
	Get a good night's sleep the two nights before the test.
4. Before the test:	Eat breakfast if the test is in the morning.
	Collect everything you need for the test.
	Be sure you know when and where the test will be held.
	Arrive early. (arrive late, and you invariably start off poorly.)
	Arrange your materials to take the test.
5. Taking the test:	Take a deep breath and let it out slowly (relax).
	Write your name on the test. Read the test directions.
	Skim (preview) the entire test. Jot down any brief thoughts.
	Budget your time for each question on the basis of how important it is.
	Attack a question that you know how to answer first.
	Read the entire question again.
	Ask yourself what the professor wants.
	For essay questions, outline answers.
	Answer the question. Briefly review your answer.
	Ask yourself what is the best use of your remaining time, then move on to another question.
	If you're stuck, move on to another question.
	If you have answered all the questions and are stuck on one:
	Keep trying. Try a different approach.
	Systematically search your memory for a clue.
	If the test is an open-book test, look up key words in the index.
	If you finish the entire test early, don't leave. Check for errors.
6. Hand-in:	Arrange the test pages in order. Write your name on every page.
	Fasten the test pages together.
7. After the test:	Determine on your own the answer to questions you could not do.
	Always review the feedback on returned tests.

TABLE 8.4. Student Time Management

1. Goals:	Develop a time management system that works for you.
	Develop your written goals for college. Reviewing these goals will help when the workload seems excessive.
	Become involved as a leader in *one* extracurricular activity.
2. Schedule:	Keep a calendar or date book with all important test and project dates.
	List meetings and appointments.
	If you like detailed schedules, develop one.
	Schedule your studying at your best times during the day.
	If you have trouble getting things done, keep a detailed time log for two days. Control the time wasters.
3. To-Do lists:	Develop a to-do list every week. Update it daily.
	Be sure to look at the calendar when you prepare your to-do list.
	Check off items as you work on them.
4. Prioritize:	Not everything is of equal importance. Work on important tasks.
	Use the 80:20 rule (80 percent of the value comes from the first 20 percent of the work).
	Don't procrastinate. An early start on projects allows your subconscious to do some of the work.
	Learn to say no to distractions.
5. Writing papers:	Budget one or two days per page.
	Follow a plan: Collect information. Organize.
	Free-write (write as quickly as possible).
	Rewrite. Edit and revise. Rewrite again.
	Do footnotes, bibliography, etc.
	Read your paper again two days later.
	Break long papers into parts and work on one part at a time.
	Use a computer. Learn to compose while keyboarding.
6. Tips:	Be prepared to write down ideas at any time.
	Get to know at least two of your professors well.
	Teachers want you to think and talk as they do. Imitate them. Eventually you will learn a new method of self-expression.
	Use down time. Bring along a book or flash cards for waiting in lines or rides.
	Learn about yourself. Use the college's resources for career planning and psychological testing.
	Take classes to become computer literate.
	Arrange to have at least one success every day.
	Have fun every day.

stressed. Tell them to take a deep breath and slowly let it out (Borysenko, 1987) and then repeat this. This simple exercise may be sufficient to relax students enough that they can function. Treat severe cases, such as fainting, as emergencies (see section 7.5).

Time management tips for students are listed in Table 8.4. This table is in many ways a summary of chapters 2 and 3. Additional ideas are from Di Yanni (1997, chapter 2), Gerow and Gerow (1997, chapters 2 and 10), Kahn (1992, 38, 68–74), Landis (1995, 89, 92–93), Robinson (1993, 81–87), Traub (1994, 122–123), and Walesh (1995, 30–42). Surprisingly, I have found that the majority of students have not had (or at least they do not remember) formal instruction in how to manage their time. Even a few suggestions can help significantly.

8.7. Learning How to Learn

Ultimately, a college education must prepare students for change (Walesh, 1995, 406–407) and teach them how to learn (Ehrlich, 1995; Pope, 1995). People who know how to learn set up conditions that lead to learning (see section 4.2). This does *not* mean that they must learn things alone. There might be a course at a nearby college or on the web that will satisfy learning needs, or there may be an appropriate workshop at a professional convention. If there are no existing courses or workshops, motivated learners may organize a group to study together or hire a tutor. The ability to select appropriate courses or workshops, hire the appropriate tutor, and organize a study group are all part of knowing how to learn.

Students need to learn how to benefit from structured learning situations. This includes developing good attitudes, expecting to learn the material, becoming involved, using a deep learning style, actively processing material, generating visual images, practicing, asking questions, cooperating with other students, taking the opportunity to teach and be taught by others, and spending time on task. If the instructor does not follow learning principles, students who know how to learn can ask appropriate questions, such as, "Which concepts are key?" and "What are the best resources?" They develop a structured hierarchy of content and ask for the instructor's help improving it. If the instructor follows a deductive style, the students ask for examples. Independent learners are proactive in searching out additional learning materials by looking at other textbooks, searching the web, and using the library.

Learning alone also requires good learning principles that start with a positive "I can" attitude. The student searches for books, web pages, or other sources that will facilitate learning. He or she looks for sources that use an inductive approach, give concrete examples, guide the learner, and develop a structured hierarchy of material. If none of the sources do this in a satisfactory manner, the student develops a hierarchy, key relations charts, and examples that illustrate the principles. The student also uses good study habits—doing deep processing, developing visuals, practicing, spending time on task, asking and answering questions about the material, and evaluating his or her own work.

Since learning how to learn is an important goal, help students understand what helps them learn. Even good learners are often unaware of what they do. They need to reflectively process the steps used to learn; otherwise, these learning tools may not be consciously available when the situation changes. For example, students with excellent undergraduate records may stumble in graduate school. As an undergraduate, they had support systems available such as informal study groups. Alone at a new school they are scared and try to go it alone instead of building the same mechanisms that worked when they were undergraduates. Encourage introspection (e.g., in a journal) about learning.

Sometime during their years in college, students should learn a theory of learning styles and learning cycles such as Kolb's theory (see section 6.3), the 4MAT theory (McCarthy, 1987), right left brain theories (Herrmann, 1990; Lumsdaine & Lumsdaine, 1993), or the Learning Style Descriptor (Landis, 1995, 125–127). Any theory that they can understand and use will do. Understanding learning styles will help them be effective in groups and cope with teachers whom they see as difficult.

Students need to practice independent learning in the controlled and relatively safe atmosphere of the university. Seniors should have assignments to learn material without the guidance of a professor, and they must receive feedback not only about how well they learned the material but also about the process they used to learn the material.

8.8. Summary

Higher education in the United States serves a large, and currently increasing, number of students. Most first-year students are in the traditional age bracket and live on campus; most older students live off campus. Surveys indicate that students' academic workweeks are light, which may justify some of the faculty grumbling about student quality. Moffatt's anthropological analysis showed that students want to balance academic work with fun.

Piaget's theory of intellectual development helps explain in what ways some students are not ready for academically rigorous classes. Unfortunately, the theory does not provide a recipe to ensure that all high school graduates are ready for college or to help them develop into formal operational thinkers once they are in college. Perry's model is the prototype of theories of cognitive development in college that show students growing from a dualistic right-versus-wrong thinking to, first, a realization that the world allows multiple answers and, eventually, a relativistic view. Many students become stalled in the multiplistic range. Since there are methods that encourage student "growth" on Perry's scale, the question for professors and institutions is whether they should encourage this growth. My personal answer is yes, but I may be biased by teaching in one of the areas where little growth is observed.

Since students control their learning, motivation is important. Professors need to use the vocational interests of students to find motivating factors. Maslow's theory helps explain why actions motivate different students. Efforts focused at the levels of belonging needs and esteem needs are often effective. Academic success is often very motivating. Professors can help by varying their teaching styles, since this allows more students to experience success in class.

Students can also be motivated by involving them academically and socially in the institution. Encourage students to become involved in class and in extracurricular activities. Interact with students both in and out of class. Use teaching strategies, such as cooperative group methods, that increase student involvement. Help develop supplemental instruction for students who struggle. In my opinion, the most important factor is to expect and encourage deep approaches to learning.

Teaching students to become better learners is effective and efficient because it has a multiplier effect. If an hour of class time during the semester encourages students to study one hour more per week, for every student you gain about fourteen hours of time on task during the semester. If they also become more efficient in their study time, student learning can increase significantly. And if they learn to learn on their own, some of the content that was formerly covered in class can be learned outside of class. Spending class time on learning processes is a win–win situation for students and professors.

CHAPTER

9

Graduate Students and Graduate Programs

Professor Seth Atkins was in charge of the ad hoc committee to study his department's master's and Ph.D. programs. The number of applicants and the enrollment of new students in the master's program were at all-time highs, but there were frequent student complaints and students were quitting the program. Even more distressing, graduates and the employers of graduates reported that the program had not prepared them for their professional responsibilities. As Seth talked to the departmental faculty, he found they had very different views on the importance of the master's program, its purpose, whether there really was a problem, and what could be done.

The department's Ph.D. program was well respected and received a number of good applicants, but many of the best applicants were going to other schools, and only half of those who matriculated ever received Ph.D.s. Graduates often had difficulty finding academic positions, and those who went into other areas complained they were not prepared for the job market. The faculty agreed on the importance of the Ph.D. program but disagreed on everything else about it.

In this chapter I discuss how the education of graduate students can be made more effective and reasonably efficient. After presenting a brief statistical portrait of graduate students, I list improvements that may be made in graduate programs and explain methods professors can use to work effectively with teaching assistants (TAs) and help Ph.D. students learn how to teach. In the last section, I discuss advising students in their research.

9.1. A Portrait of Graduate Students

The biggest surprise I had in collecting data for this book is the large number of people in the United States who earn graduate degrees, particularly master's degrees. In 1990 approximately 20 percent of all adults in the United States had earned a four-year college degree. More than one-third had continued on to earn a graduate degree (Almanac, 1998, 6). In 1994–95, more than 1,160,000 bachelor's degrees, 397,000 master's degrees, 75,000 professional degrees, and 44,000 doctorates were awarded in the United States (Almanac, 1998, 26). The total number of advanced degrees is almost half the number of bachelor's degrees! The growth in advanced degrees, particularly master's degrees, has significantly outstripped the growth in bachelor's degrees.

In 1966, 40 percent of women and almost 60 percent of men entering college expected to earn an advanced degree. By 1996, these expectations had increased to 66 percent of the women and 65 percent of the men (Astin, 1998). In 1994–95, women received 55 percent of master's degrees awarded (Almanac, 1998, 24). Women also expected to earn more medical, dental, and law degrees than men. Excluding engineering and science, more than half of new Ph.D.s are awarded to women (Schuster, 1993).

The master's degree has become largely a professional degree. More than a quarter of the master's degrees are awarded in education and slightly less than a quarter are awarded in business. Education is unique since almost as many master's degrees as bachelor's degrees are earned. About 80 percent of the almost 2 million students enrolled for an advanced degree are studying to earn a master's degree (Almanac, 1998, 19; Press, 1997, 7), and about two-thirds of these students are in part-time programs (Conrad et al., 1993, xiv). More than 70 percent of the master's degrees are non-thesis degrees, and this percentage continues to increase (Conrad et al., 1993, 22).

More than half of the professional degrees were awarded in law, with another 20 percent in medicine (Almanac, 1998, 24). Doctoral degrees were split, with 35 percent in natural sciences, 16 percent each in education and social sciences, 15 percent in engineering, and 12 percent in arts and humanities. Sixty percent of the doctoral degrees are awarded to men.

In 1996, 65 percent of the doctorates were awarded to U.S. citizens and another 9 percent to permanent residents who were not citizens. Of these degrees, 0.6 percent were awarded to American Indians, 3.5 percent to Hispanics, 4.6 percent to African Americans, 11.7 percent to Asian Americans, and 78.4 percent to white, non-Hispanic Americans (Almanac, 1998, 24). Fewer African Americans received doctorates in 1991 than in 1980 (Sidel, 1994, 44). The number of doctorates per thousand of population—African Americans, 17; Hispanics, 22; whites, 65; and Asian Americans, 189 (Bowen & Rudenstine, 1992, 40)—further highlights the racial inequalities.

The number of institutions granting advanced degrees has increased as institutions have sought to raise their status (Bowen & Rudenstine, 1992, 19–20; Conrad et al., 1993, 18). Doctorate degrees are awarded by more than 350 U.S. institutions, although the lowest 20 percent of these institutions award very few doctorates (Bowen & Rudenstine, 1992, 20). The top 35 schools granted more than 40 percent of the doctorates. Master's degrees were awarded by 1,192 institutions in 1985 (Conrad et al., 1993, 18), and the number has surely increased significantly. In the United States, approximately 42 percent of full-time faculty teach at doctorate-granting institutions and another 25 percent at institutions that grant master's degrees but not doctorates (Almanac, 1998, 29). About one-third of the professoriate teach at institutions that do not offer advanced degrees.

Most students feel intellectually inadequate at the start of graduate school (Getman, 1992, 8). One positive result of this is they often study hard. In the early 1970s, first-year graduate students studied twenty or more hours per week outside of class (Baird, 1974, 67–98), which was considerably more than undergraduates. Graduate students receive about the same grades in graduate school as they received as undergraduates.

A 1999 survey of graduate students in engineering and science by the National Association of Graduate-Professional Students (NAGPS, 1999) showed that 85 percent of the students were satisfied with their education, 78 percent were satisfied with academic supervision from their advisor, 76 percent were satisfied with their program, and 74 percent thought that the teaching of graduate courses was excellent. Since professors and departments are rated mainly on the basis of research, it should be no surprise that national ratings do not correlate with student satisfaction with teaching (Friedman, 1987, 25–33). Half of the students thought they were inadequately trained for teaching assignments, and only 37 percent agreed they were adequately supervised while teaching (NAGPS, 1999). A survey of doctoral students conducted by Chris M. Golde (Magner, 2000) found more dissatisfaction: One-third were unhappy with the organization of their doctoral program and one-fourth wanted to be able to take more courses outside their department.

Master's degree programs are highly variable and range from 24 to 60 credit hours (Peters, 1992, 113). Although most part-time students enroll in programs with hours in the lower part of the range, they often take 5 to 10 years to finish and attrition is high. For these students, many of whom are taking courses by distance education, the master's degree is a relatively low priority unless it is a job requirement. The reason for the large number of master's degrees in education is precisely that it often is a job requirement.

The 50 percent attrition rate of Ph.D. students and the average time to degree, which ranges from 4.9 years for chemists to 12 years in education, are widely believed to be too high (Bowen & Rudenstine, 1992). More than half of the attrition occurs during the first two years, while students take courses. Some early attrition is inevitable as students find they have made a mistake in the field or school chosen. The attrition and delayed graduation times of ABD (all but dissertation) students is much more costly in terms of time and money. Attrition increases when the time to degree increases. Only 60 percent of graduate students who responded to the NAGPS (1999) survey thought their programs adequately controlled the time to degree. These important issues are revisited in sections 9.2 and 9.5.

9.2. Improving Graduate Programs and Graduate Courses

Graduate programs, which are controlled by individual departments, vary much more than undergraduate programs, which are controlled by the institution and outside accreditation agencies (Conrad et al., 1993; Jerrard & Jerrard, 1998; Rosovsky, 1990, 148). Master's programs in disciplines that do not accredit the master's degree (e.g., liberal arts, engineering, or science) vary significantly. Some are essentially extensions of the undergraduate program, while others require an extensive research thesis and are essentially miniature Ph.D. programs. Doctorate programs also vary significantly, particularly across disciplines. Professional programs such as medicine, law, pharmacy, and social work, which are accredited, are relatively uniform in their requirements, but there is no agreement across disciplines.

Master's Programs

In the United States, earning a bachelor's degree is now seen as necessary for economic survival and is no longer considered a mark of distinction. Thus the master's degree has become the new goal for many students. It is considered to be the first professional degree in many disciplines, has become the key to economic success, and is the next mass degree (Clark, 1995, 242–243). A 1995 National Science Foundation (NSF) workshop (see Chapman, 1997) called for the "revitalization of the MS degree."

In a major effort to make some sense of the broad range of master's programs available, Conrad et al. (1993) classified programs into categories on the basis of five questions:

1. What approach is used for teaching and learning? Teaching can be mainly *didactic,* using lectures to transfer knowledge from the faculty to the students, *facilitative,* with hands-on learning to help the students learn, or *dialogical,* with students and faculty learning from each other.
2. What is the program orientation? It can be *academic,* focusing on theory and academic values; *professional,* focusing on applied practical knowledge and professional values; or *connected,* embracing both theory and application.
3. Is departmental support weak (the bachelor's degree or doctorate is more important)?
4. Is institutional support weak (the program is not perceived to contribute to the mission of, enhance the reputation of, or provide resources for the institution)?
5. What is the student culture? It can be *individualistic* (often with considerable student competition), with the faculty perceived as the source of information; *participative,* consisting of cooperative interactions among students; or *synergistic,* with collaborative learning and active learning communities. Note that the faculty and the environment as well as the students affect the student culture.

The combinations of answers to these five questions can result in 108 patterns, which is too many to be useful. However, since answers to the questions are not independent, many of these patterns did not occur. In addition, the answers to the first three questions were considered to be more important. By employing flexibility in fitting programs into categories, the authors classified master's programs into four categories:

Ancillary (secondary to the Ph.D. program): Didactic teaching, academic orientation, weak departmental and institutional support, and individualistic student culture.

Career advancement: Didactic teaching, professional orientation, usually strong departmental and perhaps institutional support, and usually individualistic student culture.

Apprenticeship: Facilitative teaching, usually academic orientation, strong department but weak institutional support, and synergistic student culture in more than half the cases.

Community-centered: Dialogical teaching, usually connected orientation, strong departmental support, strong institutional support in half the cases, and synergistic or participative student culture.

Conrad et al. (1993, chapter 10) used this classification scheme to analyze the programs and determine what could be done to improve them. They found that high-quality master's programs are characterized by:

- Unity of purpose among administration, faculty, and students
- Students with strong commitment to learning
- Student input and a leader at the school who listens
- Strong program leadership
- Critical mass of students and faculty
- Faculty committed to master's education in discipline
- Faculty with professional work experience
- Core course work at appropriate level that provides broad understanding of field
- Doing-centered learning (students practice what they will do on the job)
- Balance between theory and practice (Clifford & Guthrie, 1988, 231, 233)
- Requirement of tangible product, such as thesis or project
- Immersion of students and faculty in an intensive, in-depth program (part-time programs use intensive weekends or summer offerings to immerse the participants, and full-time students may also benefit from immersion techniques)
- Sustained, time-intensive individual attention from faculty or advanced doctoral students
- Simultaneous cooperative support and rigorous intellectual challenge
- An atmosphere that encourages risk taking
- Strong departmental and institutional support that is necessary but not sufficient

Teaching graduate students means more than disseminating information. High-quality programs use many of the teaching methods discussed in Chapter 6. Encourage students to learn from and teach each other. Encourage student dialogue both inside and outside of class. Expect and require graduate students to come to class prepared. Students need to learn both tangible knowledge (e.g., codified content) and tacit knowledge (e.g., a questioning but positive attitude toward learning) (Clark, 1995, 232–233). There needs to be a discipline-dependent balance of education and training.

None of the ancillary programs were considered high quality (Conrad et al., 1993). Significant improvement of these programs will require a major change in attitude and support. Assuming they have strong support, career advancement, apprenticeship, and community-centered programs can improve by making sure there is a critical mass of committed students, increasing cooperative and hands-on teaching, encouraging student cooperation, providing immersion experiences, involving students in doing what professionals do, requiring a tangible product, increasing student–faculty interactions, and strengthening leadership. Note that part-time programs can be of high quality (Conrad et al., 1993). Individual faculty members who teach the courses and control field experiences can institute many of the changes needed to improve programs.

Ph.D. Programs

We can extend this analysis to Ph.D. programs by noting that most Ph.D. programs naturally have a period when students focus on courses and a period when they focus on research. I categorize Ph.D. programs as follows:

Nonsupportive Ph.D.: Didactic teaching with individualistic student culture in courses; noninteractive professors with individualistic student culture during research; academic orientation; and strong departmental and institutional support.

Research-supportive Ph.D.: Didactic teaching with individualistic student culture in courses; facilitative professors with participative or synergistic student culture during research; academic orientation; and strong departmental and institutional support.

Supportive Ph.D.: Facilitative teaching with participative or synergistic student culture in courses; facilitative professors with participative or synergistic student culture during research; academic orientation; and strong departmental and institutional support.

Weak programs: Insufficient support; few students; few graduate-level courses; and few graduates.

I have observed many departments that fit into the first two and last categories, and at least one department in the third category. As departments become more supportive, attrition will decrease.

The following characteristics of Ph.D. programs reduce attrition and the time to degree (Bowen & Rudenstine, 1992) :

Admission procedures:
- Publish attrition and average time-to-degree data regularly. Large discrepancies between the actual and initially expected time to degree may cause increased attrition.
- Admit students with adequate academic preparation.
- Admit entering cohorts of modest size, instead of admitting large entering cohorts with the intention to weed out students. However, a critical mass of students is required. Scale does matter.

Financial support:
- Guarantee that students will receive adequate financial support for a specified number of years as long as their progress is satisfactory. Self-supported students have high attrition rates and long times to degree.
- Avoid excessive graduate student teaching requirements as a way to support students. Teaching more than two years lengthens time to degree and increases attrition.

Program structure:
- Develop objectives and time lines. Specify firm early dates to complete language and other special requirements. Identify a firm date to take the qualifying exam. Set target dates for dissertation outlines, chapters, initial drafts, and final completion.
- Monitor progress.
- Minimize the number of major hurdles. Each major hurdle increases attrition and time to degree.
- Give students incentives to meet deadlines. For example, students might receive a salary increase or travel allowance if they pass the qualifying exam on time.
- Set a reasonable maximum number of years for finishing the Ph.D. Stop support at this time.

Well-organized courses:
- Provide guidance in picking courses. The more specialized courses available, the more guidance is needed.
- Cover the fundamentals of the discipline in the core courses.
- Emphasize independent work in the courses. This reduces the shock of shifting to independent research once the course requirements are completed.
- Be sure courses are well taught. Students may drop out because of unsatisfactory experiences with courses.

Effective faculty:
- Provide students with substantial individual attention and encouragement. Students strongly dislike faculty neglect.
- Develop substantial agreement, if possible, on research methodologies.
- Act in a collegial manner.

Successful research programs:
- Reduce the isolation of students doing research. This can be done with a laboratory environment, as is common in science or by starting required dissertation workshops.
- Provide students with close faculty supervision while they are doing research.
- Link student research closely to faculty research interests as much as possible.
- Show the students how to manage their time.

Many of these items are under control of individual faculty. A department with a will to get things done can put the structural items into place, and an administrative assistant can keep them in place. The teaching methods introduced in Chapter 6 can be used to introduce independent work into the courses. The faculty individually and as a group need to decide to devote time to students.

Some of these ideas, such as organizing research into laboratories, which works well in science, may not be transferable to other disciplines (Bowen & Rudenstine, 1992, 208). However, professors are creative and can develop other methods to reduce student isolation, and even if faculty are not close to students' research, they can supervise it closely. Some difficulties, such as major disagreements on methodology, may be impossible to solve and may require a faculty agreement to disagree, but in such a way that does not harm the graduate students.

Perhaps the most difficult problems are those related to finances. Money does make a difference. It is easier to support a small cohort of students who graduate relatively quickly than it is to support a large cohort with some students who hang on for a long time. Putting other reforms into place will help to reduce time to degree and make it easier to support the graduate students. Requiring students to be a TA for two years helps students learn how to teach (see section 9.4) and does not increase attrition or time to degree significantly. Since longer periods of teaching increase attrition and time to degree, other support mechanisms need to be found.

The results and discussion in Bowen and Rudenstine (1992) are corroborated by other sources. Kennedy (1997, 58) also suggests publishing attrition and time-to-degree data. He notes that institutions do this for undergraduate athletes, so why not graduate students! The effect of good, close relations with faculty is corroborated by Baird (1974, 108), Friedman (1987, 26–29), and Jerrard and Jerrard (1998, 187). Jerrard and Jerrard note that departments must communicate all requirements to the students. Money problems of graduate students are discussed by Friedman (1987, 7), Jerrard and Jerrard (1998, 203–204), and Peters (1992). Breslow (1995) suggests that departments consider cutting off support for chemistry students who do not graduate on time. The importance of courses is discussed by Cahn (1986, 95–97), Friedman (1987, 25–30), and Jerrard and Jerrard (1998, 186, 217–218). Jerrard and Jerrard and Peters (1992) emphasize time management for graduate students. Peters (55) states that graduate students identify excessive teaching as the number one reason for long graduation times. Bloom et al. (1998) agree on the need for student cooperation (44), birth control on cadre size (177), better advising (179), lower time to degree (180), more emphasis on teaching (180), and more fellowships and traineeships (180). Some departments are now controlling the size of entering graduate classes (Magner, 1999a).

An analysis of entering characteristics and educational outcomes may provide interesting results. When my department did this, we found that GRE scores did not correlate with success in our departmental graduate program and undergraduate grades and the undergraduate school attended did. A B average at some schools is equal to an A average at others. The usefulness of letters of recommendation was highly variable. Some professors were good predictors and others were not. Finetuning admission procedures resulted in reduced attrition. Each department needs to do its own analysis, because the important factors differ. The analysis may show that class sizes can be decreased with little effect on the number of Ph.D.s granted.

A final motivating factor is the availability of jobs, particularly tenure-track faculty positions. The lack of positions may keep candidates in graduate school. There is an extreme shortage of tenure-track positions in some disciplines. Although there are things the prospective assistant professor can do to become more employable (Formo & Reed, 1999), many excellent candidates will not find permanent faculty positions. Solving these problems requires major structural changes in the higher education system.

A 50 percent attrition rate of our best and brightest students is an appalling waste of talent. Since departments control admissions, TA assignments, courses, and supervision, departments—which are made up of faculty—can do something. We do not have to wait for the institution or government to act.

9.3. Working with Teaching Assistants

TAs have a major impact on both course effectiveness and professors' efficiency. If graduate students are not available, find out if undergraduate TAs can be hired. Undergraduates can be excellent TAs in lower division courses, but they should be assigned to no more than ten hours of work per week. In this section, I explore methods faculty can use to work with TAs to optimize course effectiveness without exploiting them. TA training programs are discussed in the next section.

The Advantages and Disadvantages of Being a Teaching Assistant

Most graduate students become TAs because they need the money or the TA assignment is required. Although most find the work demanding, many also find that they love teaching (Bloom et al., 1998, 15, 101). The more they interact with students, the more they enjoy and learn from the experience. They also learn the material better, become better connected to the department, and have more contact with faculty and undergraduates than do graduate students who are not TAs (Svinicki, 1994). They learn a significant amount about teaching and learning. TAs often get to know the professor in charge of the course well, which can be helpful when they are looking for a thesis advisor, committee members, and letters of recommendation. In disciplines where graduate students can easily become isolated, TAs often have higher completion rates than fellowship students do, because of increased contact (Bowen & Rudenstine, 1992, 12, 188). Because of these advantages, being a TA should be a required part of Ph.D. education, but the period as a TA should be strictly limited to two years or less (Bowen & Rudenstine, 1992).

Of course, there are disadvantages to being a TA, especially the time it takes. Students who are TAs throughout their graduate student careers take longer to earn their Ph.D.s (Bowen & Rudenstine, 1992; Peters, 1992). TAs may feel underpaid and exploited as cheap labor. If widespread, these feelings can develop into a unionization drive (Nelson, 1997). Being a TA can also be quite stressful. The first term of teaching is stressful for those who are well trained, and even worse for the majority who are not (Jerrard & Jerrard, 1998, 198). Since the TA shifts back and forth between positions of authority and subordination, there is considerable role strain in the position (Friedman, 1987, 6). Grading papers, particularly after the first time, tends to be boring. Thus, many TAs have a tendency to put off grading, which can cause conflict with the professor in charge of the course. Professors who treat their TAs as menials make the TAs' jobs more difficult.

Fortunately, most TAs start the term with a good attitude. They are anxious to do well and get along with the professor in charge of the course, but they are probably somewhat concerned about the time requirements and their teaching ability (Jerrard &

Jerrard, 1998, 198–199; Smith et al., 1992, 78–79; Svinicki, 1994). By working with them, professors can increase their effectiveness, make sure their time requirements are not excessive, and ensure that their experience is positive.

Issues to Discuss with the Teaching Assistant

Start by meeting with the TA before the term starts. Give him or her a copy of the course syllabus and course outline. Explain in detail the course procedures, including class attendance, homework, recitations, exams, and the grading procedure. Spell out exactly what you expect (Davidson & Ambrose, 1994, 83–90; B. G. Davis, 1993, 386–388; Lewis, 1994; Svinicki, 1994):

- Include the TA in the "team" that is teaching the course. As a member of the team, the TA will refrain from criticizing the professor or other TAs in front of students.
- Attendance at lectures should be required unless there is a time conflict. The TA can help with classroom management such as returning homework, passing out handouts, or taking attendance. He or she can also be asked to take notes that can be placed on reserve in the library. Finally, and most important, lecture attendance will improve the TA's performance by refreshing his or her memory of the material.
- Grading policies should be explained. Explain what items, such as homework, tests, and projects, the TA will grade; when these items will be turned in; and how quickly you want them graded. Discuss how you want them graded, and make plans to grade part of the first assignment with the TA as a training session. Determine who will keep the grade book or spreadsheet for the class.
- The TA needs to arrange office hours. Find hours that will be convenient for the TA and most of the students. If at all possible, obtain a separate office, not the TA's lab or office, for use during office hours. Discuss tutoring procedures and encourage the TA to first listen and then have students work on problems with help. Showing students the solution seems efficient, but students learn less.
- If the TA will be helping to develop course assignments or tests, discuss this aspect. New TAs need guidance.
- Delineate any available departmental or campus resources, such as secretarial support, copy shops, computer centers, and TA training resources.
- Discuss the hours per week you expect the TA to work. Approximate the number of hours the TA will need to work in an average week based on lecture attendance, grading, preparation and conduct of the recitation, office hours, and other assignments. Make sure that the TA is not overworked and exploited. It is also helpful to discuss your expectations for the TA's availability after the final exam and other times the TA may be tempted to be away from campus.
- Students should be treated fairly and respectfully at all times. The TA needs to consider interactions with students confidential, except for discussing them with others on the course team.

- Discuss university policies and procedures with the TA. In particular, discuss sexual harassment policies and make it clear that the TA is not to date any student in class until the term is over. Suggest that the TA leave his or her office door open when talking to students.
- Since international TAs may be from cultures that treat women or minorities differently, clearly inform all TAs of expected behavior (Smith et al., 1992, 12–13).
- If the TA will be in charge of a recitation section, explain the purpose of recitation. Although in many recitations the TA lectures, it is usually more effective to have the students work in cooperative groups. If cooperative groups are used, the TA will probably need some training in these techniques (see section 6.1). A selling point for the TA is that recitation sections are less work and more fun if done as cooperative groups instead of as lectures.
- For TAs teaching a recitation section (Andersen & Fabian, 1996; Sarkisian, 1990; Smith et al., 1992, 47–50, 71, 73; Svinicki, 1994): 1. Discuss the first day of class and show the TA a method, such as the "name game," for learning the students' names. 2. Expect that the TA will learn the name of every student in his or her section. 3. Arrange for some type of assessment of the TA's performance later in the term. Assessment examples include videotapes, classroom visits by the professor, peer visits, and student evaluations. 4. Briefly discuss teaching techniques, such as making eye contact, reviewing material, presenting examples, carefully listening to questions, and checking that the student's question was answered. 5. Note that enthusiasm, friendliness, politeness, frequent smiling, laughter, and a sincere desire to help students learn are often more important than pedagogical skills. 6. Give a short pep talk pointing out that this is an opportunity to finally do something about bad teaching (Ross, 1998).

This list is very up-front about what the TA will have to do. Include *all* of the duties that the TA will do during the term. Set your and the TA's expectations for performance at high levels. Honestly communicating what your expectations are will get the semester off to a good start.

During the term, meet with the TA regularly (Andersen & Fabian, 1996; B. G. Davis, 1993, 388–389; Jerrard & Jerrard, 1998, 199; Svinicki, 1994). Immediately after lectures is often a good time to talk informally. If the course has several TAs, schedule a weekly meeting to discuss the course. Ask what concepts the students are having difficulty with in recitation and what questions they are asking during office hours. Since undergraduates often identify more closely with TAs than with professors, the TA will often know about problems before you do. Ask your TA for his or her opinion about pedagogical issues such as test problems, scoring of tests and homework, students who are having difficulty, dates for assignments and tests, and grading. And listen.

Warn the TA in advance when there will be heavy grading assignments. Realize that TAs are students who may be overwhelmed by their own courses and research. Try to be flexible when assignments need to be graded. If the TA does something extra for you, such as presenting a lecture while you are out of town, express your gratitude. If the TA does an outstanding job throughout the term, write a letter to the TA detailing his or her accomplishments. Share this with the TA's advisor, and put a copy in the student's file. TAs who are treated as colleagues tend to be happy with their TA experience, and their students tend to be happy. A happy class is a good class to teach.

Teaching assistants invariably learn some practical facts about teaching. Their learning can be significantly increased if the professor discusses teaching and the pedagogical reasons for various aspects of the course. Encourage them to be observant while teaching and to reflect on it afterward (Svinicki, 1994). A modest amount of reading about teaching such as a manual for TAs (Allen & Rueter, 1990) or a book on teaching (e.g., Brinkley et al., 1999; B. G. Davis, 1993; Eble, 1988; Lowman, 1995; McKeachie, 1994; Wankat & Oreovicz, 1993), can be enlightening. Formal seminars and supervised internships are discussed in the next section.

International Teaching Assistants

Unless they were undergraduates in the United States, international TAs often have difficulties communicating and understanding U.S. culture (Sarkisian, 1990; Smith et al., 1992). There is no substitute for spending time in the United States to understand the culture and become more fluent in English. International students, particularly those whose native language is not English, should not be assigned as TAs during their first term in the United States (Wei, 1997). If new international students must be TAs, training in English and in the culture of the U.S. classroom are necessary.

At state institutions many of the undergraduates, particularly first-year students, have never had the opportunity to work with people from other countries. Although working with international TAs is a valuable part of their learning experience, they often have difficulty understanding them. When students complain, I ask them to try to "tune" their ears to the TA's language pattern for two weeks. Usually this works. If after two weeks they are still having difficulty understanding the TA, I move the students to another section if possible.

9.4. Learning How to Teach

Almost every profession except academe requires that new professionals have significant supervised practical experience before they start independent practice. New assistant professors typically find that the majority of their time is spent in preparing and delivering instruction (Boice, 1992, 2000; Menges, 1999a), yet their preparation in how to teach is often woefully inadequate (Seldin, 1990b).

One frequent result of the failure to teach Ph.D. students how to teach is poor teaching the first two or three years of professors' careers while they learn some practical pedagogy on the job. Most professors remain amateurs as far as teaching is concerned (Simon, 1994, x), and some never become good teachers, or they find they do not enjoy teaching. A second result is that new professors spend a significant amount of their time learning to teach while they are also under pressure to start their independent scholarship. Thus, during the first two or three years they often have little to show for their efforts except that they have learned some practical aspects of how to teach and how to do scholarship in the environment of their new institution.

Currently, 75 percent of professors at four-year institutions have doctorates, but only 17 percent at two-year schools do (Magner, 1999b). The majority of new professors earn their Ph.D.s from research universities, and 80 percent of them graduate from only 102 universities (Goff & Lambert, 1996). These are the "provider" institutions (Richlin, 1993b). But the majority of academic positions are at less prestigious, non-Ph.D.-granting "consumer" institutions. Community colleges are also hiring more Ph.D.s (Haworth, 1999). Unfortunately, there is a major split between provider and consumer institutions (Goff & Lambert, 1996; Richlin, 1993b, 1993c). Since the provider institutions are interested mainly in research, they educate and socialize their graduate students in research (Richlin, 1993c). In a recent survey, only 36 percent of provider institutions said that more training in teaching was needed in Ph.D. education (Richlin, 1993b). Consumer institutions, on the other hand, want to hire new professors who know how to teach, and 86 percent wanted more teacher education in graduate school (Richlin, 1993b). Learning to teach will make new graduates more competitive for faculty positions at consumer institutions. Most Ph.D. students are being educated for jobs at elite research universities that they will never hold (Goff & Lambert, 1996; Kennedy, 1997, 30).

The Need to Learn How to Teach

Many commentators believe that universities should ensure that all Ph.D.s who plan on academic careers learn how to teach (American Association of Universities [see Leatherman, 1998]; Boice,1992, 52–55; Bowen & Rudenstine, 1992, 191, 194; Brinkley et al., 1999, vii–viii; Centra, 1993, 18; Clifford & Guthrie; 1988, 324; Eble, 1988, 5, 7; Gardiner, 1994, 140; Lambert & Tice, 1992; Lowman, 1995, 305–307; Pelikan, 1992, 94; Richlin, 1993a, 1993b; Schuster, 1993; Stice, 1991; Tierney & Rhoads, 1993, 74–77; Weimer, 1990, xiii, 17). The contrary opinion was stated by Highet (1976, 112), who argued that graduate students can learn how to teach by observing professors. There are some exemplary programs, such as those at Robert Gordon University <http://www.rgu.ac.uk/subj/eds/pgcert/main.htm>, Syracuse University (Centra, 1993), the University of Colorado at Boulder ("Graduate Teaching," 1994–95), the national Preparing Future Faculty (PFF) program (Goff & Lambert, 1996) <http://www.preparing-faculty.org/>, the Preparation for the Professions initiative by the Carnegie Foundation for the Advancement of Teaching, and other programs discussed by Lambert and Tice (1992). Programs for Ph.D. students are needed at all provider institutions. Since the doctor of arts degree, the "teaching doctorate," has declined in favor (Glazer, 1993), it is even more imperative to teach Ph.D. students how to teach.

Fortunately, we know how to teach future professors how to teach (Simon, 1994, x; Stice et al., 2000), and it's not that difficult. What is needed is the will to get past professorial intransigence—the "I didn't take any teaching courses and I learned how to teach" attitude. We can learn from the pilot programs and install programs taken by the majority of Ph.D. students. An exemplary program would train teaching assistants, replace one course in the curriculum with a course in pedagogy, and have a supervised internship available for interested students.

The two major goals of education in how to teach are (1) to provide graduate students with the tools and practice to be good teachers and (2) to take them from the naive theory that teaching is information transfer to a theory that conceptualizes teaching as organizing student activities (Ramsden, 1992, 111–116). This transformation will give them the background to become good teachers and a firm basis for further growth.

Four formal methods are commonly used in teaching Ph.D. students how to teach (Wankat, 1999b):

1. Training programs for TAs before the term starts
2. TA training seminars during the term
3. Courses in pedagogy offered by education or psychology or within the disciplines
4. A supervised teaching internship within the college or at an external site

Training Programs for Teaching Assistants

Training programs for TAs are becoming common because they address a visible problem—the overuse of untrained TAs for teaching. However, only half of the graduate students who responded to the NAGPS (1999) survey reported that they had received adequate training. Training programs, which may last from a half-day to a week or more, can be universitywide, be based within a college or department, or combine these aspects. Attendance is best if professors and department chairs enthusiastically support the program. The programs should be required for new TAs, who should be paid while enrolled in the program. Black (1995) suggests that TAs should repeat the program, since their anxiety often prevents learning the first time. Research has shown that TA training programs do improve TA performance (Centra, 1993, 17). International TAs usually are required to attend additional programs that focus on spoken English and U.S. classroom culture. The programs also improve the teaching of professors who are involved in departmental programs (Black, 1995).

TA training programs should have a practical orientation. They typically cover topics such as university policies, the first class, the importance of names, leading a discussion, conducting a cooperative group session, lecturing, questioning, tutoring, use of audiovisual equipment, grading and evaluating students, sexual harassment, classroom climate, and dealing with problems (Allen & Rueter, 1990; Centra, 1993, 16–18; Davidson & Ambrose, 1994, 86–90; "Graduate Teaching," 1994–95; Smith et al., 1992, 38–43; Torvi, 1994). The presentations should model good teaching practices and require the future TAs to be active participants. For example, teach cooperative group methods using a cooperative group format. Use role plays for exploring the issues of sexual harassment, classroom climate, and dealing with problems.

Each TA should present a short, videotaped mini-lecture (microteaching) to an audience of other TAs. Split up the training class to provide time to do this. Every member of the audience should fill out a critique of the mini-lecture. This feedback is not only useful for the lecturer, but also keeps the audience involved and thinking about teaching. Since most students are embarrassed by their videotapes, have them watch the tape alone or with one staff member present.

TAs will learn more about teaching if their initial training is reinforced by seminars and feedback throughout the term and are more serious if the seminar is for credit ("Engineering TA," 1995; Centra, 1993, 16–17; Norris & Palmer, 1998; Torvi, 1994). A combination of general seminars and discipline-specific meetings works well. The general seminars can start with a presentation by one of the outstanding teachers on campus (a duty these professors are usually quite willing to do) followed by discussion. The discipline-specific meetings can focus on handling difficulties throughout the semester and providing support for the TAs. At some universities, these meetings are run by advanced or lead TAs. The participants should be encouraged to keep journals to reflect on their teaching.

A formalized method of providing feedback during the term is useful (Black, 1995). Research has shown that TA performance is improved if a trained peer watches the TA teach and privately critiques the TA's performance or if a class session is videotaped to provide feedback (Centra, 1993, 17).

Courses in Pedagogy

TA training provides a certain amount of know-how, but to develop understanding, a formal course in pedagogy is needed. A single course is a modest requirement compared to the two years of course work typically required for a Ph.D. Including a course in pedagogy in the curriculum will also help make teaching and educational scholarship legitimate topics in the discipline (Braxton & Berger, 1999). All graduate students will benefit from a pedagogy course, because they will improve their communication skills and better understand their own learning styles. Since few Ph.D. graduates have taken a course in pedagogy, those who do will stand out and have a competitive advantage for positions at consumer institutions.

The course in pedagogy should cover a broad range of topics and skills (Benassi & Fernald, 1993; Centra, 1993, 17–18; Feldhusen et al., 1998; Fernald, 1995; Rickard et al., 1991; Stice, 1991; Stice et al., 2000; Wankat, 1999b; Wankat & Oreovicz, 1993). The students appreciate practical aspects, such as microteaching and writing a test for the course. Learning the fundamentals of how students learn and how students develop during college is helpful for understanding the reasons some teaching methods work and others don't. A variety of teaching methods should be used. The students need to be active during class, they need to be encouraged to reflect through journals, and they should have the opportunity to observe exemplary teachers. Field trips can be arranged to help the students become conversant with pedagogical applications of technology, and they can do a group project. Professional topics such as ethics and obtaining an academic position (Formo & Reed, 1999) should be included. The topics covered in the engineering pedagogy course at Purdue University are listed in Table 9.1. This course was modeled after Professor John Feldhusen's educational psychology course (Feldhusen et al., 1998).

TABLE 9.1.   Topics in an Educational Methods Course for Engineering Graduate Students at Purdue University

Part I. Methods and Procedures
What Works
Efficiency and Effectiveness
Objectives and Bloom's Taxonomy
Accreditation
Creativity and Problem Solving
The Search for an Academic Position
Teaching Methods: Lecture, Co-op Groups, Discussion, Mastery Learning, Field Trips, Experiential Learning, etc.
Teaching with Technology
Mentoring Graduate Students
Testing and Grading
Cheating and Discipline
Evaluation of Teaching
Oral and Written Communication

Part II. The Student
Myers-Briggs Type Indicator
Theories of Piaget and Perry
How People Learn
Kolb's Theory
Motivation

Part III. Projects
Guided-Design Study: Ideal Graduate Program
Class Project: Ideal Undergraduate Program
Group Project: Designing an Educational Web Page

Source: Adapted from Phillip C. Wankat, "Educating Engineering Professors in Education," *Journal of Engineering Education,* 88 (1999b), 473.

A key question is, should there be a universitywide pedagogy course offered by education and/or psychology, or should there be discipline-oriented courses? A major advantage of separate courses is that the *pedagogical content knowledge* of the discipline can be developed (Lenze & Dinham, 1999; Shulman, 1986). In addition, students find that a professor in their discipline is more believable, and it is easier for students to sign up for a course in their college. The disadvantages may include less cross-fertilization of ideas and a duplication of resources. However, if major research universities are serious about teaching graduate students how to teach, the number of students taking pedagogy courses would be large enough to support courses in different colleges. The faculty who teach these courses will also benefit, since they will learn a significant amount about teaching, will become better teachers, and will enjoy teaching the course.

Interested graduate students will also benefit from more specialized advanced courses. A course in counseling skills will prove useful in advising students and facilitating group-oriented courses. Courses in quantitative and qualitative research methods in education are appropriate for students who want to become involved in educational scholarship. Courses in writing, multicultural issues, and ethics have also been offered to Ph.D. students (Leatherman, 1999). However, there is often resistance from faculty, since students will have less time for research if they take more courses (Leatherman, 1999).

New (and experienced) faculty who missed the opportunity to learn to teach in graduate school will benefit from workshops (Boice, 1992, 220–230; Kennedy, 1997, 72, 75–76; Stice et al., 2000). The little data available on the effectiveness of these programs show significantly improved teaching (Conley et al., 2000; Kennedy, 1997, 75–76).

Supervised Internships

Ultimately, learning to teach requires actually teaching. Instead of having Ph.D. students wait until after graduation, experiential-learning experiences can be arranged for interested senior Ph.D. students. Early teaching will help graduate students determine whether they enjoy teaching (Reis, 1997). Because of the time commitment, fewer students will take advantage of supervised teaching internships than will take TA training and pedagogy courses. However, in fields where there is great competition for faculty positions, a supervised internship, particularly at an institution similar to the hiring school, can make the candidate much more competitive.

Three models can be followed for supervised teaching internships (Lumsden et al., 1988; Norris & Palmer, 1998; Reis, 1997, 143–144; Sherwood et al., 1997). A formal supervision program can be modeled after programs for internships and practica in education, counseling, clinical psychology, etc. For internships within the university, a professor is listed as the supervisor for four to six students. The supervisor receives credit for teaching a course and meets regularly with the students in a small seminar to discuss their teaching. The supervisor periodically observes the graduate students teaching their classes and provides feedback. This model can be used if the teaching assignments are at a different institution, but observation is more difficult.

An alternative is to have graduate students intern at other institutions, such as community colleges. The interns teach under the watchful eye of a local professor who acts as supervisor. This approach has been successful in the PFF program (Kennedy, 1997, 284). A formal university seminar ensures that the interns reflect on and learn from their experiences. The interns teach more heterogeneous classes than they would at many universities, and since community colleges commonly hire professors with master's degrees, the interns should not be considered second-class teachers. Since the success of this approach depends heavily on the quality of the local supervisors, be sure to reward them (Bellack & King, 2000).

A somewhat different approach is for a faculty member to share a course with a selected graduate student (Sherwood et al., 1997). As a team they develop the course objectives and the syllabus, set the course schedule, develop and present lectures, write and score tests, and determine final grades. Both attend almost every class session. This is the most flexible model. Course sharing can be part of a formal internship or can be done informally, since only a private agreement between the professor and TA is needed. Since the professor is always present, political problems involved in having a TA teach the course are also avoided. However, without a formal structure there is no way to certify what the graduate student has accomplished. Since many graduate students will not know that these opportunities exist, there is also danger that some groups may be excluded. Without a formal course structure there is no possibility of developing a support seminar for the interns. In addition, I would find truly sharing my courses difficult, since I expect to be and want to be in charge.

The Role of Consumer Institutions

The role of provider institutions is clear: institute TA training programs, courses in pedagogy, and supervised internship opportunities for Ph.D. candidates. What is the role of consumer institutions? Demand a better product! Require job candidates to present an introductory teaching lecture in addition to a research seminar (Cahn, 1986, 72; A. F. Lucas, 1994, 109). Scrutinize the teaching preparation of candidates. Hire candidates who are trained and prepared to teach. Tell unsuccessful candidates and their universities that their lack of preparation to teach was a major reason they were not hired. Provide supervised internships for Ph.D. students from research universities. At the national meeting of your disciplinary organization, develop a panel session titled "What Teaching Institutions Are Looking for in New Professors." In disciplines with an excess of Ph.D.s, consumer institutions can affect their education.

9.5. Ph.D. Research and the Dissertation

Dick has been a graduate student for six years and ABD for the last four. Maybe he could have worked a little harder, but that doesn't explain how Karen can be finishing her dissertation at the end of her fourth year. She certainly hasn't sacrificed having some fun in order to graduate. Her undergraduate and graduate grades were no better than his, and he had gone to a better undergraduate school. Karen even has a faculty position waiting for her when she finishes. Life isn't fair.

Karen came to graduate school with a good idea of her research area, which helped her find an advisor quickly. Her advisor showed her how to schedule and pace her work. At first, he checked on her progress regularly and encouraged her over the inevitable rough spots. As Karen became more confident doing research, his checking became less frequent. He encouraged her to set goals and follow a regular daily schedule. Karen wrote a paper with her advisor while only halfway through her research. This was truly a joint effort, with each involved in the planning, the writing of the first draft, and the repeated rewriting. When it was time for Karen to start writing her thesis, she had a model of the process of writing to follow. Only once during one of the now infrequent checks did her advisor have to remind her to follow a regular writing schedule. Her advisor's glowing letter of recommendation helped her be invited for interviews. Karen was impressive during the interviews, and she found an exciting faculty position. Unfortunately, Dick's advisor never taught Dick how to be effective and efficient.

Although the focus of this section is on advising Ph.D. students, most of the comments also apply to advising the research of undergraduate students and master's students. However, master's students and particularly undergraduates need much more direction than experienced Ph.D. students need (COSEPUP, 1997, 21–22). Undergraduates should not be assigned to research that is highly exploratory.

Departments and professors need to impose some structure on the process of earning a Ph.D. (Bowen & Rudenstine, 1992). The procedures discussed in section 9.2. reduce attrition and the time it takes for students to become ready to do research. But they are not enough. We need to focus on the research process to help ABDs become Ph.D.s. Earning a Ph.D. should not include years with no progress.

Patterns for Earning Ph.D.s

Picking advisors and research areas, doing research, and writing dissertations to earn a Ph.D. differ dramatically among the disciplines. Bowen and Rudenstine (1992) found that physics and mathematics form a natural grouping, as do English, history, and political science. Economics straddles these two groups. Bloom et al. (1998) give a complete picture of graduate research in the sciences and note that in these disciplines, departments and faculty *need* graduate students (7). Peters (1992, 33–34) discusses the great differences in advising between the humanities and sciences, and also notes that science professors need graduate students.

In the "*independent*" camp (loosely, the humanities) graduate students develop their own research topics, usually after completing two years of courses. They then find an advisor, who may have little connection to the topic. Graduate student support is unconnected to the advisor chosen. The students do their research independently, write their dissertations with varying amounts of feedback, and write papers as the sole author.

In the "*connected*" camp (loosely, the technical fields), students usually pick a research area offered by their advisors. This is often done fairly quickly, with firm deadlines. Students work on research while still taking courses. They are often supported by their advisors' research contracts and work in their advisors' laboratories with other graduate students and often postdocs. Students work relatively closely with their advisors on research and publish papers with them. A large part of the students' dissertations may be published in journal articles before they finish.

Either system can work very well or can lead to abuse and failure. In independent programs, the classical student problems are isolation and loneliness, the inability to pick a topic, a lack of attentive advising, and excessive confusion (Bowen & Rudenstine, 1992; Brown & Atkins, 1988, 126; Friedman, 1987, 45–55; Peters, 1992, 188–193; Rosovsky, 1990, 153–154). These problems can lead to wasting a number of years, a high attrition rate, and a long time to degree. More structure, firm deadlines, and more interaction with professors and other students are appropriate remedies (Bowen & Rudenstine, 1992).

In connected programs, the classical student problems are insufficient independence, with advisors who are too controlling, demand work that is not thesis related, and treat students as technicians, and no opportunity for the student to learn to define problems (Bloom et al., 1998, 27, 71; COSEPUP, 1997, 34–35; Reis, 1997, 120–121). Although students who suffer through these problems often graduate, they have not benefited from the independent research that is expected of Ph.D.s. Increased freedom and requirements for independent research would help. The two approaches need to adopt some of the good points of the other without loosing their own strengths.

Preparing to Become an Independent Scholar

One of the paradoxes of education is that becoming an independent learner is easiest in a structured environment with appropriate deadlines and supervision. Ideally, students start to learn to be independent while they are undergraduates through independent projects in courses and undergraduate research. Independent research projects need to be continued in graduate courses (Bowen & Rudenstine, 1992, 254–255) so that when the graduate students start their dissertation research, they will have some experience in picking a topic and doing research. Departments that require independent research should repeatedly encourage graduate students to explore the possibilities for dissertation topics in their courses. Students should look for areas that are inherently interesting, since interest will help them overcome the frustrations of research. The requirements for a course project could include a brief exploration of turning the project into a dissertation.

After they have finished their courses and other requirements but before they have chosen a dissertation topic and advisor is often the most difficult time for graduate students (Bowen & Rudenstine, 1992, 254). Most students are unprepared to pick a research topic and advisor (Bloom et al., 1998, 20–34; Bowen and Rudenstine, 1992, 260–262; COSEPUP, 1997, 24; Friedman, 1987, 34–38; Jerrard & Jerrard, 1998, 205–206; Peters, 1992, 34–43; Rosovsky, 1990, 151–153).

One way to help students during this transition is to require their attendance at a pre-research seminar. Discussion, particularly of the merits of different research advisors, is less inhibited if the seminar leader is a senior Ph.D. student. A graduate student leader is likely to be closer to the new students, more empathic, and more believable than a professor. The leader can encourage exploration by asking a series of open-ended questions (Chapman, 1988). How much direction, contact, pressure, and emotional support are desired? Is the student interested in a large or small research group? Is the advisor noted for helping students after graduation? The leader may also be able to lower the students' expectations for their dissertations. Lowering expectations may sound like contrary advice, but the belief that one must produce a *magnum opus* can be overwhelming and prevent students from starting (Bowen & Rudenstine, 1992, 255; Levine, 2000). Firm deadlines for selection of research topic and advisor help prevent excessive procrastination.

Since I was socialized in the connected way of doing research, it appears to me that many professors are more motivated to advise graduate students when the students' research is directly connected to their own. Politics aside, it seems reasonable for departments with a tradition of independent research to *experiment* with joint faculty–graduate student research and joint publications for a portion of the dissertation research. This is likely to result in an approach toward an apprentice–master relationship.

In disciplines with a tradition of connected research, the challenge is to make sure that all graduate students are required to do independent research. Professors with research grants and contracts often feel pressure to produce results and may not give students enough freedom to explore their own ideas. A proven method is to require all graduate students to develop and defend an independent research proposal outside their research area (Braxton & Berger, 1999; Breslow, 1995). The students are assigned temporary advisors for this proposal. The proposals need to be completed and approved before the students are allowed to take the preliminary examination. Although time-consuming, departments that use this procedure are convinced that it pays dividends in improved research for the doctorate and better prepared graduates.

Research Supervision: The Ideal Advisor

Although the research on effective supervision of graduate students is inadequate (Brown & Atkins, 1988, 116), it is obvious that professors vary significantly in their ability (Bowen & Rudenstine, 1992, 260). A few seem to be effective with all students, most are effective with some students, and a few seem incapable of advising anyone. Twenty-two percent of the graduate students who responded to the NAGPS (1999) survey were unsatisfied with their advisor's academic supervision. The same faculty appear to have difficulty with graduate students again and again. Some faculty are better advisors of undergraduates and master's students, who typically receive more direction, than they are of Ph.D.s, whereas the opposite is true of other faculty. Fortunately, many professors become better advisors as they gain experience. Faculty do not agree what constitutes good advising and norms are not agreed on (Friedman, 1987, 8).

Doing research in graduate school is a form of experiential learning, and advisors are engaged in a form of teaching that is closer to supervision than to usual classroom teaching. Brown and Atkins (1988, 115–149) offer a detailed and useful discussion of research supervision. In surveys done in England, graduate students said they disliked unstructured, cold advisors and liked structured, warm advisors. Their second choice was structured, cold advisors. Thus students prefered structured, approachable advisors, but structure was more important than the advisor's personal characteristics. Structure itself is supportive, as long as there is not too much of it (Strauss & Sayles, 1980, 86–90). There is probably less need to provide structure if the program itself is very structured. Brown and Atkins (1988, 122) state that first-year students wanted to develop a personal relationship with their advisors, while students in the second and third years wanted expertise and regular contact (availability). As the students become more involved and professional about their research, they want their advisors to adjust. Students tend to interpret a *laissez-faire* attitude as neglect.

Students may want actions from their advisor that are not in their best interests. For example, advisors often need to push students to be more independent and refuse to direct them, even though the students ask for direction. In this situation, the art of advising is knowing when more independence is appropriate and pushing the student to be more independent in a supportive, even loving way. Unfortunately, what an advisor sees as purposeful behavior to push a student to take initiative the student is likely to interpret as neglect (Friedman, 1987, 66, 69). To prevent misinterpretation, explain to the students what you are doing and why.

I have developed a portrait of an ideal advisor from my experiences as a graduate student and advisor and from the descriptions of good advising and mentoring in Bloom et al. (1998, 24–32, 64–66), Bowen and Rudenstine (1992, 261, 264, 283–284), Brennan (1999), Brown and Atkins (1988, 118–122, 130–137), Cahn (1986, 100), COSEPUP (1997, 5, 7, 34–35, 53–63), Davidson and Ambrose (1994, 95–109), Friedman (1987, 8), Jerrard and Jerrard (1988, 206–207), Kennedy (1997, 97–116), Peters (1992, 32–33), Reis (1997, 120–122), and Scott (1978). The ideal advisor's *guiding principle is to do what is best for the student at all times*. Advisors who use other guiding principles are likely to encounter difficulties.

The ideal advisor is actively involved in research. He or she sees research as a mechanism for student learning and growth, not as an end in itself. This advisor has a balanced view of the student's research as quite important but never more important than the student's welfare. This advisor sets up a warm climate, is available to meet with students, and is supportive and encouraging during the usual frustrations and disappointments of research.

The ideal advisor plans regular meetings with the goals of determining what the student has done and helping the student plan the next step. The advisor uses skills such as questioning, probing, listening, silence, and explaining during meetings. He or she provides feedback and helps students learn to judge their own work. The advisor takes notes and uses them in planning the next meeting. Peters (1992, 33), who invariably takes the student's side on issues, states that a rigorous advisor who requires a professional standard is preferred, since rigor helps the student obtain an academic position.

The ideal advisor creates a research climate that encourages students to try independent ideas, since failures are seen as opportunities to learn. He or she is a good role model of ethical behavior and explicitly discusses ethics with students. The advisor expects the students to make regular progress in writing their dissertation and reads and comments on chapters in a timely fashion. When the students graduate, they are proud of their dissertations and prepared to be independent researchers. Their advisor helps them find their first position and maintains contact with them. The new Ph.D.s *almost* think they did it by themselves.

I have yet to meet any professors who meet all of these criteria, although a few have come close. In reality, graduate students sometimes believe their advisor is the advisor from hell. The sins of advisors include ignoring students or mildly abusing them psychologically, requesting work on projects not connected to dissertation research, and not crediting students in papers and grant applications (Peters, 1992, 164–165, 167, 170, 173, 175). Friedman (1987, 69, 84) notes that foreign students react much more strongly to supervisor neglect than American students. Women are more likely to have weak mentoring in graduate school (Trautvetter, 1999). More severe but infrequent problems include requests for personal service, severe psychological abuse, and sexual harassment (Leatherman, 1997). The department needs to deal with ethical lapses as they occur. Subtler problems can linger for years, since most departments do not evaluate the performance of advisors. Brennan (1999) discusses some of the extreme behavior, such as murder and suicide, that can result from the pressures on graduate students.

One simple method to evaluate advisors' performance is to track the performance of all Ph.D. candidates (Bowen & Rudenstine, 1992, 265–267; Brown & Atkins, 1988, 130–131). If over a number of years the students of an advisor have a significantly higher mean attrition rate or longer time to degree than the departmental mean, attention needs to be paid to that advisor. Brown and Atkins (1988, 130) state, "Nor is it taken for granted that any member of academic staff is capable of being a supervisor." Removal of a professor's advising privileges is a highly political act that should not be done lightly.

Student Failures

Brown and Atkins (1988, 123–128) identified the following as the most common problems that cause students to fail to complete the dissertation or to be late:

Methodological difficulties: The original project was too difficult or unmanageable in the time available, or the student lost interest. This was the number one problem. Advisors need to help students do reality checks to be sure their projects are well focused (Levine, 2000).

Student isolation: Students need to discuss their research and receive input from others. Otherwise, motivation and sometimes the student's objectivity suffer. This was the second most critical problem. Require attendance at regular weekly meetings, if only to discuss things other than research. Otherwise, students who miss one meeting are tempted to miss another and the problem rapidly snowballs (Brennan, 1999). Regular group meetings, working in a laboratory, and research seminars also help combat isolation.

Poor planning and project management: If students did not pick up these skills previously, they need to be taught at least rudimentary skills now.

Writing the dissertation: This is a frequent problem that leads to significant stress and frustration. Require graduate students to write throughout graduate school. Encourage students to write and submit papers during the course of their research. Nothing is as motivating to graduate students as having a paper published, and early publication is a good predictor of later publication (Wilbur, 1988). Early publication also makes students more competitive when they search for a faculty position. Students who write and turn in parts of dissertations while they are still working on their research are much less likely to have major problems finishing. Refer the students to a guide on dissertations such as Levine (2000), Peters (1992, 195–241), or Zerubavel (1999). Leatherman (2000) has an extensive annotated bibliography for dissertation writers. Some of the ideas discussed in sections 10.4 and 10.5 may be useful for graduate students.

Personal problems: Almost one-fourth of students who reach ABD status but never finish cite lack of money as the reason (Friedman, 1987, 7). A guide for graduate students states that finding sufficient financial support is one of the advisor's roles (des Jardins, 1994), but I think it is more a system problem. Excessive anxiety is a widespread problem and graduate school may be the most anxiety-laden part of an entire career (Getman, 1992, 11–12). Anxiety and other personal problems may require professional assistance.

Inadequate or no supervision: Brown and Atkins (1988, 127) state that this occurred only for a minority of students in Britain. Davidson and Ambrose (1994, 109) and the NAGPS (1999) survey indicate this problem is more common in the United States. In both cases it was significant when it occurred. Professors should receive credit for advising research students, and they should be evaluated on their performance as an advisor. Departments should establish procedures to allow students to switch advisors.

Students rarely crash and burn with no warning. The following are warning signs (Brown & Atkins, 1988, 128–130):

- Postponing or missing meetings continually
- Making excuses for not finishing work
- Procrastinating on tasks and doing other things instead of important tasks
- Lacking focus on current task
- Intellectualizing practical problems
- Resisting advice or criticism
- Blaming others
- Failing to integrate earlier work
- Changing topic or method frequently
- Being absent frequently
- Refusing to socialize with the other graduate students
- Making suicidal comments (Brennan, 1999; Schneider, 1998b)

When warning signs occur, advisors need to respond. Serious problems seldom cure themselves. As long as the professor does not accuse the student of malingering or other sins, there is no harm in asking about any of these signs. There may be legitimate reasons for a temporary lack of progress, and students usually feel better after they have talked about them. When personal problems are cutting into the student's research efforts, often the best thing the advisor can do is ease the pressure (Kennedy, 1997, 109).

Learning to Be a Good Advisor

Instruction on becoming an effective research advisor is in a worse muddle than that on how to teach. New professors have taken classes with dozens of teachers who can serve as teaching models, but they have had only one or two research advisors. Research has identified many of the things an effective teacher does, and there are proven models available for teaching students how to teach. Much less is agreed about effective research advising, and no courses are available to teach Ph.D.s to be research advisors (Bloom et al., 1998, 34). New faculty often assume that they know more about advising graduate students than they actually do (Haring, 1999). However, some fortunate graduate students and postdocs do get the opportunity to mentor undergraduates or new graduate students in research. To make the most of this opportunity, the neophyte mentors need to receive feedback on their mentoring performance from their research supervisors and from the students they mentor. Then they need to reflect on the experience. Provider institutions need to develop methods to teach graduate students how to advise effectively.

9.6. Summary

Most graduate students are enrolled in master's programs. Unfortunately, some of these programs are not receiving the attention from faculty, departments, and universities they need to be first-rate. Excellent master's programs are characterized by a clear purpose, simultaneous support and rigorous intellectual challenge, required broad core courses, a balance between theory and practice, immersion experiences, individual attention, and strong departmental and institutional support.

Most Ph.D. students learn how to do disciplinary research. We need to retain this capability while trimming the excessively high attrition rate and long time to degree. Relatively structured programs with personal attention usually have lower attrition rates and shorter times to degree. Students should have independent, group learning, and written assignments in graduate courses. Structure Ph.D. programs to encourage timely completion of all tasks required before the dissertation research. Since students often have difficulty in the period after they have completed their course work and before they have selected a project and advisor, a structured program at this time can reduce student frustration and attrition. Reduce the isolation of students doing research. Graduate students will probably benefit from learning time management principles. One of the most important but difficult problems is to ensure that students have adequate financial support without being required to teach for more than two years.

Excellent research advisors try to do what is best for the student at all times. Students prefer research advisors who are both structured and warm. Since the needs of students change as they become proficient at research, advisors need to adjust by slowly increasing students' independence. Advisors need to check on student progress at regular intervals. Difficulties that are caught quickly are less likely to blossom into crises and result in withdrawal from the program. Not all faculty are equally skilled at advising. Departments can keep records of the graduation rates and the time to degree of students advised by different professors. When these records show there is a problem, the department needs to act to correct the situation.

Since most Ph.D.s want academic positions, graduate students need to learn how to teach. In addition to serving as a TA, they will benefit from TA training programs before and during the term, courses in pedagogy, and a supervised teaching internship. Helping graduate students learn to become effective research advisors is also a laudatory goal, but methods to do this need to be developed and tested.

Graduate school is considered by many to be the jewel of the U.S. system of education (Clark, 1995, 116). Although graduate school is most often effective, the jewel could stand some polishing.

10 Scholarship and Writing: Still the Path to Fame and Promotion

Assistant Professor Alonzo Jefferson really did want to write. It wasn't his fault there was never time. Since he believed students were the reason the university existed, he devoted time to them. He enjoyed spending time with them and his teaching ratings were good and getting better. Alonzo squirmed as he looked at his mentor again. Her questions hung heavily in the air. Why was she pushing him so hard today? He was sure that this summer he would find time to write. There was certainly no time now, since he was already working seven days a week. His arguments that the university should reward good teaching with promotion and tenure had been met with a cold dose of reality: "You can argue *should* when you are a full professor and vote on promotion and tenure cases," she had said. "For now you have to be concerned with what *is*. The university rewards assistant professors with promotion and tenure for adequate teaching and excellent scholarly publications. We are pleased that you have more than satisfied the first criterion, now is time to start satisfying the second." She had softened the blow a bit by adding, "I know that you have been able to find the time to do some very good scholarship. You have to publish it to show the promotion committees." Then she had asked, "*What* is preventing you from writing?"

Alonzo had many answers, but none of them seemed very convincing. He did not have any more classes than she did, and she had won a university teaching award two years ago. He was on the curriculum committee, which was a significant time commitment, but she was the chair of that committee. She had one more graduate student than he did and was at least as active in professional societies as he was. Somehow, she was finding time to write and publish a steady stream of papers, and she had a book in press. Although it was true that Alonzo's children were younger, that did not seem to be a good reason for not writing. Alonzo did not want to talk about how hard writing was. He did not want to mention his tendency to procrastinate and do anything else instead of write. Since everybody was busy, that seemed to be a safe topic. He had told her he was too busy and could never find a long enough period to write. That quick mind of hers had pounced on this. "How long do you need?" And now his back was to the wall. How much time did he really need to write?

Two common myths about writing are that large blocks of time must be set aside for writing and that even larger blocks of time are needed for writing books. In fact, a number of short periods are usually more effective than a single long period of writing. Unless one is quite disciplined, large blocks of time rarely materialize. Moreover, when a long stretch of time to write does open up, there is more pressure on the professor to produce, so it is easy to fear failure and procrastinate. Professors write more when they are in the habit of writing every day or every other day. A half-hour or hour every day can be highly productive. What is preventing Alonzo from writing is Alonzo.

In this chapter, I offer methods that professors can use to increase their productivity in scholarship and writing in any institutional setting. Currently, the majority of American faculty stop publishing after their dissertation material (Richlin, 1993a, 1). With Boyer's (1990) broadening of the meaning of scholarship, there is no reason that this should remain true. And modest efforts on scholarship will not negatively affect teaching.

10.1. The Effect of Research on Teaching Quality

Many professors worry that a focus on research will reduce the quality of teaching. The results of many studies can be summarized as follows:

At the level of the individual professor, there is either no correlation or a slight positive correlation between research activity and teaching effectiveness. The effect of research on teaching was analyzed in detail by Feldman (1987). His meta-analysis of 29 studies found a small positive correlation of .12 between teaching effectiveness and research productivity. Other studies showed a positive correlation between research and teaching in psychology and sociology but not other areas (Centra, 1993, 139–143). These studies were done before Boyer's (1990) work and refer to classical research. Of course, in some cases research may very positively affect teaching (e.g., when the brain-dead become alive again) or may very negatively affect teaching (e.g., when the professor becomes too busy to bother with undergraduates). It is important for professors to keep current in their fields, and there is modest evidence that research helps (Fairweather, 1996, 112–113); however, professors can remain current through practically any type of scholarship, not just classical research (Boyer, 1990; Centra, 1993, 143; Rosovsky, 1990, 86–95).

On the other hand, *at the institutional level, a heavy emphasis on research negatively affects the emphasis on teaching* (Astin, 1993, 66–67, 410–423). When research becomes very important, the number of hours per week that professors devote to undergraduate students decreases, the use of teaching assistants (TAs) increases, fewer faculty use active learning strategies, and the undergraduates are neglected. At research universities, approximately one-third to one-half of a professor's time is spent on research and about half of the teaching time is spent teaching graduate students, which Clark (1995, 135, 227) considers a subsidy of research. A few schools, such as the University of Chicago and Columbia, Cornell, Harvard, Princeton, Stanford, and Yale Universities, have been able to maintain a high focus on both teaching and research (Clark, 1995, 133), but most institutions do not have the resources to resolve the dilemmas that result from too many goals. Note that Astin's finding refers to a heavy emphasis on research. Modest research does not negatively affect teaching.

This is good news and bad news. Professors can be both great researchers *and* great teachers, but few institutions have the resources to be great at both. Although institutional change is not the focus of this book, there are incremental yet cumulative ways that individual professors affect their institutions. Faculty profoundly affect the implementation of hiring, promotion, and tenure policies. At many institutions, the allocation of budget dollars within departments is largely under the control of the department chair. Most chairs do not stray too far from the collective wishes of the faculty. Although there are instances of new deans or presidents or the board of trustees unilaterally changing the mission of a college or university, usually the faculty have implicitly acquiesced.

10.2. Scholarship: Classification and Rewards

According to Newman, who wrote *The Idea of the University* in 1891, the university "is a place of *teaching* universal *knowledge*" (Newman, 1996, 3). With the advent of the research university, these goals have been widened to include "the advancement of knowledge through research, the transmission of knowledge through teaching, the preservation of knowledge in scholarly collections, and the diffusion of knowledge through publishing" (Pelikan, 1992, 16–17). A mix of scholarship and teaching is now considered ideal. Although regular publishing is not necessary, all professors should be scholars (Boyer, 1987, 131).

At many colleges and universities, the rewards for research have become considerably greater than those other activities (Tierney, 1998). In an attempt to redress this imbalance, Ernest Boyer, president of the Carnegie Foundation for the Advancement of Teaching, redefined scholarship to include four kinds—discovery (research), integration, application, and teaching. Boyer's book, *Scholarship Reconsidered* (1990), was based on a formulation originally developed by R. Eugene Rice, a scholar in residence at the Carnegie Foundation (Edgerton, 1993). The success of *Scholarship Reconsidered* was greater than Boyer's and the foundation's wildest dreams (Boyer, 1993). It touched an exposed nerve.

The Scholarship of Discovery

"What is to be known, what is yet to be found?" (Boyer, 1990, 19). The scholarship of discovery is classical research. This scholarship includes new findings, investigations, and research, plus the dissemination of the results through oral presentations, papers in print journals, electronic publication, databases, and so forth. Since universities in the United States have been heavily rewarding research for more than one hundred years (Lucas, 1994, 173–180) and educating Ph.D. students in how to do research for longer than that, this type of scholarship represents little difficulty within the university.

However, outside the university research is often attacked. For example, James F. Carlin, the chairman of the Massachusetts Board of Higher Education, stated, "At least 50 percent of all non-hard sciences research on American campuses is *a lot of foolishness!*" (Honan, 1998). The audience loved it. Kay M. McClenney, the vice president of the Education Commission of the States, said the governors are drawing distinctions between research "that is fundamentally important to society *versus* the stuff that is generated to promote tenure" (Schmidt, 1998). Even Bowen and Schuster (1986, 284), who are friends of the university, wrote, "Some of what passes for research among academics is trivial."

There have also been well-advertised cases of misconduct and fraud in scientific and engineering research that tarnishes the public image of research (Alberts & Shine, 1994; LaFollette, 1992). Faculty need to clean their own house, and we must explain to the public why research in all disciplines is important (Lewington, 1998).

Ehrlich (1995, 69) claims that only a limited number of faculty, mainly at research universities, are able to do groundbreaking research. The other forms of scholarship are critically important, since they cover areas of scholarship that are currently neglected, are valued by consumer institutions (Goff & Lambert, 1996), and are easier to do in a variety of settings.

The Scholarship of Integration

"What do the findings mean?" (Boyer, 1990, 19). The scholarship of integration involves interpretation, integration, and synthesis. This scholarship includes meta-research and interdisciplinary work that often do not fit into the current restricted definition of research. Textbooks, computer teaching programs, and popular books in the field are examples of the scholarship of integration.

Professors do this scholarship now. Unfortunately, many universities do not fund or reward it nearly as well as research, and sometimes not at all. As Jerry Goldman, an associate professor of political science at Northwestern University, has remarked, "You don't get a leave around here for writing a textbook or software" (quoted by DeLoughry, 1993, 11). The generation of instructional materials is counted at promotion and tenure time, but it is often lumped as part of teaching (Diamond, 1994). A 500- to 800-page textbook is often counted as one publication, putting it on par with a 5- to 10-page research paper! At some universities textbooks count little, while promotion committees at other institutions are delighted by these efforts. However, well-written books that integrate knowledge do considerably increase a professor's national visibility (Creamer, 1998, 42).

Writing a successful textbook can have other rewards, such as affecting students throughout the world and bringing one name recognition and money, and recent national awards for outstanding software (EDUCOM) and textbooks (Text and Academic Authors Association) have further increased the prestige. However, using one's own textbook in teaching may be viewed negatively by one's students (Silverman & Murphy, 1993). Professors who adopt their own textbook can counter students' cynicism about the conflict of interest by donating royalties earned from the book sales from their own course to the university (Kennedy, 1997, 87). At least this form of integrative scholarship counts somewhat in the university. Popular books are often scorned, and only count on the way to the bank.

The Scholarship of Application

"How can knowledge be responsibly applied to consequential problems? . . . Can social problems *themselves* define an agenda for scholarly investigation?" (Boyer,

1990, 21). The scholarship of application seeks to connect theory and practice. Disci-plinary scholarship is applied as service while contributing to knowledge. The scholar-ship of application includes consultation, technical assistance, policy analysis, program evaluation, outreach in the public schools, and so forth. This "practice and professional service" must include contextual factors while applying disciplinary knowledge (Braskamp & Ory, 1994, 42–48). What faculty often call service—committee meet-ings and administrative functions—is not included.

Rice (see Richlin, 1993b, 44) noted that the scholarship of application is the "most distinctly American" form of scholarship. The Morrill Acts of 1862 and 1890 established the land grant universities with an ethos of outreach and application (C. J. Lucas, 1994, 147–153). In the late 1870s the University of Wisconsin served as the model of a university directly searching for solutions to public problems. Although this scholarship is still healthy and fully functioning in many professional schools and land grant institutions, particularly in schools of agriculture, its importance has been eclipsed by the rise of classical research. More attention to and rewards for the scholar-ship of application are appropriate (Clifford & Guthrie, 1988, 331). However, there are possibilities for abuse if professors find consultation more exciting and lucrative than teaching and other duties on campus (Ercolano, 1994).

The Scholarship of Teaching

The scholarship of teaching is an effort to improve teaching and learning (Hutchings & Shulman, 1999). It starts with the teacher's extensive knowledge base, which helps to create a common ground of intellectual commitment. Faculty need to transmit, trans-form, and extend knowledge while in the classroom. Admittedly, this may be difficult in introductory classes. Professors need to experiment to develop and evaluate new *pedagogical content knowledge* within their disciplines (Lenze & Dinham, 1999; Shul-man, 1986). In addition to improving teaching and learning in their classrooms, schol-ars of teaching must aim to improve teaching and learning in other classrooms through presentations, articles, and books within their disciplines (Cambridge, 1999).

Through experience many teachers have learned teaching patterns that are effec-tive in their courses. They are usually not scholars of teaching. There is a clear differ-ence between gaining knowledge from experience (know-how) and understanding the concepts (Hewitt, 1995; Sparkes, 1994; Wankat, 1999b). The difficulty with know-how is that it often fails in novel situations—the professor who became a good teacher through experience has no generally valid concepts to build on. He or she must experi-ment to find a way that works. Understanding the concepts distinguishes the profes-sional from the amateur. Focusing on the scholarship of others to become "scholarly teachers" (Cambridge, 1999) or becoming scholars of teaching will make professors more professional teachers.

There are clear dangers in an attempt to codify the scholarship of teaching. First, it is possible to understand all the concepts of good teaching but not be able to apply them. The "scholarship of teaching is *not* synonymous with excellent teaching" (Hutchings & Shulman, 1999). The craft and skills of teaching are not part of the scholarship of teaching (Braskamp & Ory, 1994, 37). Professors need both an understanding of the concepts and know-how. Second, items that can be counted, such as presentations, papers, and books, may well push out items that cannot be counted—the teaching itself (Wilshire, 1990, 214–216). One difficulty is that a professor's accomplishments as a teacher cannot be replicated elsewhere, but studies of learning and teaching often can be (Wilshire, 1990, 79). Some scholars who seldom teach have become well known for their interest in teaching because of their studies of learning and teaching. Faculty need to develop imaginative ways to evaluate and value teaching and other uncountable forms of scholarship despite the numerous difficulties involved (Glassick et al., 1997). A final danger is that becoming famous often reduces a teacher's effectiveness (Nagel, 1994, 3).

Evaluation of Scholarship

If these new areas of scholarship are to change the paradigm of scholarship in universities, they must be incorporated into the allocation of resources and the faculty reward system. First there needs to be agreement that these types of scholarship are possible and valuable within the existing environment (Schon, 1995). Second, appropriate evaluation procedures need to be developed. Glassick et al. (1997, 22–36) came up with the following six evaluation standards:

1. Clear goals
2. Adequate preparation
3. Appropriate methods
4. Significant results
5. Effective presentation
6. Reflective critique

Although these authors attempted to develop universal evaluation standards, it is inevitable that many disciplines will develop their own standards.

While the evaluation of teaching and the scholarship of teaching have been extensively studied, evaluation of other forms of scholarship has been essentially ignored (Braskamp & Ory, 1994; Edgerton, 1993). To some extent, published scholarship can be evaluated through citation analysis and journal acceptance ratings (Braskamp & Ory, 1994, 286–288; Centra, 1993, 138–139; Creamer, 1998, 33–45). Unfortunately, many journals are not included in any citation index (Creamer, 1998, 31), and investigators may need to develop a citation listing for the journals of interest.

Paradigm Shifts

The idea of paradigm shifts became popular after Kuhn's (1971) analysis. The signs of a crisis that may lead to a paradigm shift are "the proliferation of competing articulations, the willingness to try anything, the expression of explicit discontent, the recourse to philosophy, and to debate over fundamentals" (Kuhn, 1970, 91). Since these conditions appear to be met at many colleges and universities, the efforts Boyer started in

Scholarship Reconsidered will probably help change the paradigm of scholarship at these institutions. Some institutions, such as Syracuse University, have made this shift (Armour, 1995). Will this paradigm shift restore teaching to primacy at institutions that claim teaching is their primary mission? I believe that the answer will be no at many institutions. Most teaching (and advising and professors' service) is not a form of scholarship. A second, more difficult, paradigm shift is also needed.

10.3. Efficiency in Scholarship: Synergy and Balance

Synergy

Returning to one theme of this book, individual actions and control, what can professors do to increase their efficiency in scholarship activities? First and probably most important is to avoid thinking of scholarship activities as isolated from each other, from teaching, and from life. Search for *synergy*.

Synergies can be developed between the various types of scholarship, teaching, and service (Pelikan, 1992; Rosovsky, 1990; Wankat, 1997). Synergy is possible between teaching and the scholarship of teaching. "Classroom research" can be used to improve instruction, and this scholarship can be developed into presentations and papers (Angelo & Cross, 1993). However, not everyone sees the interactions between teaching and scholarship in a positive light (Barber, 1992; Fairweather, 1996; Smith, 1990; Sykes, 1988).

When professors start doing scholarship on teaching, they often find they have no knowledge of appropriate pedagogical theories, previous work, or the education literature in general. It is impossible to be a scholar without a scholarly understanding of the field. Ideally, this problem is addressed in graduate school (see section 9.4), but professors can learn the missing knowledge. Self-directed reading in disciplinary education journals can help. More systematic ways to start are to read some of the excellent textbooks on teaching and learning (see Chapters 4 to 7), and take a course or workshop on teaching methods.

I can illustrate the synergy between teaching and the scholarship of teaching with a personal story. While working on an education degree (as a full professor), I took an educational psychology course. I used the Personalized System of Instruction course I was teaching as a test bed to produce data for the course project. The analysis of this data helped me improve my quizzes, gave me a better understanding of the students who struggled, and earned me an A on the course project. Then I submitted an abstract for presentation at a national meeting, polished the final paper, and published it in the proceedings (Wankat, 1983b). Adding this scholarship activity was a modest increase in workload. With a little creativity, professors can do teaching scholarship, write a paper, and make a presentation.

> TIP: Search for ways to combine teaching and the scholarship of teaching through classroom research.

Writing a textbook or developing multimedia involves synergies between teaching and the scholarships of integration and teaching. Writing advanced textbooks can be synergistic with the scholarship of discovery, and writing textbooks for experiential practice, design, or service learning can be synergistic with the scholarship of application.

Much has been made of the synergism between research and teaching (Pelikan, 1992; Wankat, 1997). There is obvious synergism between a professor's research and teaching an advanced graduate course in the same area. Student comments lead to deeper insights, and student projects can eventually blossom into joint papers. Offering a graduate elective in one's research area can force the professor to read the literature. Since courses are usually broader than research specialties, professors are forced to learn new knowledge. Teaching the material results in even better understanding. *Synergy results because knowledge, once learned, is available for any purpose.* The knowledge can be used not only to teach but also to enrich literature reviews and launch new research areas.

While professors mentor graduate and undergraduate students in research, they help the students learn how to do research. Mentoring is a form of teaching that is quite likely to affect students' lives. The critics of university research appear to have forgotten that graduate students are students. However, it is essential to maintain balance between mentoring graduate students (and those fortunate undergraduates who do research) and teaching undergraduate students.

Synergy between teaching an introductory undergraduate course and research is more difficult to achieve, but it can occur. Teaching an introductory course for the first time or after a long lapse forces a thorough review of the material. Although the material may not have changed since the professor's college years, the presentation style and emphasis will have changed. The review will revive old memories and possibly result in the professor's learning knowledge that was missed the first time. This knowledge is then available for making new connections and analogies that may help any area of scholarship.

The scholarship of application also has synergies with teaching and other forms of scholarship. Professors who consult can share these real-world applications with students as "war" stories or as projects. Application experiences may lead professors to entirely change their teaching styles and incorporate experiential learning into courses. The scholarship of application can lead to the scholarship of discovery.

The contacts a professor makes in any activity can be synergistic with other activities. Even university committee work can be synergistic with scholarship or teaching, since it mixes together professors from different disciplines. It is not uncommon to find common interests that can lead to joint scholarship activities or team teaching.

You will be more synergistic if you actively look for connections. Can a hobby affect your teaching or scholarship? Can your interests in the scholarship of application lead to greater community involvement, such as serving on the board of a local charity? Can presentation of scholarship at meetings lead to travel that will enrich your teaching and scholarship?

Balance

Appropriate *balance* between activities is critical. All teaching and no scholarship can dull one's mind. On the other hand, all scholarship and no teaching is possible for only a few professors at research universities. The dangers to higher education of eliminating scholarship are probably worse in the long run than the problems caused by excesses of research. The key, as in many human activities, is proper balance.

For many experienced professors at research universities, the danger is that balance will be lost and too much time will be spent on research. Riding herd on graduate students, raising money, writing scholarly papers, and presenting papers at meetings can easily occupy almost all of a professor's time. To maintain balance, professors must set aside time for class preparation and interactions with students. At community colleges and liberal arts institutions, the danger is that scholarly activities will be lost as one struggles to keep up with classes and student demands. I believe that balance can be maintained, but Barber (1992) thinks that balance is never achieved and research receives more attention, effort, and money than teaching receives.

Paradoxically, new professors, despite being well aware of the reward structure of the university, tend to spend too much time preparing to teach and not enough on scholarship activities (Boice, 1992, 2000; Menges, 1999a). They are often totally untrained in how to teach and receive little or no guidance in teaching. Learning to teach by trial and error is enormously time-consuming. Partly because teaching seems to be so urgent, they postpone other activities such as writing. One result is that assistant professors publish less than other professors (Blackburn & Lawrence, 1995, 158–159). Second, new professors have had little experience with time management and juggling many tasks that appear urgent. After completing their courses, Ph.D. students have the luxury of focusing on their research and perhaps their TA assignments. When they write their dissertations, that is often all they do. They believe that scholarship and writing require large, uninterrupted blocks of time. When they become professors, they find their attention distracted by a host of issues—moving, settling in to a new location, settling in as a professional, learning to teach, student interruptions, learning to be a research advisor, setting up a new research program, writing proposals, attending to committee duties, and so forth (Dinham, 1999). A large, uninterrupted block of time? What's that?

Boice (1992, 135–136) recommends that new professors first establish a balance among teaching, scholarship, and networking and then work to establish comfort in teaching. The following steps will help any professor gain balance:

1. Make a detailed log of exactly what you do during the day. (This process was described in section 2.4.)
2. Set minimum and maximum amounts of time for classroom preparation. New faculty need a maximum amount of time, while experienced faculty may need a minimum.
3. Spend at least two hours per week on social networking related to teaching and scholarly activity. There needs to be some balance between networking on scholarship and networking on teaching.

4. Boice (1992, 169–174) recommends daily scholarly writing while Zerubavel (1999, 31) recommends at least every other day. At a minimum, schedule scholarly writing at least twice and preferably more times per week. Sessions need to be long enough to produce some flow. Thirty minutes per session is an absolute minimum, although an hour or more is preferable. Do not schedule marathon (say, more than four hours at a stretch) writing sessions. With a little practice, professors can learn to pick up the thread of their thought and start writing quickly. Another advantage of frequent writing is that the subconscious appears to be more effective when a task is worked on frequently (see section 10.4).

5. Work to integrate scholarly and teaching activities. This is the synergy I discussed earlier.

6. Get a life! Balance requires spending time with one's family and friends. Most people maximize their total work output if they work six days a week. Take at least one day a week off and do *no* work. I'm *not* saying you *should* work six days a week. I'm saying don't do seven on a regular basis. At least one week of vacation per year is also beneficial. Leave the work at the university.

7. Try it! Instead of complaining how this cannot work for you, jump in and try it. Cultivate a "results first" attitude (Peters & Waterman, 1982). When we have a negative attitude, we can always find reasons why something will not work.

TIP: Pick one of the first six items in this list and try it for at least one month.

It is also important for new faculty to balance the scholarship they do alone and the scholarship they do with other faculty. Collaboration should be an agreement among equals. We collaborate when we do scholarship and writing with other professors. Collaborating is trickier than delegating and requires a certain amount of diplomacy to negotiate without Negotiating. Professors need to find balances between giving and receiving and between leading and following. This requires communicating and following some commonsense rules:

- Do your fair share and then a wee bit more.
- Don't always take the lead when working out collaboration agreements, which are often informal.
- Don't always do the fun things.
- Don't always be the cleanup crew unless you enjoy it.
- Give credit generously.
- Don't throw your weight around.

Alonzo stopped working on Sundays and restarted his Sunday tennis matches. If the weather was nice he would take his family to the beach or a state park. When the weather did not cooperate, they went to a movie or bowling. His daughter stopped asking, "Why does Daddy work all the time?" He started feeling better and was less grouchy. And he was getting just as much, if not more, work done.

10.4. Tips for Efficient Scholarship

General Tips

Since the details of how to do scholarship depend on the context, I offer here only proven general tips plus procedures for large projects. The first six tips are adapted from Peters and Waterman (1982, 13–16).

1. Be action oriented. Cultivate a results-first attitude. Get things done.
2. Develop productivity through people. Show respect for the people who help you with the scholarship. This includes secretaries, technicians, graduate students, and other professors. Give them some control, autonomy, and responsibility within broad guidelines (Vogel, 1999). Give the basic rules and guidelines, but do *not* spell out the nitty-gritty details. Be respectful of their abilities and give them due credit. Note that disagreements about what constitutes due credit on publications are common (Kennedy, 1997, 100–106). Some generosity in assigning credit will foster collegiality.
3. Establish group values. For example, checking all citations is a good rule that follows from the value "be accurate."
4. Stick to the "knitting." Stay close to your field of expertise. Some branching out is necessary for growth, but be sure you have the skills, time, and energy to complete the job. Although continually starting and abandoning projects is inefficient, occasionally abandoning a project or scholarship area may be wise.
5. Keep a simple form and a lean staff. Do not build an empire. Empire builders spend all their time managing and raising money. These tasks are not what most of us became professors to do. This advice applies to most professors, but not for the superstars at research universities (e.g., see Vogel, 1999).
6. Stay close to the customers. When applied to the university this typical business advice needs considerable translation. In scholarship, exactly who are the customers? Since granting agencies and foundations pay money, they are customers. Learn what they want and provide it as long as it doesn't violate your or the university's values and is within your "knitting." In another sense, publishers and editors of books and journals are customers. Follow their style guidelines. Don't create extra work for the editor. Finally, our peers who read our articles and books are customers. Give them value for their time.
7. Complete the work, write the article or book, and publish. Scholarship is not complete until the results have been presented or published (Glassick et al., 1997). Before the advent of the web, publication rate was the best predictor of ratings of quality by peers (Sonnert, 1995, 174). The effect of self-publishing on the web on scholar's reputations is not yet clear. Publication rates also obviously affect promotion and tenure (Whicker et al., 1993, 69–78).
8. Remember that everything can be done in small doses. Scholarship does not require large, uninterrupted time blocks.
9. Follow your heart—do what turns you on (Holden, 1999).

10. Get ahead of the curve (Holden, 1999). If you wait until an area is hot to become involved, you are likely to stay one step behind the leaders. (Note that items 9 and 10 may well be conflicting advice.)

11. Do what is necessary, even if you don't enjoy it. If you need funds to support research, write proposals.

Efficient reading and skimming are discussed by McCay (1959, 137–141), Mayer (1990, section 20), and Parker-Gibson (1998). "What is most important is not to be able to read rapidly, but to be able to decide what not to read" (McCay, 1995, 137).

- Read with a goal in mind. Make tentative hypotheses and try to bolster or disprove the hypotheses as you read. Medawar (1979, 39) cautions that "the intensity of the conviction that a hypothesis is true has no bearing on whether it is true or not." It is easier to skim or pay close attention as needed when you have an immediate goal and purpose for reading.

- Read or skim at the level required by the source. Books that do not require much reflection, such as the time management books by Mayer (1990), McGee-Cooper (1994), and McWilliams (1991), can be skimmed quickly and notes immediately jotted into the appropriate computer file or on a note card. Books that require reflection should be savored first. Take notes as you read and, after reflection, transcribe the notes into a computer file or on a note card.

- Find a good review article to use as a guide to the literature.

- To avoid boredom, look for things that are new or different.

- Cast aside your "infoguilt" and realize that there comes a time when you have enough information and can now start the work ("Melange," 1998).

- Be prepared for surprises. If you find an interesting source for a different project, either read it now or record the source for later.

- Magazines and journals accumulate. Skim the issue, write the page number of important articles, and tear out or copy the article.

- Skim for the highlights in newspapers. Write page numbers of important items on the front and reread later. Cut out important items.

- Plan some reading for trips.

- Take notes on all publications and web sites as you read or skim. These notes can be on paper or in the computer. One source per piece of paper or per file allows for easy sorting and arranging of notes when it is time to write. At the minimum include all the information necessary to cite the work. It is also useful to record the call number for library sources, the ISBN number for books, and the URL for web sites. Notes in a book are useful, but the locations of important ideas need to be recorded in the back of the book or with your other notes. Without this additional effort, it becomes difficult and time-consuming to find comments two or three years later. Date your notes.

- Although all sources are suspect, the web is particularly suspect. Try to verify your sources (Conley, 1996; Jacobson & Cohen, 1997).

Creative Scholarship

In addition to luck, serendipity requires "an educated, prepared, and clever eye to rec-ognize the observation for what it is, and not disregard it" (Bloom et al., 1998, 131). "Luck" often comes to those who have patiently been looking for something for years. The subconscious seems to work on the most pressing problem, and it appears to become convinced that a problem is pressing only after a strong conscious effort (Kill-effer, 1969). Once the subconscious is focused, an answer may come while you are not thinking about the problem. I find that answers often come to me while I'm walking in the woods or taking a shower, probably because my conscious mind is quiet enough that I can hear the voice of my subconscious. Usually this voice talks about small things—how to change a phrase, analogies between two topics, or another way to look at things—but occasionally the ideas are more significant.

Look for a viewpoint, solution method, hypothesis, and questions different from others in your research area. Be creative on purpose (Maurice Nelles in Killeffer, 1969, 139). Don't always follow what the stars in the discipline are doing. Bring in ideas from other disciplines. In this way you'll avoid "tunnel vision" (Clark, 1987, 199; Lucas, 1994, 179). What is old hat in one discipline may be new, exciting, and publish-able in another. For example, ideas that are well known in education may be novel when applied to education in your discipline. This approach is a good way to get work published. The papers may be ignored because they don't fit into the discipline's stan-dard paradigm for scholarship, but paradoxically, there is also a better chance that a paper will have high impact. Although searching for creative ideas does not appear to be efficient, once the ideas occur, carrying out the nitty-gritty details of the research may be relatively straightforward and efficient.

The Impact of Scholarship

Young faculty routinely expect their first publication to be a momentous event and are disappointed when it isn't (Getman, 1992, 50). It often takes years and a number of publications to have scholarly impact, and some professors' scholarship never has impact. Impact is affected by many things in addition to the quality of the scholarship. According to Medawar, (1979, 13, 77, 91–93) and Sonnert (1995, 172–178), you'll increase the impact of your scholarship if you

- Work hard. Hard work is more important than intelligence. Professors who work hard on scholarship get more done.
- Publish it. "Fewer, better papers" are more likely to be cited and have impact (Davidson & Ambrose, 1994, 143).
- Persist. Don't let rejections depress you for more than a few hours or at most one day. Use the reviewers' comments to improve the paper, book, or proposal and submit it to a different journal.
- Be patient. Scholarship that creates paradigm shifts is often initially neglected because it is different. For an example, see Palmer's (1998, 54–56) story about Barbara McClintock.

- Select a publication medium where it is likely to be read. A mentor can be helpful in suggesting where to publish.
- Send your material to a web site to be posted. In some disciplines, such as physics, web sites are effective for disseminating information (Wilkinson, 1998). However, some journals refuse to consider papers that have been posted on the web (Guernsey & Kiernan, 1998). Check before you post. Send other researchers copies of preprints. Articles are more likely to be cited if other scholars have copies.
- Connect your research to the work of others. Giving credit when it is due is one way to help ensure that you will receive credit when it is due. Network and get to know other scholars in the field. Professors tend to notice, read, and cite articles by people they know and like. A mentor can help with introductions. Be positive in interactions with other scholars.
- Are lucky. Luck and timing often play a big role in the success of scholarship. This may be worthless advice, but it is a useful explanation if you don't want to admit that another professor works harder or is cleverer than you.

Worthy scholarship may be neglected. Although recognition of women's scholarship has improved, the contributions of women generally are still neglected (Creamer, 1998; Schneider, 1998a; Sonnert, 1995).

Cost–Benefit Analysis

Before starting scholarship, decide whether you really have the energy and time required. Scholarship always seems to take at least three times as much energy and time as first estimated. Be selective. Work is more enjoyable when you are intrinsically motivated and believe that the results will have impact. Don't automatically refuse to work on projects for the department or university; pick and choose projects that interest you.

Informal cost–benefit analyses can help clarify decisions. Suppose you are asked to write two articles, but given the deadlines, you can write only one. One is a short article for a prestigious handbook, and the other is a longer article for a new journal. Assuming that your interest in the topics is equal, the handbook article appears to have a significantly higher ratio of benefit to cost. Of course, decisions are seldom this obvious. For example, this cost–benefit analysis does not take into account that the editor of the new journal is an old friend who has asked you for the article as a personal favor. Quantitative tools are limited, and there are times when other factors are more important.

When money is involved, use a simplified quantitative cost–benefit analysis. Suppose two different sources fund the type of scholarship you are interested in. You can calculate the benefit: cost ratio for each source as follows:

(benefit:cost, $/hour) = (probability of being funded) × ($ of grant) / (hours to prepare)

The time to prepare a proposal is often roughly proportional to the number of pages:

(hours to prepare) = k (number of pages in proposal),

where the proportionality constant, *k*, depends on the individual and the type of writing. Consider the following example:

> **SOURCE A:** This source funds $10,000 grants and requires a ten-page proposal. From past experience you know there is roughly an 80 percent chance of being funded.

(benefit:cost) = (0.8) × ($10,000) / (10k) = 800/k in $/hour

> **SOURCE B:** This source provides $150,000 over a three-year period. A twenty-page proposal is required. The expected probability of funding is 25 percent.

(benefit:cost) = (0.25) × ($150,000) / (20k) = 1,875/k in $/hour

All things being equal, write a proposal for source B, since the benefit:cost ratio is significantly higher. If all things are not equal, there may be reasons to write a proposal for source A. For example, the grant from source A may

- be prestigious,
- be a planning grant that makes you eligible for a much larger grant later, or
- represent money that goes directly to you, not to the university.

With a little creativity, benefit:cost ratios can be estimated for a variety of situations.

Rosovsky (1990, 221) notes that "before World War II, government and private research sponsorship was virtually unknown. It is amazing, how many scientific discoveries were made at that time with only tiny research budgets." This statement accurately describes the current situation in the humanities. If you don't have money, do scholarship anyway. Scholarship is done differently—not necessarily worse or better, just differently—when there is little money.

Project Scheduling

Large projects often require detailed planning. A variety of planning tools, such as chronological lists, critical path methods, and Gantt charts, are available (Walesh, 1995, 155–182). If you need to do detailed planning, these methods are not difficult to learn, and there are user-friendly computer programs for most of them. But for my scholarship these methods seem to be overkill. I do find it useful to break projects into parts and subparts. Find a planning procedure that works for you and use it.

Time lines help sell proposals to funding agencies and book publishers. The time line is a list of dates by which activities will be finished. By working forward from the start and backward from the finish, it is possible to get a feel for when parts of the project need to be done. For example, if a particular piece of equipment is needed for research and there is a nine-month wait to receive the equipment, the time line shows when the order for it must be placed. A time line is a useful fiction.

Be sure to schedule project tasks on your to-do lists and your calendar. It is useful to develop a to-do list for the project and maybe even each part of it. Checking off items on a to-do list should give you a motivating sense of accomplishment. Plan to work on an important project at least every other day. However, excessive planning can be detrimental. Planning instead of actually doing a project can be a subtle form of procrastination. It can also be depressing to see the mountains of work that must be done to complete a project. Sometimes it is better to just jump in and get started.

In graduate school, Alonzo had acquired the bad habit of reading everything very carefully. Often when he was finished with an article he didn't bother to take notes because the article was not useful to his scholarship. And for some articles, which were of minor interest, his notes consisted of the reference and a line or two. Alonzo has come to realize that some of his graduate school habits are counterproductive. He forces himself to skim articles and not read those that will not further his scholarship. Although he still always has a backlog of reading, this method reduces the stack of journals in his office.

10.5. Effective, Efficient Writing

Effective presentation is one of the standards applied to judging scholarship (Glassick et al., 1997). Articles and books usually carry the most weight during promotion and tenure decisions and influence decisions regarding merit raises. Outside the university much of what a professor does, particularly teaching, is hidden, but the written record stands out and controls the professor's reputation (Blackburn & Lawrence, 1995, 115–116).

The majority of professors have never written or edited a book or monograph. More than 40 percent have not published any writings in the last two years, while more than 20 percent have never published an article in an academic or professional journal. At the other end of the spectrum are the 4 to 6 percent who have written or edited more than five books (Bowen & Schuster, 1986, 18; Boyer, 1987, 129, 1990, tables A-19 and A-20; Magner, 1999b; Schneider, 1998a). These are professors who have developed "a lifestyle with work as its central organizing principle" (Creamer, 1998, 67). Professors who have not published may be capable in scholarship and writing but have chosen to focus on teaching or service (Getman, 1992, 126).

This section addresses the process of starting with a clean piece of paper or a blank computer file and finishing with a publishable work. In the next section I extend this discussion to the problems peculiar to writing books.

Resources for Writers

Proper use of language is important. Grammar, punctuation, spelling, and style all need to be considered. Refer to the many excellent reference works on these topics. Start with a good dictionary and thesaurus. Classics on the proper use of English include *The Elements of Style* by Strunk and White (1979), Fowler's *Modern English Usage* (Burchfield, 1996), and *The Chicago Manual of Style* (University of Chicago Press, 1993). The *Handbook of Technical Writing* by Brusaw et al. (1997) and *Effective Writing: Improving Scientific, Technical and Business Communication* by Turk and

Kirkman (1989) are useful. Readability formulas can help you write concisely using common words (Flesch, 1949; Stone, 1997). Web sites developed by professional writers may be useful for academic authors (Crawford and *Writer's Digest* staff, 2000).

> TIP: In addition to a dictionary, find one or two sources that help you and use them.

Use the tools in the word processing program on your computer to improve your writing. The spell checker is a valuable aid. The thesaurus will help you find the right word. With grammar checkers you can locate sentences that may need more work. The word count is particularly useful when the length of the paper is constrained. Unfortunately, these tools can make the writer complacent. They do not replace careful proofreading and editing.

Writing Steps

These resources, valuable as they are, barely scratch the surface of the key parts of writing—organizing ideas and putting the words down on paper (Boice, 1992, 162–183; Boice, 2000; Elbow, 1986; Zerubavel, 1999). Writers are people who write. A widely believed myth is that good writers sit down and produce a lovely, stylistically perfect first draft. This myth implies that if you can't do this you are not a good writer. Almost no one writes this way. Attempts to emulate this myth will result in extremely slow progress or failure.

This myth fails because writing requires several different functions:

- Discovering
- Organizing
- Writing
- Editing and rewriting

The myth would require doing all of the functions simultaneously, which is impossible. Every time you stop to switch functions, you have to start over. For example, suppose you have developed flow and are writing well and quickly. When you come to the end of a thought, the brain asks, "What next?" This requires switching gears and halts the flow.

One solution is to separate the process into steps (Zerubavel, 1999, 38–39). First, *discover* what you want to write about. Do the appropriate scholarly work. Many writers find free writing to be useful (Boice, 1992, 162–183; Elbow, 1986). I prefer to write from an outline, but this does not always work. If I don't know what I want to say, invariably I am unable to develop a logical organization. Free writing helps me discover what I have to say. I open a new file in my word processor, label it "Rough Ideas," and type everything I can think of on the topic. This is a dump of everything I know on the topic. No attempt is made to generate paragraphs or complete sentences. These Rough Idea (Discovery) files may be longer than the finished paper. Since no attention is paid to the finer aspects of writing, producing this draft is rapid. If I am really confused about the topic, I will add additional ideas the next day and continue day by day until the ideas dry up. Free writing is a process of clarifying your thinking about the topic.

Second, *organize* all your resources such as your free writing, notes, papers, books, and so forth. Develop a tentative overall outline of the paper or book and then tentative outlines of each section (Zerubavel, 1999, 39–46). These outlines should be targeted for a particular journal or publisher, but be sure to have at least one backup in mind in case your submission is eventually rejected. Once the sections have been organized, rewrite the overall outline. If you have previously written a lecture on the topic, that serves as a very good start on the outline (another synergism between teaching and scholarship). If you did free writing, edit and organize it. Move ideas to see what fits together and rearrange these groupings until the organization seems logical. Ideas that don't survive editing can be saved in a temporary trash file. The result of this free writing, rearrangement, and editing is a detailed word outline in a logical order. There is no need to worry about grammar, spelling, and style in this outline. However, there is a need to rewrite it. The clearer the organization of the outline, the easier and clearer the writing will be. Outlines do not work for everyone. Some people prefer concept maps (Novak & Gowin, 1984), and others use audiotapes or stenographers.

After taking a break, the next step is to *write*. "Don't wait for inspiration, ever. Write. Don't aspire to perfect openings. If you do, you'll never finish. Just write" (Kluge, 1993, 40). Write rapidly. Ignore spelling, punctuation, and grammar rules. Get the words down on paper or in the computer. If you like a phrase from your outline or free writing, use it. If the flow of the writing takes you away from the outline, that's fine. The outline is labeled "tentative" to allow for this. While writing, talk to yourself. Tell yourself how well you are doing. "I'm really cooking today." Think of the work as meaningful and clever. Keep your editor function out of sight and out of mind.

One absolutely key idea is that *writing is rewriting* (Boice, 1992, 2000; Elbow, 1986; Kluge, 1993; Zerubavel, 1999). Let the draft sit for at least a day and then rewrite. It is now time for the editor in your brain to have fun. React to the writing as if a stranger wrote it—and sometimes it will look that way. Write a better opening if your original one is trash. Make sure that each section makes sense. Throw away parts that don't withstand the cold logic of editing. Remove redundancies. Use your word processing program to correct the spelling, style, grammar, and so forth. Move phrases and paragraphs around. Savor the words and search for the best word.

The next day, print a hard copy and edit again. Text looks different on paper than on the computer screen. Continue rewriting until the draft seems finished. Look at the big picture. Is everything finished, including the title, abstract, examples and stories, figures, tables, and so forth? If not, develop the missing pieces. The abstract deserves extra attention, since many more people will read it than will read the paper (Davidson & Ambrose, 1994, 132).

When you think you are finished, let the paper sit for a couple of days. Your subconscious will mull it over. If you still think it is done, then it is time to *ask someone else to review and edit it* (Boice, 1992, 178–181). This can be a painful process. External editing can greatly improve your writing if you can control your ego and investment in the paper. Since many journals and book publishers no longer do copy editing, have papers and books copy-edited before you submit them.

Finally, check that everything is in the format required by the journal or publisher you plan to submit to. As a journal editor, I always took papers less seriously if they ignored my journal's style guide. Learn what the journal wants and then provide it.

If your paper is rejected, let it sit for a few days to give yourself time to calm down. Then modify the paper for resubmission or submission to another journal. Read the reviews and incorporate any ideas that will improve the paper. Be sure to change the format to fit the style guidelines of the new journal.

Writer's Block

The effects of *writer's block* can be minimized (Boice, 1992, 162–183; Day, 1992a, 1992b; 1993; A. F. Lucas, 1994, 164–165; Zerubavel, 1999, 2, 10). The procedure outlined above tends to prevent writer's block. The early organizing steps don't require formal writing. Success in discovering and organizing leads to a positive attitude that helps when you write. And the writing is purposely not perfect. Forcing yourself to write whether you're inspired or not eventually leads to fluency. Writing regularly minimizes writer's block (Boice, 1992, 163–167; Zerubavel, 1999, 10). Infrequent writers become rusty and feel more pressure to be inspired and perform when they try to write. It may also be helpful to establish *rituals* related to writing such as sitting down at the computer early in the morning with a cup of coffee (Silverman, 1996). Finally, you can use behaviors you want to do, such as reading the newspaper, as a reward for writing (A. F. Lucas, 1994, 164).

However, *fear* can cause writer's block. Getting started on anything new can be difficult. The procedure outlined above alleviates some fear, since relatively easy steps are done first, and near-perfection is not aimed for until late in the process. Yet fear can prevent one from starting. We are afraid of being blocked, being unable to finish the paper, finding out that we don't understand the area, getting in over our heads, having the paper be rejected, having the paper (and thus by implication us) be ridiculed or neglected, receiving faint praise from administrators and demands for more work, being unmasked as an inadequate fraud, or finding that we hate our discipline. If we never start, we never have to face our fears. Because of fear, I have procrastinated, sometimes for years, before starting to write each book. Writing the first paper from your dissertation and your first postdissertation paper are occasions ripe for fear. Fear is a major cause for writer's block experienced by Ph.D. students writing their dissertations (Duggins, 1998).

It's almost impossible to eliminate this fear. Instead, acknowledge that you are afraid and write despite the fear. To acknowledge the fear, discuss it with a trusted friend, counselor, or psychologist, or serve as your own psychologist by honestly writing down what you are afraid of. Getting the fear out in the open makes it more manageable.

Daily Writing

The reasons for limiting marathon writing sessions need to be explored further (Boice, 1992; Boice, 2000). First, writing is difficult, draining work. Most people, even professional writers, cannot write productively for longer than four to six hours. Second, startup time is cut significantly if we are in the regular habit of writing. Zerubavel (1999, 83–84) suggests ending each writing session by prepping for the next. Write down a few ideas that sketch out where you plan to go. Third, scheduling a marathon tends to make it *too* important. If all the writing that will get done in a week or a month must be done during the marathon session, there is great pressure. Pressure to perform often causes procrastination. And a bad day really cuts into productivity. You will write more and better by writing frequently for short periods. If the time is available to write more, say, during the summer or a sabbatical, write for four to six hours a day, but do it five or six days a week.

Progress in writing is erratic and unpredictable. Some days, the words flow and a great deal is accomplished. Avoid seeing these wonderful days as the benchmark of what *should* be accomplished every day. There will be days when you sit down to write and find that other things need to be worked on that although necessary, don't feel productive. Perhaps the outline has to be revised or references have to be recorded. Another advantage of writing regularly is that it is easier to see these ups and downs in a philosophical light. Writing can become a difficult but enjoyable occupation (Boice, 1992, 177–178).

At the urging of his mentor, Alonzo started writing at home for an hour before he came into his office. Much to his surprise, he found that he was getting just as much done at work as before. Somehow, he was wasting less time at work. And an hour a day of writing worked pretty well. After two months, he had written his first article and sent it to a journal. This was more than he had written in the previous three years!

10.6. Writing a Book: The Quintessential Large Scholarly Project

Writing a book and getting it published is often a defining point in a professor's career, but most professors never publish a book. Most of the comments in this section also apply to multimedia, which in the future may *share* the limelight with books.

Why Books?

Books are a natural way to report significant scholarship, since writing forces one to think deeply about the topic. Scholarly books can have significant impact, and widely adopted textbooks have an enormous impact on teaching, although they often receive little respect in academe. In addition, writing a successful textbook or popular book can be the path to owning a new Porsche or Mercedes.

Guides for book writers that may be helpful include Benjaminson (1992), Smedley et al. (1993), and Zerubavel (1999). Derricourt's (1996) guide to scholarly publishing is useful for seeing the publisher's viewpoint. Writing a book is more difficult than writing a journal article for many reasons:

- The project is very large. A typical book may be equivalent to writing 10 to 15 critical review papers. It is not unusual for professors to spend 10 years writing a textbook. Fedler (1992) suggests estimating the time it will take to keyboard your book and then doubling this figure. For textbooks a factor of three or four is probably more appropriate, because of the time required to develop examples and homework questions. Zerubavel (1999, 56–80) explains more detailed methods for estimating manuscript length and the time required to finish. Most professors who write books put an enormous amount of their own time into the effort.

- Other duties must be performed while writing. Except during sabbatical, professors cannot focus solely on the book.
- Books must be "sold" to publishers. The publisher must believe that there is a market of potential readers. This is not a criterion for dissertations or articles in scholarly publications.
- Production may require additional work (Derricourt, 1996). The author must work with the editors to improve the book. Books that are camera-ready or computer-ready may require significant extra work by the author.
- Books are very public. Any mistakes or fuzzy thinking can set the critics howling.
- In some disciplines, books have a major impact on a professor's career.
- Controlling fear and other demotivating forces is critical. Because of the importance of the book and the length of time it takes, it is easy to become demotivated and abandon the project. Approximately half the textbooks that are contracted for are never delivered.

Writing a book requires a major commitment. How do you know you are ready? If progress is to be made, *the book must be your major goal*. It will devour all of your free time for several years. Are you willing to make writing the book your major goal? Do you have the time and energy for this major commitment? Have you established a pattern of writing regularly? Do you have staying power for the long haul? Do you have something important to say that people will pay to read? Do you have a reputation in the area? Does writing a book at this time fit into your career plans? In some disciplines publishing a quality book is a major step toward tenure, whereas in other disciplines assistant professors are told to wait until they have tenure to write a book (Whicker et al., 1993, 81). Perhaps you should delay for a year or two when you have a sabbatical scheduled. Finally, and in my opinion the most important question, do you have an *overriding compulsion* to write the book (Lewis, 1992)?

Procedures for Writing Books

Other duties, such as teaching, committees, and working with graduate students, must be done, but whenever you have discretionary time you will spend it working on the book. Fortunately, books can be written in a variety of patterns.

Sabbaticals and leaves of absence: Write for half a day and do scholarship for the book the other half of the day. With this schedule, a one-year sabbatical may be sufficient time to finish.

Summer: Follow a schedule similar to the one for a sabbatical, but expect the book to take more than two summers.

During the term: Find at least an hour a day, three or more days a week, to write. The book may take several years to write, but it will get done if you are persistent.

Or you can use a combination of the above.

Writing textbooks is synergistic with teaching. Textbooks usually require examples, questions, problems, and a solution manual. Fortunately, most of this material can be written and solved as assignment and test problems while teaching. Over a period of several years this part of the book can be completed with a modest amount of extra work. New chapters can be used and tested in the course. One can become well involved in writing a textbook without making a commitment to write. Since finishing the book looks easy (it isn't), the professor may decide to go forward, particularly if approached by a publisher.

Once you decide to write a book, the first step is to select a working title. This gives you a way to refer to it to yourself and others. Since editors want to make their mark on books, often by changing the title, be willing to be flexible later when you find a publisher. The title is a more important consideration for popular books than for textbooks.

Should you write the book by yourself or with one or more co-authors? Single authors retain control. Sharing the work with co-authors reduces the effort required, but the reduction is modest, since considerable time is necessary to integrate parts written by different authors. Two authors together spend probably 50 percent more time writing a book than a single author spends—about a 25 percent reduction in each author's time. Hopefully, the co-authored book will be a better book because of the added expertise and increased rewriting. But be careful. All co-authors must make the book their number one priority (Olds, 1991). If one of the co-authors does not do his or her share of the work, tension can escalate. Removing a co-author may be difficult, unless he or she voluntarily withdraws. I had a co-author withdraw in a way that we stayed friends, but friendships have been destroyed. In the best of all possible worlds, each co-author adds to the book and encourages the other co-author(s) to write. But even in the best of worlds all money matters need to be decided in advance and written down (Olds, 1991).

Develop an outline for the overall book and then an outline for each section. In most books, particularly textbooks, the chapters follow a pattern. The following is a common pattern for a textbook chapter:

Introduction including goals and objectives
Text, figures, and tables for section 1
Example (or case study) for section 1
Text, figures, and tables for section 2
Example (or case study) for section 2
               . . .
Summary, including key points
References
Study questions and problems

Alternatively, an example that illustrates the importance of the material may appear at the beginning of each section or chapter (Hillier, 1996). Establishing a pattern early helps keep the book consistent. Structure the chapters so that each section is fairly small and one topic is discussed at a time. Use changes in margins, spacing, and type fonts to highlight important items for the students.

Zerubavel (1999, 46–55) strongly recommends writing a complete draft of the entire book *before* you begin editing or polishing any sections. Once an entire draft is finished, you will probably finish the book. If you write a couple chapters and start polishing them, it feels as though much less has been accomplished, and you are more likely to abandon the writing effort. In addition, it is easier to see how well chapters fit together once you have completed a draft of the entire book. Although this is not the method I have used, his arguments make sense.

Publishers

Once you have written and revised a portion of the book, it is time to write a prospectus and find a publisher. The prospectus typically includes the following (Derricourt, 1996, 52):

1. Title page
2. A synopsis of the book
3. A brief biographical sketch of the author
4. An analysis of the market, including competing books
5. A proposed table of contents
6. One or two typical sample chapters

Writing the prospectus is a significant amount of work. Some, but certainly not all, of this work is synergistic with writing the book.

Contact publishers. With textbooks it is common to contact several publishers at the same time. It helps if you know the acquisitions editor or he or she knows you by reputation. It is easier to obtain a book contract if you are a well-known scholar (Stone, 1994). It is also easier to get a contract once you have published a successful book. My first attempt to find a publisher for a textbook failed. A year later, I tried another group of publishers and was successful. After the first textbook was successful, the publishers competed with each other to publish the second textbook.

Commercial publishers are in business to make money. Even university presses now must make money and limit losses. This preoccupation with money greatly affects what books publishers will accept, creating a Catch-22 for the author. If, as is usually the case, similar books have already been published, publishers worry that the new book will not be able to compete. If there are no books in the area, publishers worry that there is no market. One way to fit a textbook within these constraints is to pay special attention to making it student friendly (see section 4.4). Study your reference list to determine publishers that might be interested in your book.

Timing is important. Publishers may decline an excellent book if they have just signed a competing book. If the publisher has made the business decision to move into a new area, they might be aggressive in signing new authors. But it is important to try to determine how deep their commitment is to this new publishing area.

When you receive an offer to publish your book, the publisher will ask you to sign a contract. Don't sign immediately. This contract, written by the publisher's lawyers, is biased in the publisher's favor. Author's attorney Michael Lennie (1990, 3) writes, "The first thing to remember when negotiating an author-publisher contract is 'You can't make it any worse.' This is unusual in life. . . . Even random changes are likely to render an improvement." Most professors are not trained to deal with contracts. One option is to join the Text and Academic Authors (TAA) Association (you can call them at 813-553-1195, visit their website <www.winonanet.com/taa>, or write TAA, University of South Florida, 140 Seventh Avenue South, St. Petersburg, Florida 33071) and use their resources to find a lawyer who specializes in author's contracts. Practically everything in the contract is negotiable, and a good lawyer will help pinpoint items with maximum leverage. My failure to negotiate the contract for my first book cost me about $8,000. And there are many items in the contract, such as reversion clauses, copy editing, and rights to electronic forms, that may be more important to you than royalties (Lennie, 1990, 1991, 1992; Levine, 1988).

At most universities books are usually exempted by historical tradition from university control and ownership (Kennedy, 1997, 100, 243). An unwelcome deviation from this tradition that will affect the contract is the demand by a few universities to own the copyright and receive a major share of the royalties. This change from a long and honorable tradition seems unfair, since books, multimedia, and works of art usually represent long hours of work well beyond what the professor is paid for.

Once the contract is signed, the book needs to be finished and delivered in appropriate form (Derricourt, 1996). Be sure that the appropriate form is spelled out in the contract. Write for permission to use copyrighted material unless it is covered by fair-use doctrine (Orlans, 1999). Unfortunately, the dimensions of fair use are imprecise. Many presses use a maximum of 500 words or 10 percent of the document. Permission is usually necessary to use figures, photographs, maps, tables, and other items that are a complete entity (Orlans, 1999). Work with your editor to decide when permission is required.

Many publishers require payment for use of copyrighted material, and the typical publisher's contract, which is negotiable, lists the author as the one who pays. The publisher may be willing to pay for drawing the figures if asked before the contract is signed. Previously, preparation of the index was the responsibility of the publisher, but it is more and more often being pushed onto the author. If the publisher will not prepare an index, the author either needs to do this or contract for the work. Again, who pays can be negotiated. Solution manuals, computer disks, and other supplementary teaching materials may need to be prepared for textbooks.

If you're going to do all this work, why not self-publish? With the advent of personal computers and a variety of software, self-publishing has become easier (Derricourt, 1996; O'Hara, 1998; Ross & Ross, 1994). However, there are many steps that authors need to become familiar with. There is no doubt that copy-editing adds value (Rodberg, 1992a, 1992b), and self-publishers need to plan on paying for this service. Perhaps the biggest consideration is that self-published books do not carry the imprint of acceptance and quality that being signed by a publishing house confers. Thus, self-published books may not count in promotion and tenure decisions. Second, it is convenient to let a publisher advertise and distribute your books. Professors should probably publish their first book through normal channels. Consider self-publishing, if at all, only for subsequent books.

With the exception of reference works such as encyclopedias, a special case because paper and binding costs are very high, it is too early to tell how soon or even if commercial digital publishing of books will have an impact. Consumer acceptance of digital books other than reference books is not assured. Digital publishing of books will probably become important for small print runs because of cost savings (Jensen, 1999). If publishing your "book" is critically important to you even though there are only a few hundred potential readers worldwide, consider digital publishing either by yourself or through a noncommercial publisher. Once the master has been made, mass-produced CDs are less than one dollar each and web distribution is essentially free for most professors. Some granting agencies will pay for dissemination costs if costs are included in the proposal. Digital books will probably have a niche in the publication of out-of-print books for which there is a steady but small demand.

> TIP: If writing a book is in your future, make a plan of when you will have the time and energy to work on it.

10.7. Summary

Many research studies have shown that for individual professors, there is either no correlation or a slight positive correlation between research activity and teaching effectiveness. However, at the institutional level, there is a negative correlation between a heavy emphasis on research and the emphasis on teaching.

The work by Boyer and Rice has expanded the acceptable definition of scholarship at many institutions. Faculty can publish a slow but steady stream of scholarly writings. This scholarship will enrich the literature, but, more important, it will help keep the authors intellectually alive. Scholarship and publication are possible for all professors, because they can be synergistic with teaching and be done a little at a time.

Professors can ensure that their scholarship does not negatively affect their teaching by continually searching for synergies and balance. Some synergies, such as between research and teaching an advanced graduate elective or between writing an undergraduate textbook and teaching, are relatively obvious. Professors who search for synergies can find them even between very different activities, because knowledge is useful regardless of when and why it was learned and networks can result in unexpected interactions. The balance among teaching, scholarship, and personal activities needs to be continually adjusted.

Scholarship is more likely to be productive if one has an action-oriented, results-first attitude. Insist on completing the work and publishing. Use self-discipline while reading to avoid squandering time on irrelevant items. Although it may not appear to be efficient, the effort to be creative will often be efficient in the long run. Scholarship is more likely to have impact if some attention is paid to dissemination. A steady publication rate is also more likely to have an impact on one's field. It is important to have enough time and energy to complete scholarship projects. Doing a cost–benefit analysis can often help you determine which projects to work on. Although the amount of planning needed depends on the scope of the project, plans and time lines will help you sell proposals to sponsors and publishers.

Writing well is a difficult task. At many institutions the importance of the task is magnified by a promotion and tenure system that demands publication. As a result, writing becomes even more difficult and many faculty develop a resistance to writing. Having regularly scheduled writing periods helps most people overcome writer's block. Although difficult for some professors, free writing a purposely imperfect rough draft can be effective. Once a rough draft is available, completing it through incessant rewriting is easier than producing a perfect result from a blank screen or piece of paper. Even a polished draft can be improved by letting it age for a while before rereading it and by asking someone to read and comment on it.

Writing a book is more difficult than writing an article because of the length and the need to consider economics. Yet writing a book is often the defining moment of a professor's career. The key, particularly for first-time authors, is to commit to finishing and publishing the book. Book rejections are particularly disheartening because we put so much of ourselves into books. If you use the publisher's feedback to improve the book and prospectus, dogged persistence and refusing to give in to rejections will usually be rewarded eventually.

Will Professor Alonzo Jefferson be able to publish enough of his scholarship to receive tenure? Yes, if he can stay the course and keep writing on a regular basis. He has reduced the number of hours he is working, but he has become more efficient and is getting more done. He is doing this without neglecting his students, and life has become more enjoyable. Is he ready to write a book? Probably not, since he hasn't fully developed the habit of writing yet, he doesn't need that credential for tenure in his field, and he doesn't have the driving desire to do so.

11 Service and Administration: Citizenship in the Institution

Professor Edward White didn't exactly enjoy being the chair of the undergraduate curriculum committee, but he thought the work was important. The committee not only did all the long-term planning for changes in the curriculum, but also served as the last appeal board for students. Because it was important, Ed always sent around an agenda a week before the meeting, had the departmental secretary send e-mail reminders the morning of the meeting, made sure the meeting started on time and stayed on track, and circulated the minutes shortly after the meeting. Professor Nancy Garcia, his department chair, kidded him that if he kept doing such a good job, his "reward" would be election as the next department chair.

Nancy thought her most important duties were overseeing the hiring and nurturing of new faculty. Her next priority was the nurturing and development of the other professors, professionals, and secretaries in the department. To have time for people, she made sure that all the routine administrative tasks were done efficiently and accurately, usually by her administrative assistant. She wanted to continue teaching and research, which were her reasons for becoming a professor, but she accepted that her current position took time away from them.

Generally, service is less important than research or teaching for promotion and tenure (Edgerton, 1993; Ehrlich, 1995, 77; O'Brien, 1998, 127), but, faculty who refuse to do their share of service and those who cause dissent may not be promoted, regardless of their research and teaching records (Tobias, 1992, 47). Untenured faculty are often advised to do enough service but not too much, and chairs are urged to protect new faculty from too much service (A. F. Lucas, 1994, 171). A survey of faculty by the Carnegie Foundation for the Advancement of Teaching corroborates these opinions (Boyer, 1990, tables A-12 and A-14). To both the question "How important is service within the university community for granting tenure in your department?" and the question "How important is service within the scholar's discipline for granting tenure within your department?", 51 percent of the faculty responded that service was very or fairly important in the tenure decision. Student evaluations of teaching (67 percent) and the number of research publications (57 percent) are considered fairly or very important by more respondents (Boyer, 1990, tables A-6 and A-5, respectively). University service is most important at liberal arts colleges (78 percent said very or fairly important) and least important at research universities (26 percent), while service within the discipline is most important at comprehensive institutions (64 percent) and least important at two-year colleges (36 percent) (Boyer, 1990, tables A-12 and A-14, respectively).

11.1. The Commons: Unassigned Service Duties

Every department and institution has a host of duties that are not assigned, and do not result in personal glory or a sentence in the curriculum vita, but need to be done. These include talking to visitors, attending seminars, attending honor's convocations and receptions, mixing with parents on parent's day, visiting with alumni during homecoming, grading qualifying or general examinations, serving on graduate students' committees, informally advising students, advising student organizations, writing letters of recommendation, recruiting students, judging in competitions, assisting in departmental and institutional governance, attending faculty meetings, mentoring new faculty, helping other faculty with teaching and research questions, reading drafts of manuscripts for colleagues, interacting socially with colleagues, and so forth. It is unnecessary and probably unwise for any professor to try to do all these tasks. In most departments, if all faculty members do their share of these common tasks cheerfully and with good will, the department will function well and be collegial.

External service activities may also be important. Some departments expect faculty to be involved in civic activities (Tobias, 1992, 23–37). Consulting, serving as an expert witness, reviewing papers and proposals, serving on boards of organizations, and practicing one's profession all help inform teaching and scholarship, but they also can conflict with it. Some outside activity can help prevent the deadening effect of academic life, but intense involvement robs time from teaching and research (Getman, 1992, 209–218). Balance is needed.

Most professors belong to at least one broadbased disciplinary organization, such as the American Chemical Society or the Modern Language Association. These organizations can help faculty advance their research, teaching, and service agendas. Stewart (1995) suggests that professors should attend professional society meetings and work the territory. Volunteer for some of the nonglamorous tasks, such as reviewing papers or serving on the local arrangements committee for meetings. If you are a diligent and pleasant worker, these efforts will often lead to more glamorous assignments.

Reviewing papers and proposals is time-consuming but critically important for the functioning of peer review systems. Reviewing proposals can help faculty, particularly new faculty, improve their proposals (Davidson & Ambrose, 1994, 145, 150) and reveals the direction of research in your discipline. Serving on proposal review panels is particularly useful. Not only do you see how others analyze proposals, but also you have the opportunity to network.

Professors can learn to reduce the time spent reviewing papers and proposals while still producing useful reviews. Davidson and Ambrose (1994, 155–156) offer the following suggestions:

1. Don't rewrite portions of the paper. Note if this needs to be done, but let the authors do it.

2. A few sentences of discussion suffice for each point. There is no need for lengthy discussion.
3. If you find a fatal error that invalidates the paper, you can stop searching for other problems.
4. Inform the editor of critical ethical problems, such as republishing already published work or plagiarism.

Although Davidson and Ambrose (1994, 155) suggest not being too selective in what you choose to review, I suggest the opposite. If the paper is not in your research area and you don't publish in the journal that has asked you to do the review, strongly consider refusing the request.

Faculty Governance

Faculty governance affects both the common and assigned service tasks. At the very least, faculty need to attend departmental faculty meetings. And it seems that most do: In Boyer's (1987, 243) survey, 86 percent of those responding said they usually attended departmental faculty meetings, 11 percent attended sometimes or rarely, and 3 percent never attended. Attendance at faculty senate meetings was much less robust, with 18 percent usually participating and 44 percent never participating. Two very important parts of governance—hiring new faculty and participating in promotion and tenure decisions—are discussed in section 11.3.

Mentoring

Mentoring helps new faculty learn to balance their workloads and provides significant social and emotional support that reduces the loneliness and stress commonly reported by faculty (Boice, 1992, 108–121; Menges, 1999a; Tierney & Rhoades, 1993, 27–36). Boice (1992, 116) reported that mentoring contributed to the success of the new faculty who received it, but Bode (1999) found little evidence that mentoring or collegiality was connected to successful outcomes. Nevertheless Bode thought that there are many reasons to foster mentoring. Surprisingly, mentors report more benefits than mentees (Boice, 1992, 116–117). Apparently, mentors alleviated their loneliness, had a chance to reflect on academic life, and felt cared for.

Since most new faculty do not find mentors on their own, systematic programs with a paid coordinator are recommended (Bode, 1999; Boice, 1992,107–121; Haring, 1999; Sorcinelli, 1995). Formal mentoring programs can be mainly "grooming," with one-way communication from the mentor to the protégé, or "network mentoring," with two-way communication and an opportunity for both mentor and protégé to learn (Haring, 1999). Initial orientation programs for mentors and mentees are helpful. Mentors often want to talk but may need to learn how to use small talk and listen (see section 7.4).

Mentors and mentees do not have to be in the same department, and there is less possibility of conflict of interest between unmatched pairs regarding evaluation versus support (Boice, 1992; Sorcinelli, 1995). In my experience, another advantage of unmatched pairs is that the relationship can reduce both professors' parochial outlooks and beliefs that all departments function in the same manner. You may find, as I did, that the grass isn't greener on the other side of campus. The relationships between matched and unmatched pairs may be quite different, but this aspect was not studied. Bode (1999) found that mentoring pairs in which one party sought out the other lasted longer than assigned pairs, but the least successful pairs were those in which the pair had an established friendship (Boice, 1992, 114). Mentees in these pairs often complained when the other person assumed the role of mentor.

Mentor-mentee pairs met more often and were more satisfied with the relationship when they were initially goaded by the program coordinator to meet (Boice, 1992). The usual excuses for not meeting were a lack of time and nothing to talk about. Pairs who used small talk developed friendships and started to meet without being goaded. In addition to small talk, pairs discussed scholarly productivity, classroom management and students, conflicts and politics, and tenure (Boice, 1992, 114–116). Mentees were often hesitant to try to change their teaching styles or their writing habits on the basis of the comments of their mentors. They did seem to develop relaxed styles in class quicker than new faculty who were not mentored. Professional conferences can be stressful for new faculty, who in one study reported that mentors from the same discipline were helpful to them before and during their attendance at conferences (Tierney & Rhoades, 1993). The contradictions reported in the research on mentoring show that there is much left to learn.

Experienced faculty can also help new faculty informally. Be friendly and interested in what new faculty are doing. Don't sit and wait for them to ask for advice. Many will never ask. Volunteer assistance at times when it might be useful. Offer a copy of your syllabus and course outline. Volunteer to introduce the new professor to people at a professional meeting. If you are comfortable with visitors in your classes, suggest that the new professor visit your classroom and discuss the class with you afterwards. Offer to read proposals or articles before they are submitted.

> TIP: Ask someone to be your mentor for either research or teaching, or volunteer to be a mentor. Most professors wait to be asked.

The Negative Side

Few departments approach paradise, and few faculty believe collegiality exists on their campus (Bode, 1999, 122). Trouble can result when those who are doing more than their share of the common service activities realize that there are freeloaders (Cahn, 1986, 52–55). Many faculty refuse to become involved in governance (O'Brien, 1998, 132), and university administrations are universally becoming more important (Kerr, 1982, 28). Professors may insist on belittling colleagues, even though this does not give the name-caller a good reputation (Stewart, 1995). Failure to support the commons rarely causes low raises or lack of perks such as travel money. Untenured faculty are often advised to refrain from helping in the commons, since time spent on these activities takes away from research and teaching. No amount of service will overcome a lack of research at promotion and tenure time (Colton, 1988).

Working toward Improvements

If collegiality, faculty governance, the commons, and a willingness to work for the common good are important, and I believe they are, individual professors, departments, and institutions need to work for controlled balance. Expect that everyone will do his or her fair share of these and assigned service activities (Tobias, 1992, 23–37). Perhaps the critical step is hiring the right people. There are certainly enough excellent teachers and good scholars available that arrogant, crabby, selfish, or nasty candidates do not have to be hired. The only possible exception is hiring a star, but I believe certain personal traits should disqualify even these candidates. However, to avoid the ever present danger that biases may lurk behind the issue of collegiality, objections must focus on matters that are pertinent to faculty duties (Cahn, 1986, 73–74). Senior faculty should lead by example and be involved in faculty governance and the commons. If senior faculty work hard and are collegial, junior faculty will follow their example (Tobias, 1992, 36–37). Mentors can encourage junior faculty to do their share, but not too much. A reasonable balance for untenured faculty is involvement in one substantial service capacity in addition to the common activities (Pye, 1988).

11.2. Assigned Service Tasks

Every department and institution has a host of service tasks that are typically assigned. Although assignments to the university senate and college promotion committee are usually based on a vote by the faculty, most other service assignments are made by the department chair or, for university and college committees, by the dean. The most commonly assigned service is serving on committees. Committee assignments are at two levels—the committee chair and everyone else. Most departments also have quasi-administrative faculty offices, such as director of the Undergraduate Program, director of the Graduate Program, and associate chair. Since these positions may involve a significant time commitment, there may be a modest amount of release time associated with them. There are also assigned tasks, such as academic advising and seminar coordinator, that are in the gray area between teaching and service. All professors "should have a meaningful assignment in support of departmental goals and another in support of institutional goals" (Rezak, 2000, 7). Many departments purposely assign new faculty to fewer duties to give them time for research and teaching. However, there can be a tendency to appoint women and professors of color to more committees to obtain "representation." It is unfair to expect them to represent all members of a group (e.g., women, Hispanics, or African Americans), and excess service can be detrimental at promotion time (see section 11.3). Since these tasks are assigned, it is easier for the chair (and everyone else) to see if all faculty have roughly fair service loads. Of course, the quality and quantity of service actually done vary enormously.

Faculty Governance

At most institutions faculty governance, typically a faculty senate, is responsible for educational matters such as the curriculum and the academic calendar, while the administration is responsible for finances (Gilmour, 1991; O'Brien, 1998, 111). Faculty governance serves as a necessary check and balance on the administration. Rosovsky (1990, 13) states, "I am personally certain that the quality of a school is negatively correlated with the unrestrained power of administrators." In a recent survey, 91 percent of responding institutions had a participative governance organization (Gilmour, 1991). The response was over 98 percent at institutions with more than 10,000 students, but only 64 percent at colleges with fewer than 2,000 students. Faculty need to participate in university governance as part of their good citizenship (Getman, 1992; Pye, 1988).

On the other hand, faculty governance is often boring, frustrating, and inefficient. Faculty senate meetings are too often a faculty debate. Standing committees without a clear charge may meet and discuss topics with no need or desire for closure or action. A surprising number of faculty list committees and administrative assignments as the worst part of academic life (Getman, 1992, 94). Unfortunately, many professors refuse to be involved (O'Brien, 1998, 132) or, even worse, express disdain for those who spend their precious time in faculty governance (Eble, 1988, 215). If faculty refuse to be involved in governance, the administration will fill the vacuum. Although an administrative takeover may result in a short-term increase in efficiency, the long-term educational and research effectiveness of the institution will probably plummet.

There are many approaches to handling this dilemma. A balanced approach can retain the benefits of faculty governance without requiring large amounts of one's time.

- First and foremost, do not appoint or elect untenured assistant professors to faculty governance positions (Stewart, 1995). These positions take up time they need for research and teaching. And votes on controversial issues could cause problems in promotion committees. Professors with tenure, which is designed to protect individuals involved in controversial issues, should fill faculty governance positions.
- Consider the departmental senator your elected representative. Keep personally informed of the issues and give your opinions to the senator, but let the senator do the work.
- Support the faculty who are involved in faculty governance while you enjoy the benefits of their work on the sidelines.
- When it is your turn to be senator, accept gracefully. If you become interested in faculty governance, by all means become involved as a committee chair or senate officer. Otherwise, at least attend senate and committee meetings diligently and represent your department.

Improving Committees

Committees provide for the group deliberation and action required for complex problems such as curriculum revision. Committee work can be satisfying if reasonable aims and firm deadlines are set (Eble, 1988, 215). Although the chair is the key to relatively efficient committee meetings, all members have a role to play. Since members need to know the purpose of the committee, the person constituting the committee should give it a clear charge with appropriate constraints and a reasonable, firm deadline (Tucker, 1984, 61–65). The charge should be in writing, and the entire committee should have the opportunity to ask questions about the committee's charge. Committees need to know from the beginning if they are *advisory* or *decision-making* committees. Confusion on this aspect can cause later charges of bad faith. Standing committees also need a clear charge if they are expected to perform tasks other than routine duties.

Smelser (1993, 2–10) delineates the charge of committees into five functions:

Collective thinker—The committee gathers information, brainstorms, reflects, and either suggests or decides alternate courses of action.

Umpire—The committee serves as judge when rules are ambiguous.

Unifier—The committee builds consensus within the organization for certain actions.

Rubber stamp—Administrators may occasionally expect a committee to approve a policy that has been already decided on.

Competitor in power game—Administrators may wish to deflect criticism by having a committee decide on unpopular actions.

Do not assign untenured assistant professors to committees that function as an umpire, rubber stamp, or competitor. Since assistant professors feel vulnerable and may not refuse assignments, the departmental chair and dean need to protect them (Alexander-Snow & Johnson, 1999). Tenured professors have protection in any controversy. Even tenured professors should think twice before accepting assignment to one of these three types of committees. Unlike in industry, serving on academic committees is essentially a voluntary act for tenured professors (Smelser, 1993, 39–42). Of course, committee assignments do not come neatly labeled, and you have to read between the lines. If you're asked to be committee chair, think about the charge and the resources that will be needed and negotiate both before deciding (Smelser, 1993, 71–75).

Once they receive the charge, faculty committees invariably return to square one and debate the fundamentals (Smelser, 1993, 24–31). The chair should encourage this action early in the process—if this step is skipped, the committee will eventually return to it later when it may be disruptive. One of the prime tasks of the chair is to have the committee redefine vague or overly ambitious charges to something that can be accomplished in a reasonable timeframe. Unanimous agreement on the actual charge the committee will work on will make agreement later, when the report is written, much easier.

The committee chair has significant responsibility for smooth functioning of the committee. The chair can improve committee functioning by (Mayer, 1990, 94–103; Smelser, 1993)

■ Finding a time everyone can meet. Ask all members for the times they *absolutely* cannot meet. This is likely to provide more possible times for meetings than asking when the members *can* meet. If possible, avoid early morning and Friday afternoon meetings.

- Scheduling a regular meeting time and location. Be sure the room has a clock. Inform everyone.
- Developing an agenda before each meeting. Send it to the committee members a few days before the meeting. Bring extra copies to the meeting.
- Sending an e-mail reminder of the meeting on the morning of the meeting.
- Starting and finishing meetings on time. More than anything else this gives meetings a businesslike aspect. Announce that the ending time has arrived, but be flexible. You might call members personally and ask them to arrive on time for the first meeting to set a good precedent.
- Finding a volunteer to serve as committee secretary at the beginning of the first meeting.
- Following the agenda, but giving the committee members a chance to add items for later meetings. Although time-consuming, it is important to be open to alternate viewpoints.
- Being permissive and letting everyone have a say during initial meetings. When it is time to move the committee forward, ask for permission to become directive. The threat of more frequent and longer meetings will often focus members on the task at hand. Time limits for discussion of each topic may work during the directive phase.
- Dealing with conflicts openly. Try for compromise. There may be alternatives that are more acceptable to everyone. Voting is a last resort, because it produces losers.
- Writing the first draft of the report. The person who writes the draft controls the tone and much of the meaning of the report. Submit the draft to committee members a few days before the meeting scheduled to amend the draft.
- Avoiding defensiveness when the draft is amended.
- Obtaining psychological closure when the committee disbands.

TIP: Learn to chair efficient committee meetings.

Committee members also have responsibility for the smooth functioning of their group. Mayer (1990, 100–103) and Smelser (1993, 60–69) suggest that committee members

- Arrive early. Call if you must be late.
- Don't schedule anything for at least fifteen minutes after the meeting is supposed to end.
- Take notes. It will help keep you awake and serves as a check on the minutes.
- Read the minutes before the meeting.
- Follow through on anything you volunteer to do.
- Time your interventions and keep your comments in context. Academics are prone to bringing up irrelevant items (Tucker & Bryan, 1988, 33). Avoiding this sin will help the process.
- Never attack another committee member. It invites revenge, which invites more revenge, and the meeting rapidly deteriorates.

■ Use humor. It helps release tension and soothes the working of the committee. However, humor can be overdone, particularly if it is irrelevant.

TIP: Becoming an effective committee member can make your service less painful.

Director and Assistant Chair Positions

Faculty in positions such as director of Graduate Studies, director of the Undergraduate Program, and assistant or associate chair have significant administrative duties. These positions often serve as a preliminary training ground for future department chairs. With some thought and planning, the occasionally heavy administrative duties can be reduced.

Before accepting the position negotiate the amount of clerical assistance and any appropriate reduction in course load. If full-time clerical assistance is not available, it may be possible to convince the department chair to pay for a part-time student assistant.

Study all of the paperwork and administrative duties involved in the position. All routine tasks or tasks that can be made routine should be *delegated* to your assistant with directions to ask you about nonroutine matters. If at all possible, each time you make a decision, create a policy statement. If faculty should be involved in the decision, which is often the case in policies affecting the curriculum, ask for input or a vote of the faculty. The purpose of policy statements is to make nonroutine questions routine. Be sure your assistant has an updated copy of all policy statements. Policy statements should also be shared periodically with student groups they affect. It is important to remain flexible and caring in application of policy statements, or they can harden into a bureaucracy. There should always be an appeal procedure that will force an in-depth look at the merits of any particular case.

Communicate your decisions and activities on a regular basis to the department chair and the faculty. *Poor communication is the greatest management flaw in colleges and universities* (Tucker & Bryan, 1988, 30–32). Use letters when writing to one or at most two people. Memoranda are appropriate for straight information transfer to large groups of people, such as the faculty, all graduate students, or all undergraduates in the department. If there are due dates, list them twice on the memo. Be sure memos are clear. Everyone tries to soften bad news, and the resulting memos are often ambiguous (Tucker & Bryan, 1988, 31–32). Readers of short memos are prone to read between the lines and overinterpret. Ask someone who does not know the situation to read the memo and discuss his or her interpretation of it with you.

11.3. Promotion and Tenure Procedures

Hiring, promotion, and tenure are the most important decisions faculty are involved in. At most schools, "the faculty decides who shall be on the faculty" (Kingman Brewster quoted by Kennedy, 1997, 127). An effective, fair promotion procedure starts at hiring and continues throughout the probationary period. Helping the administration decide whom to hire is an important responsibility for all faculty (Kennedy, 1997, 128). Cahn (1986, 73–74) suggests

1. Judging candidates "as potential teachers, scholars, and contributors to the academic community." If teaching is important, it should be important in the hiring decision (see section 9.4).
2. Considering personal traits that will affect the candidate's performance as a professor.
3. Expecting a solid commitment to academic ethics.

Faculty need to study the candidate's scholarship and attend the teaching performance. Unfortunately, hiring committees may become acrimonious. A department that reaches a consensus on its mission can usually avoid this problem. Lack of agreement on fundamental issues can lead to endless debate in the hiring committee as the issues are argued again and again.

Selective hiring based on promotion criteria, mentoring new professors, and yearly feedback throughout the process reduces surprises for both promotion committee and candidates. If faculty want to change the reward system, they can start to change it in promotion committees. This particularly applies to teaching, since it is undervalued in most promotion committees (Seldin, 1990b). However, evaluation of teaching based solely on student evaluations is risky. High initial teaching ratings may be the result of beginner's enthusiasm and camaraderie with students, not on fundamental pedagogical skills that will sustain good teaching (Cahn, 1986, 77–78). On at least one occasion, I misinterpreted the meaning of a candidate's teaching record and urged promotion when saying no was probably the wiser choice. I also feel that very meritorious, long-term service by associate professors may merit promotion to full professor, but I realize this does not happen at many research universities.

A fair process must give all assistant professors equal opportunities to excel. Since teaching upper division and graduate courses is more conducive to publishing (Creamer, 1998, 26), assistant professors need equal assignments in these courses. There is a tendency to give women fewer of these assignments (Creamer, 1998). All professors need to be advised early in the process which activities will and will not count for promotion. The promotion committee or, in large departments, subcommittees should evaluate the progress of all assistant and associate professors every year, whether or not a vote is taken. Written and oral feedback should be given to the candidates. Although the department chair will usually provide this feedback, this duty can be delegated to a member of the promotion committee.

The development patterns of women and professors of color are likely to be different than those of white males. For example, the productivity of women often peaks later than that of men (Creamer, 1998, 27). Since they are often more interested in service and advising, it is not unusual to give female professors and professors of color more committee and advising assignments than white males are given. This practice is unfair if these activities don't count at promotion time (Alexander-Snow & Johnson, 1999). These patterns need to be considered in interpreting candidates' records.

Promotion committees should operate with the highest ethical standards. One ethical issue is the confidentiality of votes. Cahn (1986, 86–87) argues against confidentiality at the departmental level, since everyone's position is essentially known, but argues there should be a secret ballot at the next level to protect the volunteers on the committee. I believe secret ballots should be used throughout the process since in close calls—and most denials of promotion and tenure are close calls—final votes are often not known. In any case, committee members should strictly follow departmental and university rules about confidentiality. Votes, particularly at the departmental level, should be accompanied by a detailed assessment of the candidate (Cahn, 1986, 86). Provide the candidate with both positive and negative feedback. When the votes are confidential, the comments need to be suitably disguised.

A second issue with ethical overtones is how much collegiality should count in promotion and tenure decisions. If a faculty member is very disruptive and reduces the effectiveness of the department, then denying tenure on the basis of collegiality can be justified. However, a high threshold needs to be breached before collegiality is invoked as a reason for denial of tenure.

Typically, candidates should demonstrate excellence in research, teaching, or service; however, at many institutions teaching and service are undervalued (Getman, 1992, 117; Tierney, 1998) and publication has become "a surrogate for excellence" (Getman, 1992, 100). The downsides of denial of tenure to a meritorious assistant professor are that it blights his or her life, at least temporarily, and other untenured professors become obsessed with earning tenure (Getman, 1992, 112). The other side of the argument is essentially that granting tenure to marginal candidates is more likely to result in deadwood and a mediocre department (Cahn, 1986, 77–88). Cahn (1986, 80) argues that saying no when yes is appropriate is probably less damaging to the institution than mistakenly awarding tenure and suggests that the institution consider whether it could hire a better person. He even suggests a rule of thumb: "When in doubt, say no" (79). Unfortunately, a bad decision either way can become a tragedy. Institutions need to clearly state their mission and then follow it in promotion and tenure cases. Formulas are inappropriate, since fair process requires that every case be considered individually. Special consideration must be made for any professor who is caught in a change of institutional mission (Getman, 1992, 112–129).

Serving on promotion committees is not enjoyable when candidates, particularly friends, are denied promotion and tenure. However, this service is critical, since it is a fundamental faculty governance activity. The tenure process changes people (Getman, 1992, 160). We need to work to make the changes positive.

11.4. Department Chairs: The Bridge between Faculty and Administration

The estimated 80,000 department chairs in the United States are crucial for the long-term success of departments and deans (A. F. Lucas, 1994, 6, 1999). Because chairs are partly administration and partly faculty, the position is ambiguous and often stressful (A. F. Lucas, 1999). Despite this, most chairs find a great deal of satisfaction in serving. Bennett (1983, 176–177) and Tucker (1984, 58) report that 80 and 90 percent, respectively, are willing to serve another term. Those who did not want another term had already served for a number of years, were itching to get back to research, or were at institutions with financial difficulties. Department chairs average a 55-hour-per-week workload, spending approximately 26 hours on departmental leadership and administrative tasks, 10 on teaching and advising students, 9 on research and personal development, and 4 on college and university activities (Tucker, 1984, 58–59). Major causes of satisfaction are the chair's influence and attention from departmental faculty.

Roles and Responsibilities of the Chair

Gmelch (1995) maintains that the four roles of the chair are to

1. Serve as *manager* with fiduciary responsibilities. This is the dean's idea of the most important role, and it is the most time-consuming because of paperwork and meetings. However, it is usually the least liked.
2. Be the departmental *leader,* providing long-term vision and direction to the department. This is a challenging but enjoyable role for most chairs.
3. Retain one's *academic identity* by continuing to teach and do research. Since it is familiar, this is the most comfortable role; however, chairs are frustrated by the lack of time. It is not uncommon for them to stop doing research.
4. Serve as the department's director of *faculty development* and be in charge of recruiting, selecting, evaluating, training, motivating, and regenerating faculty. The most important single task, which is shared with the faculty, is selection of new faculty. Since 85 to 90 percent of departmental budgets typically go to salaries, faculty development is important. But chairs are neither trained nor prepared for this task. Gmelch (1995, 154) notes that "the choice is to hire superstars or to develop faculty."

A. F. Lucas (1994, 25) argues that leadership and faculty development are the most important roles of department chairs.

Chairs are ultimately responsible for the operation of their departments. Developing the instructional and research programs, assigning the duties of faculty and staff, dealing with issues of unsatisfactory performance, developing the departmental budget, selecting and evaluating faculty, planning and developing a vision for the department, and serving as the office manager and maintenance supervisor are only a few of their responsibilities. Above all, since they work for and with the dean, good communication and a good relationship with the dean are essential.

Selection of the Chair

Institutions use a variety of procedures to select new chairs. Regardless of how it is done, selection of a new chair is often a period of high anxiety for faculty and staff as well as for the dean (Colton, 1988). Untenured faculty and departmental staff have the most at stake, since they are unprotected by tenure. The decision is also important for tenured faculty, since the chair controls many perquisites and usually has a major say in merit raises. From the point of view of the department, a good chair is fair (which has many interpretations) and is a good advocate for the department with the dean.

In a typical process, the dean picks a selection committee composed of professors in the department and perhaps a student representative or professor from another department. The committee is usually chaired by a senior professor in the department, although the dean or his or her representative may chair the committee. The purpose of the committee is to develop a short list of acceptable candidates who are interested in the position. Candidates for interviews are selected from this short list. The committee may develop the interview schedules and host the candidates. After the interviews, the dean, with advice from the department, selects. As long as the dean selects someone from the list, this procedure gives the committee, and hence the department, initial selection and veto power.

The dean tells the committee the number of names he or she wants on the short list; whether the search should be internal, external, or both; the appropriate rank of candidates; a general idea of the qualifications expected; perhaps a salary limit; and the desired date. Politically, the most interesting part of this list is the type of search to be conducted. An internal-only search may mean the dean thinks there are several good internal candidates or that the dean does not want to increase the size of the department. At research universities, combined searches are common. An external-only search may signal that the dean believes there are major problems in the department.

Finding good candidates who are willing to become chair is often difficult. Fortunately, everyone considers being asked a compliment. External candidates may refuse for a variety of reasons that are unconnected to the department. However, there are times when professors are movable. The professor who wants to become chair but has been passed over may be ready to move. Associate professors can occasionally be lured by the promise of early promotion to full professor. The professor's spouse may be unhappy and encourage moving. The seven-year itch and midlife crises often make faculty ready to leave. Since these issues are usually not known to the committee, all the committee can do is create their list and talk to potential candidates.

Lists of external candidates usually start with people who can almost walk on water. Since there doesn't seem to be any *a priori* way to make selection committees realistic, do this initial screening quickly. Then do a second, more realistic screening. Check references of interested candidates *by telephone*. People are often much more honest in a conversation than in writing. Unfortunately, some external candidates will use the potential job offer to exert leverage over their administrations.

External candidates provide a fresh start for the department, help prevent stagnation, and can sometimes bring an excellent professor to the department. Internal candidates are not as exciting as external candidates, but they often have a number of advantages (Tucker & Bryan, 1988, 42–43). They are well known and thus less risky, lend an air of stability and continuity to the department, and will get off to a faster start. Great teachers, who often make good chairs (Eble, 1988, 193–194; Tucker & Bryan, 1988, 47), are more likely to be nominated in an internal search. External searches invariably take longer and cost more than internal searches. If the department is almost unanimous about an internal candidate, the search committee may save a lot of time and effort by strongly urging the dean to select on the basis of the internal search.

The research and teaching of new chairs invariably suffer. Why do professors want the position? First, most candidates believe they can do it all and do not realize how much their teaching and research will suffer. Second, the chair is important, receives significant respect outside the institution, and has a certain amount of clout inside. He or she has an opportunity to lead the department in new directions. Third, the position presents an opportunity to do one's duty and be of service, which is appealing to many professors. Fourth, becoming the chair is a change of pace that may be desirable after a number of years of teaching and research. Finally, some professors accept the position to prevent rival candidates from taking the job (Colton, 1988). The reasons are appealing enough that the refusal of several good internal candidates to accept the position is a clear warning that the department has significant problems (Tucker & Bryan, 1988, 43).

The dean may select a new chair for reasons different from the departments' (Tucker & Bryan, 1988, 35–36). If the department is important and has high prestige, the dean will want a strong chair who will enhance its reputation. If the dean perceives that the department has a specific problem, a chair who addresses that problem will be selected. If the department is not a high priority and is not slated for growth, the dean will select a chair who will accept institutional priorities and is comfortable with a no-growth policy.

> TIP: The search committee exercises its veto power by leaving names off the list. *Never* place the name of an unacceptable person on the short list. If necessary, give the dean a shorter list than requested.

Working with the Dean

Dealing with the dean is never far from the chair's mind (Bennett, 1983, 153). The chair will be most effective if he or she is respected by the dean and has a good working relationship with and can communicate with the dean (Tucker & Bryan, 1988, 30). Chairs who help the dean by being cooperative and accepting compromise will ease the dean's burden and be appreciated. At the same time, chairs must represent their departments assertively. All deans want cooperative chairs; good deans want them to be strong advocates for their departments. Chairs need to learn to align their department's goals with the dean's goals and support the dean once a decision has been made (Tucker & Bryan, 1988). And they must learn when to choose their battles. Some issues are not important enough to argue about, while a few need to be argued as forcefully as possible.

The departmental budget is often the primary area of contention. The dean's first and most important lesson, "there is never enough money" (Tucker & Bryan, 1988, 65), is also true for departments. Deans should avoid micromanaging the budgets below their level and give the chairs authority to spend as appropriate. Chairs should do the same when allocating (much smaller) budgets within their department. For example, if there is a departmental travel budget, it will stretch further if faculty are given a dollar amount they can spend instead of being told they can take one trip. In the latter case, saving money is not of direct advantage to the professor, while in the former it is. Guarantees of money to attend meetings to deliver papers lead to higher professorial productivity (Creamer, 1998, xi).

Communication with the dean is critical. Early involvement of the dean in major departmental plans gives him or her time to buy in to the ideas (McCay, 1995, 118). Be sure the dean has all the information needed to make decisions. Information, preferably statistics, needs to be arranged in a compelling and easily understood fashion (Bennett, 1983, 160). The most compelling information is data obtained from the provost's office and presented in a way that supports your department's request. The request may get to the president, who will know much less about your department and will rely on the dean's presentation and the strength of the information.

The chair's ultimate weapon in a disagreement with the dean is to threaten to resign. Even if the threat is serious, it is easily overused since "the impact falls off quickly after the first time it is mentioned" (Bennett, 1983, 159). An often more effective approach is to imply that you may resign. This escalates the crisis much less, feels less like blackmail, and can be effective if the dean is perceptive.

Leadership

Professors often become chair because they want to exert leadership. They fairly quickly realize that faculty require a different leadership style than is used in the army or business. In those arenas, the leader's *power of position* is often sufficient. In academe, the chair usually finds that *personal power* is more effective, although the negative side of personal power is coercion (A. F. Lucas, 1994, 14). Persuasion works best (Bennett, 1983, 13; Tucker, 1984, 7–9). The wise chair shares authority with the senior professors in the department, either through a committee structure or informally (Colton, 1988).

The appropriate leadership style depends on the context. Some professors always need significant support, and some seldom want it. New professors may first desire direction and later reject it. Faculty may show different maturity levels for different objectives. Even brilliant professors occasionally act like little children, and the chair needs to mediate conflicts quickly before they escalate. Fairness often involves treating individuals differently.

Chairs make a huge number of decisions (Tucker, 1984, 99–116). Some of these are small and should be made quickly (e.g., should a travel request be approved?), others require input from the faculty before the chair decides, and still others should be decided by the faculty. If the decision requires allocation of the budget, the chair wants input but needs to keep control of the final decision. By tradition, the faculty usually expects to make curriculum and other academic decisions. Unless there is an overriding reason not to, the faculty should make these decisions within broad limits.

To institute change, the chair must be persuasive, particularly if faculty participation is needed for success. Explain why change is desirable and then let the faculty develop an implementation plan. A diverse faculty committee will often develop more innovative plans than the chair, although the committee route is invariably slower. Tucker (1984, 135–136) suggests the following steps for starting new programs:

1. Aim for faculty cooperation.
2. Think big, but start small.
3. Involve faculty in planning from the beginning.
4. Be eclectic. A variety of approaches works best.
5. Pick methods that are likely to succeed.
6. Institutionalize the change.

The prickliness of faculty makes faculty development and evaluation tricky. Share the responsibility for development of junior faculty with senior faculty (Gmelch, 1995). A good teacher can be encouraged to become a scholar of teaching and share knowledge with junior faculty. Research scholars can share their knowledge of funding sources and help junior faculty network. A politically savvy professor can help junior faculty understand the maze of university politics. The chair should try to keep administrative trivia and political aggravation away from junior faculty. Finally, senior faculty who make an effort to work with new faculty should be rewarded (Alexander-Snow & Johnson, 1999). Note that there are a variety of ways to reward individuals besides money (Lucas, 1999). These include attention, private and public praise, attention, favorable course scheduling, attention, resource allocation, and attention.

Performance reviews were my least favorite part of being the chair. Faculty, particularly senior faculty, don't like to be told they are ineffective or wrong, and they dislike being told what to do. However, since problems or lack of productivity seldom get better by themselves, the chair needs to confront them (Bennett, 1983, 73). Ask each faculty member to devise a development plan showing his or her areas of strength and weakness for the upcoming year (Gmelch, 1995). Problem areas are much more palatable if the faculty member brings them up first. Always discuss the areas the professor is doing well in and praise successes. Then discuss areas where improvement is suggested. Mix positive feedback with challenges (Rezak, 2000). Since few professors are stars in teaching, research, and service simultaneously, chairs should look for group approaches to increase departmental productivity (Fairweather, 1999). For example, if a service-oriented professor can be given heavy service assignments with a reduced expectation for scholarship, this will provide research-oriented professors more time for research. Of course, if this is done and the service-oriented professor fulfills expectations, he or she needs to be rewarded. After the performance review, provide a written summary that includes the major positive and negative points. Written summaries protect faculty if nontraditional roles are suggested, and they make it much more difficult for professors to rationalize or avoid uncomfortable truths.

One of the most difficult leadership tasks for chairs is the rehabilitation of burned-out, alienated colleagues. A. F. Lucas (1994, 89–95) describes a system that has a high success rate. The chair starts by greeting the colleague in a cheerful voice. After several days of greeting, the chair engages the colleague in small talk. After several weeks, the chair starts to try to involve the colleague in the department with requests for his or her opinion and then requests to do small tasks. If the burned-out individual starts a tirade at any point in the process, *the chair should not defend the system.* The chair should actively listen and accept the feelings.

Major problems such as alcohol and drug abuse or sexual harassment need to be confronted immediately. Don't wait until the annual performance review. Since these issues may eventually involve litigation, follow your institution's guidelines. If you are unsure of how to proceed, ask for help.

11.5. Some Thoughts from the Trenches for Administrators

This section is not a manual for administrators. Readers searching for a how-to on administration will probably find what they need in some of the many books written by and for deans (Rosovsky, 1990; Tucker & Bryan, 1988), provosts (Martin et al., 1997), and presidents (Birnbaum, 1992; Bogue, 1994; Ehrlich, 1995; Fisher & Koch, 1996; Kennedy, 1997; Kerr, 1982; Murphy, 1997; O'Brien, 1998), plus general books on academic administration (Balderston, 1995; Bergquist, 1992; Birnbaum, 1991; Seldin, 1990a). What I hope to do in this section is to provide a picture of what professors want senior administrators to be concerned with. I will assume that teaching is the primary mission of the institution.

The board and the upper administration should set the tone for the institution (Hecht, 1995). "Symbolism embedded in *action* is far more convincing to faculty than symbolism embedded in *rhetoric*" (Fairweather, 1996, 181). If education is indeed the highest priority, that should be clearly stated in print and the priority of teaching should be discernible from the budget and from hiring, promotion, and tenure actions (Armour, 1995; Rice & Austin, 1990). A major component in the hiring decision should be based on teaching, good teaching should be a major component of the promotion and tenure process, and there should be distinguished professors based on contributions to teaching and the scholarship of teaching.

Higher level administrators should be directly and personally involved in teaching, advising students, or other interactions with students. Green (1990, 56) states that administrators below the president should "make every effort to teach." This does not go far enough. The president and all academic administrators should teach at least one class or seminar a year. If the president needs to meet with donors, he or she can invite the donors to attend class. Nothing will convince donors that teaching *is* important more than seeing the president enjoy teaching.

Administrators whose departments directly serve students should be involved on a regular basis with direct service. For example, the bursar should regularly do a shift "on the floor," collecting payments and dealing with student problems, the director of counseling should counsel, and so forth. All administrators need to develop ways to interact with students formally and informally.

A scholastic atmosphere should permeate the entire institution. Everyone should be encouraged to continue his or her education either formally or informally. Negative rules do not help create an atmosphere of growth.

Presidents, provosts, and deans need to know their subordinates at least two levels down. Presidents need to work regularly with vice presidents and deans and on an occasional basis with department chairs. This is true even at very large institutions.

Methods to gain rapport with faculty are similar to the methods faculty can use to gain rapport with students (see sections 7.1 and 7.2). Learn and use names, be friendly and interested in individuals, and be available. All administrators need to be available so that anyone (faculty, students, and staff) who wants to can make an appointment or drop in at specified times. This access can be strictly limited in many ways, but it is an important safety valve. And the single most important lesson is *listen* (Ehrlich, 1995, 2).

Although the need to limit deadwood has been claimed to be greatly exaggerated (Kennedy, 1997, 131; O'Brien, 1998, 44), deadwood can cause severe morale problems and major public relations disasters. Most faculty want to see deadwood humanely trimmed. Universities cannot afford to allow professors, administrators, or staff to retire in place. Tenure does not prevent removal of faculty for adequate cause but does require due process (Van Alstyne, 1971; Firkin, 1996, 92–97). Adequate cause can include failure to meet specified norms of productivity or performance and specific misconduct. Enlist the faculty senate, union, and the American Association of University Professors to help develop expeditious methods for removing professors, administrators, and staff *for cause*. So that age discrimination is avoided, some type of periodic review needs to be developed. At least the first level of this review process for faculty and staff could be the annual evaluations that chairs should be doing already. Wegner (1999) gives an example of an apparently successful process of instituting posttenure review at Arizona State University.

Calls for increased productivity must be led and modeled by administrators, starting with the president. That is, they must become more efficient and effective also. One efficiency that would be much appreciated by professors is the development of programs on conducting effective, efficient academic meetings.

Most important, administrators must set the highest ethical standards. There should be an attitude of trust and honesty toward all students, faculty, staff, and administrators (Rezak, 2000). When an administrator makes a mistake, he or she must come clean (Rosovsky, 1990, 254).

11.6. Summary

Although almost always considered less important than teaching and research, service in its many guises is important. Colleges and universities would be much more bureaucratic without the many hours of service done by dedicated faculty.

Unassigned service is done in the "commons." Although there is usually no credit attached to it, this service is important for the smooth functioning of the department and the university. Professor Nancy Garcia always volunteered to do the service that she enjoyed and made sure that she did more than her fair share; perhaps this partly explained why she was strongly supported to become the chair.

Assigned service is certainly more visible than the commons, but it can also be more frustrating and irritating. Professor Ed White was able to ease the frustration by working hard to chair an efficient undergraduate curriculum committee. Professors who learn to be good committee members and good chairs can help the service function enormously.

All faculty can help their institution run smoothly by being collegial and supporting those who are involved in service and faculty governance. "Support" does not imply agreement with everything they do but includes appreciation of their efforts. If you think you can do better, run for the senate or ask your department chair to give you significant responsibility as a committee chair or director of undergraduate or graduate affairs.

At most institutions, faculty have a major say in hiring, promotion, and tenure. Professors are usually serious about these functions, although they do not always act professionally. The process will be smoother and more effective if the department can agree in writing what characteristics are required of new hires and for promotion. During the hiring process, candidates should be judged on essentially the same criteria that will be used for promotion and tenure. If teaching is important, faculty candidates should be asked to teach a class in addition to presenting a research seminar.

I believe that it is important to continue to draw departmental chairs, deans, and higher academic administrators from the faculty. The president and higher administrators need to continue to be involved in the highest priority of the institution—teaching or scholarship—or they will lose touch with it. Department chairs would benefit from more training in aspects of the job such as leadership, working with an administrative assistant to handle routine functions, faculty development, mediating conflicts, rejuvenating burned-out faculty, and communicating with the dean.

"The root condition of college professing is that it is a service profession, whether one thinks of serving humankind by advancing truth or by serving students" (Eble, 1988, 221). Devoting time to service functions is congruent with this view.

CHAPTER

12 Closure: Making Changes

Professor Alan Atkins was talking to me the other day. "I understand everything in this book. I agree with ninety percent of it. But I am no more efficient than I was before I read the book." Understanding the approaches is easy. The difficult part is applying the principles. In this short chapter, I discuss proven methods for changing habits.

12.1. Start NOW

Perhaps the biggest barrier to successfully changing habits is grandiose plans. Trying to change everything at once will lead to failure, disappointment, and abandonment of the entire effort. This is why New Year's resolutions often fail. Work on one major goal at a time in small doable steps. Be sure that changes have become new habits—which takes approximately three months (McCay, 1995, 153–159)—before moving on. Don't wait for the perfect moment to start. It will never come. Start now.

To be successful, plan changes that minimize the possibility of failure. This is not a tautology. *Most efforts to change fail because the effort is structured in such a way that failure is almost inevitable.* For example, Professor Atkins may decide to diet, with the goal of losing 40 pounds. He starts a strict 1,000-calorie-per-day diet with no desserts or other goodies. Even more unrealistic, he decides to quit smoking and start an exercise regimen at the same time. The only built-in reward is weight loss. The new lifestyle is started cold turkey. Well, it can't be done. Alan will fail, because the change is too strict, too big, and without immediate reward, and he must be perfect. When he cheats, which is inevitable, he claims he has failed, binges on food, stops exercising, and starts smoking again. To be successful, include rewards and expect occasional relapses.

Covey (1989, 48–56, 72–77), Johnson and Johnson (1986), Lakein (1973, 140–157), McKeachie (1994, 303–311), Menges (1999b), and Weimer (1990, 34–42) suggest the following methods to change habits:

- Start with a positive attitude. You are an adult and you can do this.
- As part of getting ready:
  - Develop awareness and understanding of work methods.
  - Look for new ideas.

- Choose what to change:
  - Pick clear goals.
  - If the goal is measurable, such as weight loss, pick a target.
  - Plan to try some small changes that you believe will work.
  - Plan some challenging but attainable goals.
  - Avoid resolutions that you expect to break.
  - Be selective. Plan to make changes that fit with your life mission and goals. It is easier to make changes if there is a noble purpose.
  - Pick changes that will make a difference.
  - Talk to your doctor first if the changes will affect your health. He or she can also provide valuable motivation.
  - Avoid attempts to change everything at once.
  - Seek balance.
  - Be willing to accept the risk of leaving your comfort zone. Try some things that you wouldn't normally do.
  - Be willing to make mistakes. If you try something and it does not work, you have learned something.
- Start now with a plan:
  - Give yourself some flexibility. Don't expect to do the change every day. You are much less likely to fail if you expect to change your behavior only part of the time, and intermittent reinforcement is powerful.
  - Write your plans down, carry them with you, and refer to them occasionally. Formal resolutions can work.
  - Consider making a public commitment. A friend or relative can help to motivate you and keep you on the straight and narrow.
  - Consider working on changes privately. There is something delicious about having friends notice the effect of your diet without knowing you were trying to lose weight.
- Persist. To change habits, three months is required. Plan to stay with the changes for a long period of time:
  - Exercise your self-discipline. Do this when you don't really need it so that you will be disciplined when you do need it.
  - Tell yourself you have to wait five minutes when you are tempted to backslide. For example, wait five minutes for that piece of candy. Then try to stall again. This is a case where procrastinating is good.
  - Expect relapse. Think of backsliding as a learning experience, not failure, and return to the plan.
- Monitor each change for at least one month, and preferably three:
  - Keep a record. I record every time I exercise in my pocket calendar to be sure I am meeting my goals. If I don't write it down, I forget.
  - Seek appropriate feedback. Monitor the results of the change. If the change affects others, ask for feedback.
  - Accept a lack of obvious progress. Weight loss, improvements in student learning, and increased writing productivity all take time.

- Celebrate the little victories. Define even small progress toward the goal as success. For example, exercisers need to congratulate themselves every day they exercise, even if the exercise was not as vigorous as planned.
  - Reward yourself for the milestones along the way to big victories.
- Institutionalize the change. In other words, make the change a permanent part of your new work habits or new lifestyle.
- Slowly add additional changes as you see progress.
- Stay the course.

Work habits are difficult to change; however, once new habits are acquired, they will be equally persistent. If you can stick with the new habits for three months, you will have a firm basis to build on for future change.

12.2. The "One-Minute" Approach to Change

The *"one-minute"* method (Johnson & Johnson, 1986) involves writing specific goals, reviewing them every day, praising yourself when you accomplish a goal, catching yourself in errors, and praising yourself after recovering from an error. Briefly, the steps are as follows:

1. Write brief, specific, positive goals in the first person. Carry these goals with you.
2. Take one minute to review your goals several times per day.
3. Monitor your behavior throughout the day.
4. When you do something right or close to right, praise yourself *now.* Be specific about what you did right. Pause and feel good about doing it right. Decide to repeat the positive behavior.
5a. As soon as you see that a behavior does not match your goals, be specific about the fumble. Silently feel bad about not following your goals.
5b. Remind yourself that you can recover from fumbles by redirecting your behavior. Praise yourself for recovering and feel good about yourself.

Professor Atkins decides to use the one-minute procedure for two goals. First, he wants to improve his teaching by including activity breaks in his lectures (see section 5.3). He writes his goal on a slip of paper: "I will include one 3- to 5-minute student activity break in the middle of my lecture at least twice a week." He staples this slip of paper on his pocket calendar, where he will see it often. After preparing a lecture, Alan routinely looks at his calendar to see what to do next and thus automatically reviews his goal. If he has included an activity break in the lecture notes, he praises himself, feels good about it, and proceeds to the next task. If he has not included an activity break, he lets himself feel bad and then recovers from the fumble by inserting a break at an appropriate spot.

Alan also reviews his goal before class to remind himself to include the activity break. After class he checks to see if he actually did it. If he did, he praises himself, feels good, and resolves to continue his good work. If during the rush of class the activity break was shunted aside, Alan feels bad about fumbling this opportunity. He then decides to be sure to include an activity break next time and feels good about his resolution. At the end of the week when he reviews his goal, he has been successful if he included an activity break in two of the three lectures. Thus, most of the time he is successful and can praise himself and feel good about his accomplishment that week.

Alan has the reputation for being disorganized. He often loses papers he is supposed to sign and return to his department chair. This exasperates her, and she frequently complains to Alan about this. Since Alan gets along well with the chair in other respects, he decides that it is silly to let such a small thing cloud their friendship. He realizes that if he wants to stop this problem from damaging their relationship, he has to change his behavior. Alan obtains an in box and labels it "papers to sign." This is the easy part. The hard part is to remember to use it.

To change his behavior, Alan uses the one-minute approach. On a slip of paper he writes the following goal: "I will put all papers requiring my signature in the box, and I will sign every paper in the box at least once a week." Alan reviews this goal several times a day. If he has put papers in the box, he praises himself and feels good about it. If there is a loose piece of paper on his desk that needs a signature, he says "Oops!" to himself, and then recovers by putting it in the box. On Fridays reading the goal reminds him that he has not yet signed the papers in the box. He does this task and feels good about himself. Several months later, the chair's secretary remarks, "Alan, what has happened? I don't have to badger you for forms any more."

TIP: The one-minute approach works. Try it for one or two goals.

12.3. A 12-Step Procedure

The one-minute approach works well for professors who are generally satisfied with their time control and have only a few goals to work on. However, there are professors whose lives are so muddled that they are ineffective. They do not know where to start to change things, and controlling their time appears to be hopeless. Change may be affected by a *willing* embrace of a totally new social community such as joining a kibbutz or Alcoholics Anonymous (AA) (Tucker, 1984, 104). Thus, the third approach, for professors who have been totally unable to organize their lives, is a 12-step program modeled after the AA program. Most professors will see this program as overkill.

Since the AA 12-step program is explicitly spiritual and requires a religious commitment, psychologists and counselors have developed alternative 12-step programs for treating alcoholic addiction for the nonreligious (Le et al., 1995; Skinner, 1987). I have used these nonreligious programs to develop a 12-step program for people who are not in control of their time. Professors who are religious may want to refer to the original AA program and change these 12 steps to explicitly refer to a dependence on God (Beattie, 1990; Le et al., 1995; Skinner, 1987).

A 12-Step Procedure for Controlling Your Life
1. I admit that I am not in control of my time and that my life has become unmanageable.
2. I believe that I, with help from others, can restore control in my life.
3. I will turn to others for help, while continuing to work to help myself follow a new path.
4. I will look within and honestly list the obstacles to changing my life.
5. I will become fully aware of how my habits hurt those around me, and will discuss these problems with at least one other person.
6. I will accept others' help and work to change my life in a positive direction.
7. I am proud that I am an adult who can take control of my life, and with the help of others can grow and change.
8. I am willing to make peace with myself and others.
9. I will take action to make peace with and help others.
10. I will strive to be self-aware, monitor my behavior, admit my errors to myself, and follow my new path.
11. I will continue to develop my abilities by becoming fully conscious of myself and others, and I will appreciate what others have done for me.
12. I will actively help others who cannot control their lives.

I do not have direct evidence that this procedure works, as I do for most of the methods in this book. However, there is indirect evidence, since the AA 12-step program does help people who voluntarily enter the program control their alcohol addiction problems.

12.4. Closure

This is the end of the shortest chapter and of the book. Although short, this chapter is important since it explains how to actually accomplish change and use the methods discussed in the previous chapters. Understanding the methods without applying them is an academic exercise. The application of these methods can change your teaching, research, and service, and ultimately your career and life.

Many self-help books include some of the suggestions I give in sections 12.1 and 12.2. I have tried most of them and found them effective. I suggest trying an informal approach first and, if that doesn't work, something more formal. The two most effective actions I can take to help myself change are *writing down my goal* and *keeping a written record of accomplishment.* Writing the goal down forces me to admit that it really is an important goal. The written record, usually a checkmark on a calendar, allows me to monitor progress and is a surprisingly effective motivator. Sometimes the only reason I will exercise is to earn my checkmark for the day.

Improving our efficiency and effectiveness is easiest when there is something to build on. The 12-step program is an attempt to help those who do not appear to have much to build on. A person always has more strength and resources than it seems, and the 12-step program may allow him or her to use them to change.

Is it possible to have it all? Peters and Austin (1985, 496) state, "We are frequently asked if it is possible to 'have it all'—a full and satisfying personal life and a full and satisfying, hard-working, professional one. Our answer is: No. The price of excellence is time, energy, attention and focus, at the very same time that energy, attention and focus could have gone toward enjoying your daughter's soccer game. Excellence is a high-cost item." However, they also state, "There is no requirement that the cost of excellence is suffering." Since professors can, to a large extent, choose how to spend their time, balance can be achieved.

REFERENCES

Agre, P. "Networking on the Network," <http://www. jobwell.org/catapult/pagre-n.html>, August 5, 1994.

Ainsworth, L., Garnett, D., Phelps, D., Shannon, S., and Ripperger-Suhler, K. "Steps in Starting Supplemental Instruction." In Martin, D. C., and Arendale, D. R. (Eds.), *Supplemental Instruction: Increasing Achievement and Retention. New Directions for Teaching and Learning,* No. 60. San Francisco: Jossey-Bass, 1994, 23–29.

Alberti, R. E., and Emmons, M. L. *Your Perfect Right. A Guide to Assertive Behavior,* 2d ed. San Luis Obispo, CA: Impact, 1974.

Alberts, B., and Shine, K. "Scientists and the Integrity of Research." *Science, 266* (1994), 1660–1661.

Alexander-Snow, M., and Johnson, B. J. "Perspectives from Faculty of Color." In Menges, R. J., and associates, *Faculty in New Jobs: A Guide to Settling in, Becoming Established, and Building Institutional Support.* San Francisco: Jossey-Bass, 1999, 88–117.

Allen, D. E. "Bringing Problem-Based Learning to the Introductory Biology Classroom." In McNeal, A. P., and D'Avanzo, C., *Student-Active Science: Models of Innovation in College Science Teaching.* Fort Worth, TX: Saunders, 1997, 259–278.

Allen, R. R., and Rueter, T. *Teaching Assistant Strategies: An Introduction to College Teaching.* Dubuque, IA: Kendall/Hunt, 1990.

Almanac, *The Chronicle of Higher Education 1998–1999 Almanac Issue,* August 28, 1998.

Altbach, P. G. "Problems and Possibilities: The U.S. Academic Profession." *Studies in Higher Education,* 20:1 (1995), 27–44. Reprinted in Altbach, P. G., and Finkelstein, M. J. (Eds.), *The Academic Profession: The Professoriate in Crisis.* New York: Garland, 1997, 3–20.

American Counseling Association. "Code of Ethics and Standards of Practice." *Counseling Today,* June 1995, 33–40.

Andersen, K., and Fabian, K. "The Discussion/Recitation Section." In Lambert, L. M., Tice, S. L., and Featherstone, P. H. (Eds.), *University Teaching: A Guide for Graduate Students.* Syracuse, NY: Syracuse University Press, 1996, 29–36.

Angelo, T. A. "A 'Teacher's Dozen': Fourteen General, Research-Based Principles for Improving Higher Learning in Our Classrooms." *American Association for Higher Education Bulletin,* April 1993, 3–7, 13.

Angelo, T. A., and Cross, K. P. *Classroom Assessment Techniques: A Handbook for College Teachers,* 2d ed. San Francisco: Jossey-Bass, 1993.

Arendale, D. R. "Understanding the Supplemental Instruction Model." In Martin, D. C., and Arendale, D. R. (Eds.), *Supplemental Instruction: Increasing Achievement and Retention. New Directions for Teaching and Learning,* No. 60. San Francisco: Jossey-Bass, 1994, 11–21.

Armour, R. A. "Using Campus Culture to Foster Improve Teaching." In Seldin, P. (Ed.), *Improving College Teaching.* Bolton, MA: Anker, 1995, 13–25.

Arreola, R. A. "Distance Education: The Emergence of America's Virtual University." In Seldin, P., and associates, *Improving College Teaching.* Bolton, MA: Anker, 1995, 219–233.

Astin, A. W. *Preventing Students from Dropping Out.* San Francisco: Jossey-Bass, 1975.

Astin, A. W. *What Matters in College? Four Critical Years Revisited.* San Francisco: Jossey-Bass, 1993.

Astin, A. W. "The Changing American College Student: Thirty-Year Trends, 1966–1996." *Review of Higher Education.* 21:1 (1998), 115–135.

Atamian, R., and DeMoville, W. "Office Hours–None: An E-Mail Experiment." *College Teaching,* 46:1 (1998), 31–35.

Attewell, P. A. "The Productivity Paradox." *Chronicle of Higher Education,* March 15, 1996, A56.

Austin, A. E., and Rice R. E. "Making Tenure Viable: Listening to Early Career Faculty." *American Behavioral Scientist,* 41, (1998), 736–753.

Baecker, D. L. "Uncovering the Rhetoric of the Syllabus: The Case of the Missing I." *College Teaching,* 46:2 (1998), 58–62.

Baird, L. L. *Careers and Curricula: A Report on the Activities and Views of Graduates a Year after Leaving College.* Princeton, NJ: Educational Testing Service, 1974.

Balderston, F. E. *Managing Today's University. Strategies for Viability, Change and Excellence.* San Francisco: Jossey-Bass, 1995.

Baldwin, B. A. "Stress and Technology." *USAIR Magazine,* November 1989, 30–41.

Barbe, W. B., and Milone, M. N. "What We Know about Modality Strengths." *Educational Leadership,* February 1981, 378.

Barber, B. R. *An Aristocracy of Everyone: The Politics of Education and the Future of America.* New York: Ballantine Books, 1992.

Barr, R. B., and Tagg, J. "From Teaching to Learning—A New Paradigm for Undergraduate Education." *Change,* 27:6 (1995), 13–25.

Baxter Magolda, M. B. *Knowing and Reasoning in College: Gender-Related Patterns in Students' Intellectual Development.* San Francisco: Jossey-Bass, 1992.

Beattie, M. *Codependents Guide to the Twelve Steps.* New York: Simon & Schuster, 1990.

Belenky, M. F., Clinchy, B. M., Goldberger, N. R., and Tarule, J. M. *Women's Ways of Knowing: The Development of Self, Voice, and Mind.* New York: Basic Books, 1986.

Bellack, J. P., and King, C. P. "Rewarding Volunteer Educators." *AAHE Bulletin,* 52:10 (2000), 7–9.

Benassi, V. A., and Fernald, P. S. "Preparing Tomorrow's Psychologists for Careers in Academics." *Teaching of Psychology,* 20 (1993), 149–155.

Benjamin, E. "Declining Faculty Availability to Students Is the Problem—But Tenure Is Not the Explanation." *American Behavioral Scientist,* 41 (1998), 716–735.

Benjaminson, P. *Publish without Perishing: A Practical Handbook for Academic Authors.* Washington, DC: National Education Association, 1992.

Bennett, J. B. *Managing the Academic Department: Cases and Notes.* New York: American Council on Education and Macmillan, 1983.

Benson, H., (with Klipper, M. Z.) *The Relaxation Response.* New York: William Morrow, 1975.

Berger, K. T. *Zen Driving.* New York: Ballantine Books, 1988.

Bergquist, W. H. *The Four Cultures of the Academy: Insights and Strategies for Improving Leadership in Collegiate Organizations.* San Francisco: Jossey-Bass, 1992.

Berquist, W. H., and Phillips, S. R. (Eds.). *A Handbook for Faculty Development,* vol. 2. Washington, DC: Council for Advancement of Small Colleges, 1977, chapter 9.

Birnbaum, R. *How Colleges Work: The Cybernetics of Academic Organization and Leadership.* San Francisco: Jossey-Bass, 1991.

Birnbaum, R. *How Academic Leadership Works: Understanding Success and Failure in the College Presidency.* San Francisco: Jossey-Bass, 1992.

Black, B. "TA Training: Making a Difference in Undergraduate Education." In Seldin, P., and associates, *Improving College Teaching.* Bolton, MA: Anker, 1995, 65–76.

Blackburn, R. T., and Lawrence, J. H. *Faculty at Work: Motivation, Expectation, Satisfaction.* Baltimore: Johns Hopkins University Press, 1995.

Bloom, B. S., Engelhart, M. D., Furst, E. J., Hill, W. H., and Krathwohl, D. R. *Taxonomy of Educational Objectives: The Classification of Educational Objectives. Handbook I: Cognitive Domain.* New York: David McKay, 1956.

Bloom, D. F., Karp, J. D., and Cohen, N. *The Ph.D. Process: A Student's Guide to Graduate School in the Sciences.* New York: Oxford University Press, 1998.

Blumenstyk, G. "Putting Class Notes on the Web: Are Companies Stealing Lectures?" *Chronicle of Higher Education,* October 1, 1999, A31–A32.

Bode, R. K. "Mentoring and Collegiality." In Menges, R. J., and associates, *Faculty in New Jobs: A Guide to Settling in, Becoming Established, and Building Institutional Support.* San Francisco: Jossey-Bass, 1999, 118–144.

Bogue, E. G. *Leadership by Design: Strengthening Integrity in Higher Education.* San Francisco: Jossey-Bass, 1994.

Boice, R. *The New Faculty Member: Supporting and Fostering Professional Development.* San Francisco: Jossey-Bass, 1992.

Boice, R. *Advice for New Faculty Members: Nihil Nimus.* Boston: Allyn and Bacon, 2000.

Bolles, R. N. *The Three Boxes of Life and How to Get Out of Them: An Introduction to Life/Work Planning.* Berkeley, CA: Ten Speed Press, 1981.

Bolles, R. N. *The 2000 What Color Is Your Parachute?* Berkeley, CA: Ten Speed Press, 2000.

Bolton, R. *People Skills: How to Assert Yourself, Listen to Others, and Resolve Conflicts.* Englewood Cliffs, NJ: Prentice Hall, 1979.

Bonwell, C. C., and Eison, J. A., *Active Learning: Creating Excitement in the Classroom.* ASHE-ERIC Higher Education Report No. 1. Washington, DC: George Washington School of Education and Human Development, 1991.

Borchardt, J. K. "Managing Time Effectively." *Today's Chemist at Work,* October 1996, 55, 56, 58.

Borysenko, J., with Rothstein, L. *Minding the Body, Mending the Mind.* Reading, MA: Addison-Wesley, 1987.

Boud, D., and Feletti, G. (Eds.). *The Challenge of Problem-Based Learning.* New York: St. Martin's Press, 1991.

Bowen, H. R., and Schuster, J. H. *American Professors: A National Resource Imperiled.* New York: Oxford University Press, 1986.

Bowen, W. G., and Bok, D. *The Shape of the River: Long-Term Consequences of Considering Race in College and University Admissions.* Princeton, NJ: Princeton University Press, 1998.

Bowen, W. G., and Rudenstine, N. L. *In Pursuit of the PhD.* Princeton, NJ: Princeton University Press, 1992.

Bowser, B. P., Auletta, G. S., and Jones, T. *Confronting Diversity Issues on Campus.* Newbury Park, CA: Sage, 1993.

Boyer, E. L. *College: The Undergraduate Experience in America.* New York: Harper & Row and Carnegie Foundation for the Advancement of Teaching, 1987.

Boyer, E. L. *Scholarship Reconsidered: Priorities of the Professoriate.* Princeton, NJ: Carnegie Foundation for the Advancement of Teaching, 1990.

Boyer, E. L. "Scholarship Reconsidered: Teaching and Its Recognition." Paper presented at the annual meeting of the American Society for Engineering Education, June 23, 1993.

Braskamp, L. A., and Ory, J. C. *Assessing Faculty Work: Enhancing Individual and Institutional Performance.* San Francisco: Jossey-Bass, 1994.

Braxton, J. M., and Berger, J. B. "How Disciplinary Consensus Affects Faculty." In Menges, R. J., and associates, *Faculty in New Jobs: A Guide to Settling in, Becoming Established, and Building Institutional Support.* San Francisco: Jossey-Bass, 1999, 243–267.

Brennan, M. B. "Service Learning in Science Takes Off." *Chemical & Engineering News,* April 27, 1998, 46.

Brennan, M. B. "Graduate School: Smoothing the Passage." *Chemical & Engineering News,* January 25, 1999, 11–19. See also page 5.

Breslow, R. C. "The Education of Ph.D.s in Chemistry." *Chemical & Engineering News,* December 11, 1995, 65–66.

Bright, A., and Phillips, J. R. "The Harvey Mudd Engineering Clinic: Past, Present, Future." *Journal of Engineering Education,* 88:2 (1999), 189–194.

Brinkley, A., Dessants, B., Flamm, M., Fleming, C., Forcey, C., and Rothschild, E. *The Chicago Handbook for Teachers.* Chicago: University of Chicago Press, 1999.

Brown, G., and Atkins, M. *Effective Teaching in Higher Education.* London: Methuen, 1988.

Brown, S., Armstrong, S., and Thompson, G. (Eds.). *Motivating Students.* London: Kogan Page, 1998.

Brufee, K. A. *Collaborative Learning: Higher Education, Interdependance, and the Authority of Knowledge.* Baltimore: Johns Hopkins University Press, 1993.

Brusaw, C. T., Alred, G. J., and Oliu, W. E. *Handbook of Technical Writing,* 5th ed. New York: St. Martin's Press, 1997.

Burchfield, R. W. (Ed.). *The New Fowler's Modern English Usage,* 3d ed. Oxford: Oxford University Press, 1996.

Burns, D. D. *The Feeling Good Handbook.* New York: William Morrow, 1989.

Buxton, T. H., "Study Habits: When and How to Study for Maximum Effect." In Higgins, R. D., Cook, C. B., Ekeler, W. J., Sawyer, R. M., and Prichard, K. W. (Eds.), *The Black Students Guide to College Success,* revised and updated by W. J. Ekeler. Westport, CT: Greenwood Press, 1994, 68–76.

Cahn, S. M. *Saints and Scamps: Ethics in Academia.* Totowa, NJ: Rowman & Littlefield, 1986.

Cambridge, B. "The Scholarship of Teaching and Learning: Questions and Answers from the Field." *American Association for Higher Education Bulletin,* December 1999, 7–10.

Carnegie Commission on Higher Education. *The Fourth Revolution: Instructional Technology in Higher Education.* New York: McGraw-Hill, 1972.

Carnevale, D. "Distance Education Can Bolster the Bottom Line, a Professor Argues." *Chronicle of Higher Education,* October 22, 1999, A60.

Carnevale, D. "Study Assesses What Participants Look for in High-Quality Online Courses." *Chronicle of Higher Education,* October 27, 2000, A46.

Carskadon, T. G. "Student Personality Factors: Psychological Type and the Myers-Briggs Type Indicator." In Prichard, K. W., and Sawyer, R. M. (Eds.), *Handbook of College Teaching.* Westport, CT: Greenwood Press, 1994, 69–81.

Carson, B. H. "Thirty Years of Stories: The Professor's Place in Student Memories." *Change,* 28:6 (1996), 11–17.

Cashin, W. E. "Motivating Students." *Idea Paper No. 1.* Mahattan, KS: Center for Faculty Evaluation and Development, Kansas State University, 1979.

Centra, J. A. *Reflective Faculty Evaluation: Enhancing Teaching and Determining Faculty Effectiveness.* San Francisco: Jossey-Bass, 1993.

Chapman, D. (Ed.). "How to Do Research at the MIT AI Lab," <http://www.cs.indiana.edu/mit.research.how.to.html>, September/October 1988.

Chapman, S. "ACS Activities in Professional Training." Chemical & Engineering News, January 20, 1997, 38.

Chickering, A. W., and Gamson, Z. F. "Seven Principles for Good Practice in Undergraduate Education." *American Association for Higher Education Bulletin,* 39 (1987), 3–7.

Chickering, S. W., and Schlossberg, N. K. *Getting the Most Out of College.* Boston: Allyn & Bacon, 1995.

Chism, N. "Taking Student Diversity into Account." In McKeachie, W. J. (Ed.), *Teachng Tips,* 9th ed. Lexington, MA: D. C. Heath, 1994, chapter 22.

Christensen, N. "The 'Nuts and Bolts' of Running a Lecture Course." In DeNeef, A. L., Goodwin, C. D., and McCrate, E. S. (Eds.), *The Academic's Handbook.* Durham, NC: Duke University Press, 1988, chapter 11.

Clark, B. R. *The Academic Life: Small Worlds, Different Worlds.* Princeton, NJ: Carnegie Foundation for the Advancement of Teaching, 1987.

Clark, B. R. *Places of Inquiry: Research and Advanced Education in Modern Universities.* Berkeley: University of California Press, 1995.

Claxton, C. S., and Murrell, P. H. *Learning Styles: Implications for Improving Educational Practices.* ASHE-ERIC Higher Education Report No. 4. Washington, DC: Association for the Study of Higher Education, 1987.

Cleary, T. *The Human Element: A Course in Resourceful Thinking.* Boston: Shambhala, 1994.

Clegg, V. L. "Tips for Tests and Test Giving." In Prichard, K. W., and Sawyer, R. M. (Eds.), *Handbook of College Teaching: Theory and Applications.* Westport, CT: Greenwood Press, 1994, chapter 33.

Clifford, G. J., and Guthrie, J. W. *Ed School: A Brief for Professional Education.* Chicago: University of Chicago Press, 1988.

Colton, J. "The Role of the Department in the Groves of Academe." In Deneef, A. L., Goodwin, C. D., and McCrate, E. S. (Eds.), *The Academic's Handbook.* Durham, NC: Duke University Press, 1988, 261–281.

Conley, C. H., Ressler, S. J., Lenox, T. A., and Samples, J. W. "Teaching Teachers to Teach Engineering— T4E," *Journal of Engineering Education,* 89 (2000), 31–38.

Conley, L. C. "Research Using the Information Superhighway." In McCuen, R. H. (Ed.), *The Elements of Academic Research.* New York: American Society of Civil Engineers Press, 1996, 91–107.

Conrad, C. F., Haworth, J. G., and Millar, S. B. *A Silent Success: Master's Education in the United States.* Baltimore: John Hopkins University Press, 1993.

Cormier, L. S., and Hackney, H. L. *Counseling Strategies and Interventions,* 5th ed. Boston: Allyn and Bacon, 1999.

COSEPUP (Committee on Science, Engineering and Public Policy; National Academy of Sciences, National Academy of Engineering and Institute of Medicine). *Adviser, Teacher, Role Model, Friend: On Being a Mentor to Students in Science and Engineering.* Washington, DC: National Academy Press, 1997.

Covey, S. R. *The 7 Habits of Highly Effective People: Powerful Lessons in Personal Change.* New York: Simon & Schuster, 1989.

Covey, S. R. *Principle-Centered Leadership.* New York: Simon & Schuster, 1991.

Coyle, E. J., and Jamieson, L. H. "EPICS: Service-Learning by Design. Engineering Projects in Community Service." In Tsang, E. (Ed.) *New Approaches to Educational Design: Concepts and Models for Service-Learning in Engineering.* Washington, DC: American Association for Higher Education, 1999, chapter 1. This is part of an AAHE series on service learning in the disciplines.

Cranshaw, F. F., and Hughart, T. R. *Peer Counseling: A Program in Caring.* Dover, MA: Florence F. Cranshaw, Dover-Sherborn High School, 1985.

Crawford, B., and the *Writer's Digest* staff. "101 Best Web Sites for Writers." *Writer's Digest,* May 2000, 24–29.

Creamer, E. G. *Assessing Faculty Publication Productivity: Issues of Equity.* ASHE-ERIC Higher Education Report No. 2. Washington, DC: Graduate School of Education and Human Development, George Washington University, 1998.

Cross, K. P. "On College Teaching." *Journal of Engineering Education,* 82 (1993), 9–14.

Cross, K. P. "Classroom Research: Helping Professors Learn More about Teaching and Learning." In Seldin, P., and associates, *How Administrators Can Improve Teaching: Moving from Talk to Action in Higher Education.* San Francisco: Jossey-Bass, 1990, 122–142.

Csikszentmihalyi, M. *Flow: The Psychology of Optimal Experience.* New York: HarperCollins, 1990.

Csikszentmihalyi, M. *Finding Flow: The Psychology of Engagement with Everyday Life.* New York: Basic Books, 1997.

Cyrs, T. E., and Smith, F. A. *Teleclass Teaching: A Resource Guide,* 2d Ed. Las Cruces, NM: Center for Educational Development, New Mexico State University, 1990.

D'Andrea, V., and Salovey, P. *Peer Counseling: Skills and Perspectives.* Palo Alto, CA: Science and Behavior Books, 1983.

D'Augelli, A. R., Handis, M. H., Brumbaugh, L., Illig, V., Searer, R., Turner, D. W., and D'Augelli, J. F. "The Verbal Helping Behavior of Experienced and Novice Telephone Counselors." *Journal of Community Psychology,* 6 (1978), 222–228.

Dale, E. *Audio-Visual Methods in Teaching,* 3d Ed. New York: Holt, Rinehart, and Winston, 1969.

Davidson, C. I., and Ambrose, S. A. *The New Professor's Handbook: A Guide to Teaching and Research in Engineering and Science.* Bolton, MA: Anker, 1994.

Davis, B. G. *Tools for Teaching.* San Francisco: Jossey-Bass, 1993.

Davis, J. R. *Better Teaching, More Learning: Strategies for Success in Postsecondary Settings.* Phoenix, AZ: American Council on Education, and Oryx Press, 1993.

Day, S. X. "Emotional Aspects of Writer's Block." *TAA Report,* July 1992a, 7–8.

Day, S. X. "Cognitive Aspects of Writer's Block." *TAA Report,* October 1992b, 4–6.

Day, S. X. "The Situational Aspect of Writer's Block." *TAA Report,* January 1993, 9–11.

Deans, T., and Meyer-Goncalves, Z. "Service-Learning Projects in Composition and Beyond." *College Teaching,* 46:1 (1998), 12–15.

Dede, C. "Emerging Media for Distributed Learning: Facilitating Knowledge, Creation, Sharing, and Mastery." Paper presented at Purdue University, March 2, 1999.

Delaney, J. "The Art of Mail Management." *Sky* (Delta Airlines), November 1981, 34, 36, 38.

Delfin, P. E., and Hartsough, D. M. *Programmed Instructions for Crisis Intervention Helpers: Suicide, Drugs and Sexuality.* Lafayette, IN: Purdue Research Foundation, 1976.

DeLoughry T. J. "Professors Report Progress in Gaining Recognition for Their Use of Technology." *TAA Report,* April 1993, 10–11.

DeLoughry, T. J. "Is New Technology Worth It? Colleges Find It's Hard to Measure the Return on Investments in Computing." *Chronicle of Higher Education,* June 22, 1994, A19, A21.

Delworth, U., Rudow, E. H., and Taub, J. (Eds.). *Crisis Center/Hotline: A Guidebook to Beginning and Operating.* Springfield, IL: Charles C. Thomas, 1972.

Derricourt, R. *An Author's Guide to Scholarly Publishing.* Princeton, NJ: Princeton University Press, 1996.

des Jardins, M. "How to be a Good Graduate Student," <http://www.cs.indiana.edu/how.2b/how2b.html>, March 1994.

Diamond, R. *Serving on Promotion and Tenure Committees: A Faculty Guide.* Bolton, MA: Anker, 1994.

Dinham, S. M. "Being a Newcomer." In Menges, R. J., and associates, *Faculty in New Jobs: A Guide to Settling in, Becoming Established, and Building Institutional Support.* San Francisco: Jossey-Bass, 1999, 1–15.

Di Yanni, R. *The Insider's Guide to College Success.* Boston: Allyn and Bacon, 1997.

Duffy, D. K., and Jones, J. W. *Teaching within the Rhythms of the Semester.* San Francisco: Jossey-Bass, 1995.

Duggins, K. "A Psychologist for Aspiring Ph.D.s." *Chronicle of Higher Education,* June 26, 1998, A10.

Dyer, W. W., and Vriend, J. *Counseling Techniques That Work.* Alexandria, VA: American Association for Counseling and Development, 1988.

Dziech, B. W., and Weiner, L. *The Lecherous Professor: Sexual Harassment on Campus.* Boston: Beacon Press, 1984.

Easwaran, E. *Meditation,* 2d ed. Tomales, CA: Nilgiri Press, 1991.

Eaves, B. C. "Courses for Learning the Practice of Operations Research." In Arrow, K. J., Cottle, R. W., Eaves, B. C., and Olkin, I. (Eds.), *Education in a Research University.* Stanford, CA: Stanford University Press, 1996, 231–259.

Eberts, R. "Opportunities for Technology in Engineering Education." Paper presented at Purdue University, December 14, 1998.

Eble, K. E. *The Craft of Teaching,* 2d ed. San Francisco: Jossey-Bass, 1988.

Edgerton, R. "The Re-examination of Faculty Priorities." *Change,* 25:4 (1993), 10–25.

Edward, N. S. "Granting of Academic Credit for Work Based Learning in Scottish Higher Education." *Journal of Engineering Education,* 87 (1998), 15–17.

Edwards, R. V. *Crisis Intervention and How It Works.* Springfield, IL: Charles C. Thomas, 1977.

Egan, G. *The Skilled Helper: A Systematic Approach to Effective Helping,* 6th ed. Pacific Grove, CA: Brooks/Cole, 1998.

Ehrlich, T., with Frey, J. *The Courage to Inquire: Ideals and Realities in Higher Education.* Bloomington, IN: Indiana University Press, 1995.

Ehrlich, T. "Foreword." In Jacoby, B., and associates, *Service-Learning in Higher Education: Concepts and Practices.* San Francisco: Jossey-Bass, 1996, xi–xvi.

Ekeler, W. J. "The Lecture Method." In Prichard, K. W., and Sawyer, R. M. (Eds.), *Handbook of College Teaching.* Westport, CT: Greenwood Press, 1994, chapter 5.

Elbow, P. *Embracing Contraries: Explorations in Learning and Teaching.* New York: Oxford University Press, 1986.

Ellis, A. *Humanistic Psychotherapy.* New York: McGraw-Hill, 1973.

Ellis, A., and Harper, R. A. *A Guide to Rational Living,* 3d ed. North Hollywood, CA: Wilshire, 1997.

"Engineering TA Manual. " College of Engineering, University of Colorado at Boulder, 1995.

Epstein, J. (Ed.). *Masters: Portraits of Great Teachers.* New York: Basic Books, 1981.

Ercolano, V. "Ethical Dilemmas: When Faculty Responsibilities Conflict." *ASEE PRISM,* October 1994, 20–24.

Ericksen, S. C. *Motivation for Learning: A Guide for the Teacher of the Young Adult.* Ann Arbor: University of Michigan Press, 1974.

Ericksen, S. C. *The Essence of Good Teaching.* San Francisco: Jossey-Bass, 1984.

Everstine, D. S., and Everstine, L. *People in Crisis: Strategic Therapeutic Interventions.* New York: Brunner/Mazel, 1983.

Eyler, J., and Giles, D. E. Jr. *Where's the Learning in Service-Learning?* San Francisco: Jossey-Bass, 1999.

Fairhurst, A. M., and Fairhurst, L. L. *Effective Teaching, Effective Learning: Making the Personality Connection in Your Classroom.* Palo Alto, CA: Davies-Black, 1995.

Fairweather, J. S. "The Value of Teaching, Research and Service." *NEA 1994 Almanac of Higher Education,* 1994, 39–58. Reprinted in Altbach, P. G., and Finkelstein, M. J. (Eds.), *The Academic Profession: The Professoriate in Crisis.* New York: Garland, 1997, 169–188.

Fairweather, J. S. *Faculty Work and Public Trust: Restoring the Value of Teaching and Public Service in American Academic Life.* Boston: Allyn and Bacon, 1996.

Fairweather, J. S. "The Highly Productive Faculty Member: Confronting the Mythologies of Faculty Work." In Tierney, W. G. (Ed.), *Faculty Productivity. Facts, Fiction, and Issues.* New York: Falmer, 1999, 55–98.

Farrar, R. T. *Peterson's College 101: Making the Most of Your Freshman Year,* rev. ed. Princeton, NJ: Peterson's Guides, 1988.

Fazey, D., and Fazey, J. "Perspectives on Motivation: The Implications for Effective Learning in Higher Education." In Brown, S., Armstrong, S., and Thompson, G. (Eds.), *Motivating Students.* London: Kogan Page, 1998, 59–72.

Feagin, J. R., Vera, H., and Imani, N. *The Agony of Education: Black Students at White Colleges and Universities.* New York: Routledge, 1996.

Fearing, J. "Guest Editorial: New Addiction Finds People 'Hooked on the Net.'" *Counseling Today,* March 1996, 26–27.

Fedler, F. "Coping with an Author's Common Problems." *The Academic Author,* 6:1 (1992), 8.

Felder, R. M. "The Generic Quiz: A Device to Stimulate Creativity and Higher-Level Thinking Skills." *Chemical Engineering Education,* 19 (1985), 176.

Felder, R. M. "The Myth of the Superhuman Professor." *Journal of Engineering Education,* 83 (1994), 105–110.

Felder, R. M. "Matters of Style." *ASEE PRISM,* December 1996, 18–22.

Felder, R. M., and Brent, R. "Random Thoughts . . . Getting Started." *Chemical Engineering Education,* 29 (1995), 166–167.

Felder, R. M., and Brent, R. "Random Thoughts . . . Objectively Speaking." *Chemical Engineering Education,* summer 1997, 178–179.

Felder, R. M., Felder, G. N., and Dietz, J. M. "A Longitudinal Study of Engineering Student Performance and Retention. V. Comparisons with Traditionally-Taught Students." *Journal of Engineering Education,* 87 (1998), 469–480.

Felder, R. M., and Silverman, L. K. "Learning and Teaching Styles in Engineering Education." *Engineering Education,* April 1988, 674.

Feldhusen, J. F., Ball, D., Wood. B., Dixon, F. A., and Larkin, L. "A University Course on College Teaching." *College Teaching,* 46:2 (1998), 72–75.

Feldman, K. A. "Research Productivity and Scholarly Accomplishment of College Teachers as Related to Their Instructional Effectiveness: A Review and Exploration." *Research in Higher Education,* 26 (1987), 227–298.

Fernald, P. S. "Preparing Psychology Graduate Students for the Professoriate." *American Psychologist,* 50 (1995), 421–427.

Finlayson, B. A. "Can Professors Use Technology to Teach Faster, Better, Cheaper?" Phillips Petroleum Company Lecture, School of Chemical Engineering, Oklahoma State University, Stillwater, OK, April 12, 1996. Copies are available from the School of Chemical Engineering at Oklahoma State University.

Finster, D. C. "Developmental Instruction. Part I. Perry's Model of Instruction." *Journal of Chemical Education,* 66 (1989), 659–661.

Finster, D. C. "Developmental Instruction. Part II. Application of the Perry Model to General Chemistry." *Journal of Chemical Education,* 68 (1991), 752–756.

Firkin, M. W. (Ed.). *The Case for Tenure.* Ithaca, NY: IRL Press, 1996.

Fisher, B. *Rebuilding: When Your Relationship Ends.* San Luis Obispo, CA: Impact, 1981.

Fisher, J. L., and Koch, J. V. *Presidential Leadership: Making a Difference.* Phoenix, AZ: American Council on Education and Oryx Press, 1996.

Fitch, P., and Culver, R. S. "Educational Activities to Stimulate Intellectual Development in Perry's Scheme." In *Proceedings of the American Society for Engineering Education Annual Conference.* Washington, DC: American Society for Engineering Education, 1984, 712–717.

Flacks, R., and Thomas, S. L. "Among Affluent Students, a Culture of Disengagement." *Chronicle of Higher Education,* November 27, 1998, A48.

Flavell, J. H., Miller, P. H., and Miller, S. A. *Cognitive Development,* 3d ed. Englewood Cliffs, NJ: Prentice-Hall, 1993.

Flesch, R. *The Art of Readable Writing*. New York: Harper Brothers, 1949.

Floyd, B. P. "Bookmark." *Chronicle of Higher Education*, August 14, 1998, A25.

Formo, D. M., and Reed, C. *Job Search in Academe: Strategic Rhetorics for Faculty Job Candidates.* Sterling, VA: Stylus, 1999.

Foster, S. "Characteristics of an Effective Counselor." *Counseling Today*, December 1996, 21, 34.

Frances, C., Pumerantz, R., and Caplan, J. "Planning for Instructional Technology: What You Thought You Knew Could Lead You Astray." *Change* 31:4 (1999), 25–33.

Freire, P. *Pedagogy of the Oppressed*, translated by M. B. Ramos. New York: Continuum, 1993.

Freudenberger, H. J., with Richelson, G. *Burn Out: How to Beat the High Cost of Success*. New York: Doubleday, 1980.

Friedman, N. *Mentors and Supervisors: Doctoral Advising of Foreign and U. S. Graduate Students*. New York: Institute of International Education, 1987.

Gardiner, L. F. *Redesigning Higher Education: Producing Dramatic Gains in Student Learning*. ASHE-ERIC Report No. 7. Washington, DC: Graduate School of Education and Human Development, George Washington University, 1994.

Gardner, H. *Frames of Mind: The Theory of Multiple Intelligences*. New York: Basic Books, 1983.

Gardner, H. *Multiple Intelligences: The Theory in Practice*. New York: Basic Books, 1993.

Gardner, J. N., and Jewler, A. J. (Eds.). *Your College Experience: Strategies for Success,* 2d ed. Belmont, CA: Wadsworth, 1995.

Gazzaniga, M. S. "The Split Brain Revisited." *Scientific American*, July 1998, 50–55.

Gerow, J. R., and Gerow, N. S. *College Decisions: A Practical Guide to Success in College*. Ft. Worth, TX: Harcourt Brace, 1997.

Getman, J. *In the Company of Scholars: The Struggle for the Soul of Higher Education*. Austin: University of Texas Press, 1992.

Gibbons, J. F., Kinchelve, W. R., and Down, K. S. "Tutored Videotape Instruction: A New Use of Electronics Media in Education." *Science,* 195 (1977), 1139.

Gibbs, G. *Teaching More Students. 2. Lecturing to More Students*. Oxford: Polytechnic & Colleges Funding Council, Oxford Centre for Staff Development, Oxford Brookes University, 1992.

Gibbs, G. *Learning in Teams: A Student Manual*. Oxford: Polytechnic & Colleges Funding Council, Oxford Centre for Staff Development, Oxford Brookes University, 1994.

Gilmour, J. E. Jr. "Participative Governance Bodies in Higher Education: Report of a National Study." *New Directions for Higher Education,* 19:3 (1991), 27–39.

Gladieux, L. E., and Swail, W. S. "Who Will Have Access to the Virtual University?" *AAHE Bulletin,* 52:2 (1999), 7–9.

Glasser, W. *Reality Therapy: A New Approach to Psychiatry*. New York: Harper & Row, 1965.

Glasser, W. *Take Effective Control of Your Life*. New York: Harper & Row, 1984.

Glassick, C. E., Huber, M. T., and Maeroff, G. I. *Scholarship Assessed: Evaluation of the Professoriate*. San Francisco: Carnegie Foundation for the Advancement of Teaching and Jossey-Bass, 1997.

Glazer, J. S. *A Teaching Doctorate? The Doctor of Arts Degree, Then and Now*. Washington, DC: American Association for Higher Education, 1993.

Gmelch, W. H. *Coping with Faculty Stress.* Newbury Park, CA: Sage, 1993.

Gmelch, W. H. "The Department Chair's Role in Improving Teaching." In Seldin, P., and associates, *Improving College Teaching*. Bolton, MA: Anker, 1995, 153–166.

Goff, J. G., and Lambert, L. M. "Socializing Future Faculty to the Values of Undergraduate Education." *Change,* 28:4 (1996), 38–45.

Goldstein, P. *Copyright's Highway: The Law and Lore of Copyright from Gutenberg to the Celestial Jukebox*. New York: Hill & Wang, 1995.

Goleman, D. *Emotional Intelligence: Why It Can Matter More Than IQ*. New York: Bantam, 1995.

Goodman, J. "The Dental Model for Counseling." *American Counseling,* summer 1992, 27–29.

Gordon, T. *P. E. T. Parent Effectiveness Training: The Tested New Way to Raise Responsible Children*. New York: New American Library and Times Mirror, 1975.

Gordon, T., with Burch, N. *T. E. T. Teacher Effectiveness Training*. New York: Peter H. Wyden, 1974.

Gordon, V. N. *Handbook of Academic Advising*. Westport, CT: Greenwood Press, 1992.

Gose, B. "Many Colleges Move to Link Courses with Volunteerism." *Chronicle of Higher Education,* November 14, 1997, A45–A46.

"Graduate Teacher Program." Graduate School, University of Colorado at Boulder, 1994–95.

Green, M. F. "Why Good Teaching Needs Active Leadership." In Seldin, P., and associates, *How Administrators Can Improve Teaching: Moving from Talk to Action in Higher Education*. San Francisco: Jossey-Bass, 1990, 45–62.

Grites, T. J. "Improving Academic Advising." *Idea Paper No. 3*. Manhattan, KS: Center for Faculty Evaluation and Development, Kansas State University, August, 1980.

Groh, S. E., Williams, B. A., Allen, D. E., Duch, B. J., Mierson, S., and White, H. B. III. "Institutional Change in Science Education: A Case Study." In McNeal, A. P., and D'Avanzo, C. (Eds.), *Student-Active Science: Models of Innovation in College Science Teaching.* Fort Worth, TX: Saunders, 1997, 83–93.

Gronlund, N. E. *How to Write and Use Educational Objectives,* 4th ed. New York: Macmillan, 1991.

Guernsey, L., and Kiernan, V. "Journals Differ on Whether to Publish Articles That Have Appeared on the Web." *Chronicle of Higher Education,* July 17, 1998, A27–A29.

Hackney, H. L., and Cormier, L. S. *The Professional Counselor: A Process Guide to Helping,* 3d ed. Boston: Allyn and Bacon, 1996.

Hamelink, J., Groper, M., and Olson, L. T. "Cooperation not Competition." In *Proceedings of the ASEE/IEEE Frontiers in Education Conference.* New York: Institute of Electrical and Electronic Engineers, 1989, 177.

Hanna , S. J., and McGill, L. T. "A Nuturing Environment and Effective Teaching." *College Teaching,* 33:4 (1985), 177.

Hanna, F. J., Hanna, C. A., and Keys, S. G. "Fifty Strategies for Counseling Defiant, Aggressive Adolescents: Reaching, Accepting and Relating." *Journal of Counseling and Development,* 17 (1999), 395–404.

Haring, M. J. "Briefing on Mentoring." Purdue University, West Lafayette, IN, October 18, 1999.

Harper, T. "e-@mailm@n," *Sky,* October 1999, 104–107.

Harrisberger, L. *Succeeding: How to Become an Outstanding Professional.* New York: Macmillan, 1994.

Hativa, N. "Clarity of Explanation/Development in Lectures." Presentation at Purdue University, West Lafayette, IN, October 25, 1995.

Hatton, D. M., Wankat, P. C., and LeBold, W. K. "The Effects of an Orientation Course on the Attitudes of Freshmen Engineering Students." *Journal of Engineering Education,* 87 (1998), 23–27.

Haworth, K. "More Community Colleges Push to Hire Ph.D.s as Professors." *Chronicle of Higher Education,* January 8, 1999, A12–A13.

Hebel, S. "Community College of Denver Wins Fans with Ability to Tackle Tough Issues." *Chronicle of Higher Education,* May 7, 1999, A37–A38.

Hecht, I. W. D. "Quality Teaching: What Role for Administrators?" In Seldin, P., and associates, *Improving College Teaching.* Bolton, MA: Anker, 1995, 27–36.

Henderson, S. J. "'Follow Your Bliss': A Process for Career Happiness." *Journal of Counseling and Development,* 78 (2000), 305–315.

Hendley, V., and staff. "Let Problems Drive the Learning." *ASEE PRISM,* October 1996, 30–36.

Herrmann, N. *The Creative Brain.* Lake Lure, NC: Ned Herrmann/Brain Books, 1990.

Herzberg, F. *Work and the Nature of Man.* Cleveland: World, 1966.

Herzberg, F., Mausner, B., and Snyderman, B. *The Motivation to Work.* New York: Wiley, 1959.

Hewitt, G. F. "People Processing—The Chemical Engineering Way." Phillips Petroleum Company Lecture, School of Chemical Engineering, Oklahoma State University, Stillwater, OK, April 1995. Copies are available from the School of Chemical Engineering at Oklahoma State University.

Higgins, R. D., Cook, C.B., Ekeler, W. J., Sawyer, R. M., and Prichard, K. W. (Eds.). *The Black Students' Guide to College Success,* revised by W. J. Ekeler. Westport, CT: Greenwood Press, 1994.

Highet, G. *The Immortal Profession: The Joys of Teaching and Learning.* New York: Weybright and Talley, 1976.

Hillier, F. S. "Some Lessons Learned about Textbook Writing." In Arrow, K. J., Cottle, R. W., Eaves, B. C., and Olkin, I. (Eds.), *Education in a Research University.* Stanford, CA: Stanford University Press, 1996, 261–269.

Hilton, P. "The Tyranny of Tests." *American Mathematical Monthly,* April 1993, 365–369.

Hoffman, E. *The Right to Be Human: A Biography of Abraham Maslow.* Los Angeles: Jeremy P. Tarcher, 1988.

Holden, C. "Eight Attributes of Highly Successful Postdocs." *Science,* 285 (1999), 1527–1529.

Honan, W. H. "The Ivory Tower under Siege; Everyone Else Downsized; Why Not the Academy?" *New York Times Education Life,* January 4, 1998, 33, 44, and 46.

Horning, A. S. "Helping Students in Trouble: What They Didn't Teach in Grad School." *College Teaching,* 46 (1998), 2–8.

Houze, R. N., and Simon, R. J. "Cooperative Education: Three on a Tightrope." *Engineering Education,* 71 (1981), 283–287.

Huber, R. M. *How Professors Play the Cat Guarding the Cream: Why We're Paying More and Getting Less in Higher Education.* Fairfax, VA: George Mason University Press, 1992.

Humphrey, J. H. *Teaching Children to Relax.* Springfield, IL: Charles C. Thomas, 1988.

Hunkeler, D., and Sharp, J. E. "Assigning Functional Groups: The Influence of Group Size, Academic Record, Practical Experience and Learning Style." *Journal of Engineering Education,* 86 (1997), 321–332.

Hutchings, P. *Using Cases to Improve College Teaching: A Guide to More Reflective Practice.* Washington,

DC: American Association for Higher Education, 1993.

Hutchings, P., and Shulman, L. S. "The Scholarship of Teaching. New Elaborations, New Developments," *Change,* 31:5 (1999), 10–15.

Inglis, A., Ling, P., and Joosten, V. *Delivering Digitally: Managing the Transition to the Knowledge Media.* London: Kogan Page, 1999.

Jacobson, E. *You Must Relax,* 4th ed. New York: McGraw-Hill, 1962.

Jacobson, R. L. "As Instructional Technology Proliferates, Skeptics Seek Hard Evidence of Its Value." *Chronicle of Higher Education,* May 5, 1993, A27.

Jacobson, T. E., and Cohen, L. B. "Teaching Students to Evaluate Internet Sites." *The Teaching Professor,* 11:7 (1997), 4.

Jacoby, B. "Service-Learning in Today's Higher Education." In Jacoby, B., and associates. *Service-Learning in Higher Education: Concepts and Practices.* San Francisco: Jossey-Bass, 1996, 3–25.

Jacoby, B., and associates. *Service-Learning in Higher Education: Concepts and Practices.* San Francisco: Josssey-Bass, 1996.

Jacoby, B. "Service Learning." Lecture at Purdue University, West Lafayette, IN, March 30, 2000.

Jensen, M. "Tearing Up the Limits Imposed by Paper." *Chronicle of Higher Education,* June 25, 1999, B9.

Jerrard, R., and Jerrard, M. *The Grad School Handbook.* New York: Perigee, 1998.

Johnson, D. W., and Johnson, R. T. *Learning Together and Alone: Cooperation, Competition and Individualization.* Englewood Cliffs, NJ: Prentice Hall, 1975.

Johnson, D. W., Johnson, R. T., and Smith K. A. *Active Learning: Cooperation in the College Classroom.* Edina, MN: Interaction Books, 1991a.

Johnson, D. W., Johnson, R. T. and Smith, K. A. *Cooperative Learning: Increasing College Faculty Instructional Productivity.* ASHE-ERIC Higher Education Report No. 4. Washington, DC: Graduate School of Education and Human Development, George Washington University, 1991b.

Johnson, D. W., Johnson, R. T., and Smith, K. A. "Cooperative Learning Returns to College: What Evidence Is There That It Works?" *Change,* 30:4 (1998), 27–35.

Johnson, G. R. *Taking Teaching Seriously: A Faculty Handbook.* College Station: Center for Teaching Excellence, Texas A&M University, 1988.

Johnson, G. R. *First Steps to Excellence in College Teaching.* Madison, WI: Magna, 1990.

Johnson, S., and Johnson, C. *The One-Minute Teacher.* New York: Quill, 1986.

Jung, C. G. *Psychological Types.* Princeton, NJ: Princeton University Press, 1971. First published in 1921.

Kadiyala, M., and Crynes, B. L. "A Review of Literature on Effectiveness of Use of Information Technology in Education." *Journal of Engineering Education,* 89 (2000), 177–189.

Kahn, N. B. *More Learning in Less Time,* 4th ed. Berkeley, CA: Ten Speed Press, 1992.

Keegan, A. R. "Time Is Tight for Counselors." *Guidepost* (American Personnel and Guidance Association newsletter), September 18, 1986, 1, 6, 8.

Keller, F. S. "Good-bye, Teacher . . ." *Journal of Applied Behavioral Analysis,* 1 (1968), 79.

Kennedy, D. *Academic Duty.* Cambridge, MA: Harvard University Press, 1997.

Kenney, P. A., and Kallison, J. M. Jr. "Research Studies on the Effectiveness of Supplemental Instruction in Mathematics." In Martin, D. C., and Arendale, D. R. (Eds.), *Supplemental Instruction: Increasing Achievement and Retention. New Directions for Teaching and Learning.* No. 60. San Francisco: Jossey-Bass, 1994, 73–82.

Kerr, C. *The Uses of the University,* 3d ed. Cambridge, MA: Harvard University Press, 1982.

Kibler, R. J., Barker, L. L., and Miles, D. T. *Behavioral Objectives and Instruction.* Boston: Allyn and Bacon, 1970.

Kibler, W. L., Nuss, E. M., Paterson, B. G., and Pavela, G. *Academic Integrity and Student Development: Legal Issues. Policy Perspectives.* Asheville, NC: College Administration, 1988.

Killeffer, D. H. *How Did You Think of That? An Introduction to the Scientific Method.* Garden City, NY: Anchor Books, 1969.

Kinch, M. "Technology Corner: Technology and Me: Perfect Together?" *American College Counseling Association Visions,* 4:2/3 (1996), 9.

Kitchener, K., and King, P. "Reflective Judgment: Concepts of Justification and Their Relationship to Age and Education." *Journal of Applied Developmental Psychology,* 2 (1981), 89–116.

Kitchener, K., and King, P. "The Reflective Judgment Model: Ten Years of Research." In Commons, M., Armon, C., Kohlberg, L., Richards, F., Grotzer, T., and Sinnott, J. (Eds.), *Adult Development: Models and Methods in the Study of Adolescent and Adult Thought.* New York: Praeger, 1990, 63–78.

Kloss, R. J. "A Nudge Is Best: Helping Students through the Perry Scheme of Intellectual Development." *College Teaching,* 42 (1994), 151–158.

Kluge, P. F. *Alma Mater: A College Homecoming.* Reading, MA: Addison-Wesley, 1993.

Kolb, D. A. *Experiential Learning: Experience as the Source of Learning and Development.* Englewood Cliffs, NJ: Prentice Hall, 1984.

Kolb, D. A. *Bibliography of Research on Experiential Learning and the Learning Style Inventory.* Boston: McBer, 1998.

Kolb, D. A. *Learning Style Inventory, Version 3.* Boston: Hay/McBer, 1999.

Krathwohl, D. R., Bloom, B. S., and Masia, B. *Taxonomy of Educational Objectives: The Classification of Educational Goals. Handbook II: The Affective Domain.* New York: David McKay, 1964.

Krishnamurti, J. *The First and Last Freedom.* New York: Harper & Row, 1954.

Kubler-Ross, E. *On Death and Dying.* New York: Macmillan , 1969.

Kuh, G. D., Schuh. J. H., Whitt, E. J., Andreas, R. E., Lyons, J. W., Strange, C. C., Krehbiel, L. E., and MacKay, K. A. *Involving Colleges.* San Francisco: Jossey-Bass, 1991.

Kuh, G. D., and Vesper, N. "A Comparison of Student Experiences with Good Practices in Undergraduate Education between 1990 and 1994." *Review of Higher Education,* 21 (1997), 43–61.

Kuhn, T. S. *The Structure of Scientific Revolutions,* 2d ed. Chicago: University of Chicago Press, 1970.

Kulik, J. A., Kulik, C. C., and Cohen, P. A. "A Meta-Analysis of Outcome Studies of Keller's Personalized System of Instruction." *American Psychologist,* 34 (1979), 307.

Kurfiss, J. G. *Critical Thinking: Theory, Research, Practice, and Possibilities.* ASHE-ERIC Higher Education Report No. 2. Washington, DC: Association for the Study of Higher Education, 1988.

Kussmaul, C., Dunn, J., Bagley, M., and Watnik, M. "Using Technology in Education: When and Why, Not How." *College Teaching,* 44 (1996), 123–127.

LaFollette, M. C. *Stealing into Print: Fraud, Plagiarism, and Misconduct in Scientific Publishing.* Berkeley: University of California Press, 1992.

Lair, J. *"I Ain't Much, Baby—But I'm All I've Got,"* expand. ed. New York: Doubleday, 1972.

Lakein, A. *How to Get Control of Your Time and Your Life.* New York: Signet, 1973.

Lambert, L., and Tice, S. L. (Eds.). *Preparing Graduate Students to Teach: A Guide to Programs that Improve Undergraduate Education and Develop Tomorrow's Faculty.* Washington, DC: American Association for Higher Education and Council of Graduate Schools, 1992.

Landis, R. B. *Studying Engineering: A Road Map to a Rewarding Career.* Burbank, CA: Discovery Press, 1995.

Landow, G. P. "Newman and the Idea of an Electronic University." In Newman, J. H., *The Idea of a University,* edited by Turner, F. M. New Haven, CT: Yale University Press, 1996, 339–361.

Lang, M. "Should I Choose a Black College or an Integrated College?" In Higgins, R. D., Cook, C.B., Ekeler, W. J., Sawyer, R. M., and Prichard, K. W. (Eds.), *The Black Students' Guide to College Success,* revised and updated by W. J. Ekeler. Westport, CT: Greenwood Press, 1994, 9–15.

Larson, R. E. (Ed.). *Preparing to Listen . . . A Sourcebook for Teleministry Training.* Harrisburg, PA: Contact Teleministries USA, 1978.

Laurillard, D. *Rethinking University Teaching: A Framework for the Effective Use of Educational Technology.* London: Routledge, 1993.

Layzell, D. T. "Higher Education's Changing Environment: Faculty Productivity and the Reward Structure." In Tierney, W. G. (Ed.), *Faculty Productivity. Facts, Fiction, and Issues.* New York: Falmer, 1999, 3–37.

Le, C., Ingvarson, E. P., and Page, R. C. "Alcoholics Anonymous and the Counseling Profession: Philosophies in Conflict." *Journal of Counseling and Development,* 73 (1995), 603–609.

Leatherman, C. "Should Dog Walking and House Sitting Be Required for a Ph.D.?" *Chronicle of Higher Education,* July 18, 1997, A10–A11.

Leatherman, C. "Research Universities Urged to Do Better Job of Tracking Careers of Ph.D.'s." *Chronicle of Higher Education,* November 20, 1998, A12.

Leatherman, C. "A University Decides that Its Ph.D.'s Should Be Able to Talk to Average Joes." *Chronicle of Higher Education,* October 8, 1999, A18–A19.

Leatherman, C. "A New Push for ABD's to Cross the Finish Line." *Chronicle of Higher Education,* March 24, 2000, A18–A19.

Lenier, M., and Maker, J. *Keys to College Success: Reading and Study Improvement,* 4th ed. Upper Saddle River, NJ: Prentice Hall, 1998.

Lennie, M. R. "How to Negotiate an Improved Author-Publisher Contract." *TAA Report,* October 1990, 3–4.

Lennie, M. R. "The Royalty Clause." *TAA Report,* April 1991, 3, 8–9.

Lennie, M. R. "Negotiating a Contract—Provisions Often Overlooked." *TAA Report,* October 1992, 3, 6.

Lenze, L. F., and Dinham, S. M. "Learning What Students Understand." In Menges, R. J., and associates, *Faculty in New Jobs: A Guide to Settling in, Becoming Established, and Building Institutional Support.* San Francisco: Jossey-Bass, 1999, 147–165.

Leslie, D. W. "Redefining Tenure: Tradition Versus the New Political Economy of Higher Education." *American Behavioral Scientist,* 41 (1998), 652–679.

Leslie, J. "Computer Visions: The Good, the Bad, and the Unknown." *Modern Maturity,* November/December 1998, 36–39.

Levine, A., and Nidiffer, J. *Beating the Odds: How the Poor Get to College.* San Francisco: Jossey-Bass, 1996.

Levine, M. *Negotiating a Book Contract: A Guide for Authors, Agents and Lawyers,* 3d ed. Wakefield, RI: Moyer Bell, 1988.

Levine, S. J. "Writing and Presenting Your Thesis or Dissertation," <http://www.msue.edu/aee/dissthes/guide.htm>, January 2000.

Lewington, J. "Professors in Canada Adopt New Tactics to Demonstrate Why Their Work Matters." *Chronicle of Higher Education,* June 19, 1998, A47, A49.

Lewis, K. G., "Teaching Large Classes (How to Do It Well and Remain Sane)." In Prichard, K. W., and Sawyer, R. M. (Eds.), *Handbook of College Teaching: Theory and Applications.* Westport, CT: Greenwood Press, 1994, chapter 25.

Lewis, R. "Textbook Authors Caution: Write for Love, Not Recognition." *The Scientist,* 6 (1992), 20, 22.

Light, R. J. *The Harvard Assessment Seminars: Explorations with Students and Faculty about Teaching, Learning, and Student Life.* First report. Cambridge, MA: Graduate School of Education and Kennedy School of Government, Harvard University, 1990.

Light, R. J. *The Harvard Assessment Seminars: Explorations with Students and Faculty about Teaching, Learning, and Student Life.* Second report. Cambridge, MA: Graduate School of Education and Kennedy School of Government, Harvard University, 1992.

Lowman, J. *Mastering the Techniques of Teaching.* San Francisco: Jossey-Bass, 1985.

Lowman, J. *Mastering the Techniques of Teaching,* 2d ed. San Francisco: Jossey-Bass, 1995.

Lucas, A. F. *Strengthening Departmental Leadership: A Team-Building Guide for Chairs in Colleges and Universities.* San Francisco: Jossey-Bass, 1994.

Lucas, A. F. "Myths That Make Chairs Feel They Are Powerless." *American Association for Higher Education Bulletin,* 52:3 (1999), 3–5.

Lucas, C. J. *American Higher Education: A History.* New York: St. Martin's Griffin, 1994.

Lucas, C. J. *Crisis in the Academy: Rethinking Higher Education in America.* New York: St. Martin's Press, 1996.

Lumsdaine, E., and Lumsdaine, M. *Creative Problem Solving: Thinking Skills for a Changing World,* 2d ed. New York: McGraw-Hill, 1993.

Lumsden, E. A., Grosslight, J. H., Loveland, E. H., and Williams, J. E. "Preparation of Graduate Students as Classroom Teachers and Supervisors in Applied and Research Settings." *Teaching of Psychology,* 15:1 (1988), 5–9.

Mackenzie, R. A. *The Time Trap: How to Get More Done in Less Time.* New York: McGraw-Hill, 1972.

MacKenzie, O., Christensen, E. L., and Rigby, P. H. *Correspondence Instruction in the United States: A Study of What It Is, How It Functions, and What Its Potential May Be.* New York: McGraw-Hill, 1968.

MacTaggart, T. J., and associates, with Crist, C. L. *Restructuring Higher Education. What Works and What Doesn't in Reorganizing Governing Systems.* San Francisco: Jossey-Bass, 1996.

Mager, R. F. *Preparing Instructional Objectives.* Palo Alto, CA: Fearon, 1962.

Magner, D. K. "Doctoral Programs Decide That Smaller Is Better." *Chronicle of Higher Education,* February 26, 1999a, A12–A13.

Magner, D. K. "The Graying Professoriate." *Chronicle of Higher Education,* September 3, 1999b, A18–A21.

Magner, D. K. "Critics Urge Overhaul of Ph.D. Training, but Disagree Sharply on How to Do So." *Chronicle of Higher Education,* April 19, 2000, A19–A20.

"Managing People—Notice and Avoid Fear-Instilling Behaviors" *The Pryor Report. Management Newsletter,* 12:3a (1996), 2.

Marsh, H. W. "Students' Evaluations of University Teaching: Dimensionality, Reliability, Validity, Potential Biases, and Utility." *Journal of Educational Psychology,* 76 (1984), 707.

Martin, D. C., and Arendale, D. R. (Eds.). *Supplemental Instruction: Increasing Achievement and Retention. New Directions for Teaching and Learning.* No. 60. San Francisco: Jossey-Bass, 1994.

Martin, J., Samuels, J. E., and associates. *First among Equals: The Role of the Chief Academic Officer.* Baltimore: Johns Hopkins University Press, 1997.

Marton, F. "Describing and Improving Learning." In Schmeck, R. R. (Ed.), *Learning Strategies and Learning Styles.* New York: Plenum, 1988.

Marton, F., and Saljo, R. "Approaches to Learning." In Marton, F., et al. (Eds.), *The Experience of Learning.* Edinburgh: Scottish Academic Press, 1984.

Marvin, P. *Managing Your Career: American Chemical Society Correspondence Course.* Audiotapes. Washington, DC: American Chemical Society, 1974.

Maslow, A. H. *Motivation and Personality,* 2d ed. New York: Harper & Row, 1970.

Matejka, K., and Kurke, L. B. "Designing a Great Syllabus." *College Teaching,* 42:3 (1994), 115–117.

Matthews, A. *Bright College Years: Inside the American Campus Today.* New York: Simon & Schuster, 1997.

Mayer, J. J. *If You Haven't Got the Time to Do It Right, When Will You Find the Time to Do It Over?* New York: Simon & Schuster, 1990.

Mazur, E. *Peer Instruction: A User's Manual.* Upper Saddle River, NJ: Prentice Hall, 1997.

McCabe, D. L., and Trevino, L. K. "What We Know about Cheating in College: Longitudinal Trends and Recent Developments." *Change,* 28:1 (1996), 29–33.

McCarthy, B. *The 4MAT System: Teaching to Learning Styles with Right/Left Mode Techniques,* rev. ed. Barrington, IL: EXCEL, 1987.

McCaulley, M. H. "The Myers-Briggs Type Indicator: A Jungian model for problem solving." In Stice, J. (Ed.), *Developing Critical Thinking and Problem-Solving Abilities.* San Francisco: Jossey-Bass, 1987.

McCay, J. T. *The Management of Time.* Englewood Cliffs, NJ: Prentice Hall, 1995. First published in 1959.

McCollum, K. "Students Find Sex, Drugs, and More Than a Little Education on Line, Survey Finds." *Chronicle of Higher Education,* May 14, 1999, A31.

McEwen, M. K. "Enhancing Student Learning and Development Through Service-Learning." In Jacoby, B., and associates, *Service-Learning in Higher Education: Concepts and Practices.* San Francisco: Jossey-Bass, 1996, 53–91.

McGee-Cooper, A., with Trammell, D. *Time Management for Unmanageable People.* New York: Bantam Books, 1994.

McKeachie, W. J. *Teaching Tips: Strategies, Research, and Theory for College and University Teachers,* 8th ed. Lexington, MA: D. C. Heath, 1986.

McKeachie, W. J. *Teaching Tips: Strategies, Research, and Theory for College and University Teachers,* 9th ed. Lexington, MA: D. C. Heath, 1994.

McLeod, A. "Discovering and Facilitating Deep Learning States." *The National Teaching & Learning Forum,* 5:6 (1996), 1–7.

McWilliams, P. *Do It! Let's Get Off Our Buts.* Los Angeles: Prelude Press, 1991.

"Mechanical Engineering Master's Programs Come to the Internet." *Mechanical Advantage,* 9:3 (2000), 3–4.

Medawar, P. B. *Advice to a Young Scientist.* New York: Harper & Row, 1979.

"Mélange." *Chronicle of Higher Education,* August 7, 1998, B8.

Menges, R. J. "Using Evaluative Information to Improve Instruction." In Seldin, P., and associates, *How Administrators Can Improve Teaching: Moving from Talk to Action in Higher Education.* San Francisco: Jossey-Bass, 1990, 104–121.

Menges, R. J. "Dilemmas of Newly Hired Faculty." In Menges, R. J., and associates, *Faculty in New Jobs: A Guide to Settling in, Becoming Established, and Building Institutional Support.* San Francisco: Jossey-Bass, 1999a, 19–38.

Menges, R. J. "Seeking and Using Feedback." In Menges, R. J., and associates, *Faculty in New Jobs: A Guide to Settling in, Becoming Established, and Building Institutional Support.* San Francisco: Jossey-Bass, 1999b, 166–185.

Merritt, T. R., Murman, E. M., and Friedman, D. L. "Engaging Freshmen through Advisor Seminars." *Journal of Engineering Education,* 86 (1997), 29–34.

Mettes, C. T. C. W., Pilot, A., Roosnik, H. J., and Kramers-Pals, H. "Teaching and Learning Problem Solving in Science. Part II. Learning Problem Solving in a Thermodynamics Course." *Journal of Chemical Education,* 58 (1981), 51.

Meyer, K. A. *Faculty Workload Studies: Perspectives, Needs, and Future Directions.* ASHE-ERIC Higher Education Report No. 1. Washington, DC: Graduate School of Education and Human Development, George Washington University, 1998.

Michaelsen, L. K. "Team Learning: Making a Case for the Small-Group Option." In Prichard, K. W., and Sawyer, R. M. (Eds.), *Handbook of College Teaching.* Westport, CT: Greenwood Press, 1994, 139–153.

Middendorf, J., and Kalish, A. "The 'Change-Up' in Lecture." *National Teaching & Learning Forum,* 5:2 (1996), 1–5.

Miller, D. W. "A Ghetto Childhood Inspires the Research of a Yale Sociologist." *Chronicle of Higher Education,* March 19, 1999, A15–A16.

Miller, J. E., Trimbur, J., and Wilkes, J. M. "Group Dynamics: Understanding Group Success and Failure in Collaborative Learning." In Bosworth, K., and Hamilton, S. J. (Eds.), *Collaborative Learning: Underlying Processes and Effective Techniques.* New Directions for Teaching and Learning No. 59. San Francisco: Jossey-Bass, 1994, 33–44.

Milton, O., Pollio, H. R., and Eison, J. A. *Making Sense of College Grades.* San Francisco: Jossey-Bass, 1986.

Mintz, S. D., and Hesser, G. W. "Principles of Good Practice in Service-Learning." In Jacoby, B., and associates, *Service-Learning in Higher Education: Concepts and Practices.* San Francisco: Jossey-Bass, 1996, 26–52.

Moffatt, M. *Coming of Age in New Jersey: College and American Culture.* New Brunswick, NJ: Rutgers University Press, 1989.

Moore, D. "Multimedia Technology in Teaching." Presentation at Purdue University, West Lafayette, IN, February 17, 1999.

Moore, W. S. "Student and Faculty Epistemology in the College Classroom: The Perry Schema of Intellectual and Ethical Development." In Prichard, K. W., and R. M. Sawyer, (Eds.), *Handbook of College Teaching.* Westport, CT: Greenwood Press, 1994, 45–67.

Moran, R. A. "Fast-Track Fundamentals." *Reader's Digest,* December 1993, 112–114. Excerpt from Moran, R. A. *Never Confuse a Memo with Reality.* New York: HarperCollins, 1994.

Morton, K. "Issues Related to Integrating Service-Learning into the Curriculum." In Jacoby, B., and associates, *Service-Learning in Higher Education: Concepts and Practices.* San Francisco: Jossey-Bass, 1996, 276–296.

Murphy, M. K. (Ed.). *The Advancement President and the Academy: Profiles in Institutional Leadership.* Phoenix, AZ: American Council on Education and Oryx Press, 1997.

Murray, H. G., Rushton, J. P., and Paunonen, S. V. "Teacher Personality Traits and Student Instructional Ratings in Six Types of University Courses." *Journal of Educational Psychology,* 82 (1990), 250.

Myers, I. B. *Introduction to Type.* Palo Alto, CA: Consulting Psychologists Press, 1991.

Myers, I. B., and McCaulley, M. H. *Manual: A Guide to the Development and Use of the Myers-Briggs Type Indicator.* Palo Alto, CA: Consulting Psychologists Press, 1985.

Myers, I. B., and Myers, P. B. *Gifts Differing.* Palo Alto, CA: Consulting Psychologists Press, 1980.

Nagel, G. *The Tao of Teaching.* New York: Donald I. Fine, 1994.

NAGPS, National Association of Graduate-Professional Students. "Survey of Graduate Students," <http://www.phds.org/survey/results/>, 1999.

Nantz, K. S., and Lundgren, T. D. "Lecturing with Technology." *College Teaching,* 46 (1998), 53–56.

Nathans, E. S. "New Faculty Members and Advising." In Deneef, A. L., Goodwin, C. D., and McCrate, E. S. (Eds.), *The Academic's Handbook.* Durham, NC: Duke University Press, 1988, chapter 14.

Naumes, W., and Naumes, M. J. "Case Writing: A Tool for Teaching and Research," *Journal of SMET Education,* 1:1 (2000), 24–32.

Nelson, C. (Ed.). *Will Teach for Food. Academic Labor in Crisis.* Minneapolis: University of Minnesota Press, 1997.

Newman, J. H. *The Idea of a University,* edited by Turner, F. M. New Haven, CT: Yale University Press, 1996. Based on a 1891 edition published by Longmans, Green.

Nooman, Z. G., Schmidt, H. G., and Ezzat, E. S. *Innovations in Medical Education: An Evaluation of its Present Status.* New York: Springer, 1990.

Norris, P. M., and Palmer, S. C. "Effectiveness of Woodruff School Doctoral Teaching Intern Program." *Journal of Engineering Education,* 87 (1998), 223–226.

Novak, J. D., and Gowin, D. B. *Learning How to Learn.* Cambridge: Cambridge University Press, 1984.

Nowak, M. A., and Sigmund, K. "Shrewd Investments." *Science,* 288 (2000), 819–820.

O'Brien, G. D. *All the Essential Half-Truths about Higher Education.* Chicago: University of Chicago Press, 1998.

O'Donnell, J. M., and George, K. "The Use of Volunteers in a Community Mental Health Center Emergency and Reception Service: A Comparative Study of Professional and Lay Telephone Counseling." *Community Mental Health Journal,* 13 (1977), 3–12.

O'Hara, C. "Self-Publishing Step-by-Step." *Writer's Digest,* August 1998, 20–25.

Olds, S. W. "Collaborative Writing of Textbooks." *TAA Report,* July 1991, 5, 13–14.

Oppenheimer, T. "The Computer Delusion." *Atlantic Monthly,* July 1997, 45–62.

Orlans, H. "Scholarly Fair Use: Chaotic and Shrinking," *Change,* 31:6 (1999), 52–60.

Ory, J., and Ryan, K. E. *Tips for Improving Testing and Grading.* Newbury Park, CA: Sage, 1993.

Osterman, D., Christensen, M., and Coffey, B. "The Feedback Lecture." *Idea Paper No. 13.* Manhattan, KS: Center for Faculty Evaluation and Development, Kansas State University, 1985.

Page, C. (Ed.). *The Smart Girl's Guide to College.* New York: Noonday Press, 1997.

Palmer, P. J. *To Know as We Are Known: A Spirituality of Education.* New York: HarperCollins, 1983.

Palmer, P. J. *The Courage to Teach: Exploring the Inner Landscape of a Teacher's Life.* San Francisco: Jossey-Bass, 1998.

Panitz, B. "Get the Most Out of the Annual Conference." *ASEE PRISM,* May-June 1996, 40, 42, 44.

Parker-Gibson, N. "How to Sift Citations." *College Teaching,* 43 (1998), 106–109.

Pascarella, E. T., and Terenzini, P. T. *How College Affects Students: Findings and Insights from Twenty Years of Research.* San Francisco: Jossey-Bass, 1991.

Pascarella, E. T., and Terenzini, P. T. "Studying College Students in the 21st Century: Meeting New Challenges." *Review of Higher Education,* 21 (1998), 151–165.

Pelikan, J. *The Idea of the University: A Reexamination.* New Haven, CT: Yale University Press, 1992.

Perry, W. G. Jr. *Forms of Intellectual and Ethical Development in the College Years: A Scheme.* New York: Holt, Rinehart and Winston, 1970.

Perry, W. G. Jr. "Cognitive and Ethical Growth." In Chickering, A., and associates, *The Modern American College: Responding to the New Realities of Diverse Students and a Changing Society.* San Francisco: Jossey-Bass, 1981, 76–116.

Peters, R. L. *Getting What You Came For: The Smart Student's Guide to Earning a Master's or a Ph.D.* New York: Noonday Press, 1992.

Peters, T. J., and Austin, N. *A Passion for Excellence.* New York: Random House, 1985. Reprint, New York: Time Warner, 1986.

Peters, T. J., and Waterman, R. H. Jr. *In Search of Excellence: Lessons from America's Best-Run Companies.* New York: Harper & Row, 1982.

Peterson, H. (Ed.). *Great Teachers: Portrayed by Those Who Studied under Them.* New York: Vintage Books, 1946.

Petre, M., Carswell, L., Price, B., and Thomas, P. "Innovations in Large-Scale Supported Distance Teaching: Transformation for the Internet, Not Just Translation." *Journal of Engineering Education,* 87 (1998), 423–432.

Phillips, J. L. Jr. *The Origins of Intellect: Piaget's Theory,* 2d ed. San Francisco: W. H. Freeman, 1975.

Phillips, J. L. Jr. *Piaget's Theory: A Primer.* San Francisco: W. H. Freeman, 1981.

Pintrich, P. R. "Implications of Psychological Research on Student Learning and College Teaching for Teacher Education." In Houston, W. R., Haberman, M., and Sikula, J. (Eds.), *Handbook of Research on Teacher Education.* New York: Macmillan, 1992, 826–857.

Pintrich, P. R. "Student Motivation in the College Classroom." In Prichard, K. W., and Sawyer, R. M. (Eds.), *Handbook of College Teaching.* Westport, CT: Greenwood Press, 1994, chapter 2.

Plater, W. "Using Tenure: Citzenship within the New Academic Workforce." *American Behavioral Scientist,* 41 (1998), 680–715.

Polansky, J., Horan, J. J., and Hanish, C. "Experimental Construct Validity of the Outcomes of Study Skills Training and Career Counseling as Treatments for the Retention of At-Risk Students." *Journal of Counseling and Development,* 71 (1993), 488–492.

Pope, L. *Looking Beyond the Ivy League,* rev. ed. New York: Penguin, 1995.

Press, A. "Introduction. The Road to Graduate School." *Newsweek, Kaplan: How to Get into Graduate School, 1998 Edition.* [special issue of *Newsweek*], June 1997, 5–8.

Pulley, J. L. "A Program That Believes in Going with the 'Posse.'" *Chronicle of Higher Education,* April 28, 2000, A40–A42.

Pye. A. K. "University Governance and Autonomy—Who Decides What in the University?" In Deneef, A. L., Goodwin, C. D., and McCrate, E. S. (Eds.), *The Academic's Handbook.* Durham, NC: Duke University Press, 1988, 241–259.

Quiddus, M., and Bussing-Burks, M. "Students' Study Tips Help Others in Economics." *College Teaching,* 46:2 (1998), 57.

Race, P. "Teaching: Creating a Thirst for Learning?" In Brown, S., Armstrong, S., and Thompson, G. (Eds.), *Motivating Students.* London: Kogan Page, 1998, 47–57.

Ramsden P. *Learning to Teach in Higher Education.* London: Routledge, 1992.

Rawls, R. "Tactile Diagrams Bring Chemical Structures to Blind Students." *Chemical & Engineering News,* August 16, 1999, 39–41.

Reid, L. D. "How to Improve Classroom Lectures." *American Association of University Professors Bulletin,* 34 (1948), 576–584.

Reis, R. M. *Tomorrow's Professor: Preparing for Academic Careers in Science and Engineering.* New York: Institute of Electrical and Electronic Engineers Press, 1997.

Reisberg, L. "Hollywood Discovers an Apocryphal Legend." *Chronicle of Higher Education,* September 11, 1998, A41–A42.

Reisberg, L. "Survey of Freshmen Finds a Decline in Support for Abortion and Casual Sex." *Chronicle of Higher Education,* January 29,1999a, A47–A50.

Reisberg, L. "New Study Suggests That Most Students Are Not Heavy Drinkers." *Chronicle of Higher Education,* September 3, 1999b, A80.

Reisberg, L. "Colleges Struggle to Keep Would-Be Dropouts Enrolled." *Chronicle of Higher Education,* October 8, 1999c, A54–A56.

Rezak, W. D. "Leading Colleges and Universities as Business Enterprises." *American Association for Higher Education Bulletin,* 53:2 (2000), 6–9.

Rice, R. E., and Austin, A. E. "Organizational Impacts on Faculty Morale and Motivation to Teach." In Seldin, P., and associates, *How Administrators Can Improve Teaching: Moving from Talk to Action in Higher Education.* San Francisco: Jossey-Bass, 1990, 23–42.

Richlin, L. "Editor's Notes." In Richlin, L. (Ed.), *Preparing Faculty for the New Conceptions of Scholarship.* New Directions for Teaching and Learning No. 54. San Francisco: Jossey-Bass, 1993a, 1–2.

Richlin, L. "To Hear All Voices: A Broader View of Faculty Scholarship." In Richlin, L. (Ed.), *Preparing Faculty for the New Conceptions of Scholarship.* New Directions for Teaching and Learning No. 54. San Francisco: Jossey-Bass, 1993b, 39–46.

Richlin, L. "Graduate Education and the US Faculty." In Richlin, L. (Ed.), *Preparing Faculty for the New Conceptions of Scholarship.* New Directions for Teaching and Learning No. 54. San Francisco: Jossey-Bass, 1993c, 3–14.

Rickard, H. C., Prentice-Dunn, S., Rogers, R. W., Scogin, F. R., and Lyman, R. W. "Teaching of Psychology: A Required Course for All Doctoral Students." *Teaching of Psychology,* 18:4 (1991), 178–183.

Robinson, A. *What Smart Students Know: Maximum Grades. Optimum Learning. Minimum Time.* New York: Crown Trade Paperbacks, 1993.

Robinson, D. H. "Textbook Selection: Watch Out for 'Inconsiderate' Texts." In Prichard, K. W., and Sawyer, R. M. (Eds.), *Handbook of College Teaching: Theory and Applications* Westport, CT: Greenwood Press, 1994, chapter 32.

Rodberg, L. R. "Just When You Thought You Were Done—A Production Primer for Authors. Copy-Editor Competence: An Author's Quest(ionnaire), Part 1." *TAA Report,* 6:1 (1992a), 13–15.

Rodberg, L. R. "Just When You Thought You Were Done—A Production Primer for Authors. Copy-Editor Competence: An Author's Quest(ionnaire), Part 2." *TAA Report,* 6:2 (1992b), 12–14.

Rogers, C. R. *Freedom to Learn.* Columbus, OH: Charles E. Merrill, 1969.

Rosen, S., and Paul, C. *Career Renewal: Tools for Scientists and Technical Professionals.* San Diego: Academic Press, 1998.

Rosovsky, H. *The University: An Owner's Manual.* New York: W. W. Norton, 1990.

Ross, J. "Words of Wisdom." *Chemical & Engineering News,* September 14, 1998, 3.

Ross, T., and Ross, M. J. *The Complete Guide to Self-Publishing: Everything You Need to Know to Write, Publish, Promote and Sell Your Own Book,* 3d. ed. Cincinnati, OH: Writer's Digest Books, 1994.

Rosser, S. V. "Group Work in Science, Engineering and Mathematics: Consequences of Ignoring Gender and Race." *College Teaching,* 46:3 (1998), 82–88.

Rowe, J. W., and Kahn, R. L. *Successful Aging: The MacArthur Foundation Study.* New York: Pantheon Books, 1998.

Russell, T. L. "The No Significant Difference Phenomenon." <http://teleeducation.nb.ca/>, 1999.

Ryan, A. *John Dewey.* New York: Norton, 1995.

Sacks, P. *Generation X Goes to College: An Eye-Opening Account of Teaching in Postmodern America.* Chicago: Open-Court, 1996.

Sandler, B. R. "The Classroom Climate: Chilly for Women?" In Deneef, A. L., Goodwin, C. D., and McCrate, E. S. (Eds.), *The Academic's Handbook.* Durham, NC: Duke University Press, 1988, chapter 13.

Sanoff, A. P. "Long-Distance Relationship." *ASEE PRISM,* September 1999, 22–26.

Sarkisian, E. *Teaching American Students. A Guide for International Faculty and Teaching Fellows.* Cam-

bridge, MA: Danforth Center for Teaching and Learning, Harvard University, 1990.

Sauter, S. L., Chapman, L. J., and Knutson, S. J. *Improving VDT Work. Causes and Control of Health Connections in VDT Use.* Lawrence, KS: Ergosight Associates, 1985.

Schmidt, P. "Governors Want Fundamental Changes in Colleges, Question Place of Tenure." *Chronicle of Higher Education,* June 19, 1998, A38.

Schmier, L. *Random Thoughts: The Humanity of Teaching.* Madison, WI: Magna, 1995.

Schneider, A. "Why Don't Women Publish as Much as Men?" *Chronicle of Higher Education,* September 11, 1998a, A14–A16.

Schneider, A. "Harvard Faces the Aftermath of a Graduate Student's Suicide." *Chronicle of Higher Education,* October 23, 1998b, A12–A14.

Schneider, A. "Why Professors Don't Do More to Stop Students Who Cheat." *Chronicle of Higher Education,* January 22, 1999, A8–A10.

"Scholarships for Dropouts?" *Chronicle of Higher Education,* May 28, 1999, A39.

Schon, D. A. "Knowing-in-Action. The New Scholarship Requires a New Epistemology." *Change,* 27:6 (1995), 27–34.

Schroeder, C. S. "New Students—New Learning Styles." *Change,* 25:5 (1993), 21–26.

Schulz, W. G. "Texas-Sized Challenges." *Chemical and Engineering News,* November 30, 1998, 33–35.

Schumacher, E. F. *Small Is Beautiful: Economics As If People Mattered.* New York: Harper & Row, 1973.

Schuster, J. H. "Preparing the Next Generation of Faculty: The Graduate School's Opportunity." In Richlin, L. (Ed.), *Preparing Faculty for the New Conceptions of Scholarship.* New Directions for Teaching and Learning No. 54. San Francisco: Jossey-Bass, 1993, 27–38.

Schwehn, M. R. *Exiles from Eden: Religion and the Academic Vocation in America.* New York: Oxford University Press, 1993.

Scott, N. R. "Responsibilities of the Thesis Advisor." *Compilation of Papers on Graduate Instruction for Agricultural Engineering in a Changing Society, American Society of Agricultural Engineers,* December 1978, paper 78–5516.

Seat, E., and Lord, S. M. "Enabling Effective Engineering Teams: A Program for Teaching Interaction Skills," *Journal of Engineering Education,* 88 (1999), 385–390.

Seldin, P. (Ed.). *Coping with Faculty Stress. New Directions for Teaching and Learning,* No. 29. San Francisco: Jossey-Bass, 1987.

Seldin, P., and associates. *How Administrators Can Improve Teaching: Moving from Talk to Action in*

Higher Education. San Francisco: Jossey-Bass, 1990a.

Seldin, P. "Academic Environments and Teaching Effectiveness." In Seldin, P., and associates, *How Administrators Can Improve Teaching: Moving from Talk to Action in Higher Education.* San Francisco: Jossey-Bass, 1990b, 3–22.

Seligman, M. E. *Learned Optimism.* New York: Pocket Books, 1990.

Selingo, J. "A New Archive and Internet Search Engine May Change the Nature of On-line Research." *Chronicle of Higher Education,* March 6, 1998, A27–A28.

Sherrill, J. M., and Hardesty, C. A. *The Gay, Lesbian and Bisexual Student's Guide to Colleges, Universities, and Graduate Schools.* New York: New York University Press, 1994.

Sherwood, J. L., Petersen, J. N., and Grandzielwski, J. M. "Faculty Mentoring: A Unique Approach to Training Graduate Students 'How to Teach.'" *Journal of Engineering Education,* 86 (1997), 119.

Shneidman, E. S. *The Suicidal Mind.* New York: Oxford University Press, 1996.

Shulman, L. S. "Those Who Understand: Knowledge Growth in Teaching." *Educational Researcher,* 15:2 (1986), 4–14.

Sidel, R. *Battling Bias: The Struggle for Identity and Community on College Campuses.* New York: Viking, 1994.

Silber, J. *Straight Shooting.* New York: Harper & Row, 1989.

Simon, H. A. Foreword. In Davidson, C. I., and Ambrose, S. A., *The New Professor's Handbook.* Bolton, MA: Anker, 1994, x–xii.

Silverman, F. "Authors Often Follow Rituals to Creativity." *The Academic Author,* 1996 (2), 8.

Silverman, F. H., and Murphy, T. M. "What Effect Is Using a Text You Authored Likely to Have on How Students View You?" *TAA Report,* October 1993, 21–22.

Singer, D. G., and Revenson, T. A. *A Piaget Primer: How a Child Thinks,* rev. ed. Madison, CT: International Universities Press, 1997.

Singham, M. "The Canary in the Mine: The Achievement Gap Between Black and White Students." *Phi Delta Kappan,* September 1998, 9–15.

Skinner, B. F. "A Humanist Alternative to AAs Twelve Steps." *The Humanist,* July/August 1987, 5.

Sloan, C. J. "Listen to Your Children." *The War Cry,* March 12, 1994, 10–11.

Smedley, C. S., and Allen, M., with Briggs, H., Hale, N. S., Hoffman, C., and Laughton, C. D. *Getting Your Book Published.* Newbury Park, CA: Sage, 1993.

Smelser, N. J. *Effective Committee Service.* Newbury Park, CA: Sage, 1993.

Smith, D. G. *The Challenge of Diversity: Involvement or Alienation in the Academy?* ASHE-ERIC Higher Education Report No. 5. Washington, DC: School of Education and Human Development, George Washington University, 1989.

Smith, D., and Kolb, D. A. *User's Guide for the Learning Style Inventory: A Manual for Teachers and Trainers.* Boston: McBer, 1986.

Smith, K. A. "Grading and Distributive Justice." In *Proceedings of ASEE/IEEE Frontiers in Education Conference.* New York: Institute of Electrical and Electronic Engineers, 1986a, 421.

Smith, K. A. "Cooperative Learning Groups." In Schomberg, S. F. (Ed.), *Strategies for Active Teaching and Learning in University Classrooms.* Minneapolis: University of Minnesota, 1986b.

Smith, K. A. *Project Management and Teamwork.* New York: McGraw-Hill, 1999.

Smith, P. *Killing the Spirit: Higher Education in America.* New York: Viking, 1990.

Smith, R. M., Byrd, P., Nelson, G. L., Barrett, R. P., and Constantinides, J. C. *Crossing Pedagogical Oceans: International Teaching Assistants in U. S. Undergraduate Education.* ASHE-ERIC Higher Education Report No. 8. Washington, DC: School of Education and Human Development, George Washington University, 1992.

Smithers, A. G. *Sandwich Courses: An Integrated Education?* Windsor, United Kingdom: National Foundation for Educational Research, 1976.

Solomon, R., and Solomon, J. *Up the University: Recreating Higher Education in America.* Reading, MA: Addison-Wesley, 1993.

Sonnert, G., with the assistance of Holton, G. *Who Succeeds in Science: The Gender Dimension.* New Brunswick, NJ: Rutgers University Press, 1995.

Sorcinelli, M. D. "Dealing with Troublesome Behaviors in the Classroom." In Prichard, K. W., and Sawyer, R. M. (Eds.), *Handbook of College Teaching: Theory and Applications.* Westport, CT: Greenwood Press, 1994a, chapter 28.

Sorcinelli, M. D. "Academic Honesty." *The National Teaching & Learning Forum,* 3:5 (1994b), 8–9.

Sorcinelli, M. D. "Effective Approaches to New Faculty Development." *Journal of Counseling and Development,* 72 (1994c), 474–479.

Sorcinelli, M. D. "How Mentoring Programs Can Improve Teaching." In Seldin, P., and associates, *Improving College Teaching.* Bolton, MA: Anker, 1995, 125–136.

Sparkes, J. "The Education of Young People Aged 14–18 Years." London: Royal Academy of Engineering, 1994.

Stage, F. K., Muller, P. A., Kinzie, J., and Simmons, A. *Creating Learning Centered Classrooms: What*

Does Learning Theory Have to Say? ASHE-ERIC Higher Education Report No. 4. Washington, DC: George Washington University, 1998.

Stager, R. A., and Wales, C. E. "Guided Design: A New Concept in Course Design and Operation." *Engineering Education,* March 1972, 539.

Stevens, E. H. "Informal Resolution of Academic Misconduct Cases: A Due Process Paradigm." *College Teaching,* 44:4 (1996), 140–144.

Stewart, P. "The Academic Community." In DeNeef, A. L., and Goodwin, C. D. (Eds.), *The Academic's Handbook,* 2d ed. Durham, NC: Duke University Press, 1995, 334–340.

Stice, J. E. "A First Step toward Improved Teaching." *Engineering Education,* February 1976, 394.

Stice, J. E. "Grades and Test Scores: Do They Predict Adult Achievement?" *Engineering Education.* February 1979, 390.

Stice, J. E. "The Need for a 'How to Teach' Course for Graduate Students." In *Proceedings of the American Society for Engineering Education Annual Conference.* Washington, DC: American Society for Engineering Education, 1991, 65–68.

Stice, J. E., Felder, R. M., Woods, D. R., and Rugarcia, A. "The Future of Engineering Education: Part 4. Learning How to Teach." *Chemical Engineering Education,* spring 2000, 118–127.

Stickle, J. E., Lloyd, J., Keller, W. F., and Cherney, E. "Learning Styles in Veterinary Medicine: Relation to Progression through the Professional Curriculum and Integration into the Profession." *Journal of Veterinary Medical Education,* 26:2 (1999), 9–12.

Stone, G. "Marketing Hints to Secure Your First Text." *The Academic Author,* November 1994, 8.

Stone, G. C. "On Better Writing." *The Academic Author,* 1997 (2), 13–14.

Strandberg, M. W. P. "Design of Examinations and Interpretation of Grades." *American Journal of Physics,* 26 (1958), 555–558.

Strauss, G., and Sayles, R. *Strauss & Sayles's Behavioral Strategies for Managers.* Englewood Cliffs, NJ: Prentice Hall, 1980.

Strunk, W. Jr., and White, E. B. *The Elements of Style,* 3d ed. New York: Macmillan, 1979.

Suppes, P. "Education and Technology at Stanford in the Twenty-first Century." In Arrow, K. J., Cottle, R. W., Eaves, B. C., and Olkin, I. *Education in a Research University.* Stanford, CA: Stanford University Press, 1996, 143–158.

Svinicki, M. D. "The Test: Uses, Construction and Evaluation." *Engineering Education,* February 1976, 408.

Svinicki, M. D. "The Teaching Assistantship: A Preparation for Multiple Roles." In McKeachie, W. J. (Ed.),

Teaching Tips, 9th ed. Lexington, MA: D. C. Heath, 1994, 239–249.

Svinicki, M. D. "Helping Students Understand Grades." *College Teaching,* 46:3 (1998), 101–105.

Svinicki, M. D., and Dixon, N. M. "Kolb Model Modified for Classroom Activities." *College Teaching,* 35:4 (1987), 141–146.

Sykes, C. J. *ProfScam: Professors and the Demise of Higher Education.* Washington, DC: Regnery Gateway, 1988.

Tack, M. W., and Patitu, C. L. *Faculty Job Satisfaction: Women and Minorities in Peril.* ASHE-ERIC Higher Education Report No. 4. Washington, DC: School of Education and Human Development, George Washington University, 1992.

Tally, L. H. "Helping Hands." *Purdue Engineering Extrapolations,* Spring 1997, 6–9.

Tannen, D. *You Just Don't Understand.* New York: Ballatine Books, 1990.

Tannen, D. "Teacher's Classroom Strategies Should Recognize that Men and Women Use Language Differently." *Chronicle of Higher Education,* June 19, 1991, B1.

Tannen, D. *Talking from 9 to 5: How Women's and Men's Conversational Styles Affect Who Gets Heard, Who Gets Credit, and What Gets Done at Work.* New York: William Morrow, 1994.

Tierney, W. G. (Ed.). "Tenure Matters: Rethinking Faculty Roles and Rewards." *American Behavioral Scientist,* 41:5 (1998). Special issue on tenure.

Tierney, W. G. (Ed.). *Faculty Productivity. Facts, Fiction, and Issues.* New York: Falmer, 1999.

Tierney, W. G., and Rhoads, R. A. *Enhancing Promotion, Tenure and Beyond: Faculty Socialization as a Cultural Process.* ASHE-ERIC Higher Education Report No. 93–6. Washington, DC: School of Education and Human Development, George Washington University, 1993.

Tinto, V. *Leaving College: Rethinking the Causes and Cures for Student Attrition,* 2d ed. Chicago: University of Chicago Press, 1993.

Tinto, V. "Colleges as Communities: Taking Research on Student Persistence Seriously." *Review of Higher Education,* 21 (1998), 167–177.

Tobias, S. *They're Not Dumb, They're Different: Stalking the Second Tier.* Tucson, AZ: Research Corporation, 1990.

Tobias, S. *Revitalizing Undergraduate Science: Why Some Things Work and Most Don't.* Tucson, AZ: Research Corporation, 1992.

Torvi, D. A. "Engineering Graduate Teaching Assistant Instructional Programs: Training Tomorrow's Faculty Members." *Journal of Engineering Education,* 83 (1994), 376–381.

Traub, J. *City on a Hill.* Reading, MA: Addison Wesley, 1994.

Trautvetter, L. C. "Experiences of Women, Experiences of Men," In Menges, R. J., and associates, *Faculty in New Jobs: A Guide to Settling in, Becoming Established, and Building Institutional Support.* San Francisco: Jossey-Bass, 1999, 59–87.

Tucker, A. *Chairing the Academic Department: Leadership Among Peers,* 2d ed. New York: American Council on Education and Macmillan, 1984.

Tucker, A., and Bryan, R. A. *The Academic Dean: Dove, Dragon, and Diplomat.* New York: American Council on Education and Macmillan, 1988.

Tucker, R. W. "The Virtual Classroom: Quality and Assessment." *Syllabus,* 9:1 (1995), 48–51.

Turk, C., and Kirkman, J. *Effective Writing: Improving Scientific, Technical and Business Communication,* 2d ed. London: E. & F. N. Spon, 1989.

Ullrich, R. A. *Motivation Methods That Work.* Englewood Cliffs, NJ: Prentice Hall, 1981.

Underwood, A. "Breaking the Mold." *Newsweek, Kaplan, How to Get into Graduate School, 1998 Edition* [special issue of *Newsweek*], June 1997, 24–29.

University of Chicago Press. *The Chicago Manual of Style,* 14th ed. Chicago: University of Chicago Press, 1993.

Uris, A. *Mastery of Management.* Chicago: Playboy Press, 1973.

U.S. Department of Education. *What Works: Research about Teaching and Learning.* Washington, DC: U.S. Department of Education, 1986.

Van Alstyne, W. "Tenure: A Summary, Explanation and 'Defense.'" *AAUP Bulletin,* fall 1971, 328–333. Reprinted in Altbach, P. G., and Finkelstein, M. J. (Eds.), *The Academic Profession: The Professoriate in Crisis.* New York: Garland, 1997, 128–133.

Van Blerkom, D. L. *Orientation to College Learning.* Belmont, CA: Wadsworth, 1995.

Van Dusen, G. C. *The Virtual Campus: Technology and Reform in Higher Education.* ASHE-ERIC Higher Education Report No. 25–5. Washington, DC: George Washington University, School of Education and Human Development, 1997.

Vogel, G. "A Day in the Life of a Topflight Lab." *Science,* 285 (1999), 1531–1532.

Wagschal, K., and Wagschal, P. H. "Teaching Adult Learners." In Seldin, P., and associates, *Improving College Teaching.* Bolton, MA: Anker, 1995, 235–248.

Wales, C. E., and Nardi, A. "Teaching Decision-Making with Guided Design." Idea Paper No. 9. Manhattan, KS: Center for Faculty Evaluation and Development, Kansas State University, 1982.

Wales, C. E., and Stager, R. A. *Guided Design.* Morgantown, WV: Center for Guided Design, West Virginia University, 1977.

Wales, C. E., Stager, R. A., and Long, T. R. *Guided Engineering Design.* St. Paul, MN: West, 1974.

Walesh, S. G. *Engineering Your Future: Launching a Successful Entry-Level Technical Career in Today's Business Environment.* Englewood Cliffs, NJ: Prentice Hall, 1995.

Walker, C. J., and Hale, N. M. "Faculty Well-Being and Vitality." In Menges, R. J., and associates, *Faculty in New Jobs: A Guide to Settling in, Becoming Established, and Building Institutional Support.* San Francisco: Jossey-Bass, 1999, 216–239.

Wankat, P. C. "Are You Listening?" *Chemical Engineering,* October 8, 1979, 115–118.

Wankat, P. C. "The Professor as Counselor." *Engineering Education,* November 1980, 153–158.

Wankat, P. C. "Regrading Tests: A Chance for Students to Learn." *Engineering Education,* April 1983a, 746.

Wankat, P. C. "Analysis of Student Mistakes and Improvement of Problem Solving on McCabe-Thiele Binary Distillation Tests." *American Institute of Chemical Engineers Symposium Series,* 79 (1983b), 33–40.

Wankat, P. C. "Current Advising Practices and How to Improve Them." *Engineering Education,* January 1986, 213–216.

Wankat, P. C. "Stress Reduction Methods for Professors." In *Proceedings of the American Society for Engineering Education Annual Conference,* vol. 2. Washington, DC: American Society for Engineering Education, 1993a, 1892–1896.

Wankat, P. C. "Learning through Doing: A Course on Writing a Textbook Chapter." *Chemical Engineering Education,* 27 (1993b), 208–211.

Wankat, P. C. "Synergism between Research and Teaching Separations." *Chemical Engineering Education,* 31 (1997), 202–209.

Wankat, P. C. "Reflective Analysis of a Course." *Journal of Engineering Education,* 88 (1999a), 195–203.

Wankat, P. C. "Educating Engineering Professors in Education." *Journal of Engineering Education,* 88 (1999b), 471–475.

Wankat, P. C., and Gaunt, J. G. "Freshman Advising: Putting Effort Where It Counts." In *Proceedings of the American Society for Engineering Education Annual Conference.* Washington, DC: American Society for Engineering Education, 1994, 2101–2105.

Wankat, P. C., Hesketh, R. P., Schulz, K. H., and Slater, C. S. "Separations: What to Teach Undergraduates?" *Chemical Engineering Education,* 28 (1994), 12–16.

Wankat, P. C., and Oreovicz, F. S. *Teaching Engineering.* New York: McGraw-Hill, 1993. Available free as pdf files at <http://unitflops.ecn.purdue.edu/ChE/News/Book/>.

Wankat, P. C., and Oreovicz, F. S. "What Is Good Teaching?" *ASEE PRISM,* September 1998a, 16.

Wankat, P. C., and Oreovicz, F. S. "Controlling Content Tyranny." *ASEE PRISM,* October 1998b.

Wankat, P. C., and Oreovicz, F. S. "Hit Your Mark." *ASEE PRISM,* March 1999, 18.

Wankat, P. C., Oreovicz, F. S., and Delgass, W. N. "Integrating Soft Criteria into the ChE Curriculum." In *Proceedings of the American Society for Engineering Education Annual Conference.* Washington, DC: American Society for Engineering Education, 2000, pdf file 00332.

Weaver, R. A., Kowalski, T. J., and Pfaller, J. E. "Case-Method Teaching." In Prichard, K. W., and Sawyer, R. W. (Eds.), *Handbook of College Teaching: Theory and Applications.* Westport, CT: Greenwood Press, 1994, 171–178.

Wechsler, H. "Alcohol and the American College Campus: A Report from the Harvard School of Public Health." *Change,* 28:4 (1996), 20–25, 60.

Wegner, G. R. "Arizona State University." In *Exemplars.* Philadelphia, PA: Institute for Research on Higher Education, 1999.

Wei, J. "Message from the Dean," *EQuad News* [Princeton University], spring 1997, 2.

Weimer, M. *Improving College Teaching: Strategies for Developing Instructional Effectiveness.* San Francisco: Jossey-Bass, 1990.

Weimer, M. *Improving Your Classroom Teaching.* Newbury Park, CA: Sage, 1993.

Weinstein, C. E. "Students at Risk for Academic Failure: Learning to Learn Classes." In Prichard, K. W., and Sawyer, R. M. (Eds.), *Handbook of College Teaching.* Westport, CT: Greenwood Press, 1994, 375–385.

Wertenbaker, T. J. *Princeton 1746–1896.* Princeton, NJ: Princeton University Press, 1996.

Whicker, M. L., Kronenfeld, J. J., and R. A. Strickland. *Getting Tenure.* Newbury Park, CA: Sage, 1993.

Whitman, N. A., Spendlove, D. C., and Clark, C. H. *Increasing Students' Learning: A Faculty Guide to Reducing Stress among Students.* ASHE- ERIC Higher Education Report No. 4. Washington, DC: Association for the Study of Higher Education, 1986.

Widmar, G. E. "Supplemental Instruction: From Small Beginnings to a National Program." In Martin, D. C., and Arendale, D. R. (Eds.), *Supplemental Instruction: Increasing Achievement and Retention. New*

Directions for Teaching and Learning No. 60. San Francisco: Jossey-Bass, 1994, 3–10.

Wilbur, H. M. "On Getting a Job." In Deneef, A. L., Goodwin, C. D., and McCrate, E. S. (Eds.), *The Academic's Handbook.* Durham, NC: Duke University Press, 1988, chapter 6.

Wilde, D. J. "Using Student Preferences to Guide Design Team Composition." In *Proceedings of the ASME Design Engineering Technical Conference.* New York: American Society of Mechanical Engineers, 1997, DTM-3890.

Wilkinson, S. L. "Electronic Publishing Takes Journals into a New Realm." *Chemical & Engineering News,* May 18, 1998, 10–18.

Williams, B. A., and Duch, B. J. "Cooperative Problem-Based Learning in an Undergraduate Physics Classroom." In McNeal, A. P., and D'Avanzo, C. (Eds.), *Student-Active Science: Models of Innovation in College Science Teaching.* Fort Worth, TX: Saunders, 1997, 453–472.

Wilshire, B. *The Moral Collapse of the University: Professionalism, Purity and Alienation.* Albany, NY: State University of New York Press, 1990.

Wilson, R. "Contracts Replace the Tenure Track for a Growing Number of Professors." *Chronicle of Higher Education,* June 12, 1998, A12–A14.

Woodhams, F. "State Colleges Try to Match Private Institutions with Promises of Timely Graduation." *Chronicle of Higher Education,* December 11, 1998, A50–A51.

Woods, D. R. *How to Gain the Most from Problem Based Learning.* Waterdown, Ontario, Canada: Self-published by D. R. Woods, 1994a. Available from McMaster University bookstore (905-572-7160).

Woods, D. R. *Instructor's Guide for How to Gain the Most from Problem Based Learning.* Waterdown, Ontario, Canada: D. R. Woods, 1994b.

Woods, D. R. "PBL Workshop." Presentation at Purdue University, West Lafayette, IN, February 26, 1997.

Woods, D. R., and Ormerod, S. D. *Networking: How to Enrich Your Life and Get Things Done.* San Diego: Pfeiffer, 1993.

Woods, D. R., Hrymak, A. N., Marshall, R. R., Wood, P. E., Crowe, C. M., Hoffman, T. W., Wright, J. D., Taylor, P. A., Woodhouse, K. A., and Bouchard, C. G. K. "Developing Problem Solving Skills: The McMaster Problem Solving Program." *Journal of Engineering Education,* 86 (1997), 75–91.

Wright, D. L. "Grading Student Achievement." In Prichard, K. W., and Sawyer, R. W. (Eds.), *Handbook of College Teaching: Theory and Applications.* Westport, CT: Greenwood Press, 1994, 439–449.

Young, K. *Caught in the Net: How to Recognize the Signs of Internet Addiction and a Winning Strategy for Recovery.* New York: Wiley, 1998.

Zelinski, E. J. *The Joy of Not Working: A Book for the Retired, Unemployed, and Overworked,* 3d ed. Berkeley, CA: Ten Speed Press, 1997.

Zerubavel, E. *The Clockwork Muse: A Practical Guide to Writing Theses, Dissertations and Books.* Cambridge, MA: Harvard University Press, 1999.

Zinatelli, M., and Dubé, M. A. "'Engineering' Student Success: How Does It Happen and Who Is Responsible?" *Journal of Engineering Education,* 88 (1999), 149–152.

INDEX